*Translating Property*

# Translating Property

*The Maxwell Land Grant and the Conflict over Land in the American West, 1840–1900*

MARÍA E. MONTOYA

*University Press of Kansas*

The original hardcover edition of this book was published by the
University of California Press.

Published by the University Press of Kansas (Lawrence, Kansas 66045),
which was organized by the Kansas Board of Regents and is operated
and funded by Emporia State University, Fort Hays State University,
Kansas State University, Pittsburg State University, the University of
Kansas, and Wichita State University

Library of Congress Cataloging-in-Publication Data

Montoya, María E., 1964–
    Translating property : the Maxwell Land Grant and the conflict over
land in the American West, 1840–1900 / María E. Montoya.
        p.   cm.
    Includes bibliographical references and index.
    ISBN 0-7006-1381-1 (pbk. : alk. paper)
    1. Maxwell Land Grant (N.M. and Colo.)—History.   2. New
Mexico—History—1848–  3. New Mexico—Race relations.   4. Land
tenure—New Mexico—History—19th century.   I. Title.
    F802.M38M66 2005
    978.9—dc22

                                                        2004030866

British Library Cataloguing-in-Publication Data is available.



10 9 8 7 6 5 4 3 2 1

The paper used in this publication meets the minimum requirements of
the American National Standard for Permanence of Paper for Printed
Library Materials Z39.48-1984.

*For my dad,*
*Frederick D. Montoya,*
*1936–1997*

# Contents

*List of Illustrations*                                                    ix

*Preface*                                                                   xi

*Acknowledgments*                                                        xvii

INTRODUCTION                                                                1

1.   CONTESTED BOUNDARIES                                    19

2.   REGULATING LAND, LABOR, AND BODIES:                     46
     MEXICAN MARRIED WOMEN, PEONES,
     AND THE REMAINS OF FEUDALISM

3.   FROM HACIENDA TO COLONY                                  78

4.   PREJUDICE, CONFRONTATION, AND RESISTANCE:               121
     TAKING CONTROL OF THE GRANT

5.   THE LAW OF THE LAND:                                   157
     *U.S. V. MAXWELL LAND GRANT COMPANY*

6.   THE LEGACY OF LAND GRANTS IN THE AMERICAN WEST         191

*Notes*                                                                   221

*Bibliography*                                                            261

*Index*                                                                   279

# Illustrations

Photographs

*Photographs follow page 77.*

1. Lucien B. Maxwell with Charles F. Holly and Judge John Watts, 1869
2. Emblem embossed on the Maxwell Land Grant stock certificates
3. Maxwell Land Grant Company office, Raton, New Mexico, ca. 1890
4. Deluvina Maxwell with Ida Harris Custer, ca. 1930
5. Jicarilla man and woman at the Abiquiu, New Mexico, Indian Agency, 1874
6. WPA painting of the Maxwell estate as it looked in 1865, ca. 1930s
7. WPA painting of the Maxwell home in Cimarron, New Mexico, ca. 1930s
8. Train station at Cimarron, New Mexico, ca. 1890s
9. Building the Vermejo Ditch, 1891
10. Cattle roundup for the Maxwell Land Grant and Cattle Company, 1887
11. Thomas O. Boggs, Maxwell Company land agent, ca. 1880s
12. The Stonewall Valley in Colorado, ca. 1916
13. María de la Luz Beaubien Maxwell, ca. 1890s
14. Teodora Beaubien Mueller with child, ca. 1890s
15. Juana Beaubien Clouthier with family, ca. 1890s

16. Eleanor Beaubien and Vidal Trujillo on their wedding day, ca. 1890s

17. Pablo Beaubien, ca. 1890s

18. Painting of María Paula Lobato Beaubien, ca. 1850s

19. Petra Beaubien Abreu, ca. 1890s

20. Map of Cimarron, New Mexico, 1865

21. Surveyor's sectional map of Colfax and Mora Counties, 1889

22. View of the Cimarron River valley, 1995

23. Ruins of Elizabethtown, New Mexico, 1995

24. The remains of Colorado Fuel and Iron in Cokedale, Colorado, 1995

25. Rayado, New Mexico, ca. 1930s

## Maps

1. Present-day Colorado and New Mexico border area     7

2. Jicarilla homeland     23

3. Cornelio Vigil map of the Beaubien/Miranda Land Grant     34

4. Sites of the Maxwell incident and the White massacre on the Santa Fe Trail     42

5. Property claims on the Poñil River, ca. 1885     106

6. Maxwell Land Grant in the 1890s     193

7. Sangre de Cristo Land Grant in Colorado and New Mexico     210

## Tables

1. Maxwell Land Grant Company's valuation of settlers' property on the grant, 1887     139

2. Maxwell Land Grant Company's valuation of settlers' property on the Vermejo River, 1887     141

# Preface

The paperback edition of *Translating Property* appears when land grant rights in Colorado and New Mexico are again the topic of newspaper headlines, GAO reports, and legal opinions. Two events in particular illustrate how disputes over land grants linger on. The first event was a victory for those claiming title based on land grants. In 2003, one year after the hardcover edition of this book, the Colorado Supreme Court tried once more to translate Mexican property ideals into the U.S. system of legal rights. In *Lobato v. Taylor,* the court held that the Sangre de Cristo Land Grant (discussed in Chapter 6) conveyed usufructary rights to the residents of Costilla County—rights to gather firewood, graze livestock, and hunt on the 77,000-acre ranch of their neighbor, Jack Taylor.[1] Thus, the court rejected the view of the trial judge that the casual wording of the nineteenth-century land grant could not convey title and property rights to the local communities surrounding San Luis, Colorado. Instead, the Supreme Court remanded the case back to the trial court to sort out precisely which local residents had rights to use Taylor's land by the terms of the grant.

Then, in June of 2004, the Government Accounting Office (GAO) issued a long-awaited report on land rights in New Mexico and Colorado.[2] Although the 232-page report is the federal government's most comprehensive effort ever to sort out the tangled history of land grants, the report was disappointing to many land-grant-rights advocates, especially after the 2003 victory in *Lobato*. These advocates viewed the GAO report as one

[1] *Lobato v. Taylor,* 70 Pacific Reporter 1152, April 28, 2003.
[2] Treaty of Guadalupe Hidalgo: Findings and Possible Options Regarding Longstanding Community Land Grant Claims in New Mexico, GAO-04-59, June 4, 2004.

more attempt by the federal government to justify the dispossession of thousands of Mexican-Americans from their communally held land rights when federal courts and agencies refused to enforce their titles. The report concluded that Congress had fulfilled its legal obligations to the former citizens of Mexico through the process put in place through the Office of the Surveyor General and the Court of Private Land Claims and that Congress was under no legal obligation to compensate heirs of these land grants. The report did suggest, however, that Congress might wish to give more protection to land grant claims than the law requires. The report's five options for providing such protection ranged from creating a commission to review the process of land grant confirmations to returning lands to heirs and/or monetarily compensating them. At the writing of this preface, Congress had taken no action on the report, although members of the New Mexico congressional delegation promised to review it carefully.

Critics of the report, like Malcolm Ebright, complained that it provided little new analysis, merely restating the old arguments that the federal government has consistently made about wanting to protect vested individual property rights not rooted in land grants, which it viewed as incompatible with community land grants. The GAO report merely repeats what the U.S. government has argued since the signing of the Treaty of Guadalupe Hidalgo: despite treaty obligations, the federal government could not practically adopt every aspect of Mexico's land regime because that regime was too alien to the Anglo-American system of property. One cannot read the report without a sense of déjà vu. The report's argument echoes the U.S. Supreme Court's 1885 decision in *U.S. v. Maxwell Land Grant Company,* which is the subject of a lengthy discussion in Chapter 5. Moreover, despite its length, the report expressly refused to address what it called "collateral issues" regarding land grants in New Mexico that were beyond the "scope of the report." But these "collateral issues" go to the heart of the controversy over land in the American Southwest. Thus, the report is unlikely to lay controversy to rest. For instance, the report would not consider how racial prejudice or the ideology of Manifest Destiny might have prejudiced government agents against land grantees and their families. Furthermore, the report refused to address claims about corruption or undue influence on government officials by wealthy individuals in the territory of New Mexico during the confirmation process. As *Translating Property* argues, these issues of prejudice and corruption were at the heart of what prevented Mexican Americans from asserting their property rights. To ignore these issues is to ignore the core of the historical grievances voiced by Latinos in the American Southwest.

By contrast with the GAO report, the *Lobato* opinion by the Colorado Supreme Court is perhaps the most sympathetic of any judicial opinion or government proclamation to claims made by land grant heirs about their community property rights. The court, however, was still determined to preserve as much of the Anglo-American system of property as possible. The court rejected the plaintiffs' argument that every resident of Costilla County had entitlement to use Jack Taylor's land. Instead, the court held that the Sangre de Cristo Land Grant conveyed usufructary rights only to those particular county residents who owned land in 1864, the year that Carlos Beaubien sold the grant to William Gilpin and stipulated that Gilpin had to honor the community grant. This holding meant that Costilla County landowners could use the Taylor ranch only if they could trace their title back to a particular nineteenth-century landowner to whom Beaubien had granted usufructary rights. Thus, two otherwise identical landowners owning neighboring parcels of land in Costilla County, all of which are part of the community grant, would enjoy different grazing rights on the Taylor Ranch, based on the technicality of a title search. One can only imagine the difficulty faced by the security guards watching the Taylor Ranch: if they see a neighbor entering the ranch to gather timber, they would have to leaf hurriedly through a title book to decide whether he or she is a trespasser or a rightful possessor of an easement, both persons being otherwise indistinguishable neighbors on abutting ranches. But more important as a legal matter, the court's insistence that each resident prove a chain of title back to an 1864 landowner ignored the communal nature of the grant rights. Beaubien's grant from the Mexican government obliged him to provide usufructary rights to the residents of the local community, not to specific individuals. Nothing in the grant suggested that anyone who joined the community after 1864 should not share in these communal lands.

The court's opinion, in other words, was a compromise between the Spanish-Mexican concept of land grants, which allowed vast quantities of land to be conveyed to more loosely defined communities of people through more casual methods of recording, and the Anglo-American concept of property, which insisted on specifically identified tracts conveyed to legal individuals in the form of marketable title. Like all translations of property that this book examines, *Lobato* did not fit comfortably into the language of either legal system. It was too limited to fit into the Spanish-Mexican theory and too broad to fit into American land law.

On the other hand, in terms of American principles of land title, the court's preservation of the local residents' usufructary rights was extraordinarily broad. The court held that, in order to quiet title to his land free of the neighbors' use rights, the owners of the Taylor Ranch would have to give notice to the entire population of Costilla County: only then could potential owners of usufructary rights come forward and defend their interest. But, as the dissent by Justice Kourlis indicated, ordinary principles of American property law do not normally require landowners wishing to quiet title to their land to contact personally every member of the county, notifying each of them that their communal rights to gather firewood or graze cattle, contained in an unrecorded nineteenth-century land grant, might be extinguished. To the dissenting justice, the grant system with its sweeping bestowal of land collectively on entire communities seemed alien to the entire U.S. legal tradition. How could Jack Taylor or his descendants possibly know that they were buying "use rights" land from an entire county's population rather than title from a single landowner?

Despite the seemingly limited nature of the win in *Lobato*, land grant advocates and others should take heart from the court's willingness to "cloud" individual title by acknowledging the potential of competing communal rights to the same parcel of land. One can view this willingness as an effort to reverse a massive expropriation resulting from nineteenth-century U.S. imperialism. Although it is unfamiliar to think of the American West as another site for imperialism, in fact it was an important focus of Dutch investments, and those Dutch investors regarded New Mexico as essentially similar to Indonesia—a place where title to land could be acquired from local elites and transformed into property suitable for capitalist investment in an international market. Jack Taylor's effort to cleanse his land of the use-rights of his mostly Hispano neighbors is a faint echo of similar nineteenth-century efforts to purge title of Maori, Hawai'ian, aboriginal Australian, or native Canadian claims. That his effort has been fruitless so far reflects the Colorado Supreme Court's desire to preserve the claims of history from the demands of marketability. Such a desire to respect the historical claims of the dispossessed is a recent development in North America, having existed for less time than Jack Taylor's lawsuit. Since the 1960s, lawyers have prevailed in enforcing the treaty rights of Native Canadians, aboriginal Australians, and Native Americans. The small victory of the residents of Costilla County is, likewise, a victory of historically based treaty rights over the claims of marketable title.

As *Translating Property* argues, the history of land law in the American Southwest continues to be a peculiar amalgamation of different cultures. Europeans and Yankees who occupied this contested border region assumed that they were entering virgin land, unencumbered by the mesh of property boundaries that criss-crossed the Old World or the Eastern coast of the United States. But this assumption was mistaken: the Southwest was no empty quarter waiting to be divided up. The land was already covered with a fine lattice of rival understandings of land. Jicarilla Apaches had their traditional use rights. Magnates like Lucien Maxwell claimed the traditional power of semifeudal patrons under grants from Mexican governors: they governed rather than owned vast tracts of land—but only on condition that they created and preserved communities of small farmers and ranchers. Those farmers and ranchers, in turn, made different claims. Sometimes they claimed alternatively the rights of a feudal subject to reside on their parcels so long as they paid fealty to their patron-master. Sometimes they claimed the absolute rights of a yeoman farmer under the Homestead Act. Against all of these claims, Dutch shareholders claimed the rights of capitalist investors, to use the land freely as a factor of production, mortgaging, logging, mining—and, most important—*evicting* at will. Like layers in an archeological midden, these different understandings of land piled on top of each other over time, forming a confused legal jumble for the courts to pick apart. Small wonder, then, that the *Lobato* court's effort was not a dazzling success.

One lesson learned from *Translating Property* is that these legal issues still have real meaning to thousands of Mexican Americans in the American Southwest who continue to fight to hold onto land granted to their families over one hundred years ago. The second lesson is that history matters when sorting out issues of rights and property. In both the legal opinion and the GAO report, history played an important role in deciding how the issues should be adjudicated. Both the Colorado Supreme Court and the authors of the GAO report attempted to understand how and why the land was conveyed such that people had different and competing rights held within the community land grant structure. *Translating Property* is an attempt to show why history, culture, and law matter for those interested in understanding how the property regimes of the American Southwest have been put into place over the last 150 years and how inequality has been laid out across the landscape.

# Acknowledgments

Although I did not realize it at the time, I have been writing, or at least thinking about, this book since I was a kid. I grew up visiting my grandparents on their cattle ranch in Torres, Colorado, which sits within the northern edge of what was once the Maxwell Land Grant. In the early morning, after my grandfather fed the woodstove and made my grandmother and I coffee that was more sugar and Petmilk than coffee (a bad, but comforting, habit I still indulge in), he would tell me stories of growing up on the Torres Ranch and the changes he had seen. He told stories that his father, Luís Torres, who makes a brief appearance in the last chapter of this book, had told him about fighting the Maxwell Land Grant Company and the Colorado Fuel and Iron Company to keep his vast estate intact. Somehow Luís Torres Sr. had managed to maintain his property rights to thousands of acres of land and had passed the land to his sons and daughters, who have also passed the land to their children. So, in the interest of full disclosure, I should admit that today I own a piece of land that was once part of the Maxwell Land Grant.

My scholarly and academic interest in the Maxwell Land Grant, however, dates back to college. During a particularly bleak New Haven winter I took a course from Katherine Morrissey, "Creating a Home in the American West," because I was so homesick I thought I would have to leave Yale. It was from Kathy that I got my first taste of how fabulously fun and invigorating historical research can be. I owe a big thank-you to her because she encouraged me to think about history graduate school. She has, through the years, been a great mentor and friend. Thanks to her, a chance encounter with George Miles at the Beinecke Library, and my fabulous friends, who were just as lost as I was that summer after graduating from college, I managed to avoid going to business school and found my way into graduate school.

At the University of New Mexico, where I began my graduate school career, I had access to the institutional papers of the Maxwell Land Grant Company as well as one of the country's best collections of New Mexicana and Borderlands materials. Bill Tydeman, Rose Díaz, and Nancy Brown were all very helpful in making me feel comfortable in what was the old Coronado Room of Zimmerman Library. I also had the great pleasure of working with Richard Etulain, the late Gerald Nash, the late Howard Rabinowitz, Jane Slaughter, and Paul Hutton, each of whom taught me some important lessons about working in Western history. I was also lucky enough to have a great group of fellow graduate students. Michael Stanfield, L. Durwood Ball, Dan Churchill, Charles Rankin, and Kevin Fernlund, over the years, have all been great friends and colleagues as this book has slowly come to completion and we have all found our places in this profession.

Over the last ten years of working on this book, I have racked up a considerable debt to archivists and librarians across the country. I am indebted to the librarians at the National Archives Centers in Washington, D.C., Suitland, Maryland, and Denver, Colorado; the Huntington Library; the University of Colorado; the University of Michigan; the Denver Public Library; and the Colorado Historical Society. I owe a special thank-you to Sandra Jaramillo, Robert Torres, and Al Regensberg at the New Mexico State Records Center and Archives in Santa Fe. The old archives on Montezuma Street seemed like my second home at times, and they were all gracious in the help they gave me.

Gathering the photos for this book turned out to be one of the more interesting and challenging parts of the project. Steve Zimmer at the Philmont Museum and Arnzaiz De León at the New Mexico State Records Center and Archives were a pleasure to work with as I gathered photos. I especially want to thank Mrs. Thayla Wright at the Arthur Johnson Memorial Library in Raton, New Mexico, for letting me borrow and copy the fabulous photos of the Beaubien family. Thanks to Stella de Sa Rego, Ann Masserman, and others at the Center for Southwest Research at the University of New Mexico Library for patiently processing the complex order that involved transferring the photos from Raton.

I am also indebted to the following institutions for the financial support they gave to this project. At the University of Michigan I received a Ludolph Grant, Career Development Award, Faculty Assistance Award, and a Horace Rackham Faculty Fellowship. It would be difficult to find an insti-

tution more supportive than the University of Michigan was in funding
my research. I also received a Ford Foundation Post-Doctoral Fellowship
from the National Research Council, which provided a year off from
teaching in order to write and research. I also received an IMPART grant
from the University of Colorado, Boulder, and a Mellon Fellowship from
the Huntington Library. While I was at Yale, I was generously supported
as the Edward Bouchet Alumni Prize Fellow and the Patricia Roberts
Harris Fellow.

At Yale I had the privilege of working with Howard Lamar. I am only
one in a long line of thankful graduate students who have come to appreciate Howard more and more as we advance in our own careers. His incredible generosity, breadth of knowledge, kindness, and open-mindedness
know no limits, and I am honored to have had him advise and guide this
project when it was a dissertation. I can only hope to be half the mentor he
was for all of his students. I also owe thanks to William Cronon, Sarah
Deutsch, and John Mack Faragher, who all read this work at the dissertation stage and gave insightful comments and suggestions. I am especially
thankful for Sally Deutsch, who over the years has read this book in its
various incarnations, including as one of the outside readers for the University of California Press, and has given generous, yet critical, comments.
The book is much better because of her insights. At Yale I was part of a
rather amazing cohort of graduate students who all read parts of this manuscript and gave generously of their thoughts and comments. Thanks to
Irving Kagan, A. Yvette Huginnie, Susan L. Johnson, Gunther Peck, Emily
Greenwald, Philip Deloria, Louis Warren, David Yoo, and Dorothy Roney.

My first job at the University of Colorado spoiled me because of the
interdisciplinary set of scholars and friends who worked on the American
West and were affiliated with the Center of the American West. Patty Limerick, since the first time I met her (pre–*Legacy of Conquest*), has always
been a generous and enthusiastic friend and mentor who has influenced my
career and thinking in important ways. I thank her for helping me find and
learn my first job. I also had wonderful colleagues who helped me adjust to
the new world of academia: A. Yvette Huginnie, Virginia and Fred Anderson, Steven Epstein, Gloria Maine, Jim Jankowski, Marjorie MacIntosh,
Martha Hanna, and Padraic Kenney were all wonderful colleagues, and I
was sorry to leave them.

I always tell people that I never would have written the book I did had I
not come to the University of Michigan. I am grateful to Tomás Almaguer,
Sueanne Caulfield, Geoff Eley, Kali Israel, Sue Juster, Carol Karlsen, Val
Kivelson, Gina Morantz-Sánchez, George Sánchez, Rebecca Scott, Caroll

Smith-Rosenberg, and J. Mills Thornton for all of their time and feedback on the manuscript. I particularly want to thank Richard Candída Smith and Don Herzog, who did yeoman's work by reading the final draft and providing critical and helpful comments that helped bring the argument of the book into clearer focus. I also want to thank my junior colleagues in the department, who have made this such an intellectual and collegial place to work: Michelle Mitchell, John Carson, Mathew Countryman, John Gonzalez, and Robert Self have made this department my home. It is the generosity of intellectual exchange that has helped me to write a book that is much more focused on larger issues.

I am proud of the fabulous graduate students who have done research for me, talked about ideas, and read the manuscript both at the University of Michigan and at the University of Colorado. Barbara Berglund, Pervis Brown, Michael Droeger, Judy Daubenmeir, Tomás Hulick, Andrew Goss, Pablo Mitchell, Natalia Molina, Andrew Needham, Denise Pan, Estévan Rael y Gálvez, Tom Romero, David Salmanson, Alexander Shashko, Sonya Smith, and Martín Sul have all been hard-working and intensely smart students who, I know, will go on to great careers of their own.

Of course, one of the best things about this profession is the terrific intellectual camaraderie we get to have with others outside of our institutions. David Gutiérrez, Ramón Gutiérrez, Camille Guerin-Gonzales, A. Yvette Huginnie, Gunther Peck, Ken Orona, Neil Foley, David Montejano, Peggy Pascoe, Kathleen Underwood, Michael Welsh, Elliott West, Richard White, and John Wunder have all made quite an impression on me and this book. I especially want to thank Ramón Gutiérrez, who was also an outside reader for the University of California Press and made me feel like this was really all worth it. I also owe an incredible thanks to Virginia Scharff, who has been my confidante and an incredible intellectual mentor. Our late-night talks in hotel rooms at conferences, over the phone, and in exotic locales of the American West (Tulsa and Lincoln, to name only a few) have been invaluable to not only my intellectual development but also to my experience as a mom, spouse, and colleague. She makes the problems of juggling a husband, kids, and a job in the academy look solvable as she does it with grace and ease.

Except for my family, my friends have always been the most important part of my life. Some of them I have known since I was four, many I met in college, and a few have seen me through some long winters in Ann Arbor. I have been blessed with a wonderful set of friends who, although they have yet to read a word of this book, influenced it tremendously with words of support, hours of babysitting, hours of hitting tennis balls, and many long talks. Thanks to Myla Shepherd, Mikki MacKenzie, Cholene D. Espinoza, Elizabeth Alling Sewall, Julie Sheehan, Laura Siner, Siobhan Sharkey, Allison Hills, Laura Sagolla Croley, Luanna Vigil, and Barbara Cornblath. Without their friendship and support, my life would amount to far less. Finally, I want to thank Jack and Phyllis Zumwinkel, who have allowed me and my family to stay in their cabins every summer since I was six years old. Without the Milliken cabin's porch, I would not have been able to finish this book. The long summers outside of Rocky Mountain National Park gave me the perspective, peace, and solitude I needed.

This project has been a part of my life for way too long. It has seen me transform from a grandchild who wondered about the past to a mother who worries about the future. Through all of this, my extended family has been an integral part of this book: they have profoundly changed and influenced my life such that they shaped everything I know about myself and the work I have done in these pages. On the material side, my family from Pueblo south to Albuquerque has provided lodging, warm meals, comfort, and an attentive ear as I have traipsed across every small town in northern New Mexico and every square mile of the Maxwell Land Grant. In the broader context of life they have supported me at every turn, through the really wonderful high points as well as the depressingly low points of this process. My mother, Ruth C. Montoya, has provided too many hours of babysitting to count, but they allowed me my summers to write and re-search. Also, since the day I entered kindergarten, she has been my biggest academic backer. I only hope I can do half as well by my daughters. The only regret I have about the book is that my father, Frederick D. Montoya, did not live to see it in its final form. Although he died much too suddenly and early in life, I have wonderful memories of dragging him across the vast expanses of what was the Maxwell Land Grant so that he could take photographs, some of which appear in the book. I will cherish those memories and myriad other ones that allowed me to become the person I am today.

My husband, Rick Hills, has contributed endlessly to this book. He knows every page almost as well as I do. He was my biggest champion and my harshest critic, and it's because of his patience and view of the long-term goal that we managed to survive this process. He also provided a safe, warm, and stable family life for all of us when life seemed the most insane. It was a testament to him that our girls never cried when I left to do re-search, and felt secure with him. I couldn't have done all the research with-out his support. More importantly, he has been my best friend and true love. Finally, to my daughters, Emma Sofía and Sarah Reynalda, I owe the largest debt of all. They cheerfully tolerated a mom who was often away and more often preoccupied and distracted with work. Their smiles, wit, demanding personalities, and raw intellect, however, always reminded me at the end of every day what mattered most: my family. Thanks for reminding me about the sheer joy and adventure that each day in life brings to us. I hope this book reminds you who you are and where you come from.

# Introduction

When Denver lawyer Jeff Goldstein asked me in 1997 if I could help him with a lawsuit, *Espinoza v. Taylor*,[1] I was a bit startled to learn that conflicts over Mexican land grants still raged in the American West. To me, these land grants seemed to be arcane vestiges of a distant past. Goldstein wanted me to look at documents relating to the Sangre de Cristo Land Grant in the southern portion of Colorado. The grant had been owned in the 1840s by Carlos Beaubien, one of the parties in the Beaubien/Miranda (later the Maxwell) grant, the subject of this book. More important, he wanted me to help the people of San Luis, Colorado, regain access to a commons that their Mexican ancestors had used for hunting, wood gathering, and grazing since 1841, but which had been closed to them recently by its owners, the Taylor family.

Jack T. Taylor purchased the land in the 1960s and began logging this mountainous area, which historically had been used by the Hispanos who lived on adjoining pieces of property and in the vicinity. His logging operation not only interfered with the San Luis residents' common use rights but also caused erosion that damaged the watershed supplying the *acequias* (ditches) they relied on to irrigate their farmlands. The San Luis residents believed they possessed this right to use the land because the original owner, Carlos Beaubien, had conveyed these usufructuary rights to their families in 1863. Beaubien had received the land grant from the Mexican government in the early 1840s, and Goldstein argued that the Mexican government had given Beaubien the land on the condition that Beaubien settle this frontier location by inducing families to live there. The use of this commons was one of the most alluring aspects of living in the region.

Taylor perhaps did not understand, but in any case did not respect, the local Hispanos' historic rights of use on what the Taylor family viewed as

1

their personal private property. The Taylors believed they had the right to fence the land, keep out trespassers, and use the land's resources in any way that would benefit them. On the other hand, the residents of San Luis did not respect Taylor's assertion of his right to hold property exclusively: they had expected him to act as all previous owners had acted, by leaving the mountain tract unfenced and open to their historic uses.[2] In the more than thirty years that have passed since Jack Taylor first bought the property, both sides have continually failed to translate their conceptions of property and land use in a way that was workable with the other side's ideas about how to use the land.[3]

As I watched the trial in May 1998, it struck me that the central theme in this book had not been solved in the ensuing century and a half since these lands were granted by the Mexican government. One of the case's major issues, as well as the central issue that I explore, is how the property systems of the United States and Mexico have been in conflict with each other ever since the United States incorporated Mexico into its social, legal, and economic regime after the U.S.–Mexican War and the Treaty of Guadalupe Hidalgo in 1848. I am interested in how what we would term the "informal" property system of the Mexican frontier, which was based more on personal connections and patronage, was incorporated into the U.S. property regime of private property and public domain, which has privileged the fee simple absolute, or exclusive, form of holding property.[4] This is not surprising since the U.S. federal government found it almost impossible to embrace wholeheartedly most of the customs and institutions that had defined Mexican economic, political, and social life prior to the conquest in 1848.

The inability of the U.S. legal system to adequately incorporate the complex, yet vague, property rights of these Hispano plaintiffs was at the heart of the recent *Espinoza* case. I testified as an expert about the historic meaning of an 1863 document written by Carlos Beaubien for the people of San Luis, which granted them, among other things, access to the common areas of the vast land grant. More generally, Goldstein wanted me to talk about the cultural, social, and political context surrounding Mexican land grants and discuss my belief, based on the historical evidence, that Beaubien intended to convey usufructuary rights to the grant's inhabitants. Judge Gaspar Perricone, however, remained unsure about Beaubien's intent because of the informality of the 1863 document, which made unclear (at least to the twentieth-century reader) references to the geographic places marked for common usage by all the residents of the land grant. Moreover, the types of uses were not clearly spelled out in the document. Despite the

supposed ambiguity, however, Judge Perricone was unwilling to hear outside evidence that contextualized the agreement, ruling that the document
needed to stand on its own. He refused to hear any evidence about its
meaning in the larger context of 1840s Mexican history.

Beaubien was not an imprecise man by nature. He clearly wanted to
convey land use rights to the people of San Luis. The document's ambiguity simply exemplified the way people did business in mid-nineteenth-
century New Mexico: people knew one another, tended to trust those with
good reputations, and rarely asked for more-formal assurances. Indeed, the
document's very existence was significant because few records dealing with
settlers' rights and responsibilities in other New Mexican land grant cases
exist. To someone who studies the complexity of Mexican land grants, the
1863 document clearly conveyed usufructuary rights to the community.
And yet to the contemporary American judge who remains unfamiliar
with the complexity of Mexican land grant documents, the written evidence simply comprised a series of puzzling sentences that did not conform
to any model of conveyance with which he was familiar. In the end, the inability of the United States legal system to analyze and recognize the rights
conveyed by the 1863 document deprived the people of San Luis of their
long-held rights to use the common lands.

The *Espinoza* case is only one example of the complex issues surrounding Mexican land grants that have yet to be adequately resolved by the
U.S. legal system, or understood by many historians. In choosing not to
hear this evidence, Judge Perricone and, by extension, the U.S. legal system made it impossible to understand the San Luis residents' claims to use
Taylor's property. Instead, the court imposed artificial clarity on the document and the case in general in order to avoid serious consideration of the
San Luis residents' claims to the land. Whatever the legal merits of this
particular case, the court's disposition of cases such as this illustrates the
difficulty faced by the American legal system in translating Mexican property systems into the Anglo-American context.

In 1998, people were still dealing with the legacy of the U.S. government's war against Mexico, and Mexico's subsequent loss of half its territory in 1848. This book attempts to explain how New Mexico land grants
conveyed complex property rights to different people, and why the U.S. legal system has seen these documents as ambiguous and therefore invalid.
This book explores, in particular, the customs, property systems, and social structures that were lost when the informal property regimes of New
Mexico were subsumed into the formalistic and market-oriented U.S. legal
and property systems. *Espinoza v. Taylor*, which pitted a group of local and

relatively poor Hispano subsistence ranchers and farmers against a wealthy outsider lumberman, merely seemed to repeat the stories and themes that appear throughout this book. Perhaps we should not be so surprised by the inability of modern-day jurists, politicians, and property owners to recognize the historic legacy of Mexican land grants in the American West. As this book shows, only parts of this Mexican property system, which was based on Spain's civil law, have been incorporated into our own modern-day legal and political world, which derives primarily from English common law. As historians of labor, immigration, and politics have already pointed out, the American Southwest and its Mexican inhabitants were incorporated, assimilated, acculturated, and at times deported in order for the U.S. government and eastern business interests to wrest control of the land and natural resources from their Mexican owners.[5] Following this historiographical vein, this books shows how and why the U.S. federal government's territorial system, through the executive, congressional, and judiciary branches, succeeded in eliminating most aspects of Mexico's legal system and property regimes.

The questions that faced Judge Perricone in this 1998 case were very similar to the questions that the Supreme Court faced more than a hundred years earlier in *U.S. v. Maxwell Land Grant and Railway Company.* For example, if either court had recognized the rights of local Hispanos, how would the court then have defined the community's usufructuary rights, regulated their use, and integrated such rights with Taylor's or the Maxwell Land Grant Company's right to exploit the land's resources at will? To recognize the usufructuary rights would be to shut down logging and mining operations and other aspects of sole and often despotic dominion so tied to the fee simple absolute that American citizens recognize as private property. The failure of the courts over the last century and half to incorporate the grant system into modern American property law suggests that the problem of land grants in the American Southwest is largely a problem of translation. The Southwest has been, and continues to be, the scene of a collision between land regimes with radically different cultural conceptions of the land's purpose. The U.S. courts from before *Maxwell* and up to *Espinoza* have wanted property rights to be vested in only one owner and then expressed in clear, specific, and legally complete documents. But the Mexican property system enforced in nineteenth-century New Mexico was rooted in communal, as well as individual, ownership and was often expressed in informal, customary understandings among neighbors and in oral deals between patrons and clients. For the U.S. courts to privilege individual ownership and demand written documents to define such rights was to effectively refuse to enforce Mexican property rights.

This book addresses the larger theme of conflict over property regimes in the American West by viewing it through the lens of a single land grant—the Maxwell (formerly Beaubien/Miranda) Land Grant, a parcel of 1.7 million acres that straddled the Colorado/New Mexico state boundaries. In the hundred years covered by this narrative, the grant was transformed from an "empty" landscape that housed the semi-settled Jicarilla Apaches to a hacienda run by Lucien B. Maxwell and finally to a land company run by Dutch overseers and accommodating local officials. During this long century, Native Americans, French and Spanish officials, Mexican land grant owners, *peones*, married women, Anglo miners, American homesteaders, U.S. territorial and federal government officials, and European capitalists all vied for economic, political, and legal control of the land grant. All struggled to make a living, and in some cases a home, on this landscape. Their failures and successes tell the story of transitioning property regimes, demonstrating that the American Southwest was a complex world of interacting and conflicting property rights, race relations, and economics. Each of the grant's owners vied for control of the natural resources and people's labor in the region.

North Americans and Mexicans possessed preexisting ideas about property and how it should be allocated, used, and integrated into U.S. law and culture. This integration proved difficult, however, because of the many opportunities for mistranslation, or partial translation, that led to land loss, exploitation, political corruption, and colonial power relationships. Three particular aspects of this problem of translating property are highlighted here. First, I examine how Americans' and Europeans' perceptions of the American West as an "empty" space influenced the way they dealt with the people and land of the region. Second, this work suggests that the American West was colonized in much the same way as regions outside of North America —by dispossessing original inhabitants of land while ostensibly respecting their form of title under the indigenous property system. Finally, I attempt to understand how emerging ethnic and racial divisions were used to enforce the growing division between the landed and the landless.

## THE MYTH OF THE EMPTY AMERICAN WEST

The Turnerian conception of the American West as unsettled, unappropriated, unsocialized nature conquered by intrepid pioneers prevents ordinary observers, whether tourist or judge, from even imagining how the West could be a place where different people, much less different property regimes, collided with one another. After all, a collision presupposes at least two opposite forces. If the West consisted of unsettled land devoid of property systems, then there was nothing with which the Anglo-American conception of property could collide. Not surprisingly, the pervasiveness of this ever-popular Western myth—American westward migration moved into an area devoid of civilization, an empty natural space that shaped the migrants but no one else—still interferes with our ability to understand the complex interaction of property systems that actually occurred in the American Southwest between the sixteenth and twentieth centuries.

The U.S. legal system's failure to translate all of the cultural, social, and political meanings reflected this nineteenth-century American misconception that the West was a wide-open space ready for the taking. The myth is so pervasive that even today what most people notice about this particular landscape is that it appears empty. Except for the distinctive adobe architecture, few remnants of the Mexican past seem obvious on the present-day southern Colorado and northern New Mexican landscape of the Sangre de Cristo, the Beaubien/Miranda, and myriad other land grants. These rural spaces reveal very little of the environmentally and ethnically diverse, economically complex, and violent history of the region. Although a few small towns like San Luis, Colorado, and Cimarron, New Mexico, remain, the population in these historic spaces is sparse. A place devoid of people often leads one to believe that this place is also devoid of any meaningful history. Yet this place that today appears to be "nowhere" historically has been a real "somewhere" for the people who fought with and even killed one another over the land, its resources, and the ability to lay legal claim to them. The landscape's very emptiness encourages an amnesia about its history, which explains but does not excuse modern-day tourists', journalists', judges', and businesspeople's inability to deal equitably with competing claims to these resources.[6]

What was once the Maxwell Land Grant stretched from the Spanish Peaks, which marked the northern boundary, to the Sangre de Cristo Mountains, which marked its western edge, to the Colfax County line to the south and to the Canadian River to the east; it encompassed 1.7 million acres and in 1870 was the largest single estate in the United States (see map 1). Within these boundaries lay a varied landscape of 13,000-foot mountains, high, dry plains, scattered ponds, creeks, pine forests, and rich coal deposits. These natural resources have supported family farms, cattle and coal companies, and the tourist industry for 150 years, but the historical past has inscribed itself on this landscape only in subtle and

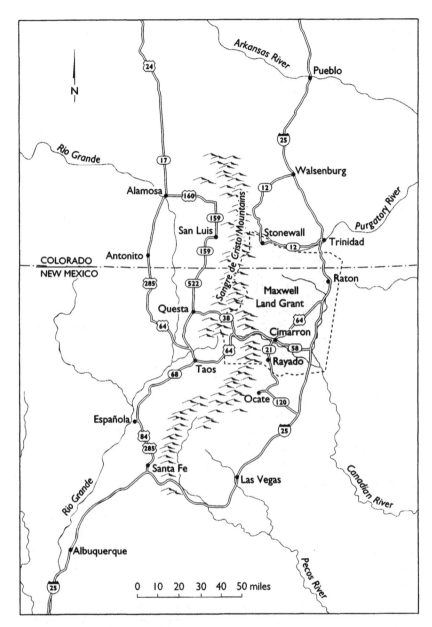

Map 1.   Present-day Colorado and New Mexico border area.

barely discernible ways. Those who used the land, whether they were Ji-carilla Apaches, Hispano settlers, Anglo homesteaders, or Dutch business-men, made very different historical and environmental impressions. The Colorado Fuel and Iron Corporation, for example, left permanent marks in the form of coal mine tailings and rusting coke ovens. In contrast, the Jicarilla Apaches left few physical reminders on the landscape they once occupied. This twenty-first-century landscape is marked in different ways precisely because of its history and the complicated relationships to land that played themselves out here. The Maxwell Land Grant Company, as-sisted by the U.S. federal government, intensified the use of the grant's nat-ural resources by overthrowing two sets of property rights—Jicarilla and Mexican—and replacing them with a new, capital-intensive property re-gime that has left its indelible mark on the landscape.

## THE UNEXCEPTIONAL AMERICAN WEST

The changes that occurred on the Maxwell Land Grant suggest that the American West was not an exceptional place. Rather, it was a region that reflected the broader trends of nineteenth-century imperial and colonial endeavors throughout the rest of the world. Colonial and post-colonial studies have been thriving intellectual fields for almost a decade, and yet few have thought to place the American West, and particularly the Ameri-can Southwest, under this rubric of analysis.[7] Perhaps this omission is because U.S. historians—and historians of the American West, in particu-lar—have excluded the United States from comparisons with other nations engaged in imperialism and colonialism because they have assumed that those themes no longer applied to the United States after 1776, when the colonies broke away from Great Britain. Only recently have historians and other academics placed events such as the era of Manifest Destiny (includ-ing the U.S.–Mexican War and westward expansion) and the Spanish-American War of 1898 within a paradigm that sees the United States for what it was—an imperial, colonizing state that incorporated the western half of its present-day territory under some rather unequal terms of entry.[8]

In this story of the Maxwell Land Grant, I want to expand the intel-lectual boundaries of the "New Western History" by making explicit comparisons to other regional and colonial histories. In placing this New Mexico case study within the context of a larger world history and other nineteenth-century case studies of land loss in places such as Hawai'i, Russia, Africa, and Latin America, this book hopes to illuminate the phe-nomenon of land loss on the United States' western frontier. In the case of the American Southwest, and New Mexico, in particular, the U.S. government acted in imperial and colonial ways that mimicked its European counterparts. By the beginning of the twentieth century, the nation had established a conquered, colonized, and dependent region of people made up of the former Mexican citizens from the provinces of New Mexico, Texas, and California. The Maxwell Land Grant and New Mexico not only possess theoretical connections to other colonial sites, but they also have specific economic and legal connections to Dutch imperial and colonial interests. New Mexico and the Maxwell Land Grant were just another stop on the colonial empire-building circuit established by the Dutch throughout the world: Indonesia, Africa, and the American West.[9] It was not a coincidence that the Maxwell Land Grant and Railway Company hired M. P. Pels, a very reputable Dutch bureaucrat from Batavia, to manage operations in New Mexico and, in particular, to remove the Anglo and Hispano squatters from the land grant. Pels had already made a successful reputation for himself in Java by accomplishing the same kind of removal and then selective incorporation of the native inhabitants into Dutch business practices.

Given this perspective, how can we continue to think of the American West as an exceptional space that creates "democratic, free, individuals" (to paraphrase Turner) when there were thousands of "new" Americans such as Indians and transformed Mexican citizens who were subjected to the colonial presence of the United States in the form of the U.S. territorial system and cavalry? By examining how the U.S. federal government came to control and tame the American Southwest in the post-1848 period, we can better understand what has been seen as the "real" American imperialism of 1898, when the United States engaged in the Spanish-American War and took control of other Hispanic peoples in Puerto Rico, Cuba, and the Philippines.[10]

And yet the American West did not develop as a colonized region in the same ways that historians have ascribed to colonial locations in Latin America, Southeast Asia, India, and Africa. Indeed, the United States did politically and economically incorporate the people of the American West as full partners, at least theoretically, into the Union. Unlike its later imperial incursions, the U.S. government did not leave New Mexico the same colonial legacy as it did the Philippines, Cuba, or Puerto Rico. Unlike these 1898 examples, the former Mexican territories eventually entered the Union on a politically equal footing: all had equal representation in Congress, and all citizens had the right to vote, although it would take another few decades of agitation, legislation, and litigation to exercise all of those rights. It is precisely because the American West had such a different trajectory from other colonial locales that it is important to look at Alan Trachtenberg's notion of "incorporation" to understand how the U.S. government and society brought this foreign territory under their control and influence.[11]

## INCORPORATING THE WEST

The book focuses specifically on the economic and political incorporation of the American Southwest into the United States. More specifically: How did the area that become known as the American West and its inhabitants become incorporated into the world-market system and into the U.S. political and legal system? This process of incorporation was a two-way street. On one side were dominant forces such as market capitalists and the U.S. federal government officials who were interested in controlling the natural resources and people (at least to a limited extent) of the American West and corralling them into the mainstream economy and body politic. William Cronon and John Agnew describe the process of pulling the U.S. West into the sphere of influence of Eastern and "gateway" cities, such as Chicago.[12] Both of these historians, however, tell this narrative from a distinctly Eastern perspective that places Eastern boosters and businessmen at the center of the story.[13] On the other side, however, were the people who were being incorporated. This book explores how the process of political and economic incorporation worked or did not work from the perspective of the Westerners who were the target of this process. It also looks at how the people on the economic and social periphery of these empire-building institutions, such as the federal government and bond-holding company, influenced and shaped policy created at the metropole.[14]

I want to understand why European investors who were searching for profitable ventures would lend their money to fund the Maxwell Land Grant Company. They were attracted by the high interest rates available in the capital-hungry West, which were considerably higher than the prevailing rates in London and Amsterdam. These creditors in Europe operated through New York and Denver brokers to purchase the western United States in bits and parcels. They were lured by dreams of untapped wealth, locked away in an allegedly untouched, uninhabited virgin land. The European investors of the grant, mostly Dutch, aided by the U.S. government, hoped to convert a wilderness into an industrial utopia manned by Dutch employees extracting timber, coal, grain, and cattle from an empty, rich, unappropriated landscape, ripe for the harvest.

The land, however, was not a wilderness without inhabitants. Nor were its people unorganized "savages" who lacked a system of apportioning rights and resources. Jicarilla Apaches, Hispano farmers, and Anglo home-steaders all had a complex network of understandings, obligations, and privileges governing their relation to the land and one another. Although this regime was not recorded in any statute or deed, it had the force of law for them.[15] When the law that the Dutch investors procured from the U.S. federal government and its territorial agents came into conflict with this local regime, the company's dream of unhampered economic exploita-tion of natural resources was shattered.[16] The investors came in search of virgin land and found a community. Hoping to build an enterprise from scratch, they eventually struggled to save their investment from a pre-existing society.

Conflicts arose because the "native" people, whether they were Indians or Hispanos, already possessed developed and workable economic, political, and property systems. These prior land regimes were bound to come into conflict with the newer ones imposed by the interlopers. Whether they were the Jicarilla Apaches who hunted and gathered, the Hispanos who worked under the *patrón*, Lucien B. Maxwell, the Anglo homesteaders compelled by the American dream of private property, or the Dutch com-pany's managers, who wanted to exploit the grant for profit in an interna-tional market, all had a specific economic and social way of dealing with and understanding the land. As we shall see, each of these uses was incompat-ible with the others.

The U.S. government's difficulty with incorporating and respecting these prior regimes was based partly on legal and structural differences. Also significant was the its reliance on local appointed officials (such as the Santa Fe Ring) to translate and mediate these differences and competing claims. The examples in this book of how Mexican married women lost property rights and how the U.S. Supreme Court dealt with the grant in *U.S. v. Maxwell* reveal how incorporation, and what has been termed "the process of liberalization," actually deprived native inhabitants of many of their prior rights. Earlier studies of the Maxwell Land Grant assumed that the federal government acted as a disinterested party and merely arbitrated the disputes between the grant's inhabitants and the Maxwell Land Grant Company. However, if one takes a close look at who controlled the territo-rial government in New Mexico and made the federal appointments, one sees an interested group of landowning politicians and entrepreneurs who had a direct stake in the outcome of the land grant conflicts. It was no accident that John T. Elkins, assigned to complete an official survey of the grant, was the brother of Stephen B. Elkins, company officer and mem-ber of the Santa Fe Ring. Nor was it coincidence that Surveyor General

Henry M. Atkinson determined the boundaries of a grant in which he owned a substantial share. Rather than the familiar battle between the settlers and company, my story illustrates how the private interests of federal officials influenced the ultimate outcome of who owned property.[17]

After 1885, however, the story of government involvement in land grants changes from the individual interests of government officials to a conflict over competing government interests in the adjudication of the grant's boundaries. State and federal governments took more of an interest in the region after the Atchison, Topeka, and Santa Fe Railroad had finally pulled New Mexico into its web of national commerce, making the Maxwell Land Grant a much more valuable resource. The State of Colorado and the U.S. government determined in 1886 that it was not the settlers who were defrauded by the company, but the government itself. The state and federal governments possessed their own interests in protecting the public domain of Colorado and their subsequent revenues from the company. In the last fifteen years of the nineteenth century, the conflict became a three-pronged controversy, with government, company, and settlers all struggling to maintain control over property that each sincerely believed belonged to them. Viewing this story through the actions of the federal government, in light of individual corruption and government interests in the land, reveals the complicated and overwhelming situation that Native Americans, Hispanos, and Anglo homesteaders faced in trying to maintain their homes. This story is not merely a two-sided conflict of Anglo versus Hispano, capitalist versus worker, or company versus settler, but rather a multisided ordeal with fluid factions and changing alliances among the many parties.

In order to fully understand the entanglement of property regimes that existed in New Mexico, one must jettison the notion that the Anglo-American system intruded into a land devoid of settlement, land appropriation, ideas about exclusive possession, and other concepts associated with the idea of "property." Indeed, when the U.S. government arrived in 1846, the land was crisscrossed with a fine network of property understandings. Already in place on this landscape were the usufructuary system of the Jicarilla Apaches, contending French and Spanish imperial efforts to secure territory, immense land grants to secure the northern frontier of the Mexican Republic, communal grants to Pueblo Indians, parcels that Hispano farmers carved along scarce waterways and centered around plazas, the civil law system to protect married women's property, and the *patrón/peón* agreements about how to fix boundaries, pay rent, and allocate reciprocal services. Anglo-American notions of homesteading and fee simple absolute were merely added to this already complex mixture of property regimes, and had to blend with it in difficult, and even violent, ways. This mix was further stirred by businessmen and territorial politicians, such as the Santa Fe Ring, who sought to profit from this legal ambiguity, idealistic federal bureaucrats who wanted to promote yeoman farmers under the Homestead Act, and Dutch investors eager to realize a competitive return on their capital by securing interest in land that was fully marketable in London, New York, and Amsterdam. The interaction of these competing property regimes suggests a story much more complex than the tale of an unsocialized nature conquered by enterprising pioneers. Undoubtedly, the Turnerian notion that the West led to a culture rooted in private property has some truth. But what *sort* of private property? What sort of ownership arose from the cultural conflict that emerged as a result of westward migration?

## RACE AND LAND OWNERSHIP

Race in the American West has also been a subject of persistent confusion —one reflected in the publicity surrounding the *Espinoza v. Taylor* case. In both newspaper articles and newsletters, the trial was often portrayed as an unambiguous controversy between local Hispanos and outside Anglos: a familiar trope about race relations in the American Southwest. But the controversy could be more accurately understood as one between the landed and relatively landless—an economic rather than a racial struggle. Indeed, there is little evidence that Hispano residents in more urbanized areas had more than a passing interest in the Taylor Ranch struggle or, for that matter, that Anglo environmentalists sympathized with Zachary Taylor (Jack's son). The few outside observers at the trial were primarily young Anglo activists from Ancient Forest Rescue, anxious to see Taylor lose and his logging operation shut down. Somewhat surreally, lunchtime often brought together an unusual coalition of older, conservatively dressed Hispanos and young hippie-like activists who found much in common when discussing the arrogance of Taylor and his lawyer, Al Wolf.

In fact, racial categories of Anglo and Hispano are relatively recent phenomena that were imposed on the people of this region during the latter part of the nineteenth century. As outsiders moved onto land grants and pushed Native Americans and Mexican Americans aside, Anglos eventually came to equate landlessness with ethnicity, and particularly with being Indian or Mexican. Indeed, it was important to conflate ethnicity with landlessness as Americans fulfilled their Manifest Destiny to occupy, liberalize, and democratize the open spaces of the American West.[18] Americans argued that both Indians and Mexicans "wasted" the land, misusing its resources. They therefore felt justified in advocating dispossession and improvement of both the land and its inhabitants. But this struggle over land was not simply about Whites removing people of color. Throughout the late nineteenth and well into the twentieth century there were economic coalitions based on landowning status that cut across racial and ethnic boundaries. For example, Miguel Otero Sr., a prominent Hispano businessman, sat on the board of directors of the Maxwell Land Grant Company when its stated policy was the dispossession of Hispano settlers. On the other hand, when violent responses reached their pinnacle on the Maxwell Land Grant, it was a coalition of Hispano and Anglos who faced down the company agents. The coalition between Ancient Forest Rescue and Hispano farmers during the *Espinoza v. Taylor* trial represents only the most recent, but certainly not a new, coalition of people overcoming racial ideologies to fight for common economic interests.

The chapters in this book are roughly chronological, beginning with the story of the Maxwell Land Grant from the Mexican period in the 1840s to the first part of the twentieth century, when the Colorado Fuel and Iron Corporation came to control the grant's economy. Chapter 1 pushes back the old Maxwell Land Grant narrative, which typically begins with conveyance of the grant from the Mexican government to Carlos Beaubien in 1841, to include an account of the land's earliest inhabitants, the Jicarilla Apaches, and their land use patterns and mental boundaries of property definition in the area. The Jicarillas' complex system of usufructuary land rights and gendered division of labor created a stable economy and environment in which they survived with little disruption for years. Their land use and labor systems stood in juxtaposition to those of later Mexicans, Europeans, and Americans, who possessed different ideas about how to economically, legally, and politically order the landscape. The Jicarillas were able to create, in their own terms, an abundant economic and spiritual life that was not successfully replicated by any of the groups who followed. Those who came after the Jicarillas pushed them aside and scorned them for their land use pattern and lifestyle. These later settlers, whether Hispanos coming east across the Sangre de Cristo Mountains or Anglos moving west, never found the landscape to be abundant, at least in the terms that they used. Ideas about how to use land and what constituted economic success were in constant flux as various groups vied with one another for economic and political control of the grant.

The confines of the grant engulfed both settled and nomadic populations who possessed clear ideas about property and land use. From the earliest arrival of the Spanish in the late eighteenth century, when they "discovered" the Jicarillas, until the late nineteenth century, it was never entirely clear which ethnic group's property system would govern the lands encompassed by the Maxwell Land Grant. To appropriate Richard White's term, the early encounters on the grant constituted a "middle ground" in which the Spanish, French, and Jicarillas all vied for control of Spain's northern boundary and the people who lived there. Perhaps more importantly, this middle ground also allowed for a constant competition between land regimes, as no one group could impose their particular view and system onto the other inhabitants or the land.[19] These early contests over land control and resources established a pattern that would continue well into the twentieth century, but with a different cast of characters acting out the roles as each new wave of immigrants appeared on the land grant.

Chapter 2 builds upon this theme of competing property regimes by examining how Mexican married women and *peones* defined their property and labor relationships on this Mexican frontier prior to U.S. occupation in 1848. In certain respects, the U.S. westward expansion marked an *erosion* of liberal individualism rather than a *perfection* of liberal ideals, as Frederick Jackson Turner argued. Turner's thesis depended on the notion that migrants encountered no systems of social ordering, or at least that they encountered no system that was worth adopting. But chapter 2 reveals that with respect to gender and property, the Anglo immigrants encountered a more liberal and individualist regime, based on the civil law. They then destroyed that regime, replacing it with their own legal and cultural common-law system of "coverture"—the right of a husband to control his wife's property. The imposition of coverture on New Mexican women reduced these independent married women to a status resembling peonage, a feudalistic status that, ironically, the U.S. government had been arguing against and attempting to eliminate in its newly acquired territories.

While the land grant came under the control of the Mexican government, the civil law governed property relationships that allowed Mexican married women a degree of legal autonomy. Mexican women's U.S. counterparts did not hold these same privileges, although the U.S. legal system was beginning to liberalize with the passage of the first Married Women's Property Acts in the 1840s. The end of the U.S.-Mexican War, the signing of the Treaty of Guadalupe Hidalgo, and the resulting move of New Mexico into the orbit of the U.S. legal system changed all of Mexican married women's prior property arrangements. The changes forced them to compromise their autonomy as they moved into a more subordinate position under the U.S. system. These changes in the property systems were very deliberate moves on the part of the U.S. government and the people who came to take over the governance and property of these newly acquired territories.

Chapter 3 picks up another strand of change as it looks at how the world of the land grant changed dramatically with the sale of the land from the Maxwell family to the English bond-holding corporation that became known as the Maxwell Land Grant and Railway Company. Under the Maxwell family, the grant had been governed by complex customary ties under which the *patrón*, Lucien Maxwell, extracted from and gave to his clients—Jicarilla Apaches, Hispano *peones*, and even Anglo miners—an elaborately complex set of duties and payments. The new capitalist investors, however, found that this prior regime was an obstacle to their use of the land as security for the cash necessary for the massive investments and improvements they needed in order to realize a competitive rate of return. In order to attract European investors, these English and Dutch businessmen marketed the land as uninhabited and immediately available for improvement and European settlement. They also used their influence over territorial government, particularly their cozy relationship with the Santa Fe Ring, to expand the boundaries of the grant. Moreover, the degree to which Maxwell Company officials were able to assert common-law rights of exclusive possession was critically affected by other federal officials, such as the secretary of the interior and the commissioner of the general land office, whom they influenced. Given the cast of characters who came to New Mexico, Dutch investment in New Mexico was similar, but not identical, to Dutch investment in Indonesia, as well as British investment in Hawai'i and the Great Mahele: all of these cases relied on expropriation of the local inhabitants in order to force these regions and their natural resources into the world market.

Chapter 4 moves away from the conflicts over the grant that played themselves out in the national and international context of world markets, Washington politics, and European boardrooms to look at how these conflicts affected those living within the boundaries of the Maxwell Land Grant itself. By looking at the violent episodes on the grant—Jicarilla removal, the Colfax County conflict, and a myriad of other guerrilla-type skirmishes—we can look at how the grant's various inhabitants aligned themselves as they tried to preserve their homes and livelihoods. The inhabitants only occasionally organized themselves along racial lines, instead tending to cross racial boundaries and ally themselves with those who had similar economic interests. Race and culture were not fixed categories exogenous to actors' strategies for economic and political success, but were tools that outsiders, such as company and government officials, used to control and understand the cultural geography of the land grant. The company officials, the federal government, and, eventually, the Anglo homesteaders themselves gradually came to use race as a proxy for landlessness, attacking Hispanos as lackeys of the company in ways similar to how Americans and Hispanos had attacked propertyless Native Americans as too dependent on the federal government to be U.S. citizens. In turn, Dutch overseers of the grant relied on tried-and-true techniques of cultural accommodation to reduce settler resistance—techniques that had been employed successfully in Indonesia and other colonial locales.

Chapter 5 returns to the familiar theme of law and property. The narrative's climax occurs with the U.S. Supreme Court's 1887 decision that all prior property regimes on the grant were void, and only the title of the Maxwell Land Grant and Railway Company to 1.7 million acres remained valid. In reaching this decision, the Supreme Court had to legally maneuver around the complexity that surrounded the competing titles to own property on the grant. How would the court balance the fee simple absolute rights of the Maxwell Land Grant Company against the ambiguous rights of the Hispano settlers and against the U.S. federal government, which was making strong claims to what they saw as the public domain within the company's claimed boundaries? Chapter 5 argues that European and eastern capitalists and the U.S. federal government did not simply expropriate settlers; rather, they manipulated the precapitalist Mexican rules of property, respecting the old regime in part (e.g., vast parcels of land) but ignoring those aspects that prevented capitalist development (e.g., *patrón*/client obligations). Why did the Supreme Court engage in what I term a mistranslation of the Mexican/civil law system of property and award sole property ownership to the foreign corporation of the Maxwell Land Grant Company? For exactly the same reasons that Judge Perricone in 1998 in *Espinoza v. Taylor* recognized only Zachary Taylor's rights: the alternative was too complex for the U.S. legal system to embrace and would have involved recognizing prior property regimes as equal to U.S. common law. Furthermore, such a decision would have compelled local, state, territorial, and federal governments to protect the property rights of former Mexican citizens, who were quickly losing status in the American West at the time. This type of recognition and protection for a people who were coming to be regarded as inferior was certainly something that the U.S. government at the end of the nineteenth century was unwilling to do as it sought to encourage European investment and development of the American West.

Chapter 6 looks at the aftermath of the Supreme Court's 1887 decision. As all of the residents on the grant came to face the reality of lost property rights, some settlers, both Anglos and Hispanos, turned to violence, the pinnacle of which was a deadly battle in Stonewall, Colorado. Simultaneously, many also turned to Populism and its rhetoric in an attempt to overturn the decision. But the agitation had few results, and eventually everyone came to accept the Maxwell Company's dominant position. Nevertheless, further dramatic economic changes were enveloping the grant as the Colorado Fuel and Iron Corporation moved onto the grant and began mining and exploiting one of the nation's largest coal deposits. With the arrival of wage labor on the grant, former small landholders lost their land and moved into the workforce as miners and steelworkers. Now the only asset they had was their own ability to work and compete with other workers in this emerging coal mining economy. This dramatic move from the land to wage work begins to explain how Mexicans, Mexican Americans, Chicanos, or Hispanos (however we choose to label them) came to be seen as landless wageworkers. This move to wage work essentially erased any prior history that Mexicans had with the land that was once theirs, but which became incorporated, both politically and economically, into the United States. Finally, the move explains why Judge Perricone, Zachary Taylor, and most Westerners have not understood the historical, economic, and legal ties that Mexican Americans in the Southwest have to the land.

This story of how New Mexico and, consequently, the land and people of the Maxwell Land Grant became a part of the United States reveals the colonial and imperial tendencies of the United States during the latter part of the nineteenth century. By studying the land grant and its inhabitants, we can begin to understand how "foreigners," whether Native American, Mexican American, or Dutch, were incorporated into the dominant economic and political system of the U.S. government. Finally, the story of the Maxwell Land Grant provides a unique glimpse into a world where outsiders sought ways to divide the inhabitants by race (Indian, Mexican, and White, to use their terms) and by class (landowners and landless). However, as the various groups of settlers made one last effort to get the company off the land grant, they overcame the racial and class differences imposed upon them by company and government officials in order to preserve their common rights and interests.

# 1    Contested Boundaries

In the beginning nothing was here where the world now
stands. . . . It was a lonely place. . . . It was then that the Jicarilla
Apache dwelt under the earth.
                    "The Jicarilla Genesis," in Richard Erdoes and
          Alfonso Ortiz, eds., *American Indian Myths and Legends*

From the moment that its first human inhabitants, the Jicarilla Apaches,
set foot on what would become known as the Maxwell Land Grant, people
told stories that marked boundaries on the landscape. These stories and
boundary markers were rooted in the particular culture of the group in-
habiting the land. The Jicarillas, in particular, marked their territory by
the natural boundaries of the four rivers that surrounded their homeland.
In turn, the Spanish explorers gave natural features (rivers, mountains,
springs) Spanish Catholic labels to mark their possession. The Mexican
government, through its grantees Carlos Beaubien and Guadalupe Miranda,
used maps and seison (the physical act of taking possession) to mark the
land grant that they and their contemporaries knew as the Beaubien/
Miranda Land Grant. And finally, the U.S. federal government used the
power of the state—through the military, office of the surveyor general,
and the federal courts—to mark the boundaries of the place they knew as
the Maxwell Land Grant. All of these competing groups labeled the landscape with a different name, marked its boundaries by different means, and
even drew different boundaries that were in constant conflict with their
neighbors' notions about property and ownership. It was a situation that
inevitably led to violent confrontations.

Past histories of the Maxwell Land Grant have typically focused on the
traditional American Western narrative of Anglo male-dominated violence.[1] But these physical and most obvious manifestations of conflict have
overshadowed the real underlying tension present on the grant since its
earliest occupation: the contest over land and property rights. However, as
Patricia Nelson Limerick astutely observed, "If Hollywood wanted to capture the emotional center of western history, its movies would be about real
estate. John Wayne would have been neither a gunfighter nor a sheriff, but

a surveyor, speculator or claims lawyer."² This history of the Maxwell Land Grant, then, goes beyond the typical narrative of violence and places different historical characters—*peones*, women, bondholders, lawyers, and surveyors—at the center of the narrative in order to reveal how the seemingly mundane acts of making a living and using property have regional and even worldwide consequences.

Two themes help us to understand this contest. First, the local inhabitants of the grant resisted "outside" control from distant invaders. When Jicarilla Apaches fought off U.S. federal troops and resisted their removal to a distant reservation, and Father Antonio José Martínez filed petitions protesting land grants to Yankee speculators, and settlers burned the homes of Maxwell Land Grant Company agents, they all voiced and acted upon their opposition to claims made by absentee landowners and government officials. Although the meaning of who was an "outsider" and what constituted an indigenous landowner changed with each passing wave of immigration, the conflicts among these fluid groups remained a constant source of tension on the grant.

Second, from the outset there was conflict over how people derived their claims to property. Local inhabitants such as the Jicarillas and Hispano settlers claimed to use the land through local custom and historic practice. On the other hand, the claims of outsiders such as homesteaders and land corporations were based on formally enacted, positive legal authority. The conflicts between usufructuary and codified legal right holders, as well as the violent episodes that ensued, were fairly inevitable. The sources of laws affecting the land grant lay beyond the grant's physical boundaries in the national capitals of Washington, D.C., and Mexico City, neither of which had an understanding of or respect for property regimes already in place on the grant. Indian removal, the Colfax County conflict, and the Stonewall Valley skirmish were the violent manifestations of the differences between outside, formally enacted laws and local, informal property regimes.

This first chapter looks at the earliest conflicts over the land that the Jicarillas saw as their homeland, the Mexican government subsequently called the Beaubien/Miranda Land Grant, and the U.S. government saw as the commercial link between the eastern states and newly acquired western territory. The chapter chronicles the arrival of the grant's first inhabitants, the Jicarilla Apaches, and their ensuing encounters with the Spanish and French empires, the later encroachments on their land by Mexican settlers, and their violent confrontations with the U.S. cavalry. As control of the land moved away from the informal and local Jicarilla power to the more formalized and distant structures of the Mexican and U.S. governments, many people protested and resisted this shift in power. These early conflicts set the stage for future contests over the land, which would become even more violent and legally entangled as the century wore on.

## THE EARLIEST INHABITANTS: THE JICARILLA APACHES

The Jicarillas used the land and its resources for hundreds of years prior to any European incursions into the area. They established successful patterns of land use by taking advantage of the region's diversity without burdening a particular parcel with overuse or mono-agriculture. It was a land use system that later arrivals to the area would have been well advised to take note of and mimic. Hispano and Anglo settlers, however, only scoffed at the Jicarillas' usufructuary practices as they established larger, permanent communities and European agricultural practices.

Much of the Jicarillas' success came because they lived in a hybrid place of sorts, between the Pueblos to their west and the Plains Indians to the east. They borrowed cultural practices from both of these groups and adapted them to their own particular environment. The Jicarillas also occupied a middle ground when, after Europeans appeared on their borders, they lived and negotiated their existence in the world between the clashing French and Spanish empires, which were both working the fur-trapping areas of the Arkansas River basin.[3] The Jicarillas also provide an important starting point because they were the first group to lose their land base in 1876.[4] Their story teaches important lessons about the role of the state in dispossessing landowners, as the U.S. federal government took a paternalistic role in finding the Jicarillas another homeland. But, as subsequent chapters will show, the federal government would not act as benevolently toward Mexican settlers, Anglo miners, and even U.S. homesteaders. The different attitudes that the U.S. government took toward the Jicarillas and the grant's later inhabitants help explain much of the confusion and difficulty in settling the land grant's boundaries.

The Jicarillas viewed their home on the eastern slope of the Sangre de Cristo Mountains as a viable and secure place for their material survival. They also viewed it as a spiritual home for themselves and their ancestors. Jicarilla creation stories explain that after the people emerged from the underworld and roamed around this world, they asked the Supreme Deity if they could live near the center of the earth. He agreed, found them a home near the Taos people, and created four sacred rivers—today known as the Arkansas to the north, the Canadian to the east, the Rio Grande to the south, and the Chama to the west—to mark the boundaries of the

Jicarillas' country.[5] (See map 2.) Although there was mutual raiding of animals and peoples among the three groups at particular historical moments, the Jicarillas lived in relatively peaceful coexistence with their Pueblo and Plains neighbors. On the other hand, prior to the Pueblo Revolt against the Spanish in 1680, many Pueblo Indians took refuge among the Jicarillas as they sought to escape the domineering watch of the Catholic priests and Spanish government.

The competing scientific narrative of how the Jicarillas came to live in the area brings us to the same, if less eloquent, conclusion: the Jicarillas arrived and lived in the area we know as the Maxwell Land Grant today. Although anthropologists dispute the exact date, sometime between the fourteenth and sixteenth centuries the Jicarilla Apaches, descendants of the southern Athapaskans, migrated south from Canada along a path between the Rocky Mountains and the Great Plains. As they reached what is now known as the American Southwest, they separated into two clans: the Moache Utes and the Jicarilla Apaches. The western group, the Moache Utes, followed the route of the Navajo Indians and settled in southwestern Colorado, where their descendants still live today. The eastern group, the Jicarilla Apaches, continued along the Great Plains and made their homes in north-central New Mexico and south-central Colorado, straddling both sides of the Sangre de Cristo Mountains.

Once settled in the area, the Jicarillas again divided into two tribes. The *olleros* (the pot-makers and mountain-valley people), known for their micaceous-clay pottery, lived along the upper tributaries of the Rio Grande as far north as the Conejos River in the San Luis Valley in present-day Colorado. While they interacted and traded with their companion groups on the other side of the mountains, they maintained a world external to the boundaries of the land grant. Most of their contact and trade, instead, was with the Pueblos of the Rio Grande and their Ute neighbors to their west. The *llaneros* (plains people), on the other hand, conformed more to the lifestyle of the Plains Indians and lived on the eastern slope of the Sangre de Cristo Mountains on the New Mexico plains—right in the heart of what would become the Maxwell Land Grant. The Jicarilla *llaneros* were relative latecomers to the Plains and adapted to the economic, social, and cultural patterns of their more-established neighbors. Both the buffalo hunting culture of the Plains Indians as well as the sedentary farming traits of the Pueblos influenced the Jicarillas as they settled themselves on the middle ground, both geographically and culturally, between the two dominant groups. According to anthropologist Morris Opler, "Jicarilla culture

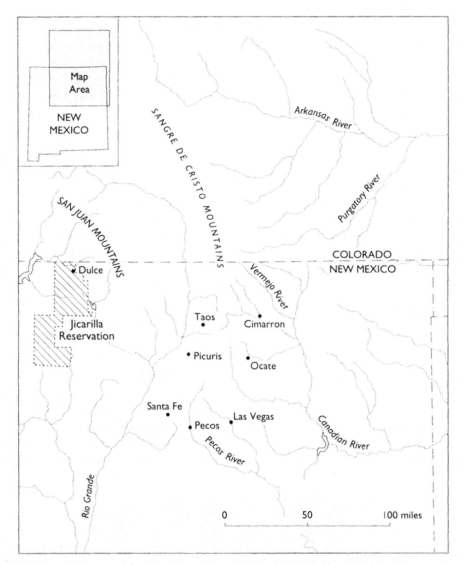

Map 2. Jicarilla homeland.

can best be comprehended as a growth and modification of the basic southern Athapaskan pattern in terms of Plains and Pueblo influences."[6]

The unique way in which both groups of the Jicarillas organized their communities had important implications for how they used the environment around them. Jicarillas' matrilocal organization, in which they lived in extended families consisting of parents, grandparents, and married daughters, in many ways dictated the way they divided their energies between agriculture and hunting. Each group member possessed two social identities, based first on the family into which one was born, and second on the family into which one married. From these relationships, a complex system of kinship developed among the many families and bound them together. Larger kinship networks, consisting of groups of extended families, traveled together in search of food and shelter and were led by an elected body of elderly men and women, who dealt with the outside world of other Indians, Spaniards, and later the Americans. Furthermore, usually a single chief for each group, descended from father to son, carried the largest burden of negotiating with outsiders. This system of loose affiliations allowed the Jicarillas the mobility necessary to adapt themselves to the sparse environment, as the groups could scatter across the countryside and come together at appointed times in the year.[7] A second advantage was that outsiders, particularly the Spanish and later the Americans, found this loose affiliation of groups frustratingly difficult to negotiate with during confrontations. In many cases, the constant shuttling that American diplomats would have to do among the various Jicarilla groups would buy the Indians time, space, and concessions in their negotiations as their opponents tired of traveling across the mountains and across the plains for treaty approval.[8] In reality, the tribal identity—Jicarilla Apache—was a European and American government construction placed upon this group of Native Americans who were loosely affiliated with one another through marriage and economic bases. Nevertheless, this construction would have important consequences for how these Indians thought of themselves and their relationship to the Mexicans and Americans who lived around them.

The harsh ecological and complex social landscapes of the area forced the Jicarillas to adopt a diversified economy. Because of the Plains tribes who raided Jicarilla settlements, the development of agriculture remained an uneven and precarious endeavor. Even so, the Jicarillas built temporary flat-roofed homes along the Cimarron, Poñil, and Purgatory Rivers, where they augmented the unreliable rainfall with irrigation to raise melons, squash, and corn.[9] Jicarilla lore attributed the origins of agriculture to a man; consequently, both Jicarilla men and women worked the fields.

Within the agricultural system, however, gendered divisions of labor were negotiated, with men preparing the fields, irrigating the crops, and harvesting while women, seeded, hoed, weeded, and helped in the fields.[10]

Although the Jicarillas practiced a limited form of agriculture, hunting was the mainstay of their existence, and the exclusive domain of men. Large animals such as buffalo, mountain sheep, antelope, deer, and elk provided not only food but also material goods. They used the hides to make housing covers, sinew for thread, rawhide for ropes and straps, and tanned skins for clothing and shoes. Smaller animals such as beaver, rabbit, squirrel, chipmunk, porcupine, and prairie dog augmented their diet. They used eagles, mountain lions, wildcats, and land turtles for feathers, furs, and body parts for religious and ceremonial purposes. Raiding and warfare infused resources into the Jicarillas' economy but came under the men's control as well.[11] Gathering efforts by the women further augmented the Jicarillas' agriculture and hunting, with wild berries and fruits, acorns, piñon nuts, and seed-bearing grasses all providing nutritious supplements to their diet. Women also gathered herbs, tubers, and leaves for medicinal purposes.[12]

The Jicarillas' success in maintaining themselves through agriculture, hunting, and gathering depended on both the diverse nature of the landscape and their gendered approach to expropriating the resources from the meager environment of New Mexico's high eastern plains. This varied land use pattern, however, was not something that later immigrants to the area imitated. In fact, in most cases Europeans disparaged Jicarilla land use for not exhibiting wealth or abundance.[13] People who later lived in the area in some ways did not take much notice of the Jicarillas because they were relatively peaceful and highly mobile. The Spanish were not particularly aware of them until the first part of the eighteenth century, after which they were constantly searching for the locus of their population so that they could trade with them and possibly establish a mission.[14] When Lucien B. Maxwell took over the land grant, he was remarkably unconcerned with their presence within his property boundaries. They were too mobile for him to worry about what they might be taking away from his land. But while this diverse use of resources served the Jicarillas well in their day-to-day existence, in the eyes of Europeans who would come to dominate the area, the Jicarillas' land use patterns gave them little claim to ownership. While not passive or static, their relationship with their environment was based on informal networks among themselves in order to exploit the land's resources while sustaining its long-term capability of providing a livelihood for them through mobility.[15] In short, their land use pattern was usufructuary, and this was not a system that Europeans or Americans counted as property ownership.

## EUROPEAN INCURSIONS

In July of 1706, the Spanish made one of their first forays into Jicarilla territory. The expedition, led by Gen. Juan de Ulibarrí, sergeant major of the territory, took to the field on behalf of the Spanish governor of the province of New Mexico. Ulibarrí's fifty fighting men and "some elements of friendly Pueblo and mission Indians from different nations" headed east to map the terrain and negotiate with the Jicarillas for the return of Pícuris Pueblo Indians who were "in the captivity and oppression of the barbarous infidel nations, the Apaches of the Plains." [16] Although the Spanish were interested in seeing their neophytes returned to the Rio Grande Valley and the Pueblos kept happy, they were also concerned about rumors that the French were encroaching on their territory via the fur-trapping rivers on the eastern plains. Ulibarrí set out to take control of this northern frontier from both the Jicarillas and the French.

Ulibarrí used the quintessentially European and Spanish way of taking possession of the eastern frontier: he made public his discovery and named—actually renamed, to be precise—every geographic object he encountered.[17] His renaming was neither an oversight nor the result of ignorance, but rather a reinscription of Spanish meaning and power over the landscape. As Ulibarrí crossed the Sangre de Cristo Mountains to the east (which had already been renamed by the Spaniards for a martyred priest), he entered what he dramatically described as *terra incognita*. He wrote, "We came to another very narrow and steep canyon, and because of the great amount of fallen trees, I ordered it to be called La Palotada (Fallen Timbers)." Ulibarrí, however, was a bit taken aback when he came upon a white cross painted on a poplar tree, which had apparently been there for quite a while given its weathered appearance. So much for undiscovered territory. But he recovered quickly and simply named the small pond next to the cross *Santa Cruz*—Holy Cross.[18] Even when Ulibarrí encountered a river that his Indians interpreters recognized and knew the name of, he remained unabashed and simply renamed it. He wrote, "We came to a large river all the nations call the Napeste. Remembering the name of the Señor Governor and Captain General, [and] in memorable praise of his Christian zeal, I gave it [the river] the name after his saint, calling it the Río Grande de San Francisco." [19] In fact, as one reads the document, it is clear that Ulibarrí and his men discover nothing. They are traveling over well-worn

Indian trading trails and being led by Indian guides and interpreters. Furthermore, not a day goes by that they do not encounter native peoples or their farming plots along the river bottoms. By the beginning of the eighteenth century, this was anything but *terra incognita.*

As Ulibarrí and his group ascended the last rise in the Sangre de Cristos and looked down across the eastern plains, he was convinced that he was now looking down upon undiscovered territory that awaited his conquest and Spanish control. He hurriedly descended from the mountains and crossed the first river, which he named "Río de San Francisco Xavier, with whose blessing I passed into unknown land, barbarously populated by innumerable infidel nations." In naming rivers, valleys, and mountains, Ulibarrí invoked the authority of the Catholic Church and Spanish Crown over the landscape by christening these sites with the names of saints (Santo Tomás, San Blas, San Nicolás, Santa Catalina) and of government officials. He even chose one particularly fertile valley to name after himself—Cañon de Ulibarrí.

In his act of crossing the land and naming places, Ulibarrí subdued and conquered the territory, which he gendered as female, with a force that was decidedly male, both in composition of its forces and in his attitude. He wrote of the fertility and fecundity of the landscape near the rivers and even marked particularly evocative aspects of the territory with references to the female body—"discovering on the right-hand side in the distance two small hills, quite similar and pointed, which I ordered named Tetas [Breasts] de Domínguez." [20] For the Spanish, and for Ulibarrí, in particular, it did not matter that they traveled over territory that had already been mapped and used by the Jicarillas and other groups. The Spanish model for mapping, and therefore taking control of a territory, was to reconnoiter, to "discover," and to name without regard to what had been placed on the landscape before them. [21]

About two weeks into the expedition, Ulibarrí came across a *ranchería grande,* a Jicarilla settlement, in which the Jicarillas "had danced over the scalp of a white man they had killed, and from whom they had also taken a long musket, a cap with red lining, and the gun powder he carried. They had also killed the pregnant woman who traveled with this white man." [22] The Jicarillas became alarmed by Ulibarrí's presence at this particular time, because they feared that he had come to take revenge for the killing of the white couple, who they assumed were Spanish. Actually, the Jicarillas did not distinguish among the Europeans they had encountered and were relieved when Ulibarrí explained that the couple was French—the rivals to the Spaniards. All seemed settled until the Jicarillas brought Ulibarrí the

musket that the dead man had been carrying. Ulibarrí wrote of the encounter: "When they brought the musket they saw the surprise it caused
us—particularly in the Frenchman we brought with us named . . . de
Archibeque. He said that he recognized the musket as belonging to his
cousin."[23] After this exchange, misinterpretation and distrust emerged
between the Jicarillas and the Spanish. Ulibarrí became concerned because
the couple's presence indicated that the French were beginning to settle in
the area, and he clearly did not hide his consternation. The Jicarillas told
them that there were other Spaniards (in reality, French) traveling with
their Indian enemies and giving muskets and powder to them. Indeed, the
couple had been killed only because they had been caught in an ambush
that the Jicarillas had made upon their enemies. Archibeque, of course, was
disturbed by the murder of his family member, which only added to the
tension.

At this point, the Jicarillas were confused and concerned enough to begin changing their story to Ulibarrí. Sensing Ulibarrí's and Archibeque's
alarm, the Jicarillas told them that the man really was not French, but
rather a "Panana chief" who just happened to have the musket. They then
"excused themselves from showing us the ladle, and cap, and the rest of
the spoils, and it was impossible to convince them to show them to us later,
making the excuse that [the items] were in other *rancherías*."[24] Perhaps
the Jicarillas had not completely understood that there were rival groups of
Europeans in their midst, and they had misinterpreted Ulibarrí's concern as
being over a dead comrade. When they quickly tried to backpedal on their
story and change the ethnic identity of the victim, their change in attitude
angered Ulibarrí, who did not want to be lied to by the Jicarillas. He began
to distrust them and became frustrated when they refused to tell him any
more about the dead couple or other "Spanish" trappers they had seen.

Ulibarrí also worried because he had seen evidence that other Europeans,
and he surmised they were French, had already been visiting and trading with the Jicarillas. When he had arrived at the *ranchería grande*, the
Jicarillas immediately took him to a large cross on the hill. He wrote, "A
Chief came and had me approach the Cross, and, having showed it to us, all
of the Spaniards and the Christian Indians dismounted and kissed and did
reverence to it."[25] The first cross that he had encountered earlier in the expedition had startled him, but did not immediately make him think of the
French. But this larger cross, combined with their pseudo-Catholic ritual,
disturbed him. Ulibarrí found what he had feared most: the Jicarillas had
encountered the French. Ulibarrí continued to question the Jicarillas, who
told him that there were more people to the east than there were in New

Mexico. "And although they can not distinguish their nation—if they are English or French," he wrote, "the Apaches buy from them many things made of iron, like hatchets, sword blades, arquebuses, and copper ladles, which, according to them, are numerous in this land." They also told Ulibarrí that their enemies sold the Jicarilla women and children to the French just as the Jicarillas sold captured slaves to the Spaniards. In these raids they had also managed to obtain three muskets. Ulibarrí worried that the French, or possibly the Dutch, were quite nearby and attempting to influence the Jicarillas.[26]

But what Ulibarrí found even more disturbing was their obvious contact with the Catholic missionaries, because it implied a more sustained relationship than the passing contact of trade. Ulibarrí wrote in his report,

> The Apaches wear many Crosses, [saints'] medals, and rosaries around their necks, and this is known to be a very old practice. . . . After making some repairs, we asked them why they wear crosses, medals, and rosaries, without knowing what they were. [They responded] that for many years they dealt with and traded with the Spaniards [Ulibarrí assumes that they mean the French], and they know that since they wear crosses, rosaries, and saints they are very valiant, and that there is no nation that can defeat them.[27]

Although Ulibarrí had misgivings about the honesty and forthrightness of the Jicarillas, he realized that he needed to act quickly and strategically in order to combat the French influence. He also needed to negotiate with the Jicarillas for the return of the Pícuris Indians, the original justification for the expedition. So Ulibarrí began to negotiate for the return of the captives. In exchange for the seventy-two Pueblo Indians and the French musket, Ulibarrí gave the Jicarillas a musket, some horses, various food staples, and the promise that the Spanish would return to the Jicarilla camps the following spring to help the Jicarillas fight their French-influenced Indian enemies. Ulibarrí's report of his reconnaissance and his conversations with the Jicarillas, who seemed content when he left them and anxious for Spanish aid against their enemies, convinced the New Mexican governor to fortify his northern frontier by creating a series of forts. Because of the Jicarillas' more sedentary lifestyle and friendliness, the Spanish government in Santa Fe tended to view them as allies against raiding Indians and the expanding French. By 1714 the Spanish employed them as an auxiliary army on their northern border.[28]

Unfortunately, there is relatively little historical material to help fill in the story of Spanish/Jicarilla relations during the eighteenth and nineteenth centuries. Through continued trade and missionary contact, the

Europeans introduced Christianity, Spanish and French words, foreign material goods, and the horse. Given their centuries-old pattern of adopting different aspects of divergent cultures, the Jicarillas selectively adopted parts of the European culture and economy. It was their adaptability and their ability to forge a lifestyle in this middle ground that allowed the Jicarillas to remain at peace with both the French and the Spanish and at an equilibrium with their Indian enemies. As Spanish and later Mexican settlers made their way north from Santa Fe and east from Taos during the first half of the nineteenth century, the Jicarillas tried to avoid conflict by living on the outskirts of the Spanish empire and the Mexican Republic. With the transfer of government from Spain to Mexico, however, and the arrival of the ever-increasing numbers of Hispano settlers from the south and Anglo traders from the east, the Jicarillas began to feel their world encroached upon.[29]

## MEXICAN BOUNDARIES: THE BEAUBIEN AND MIRANDA GRANT

The Jicarillas' troubles with outside encroachers began in January 1841, when New Mexico governor Manuel Armijo granted to Carlos Hipolite Trotier Beaubien and Guadalupe Miranda, two prominent citizens and close friends, a large tract of land in the northeast corner of the New Mexican province. In the petition that the two men sent to Governor Armijo, they wrote of the natural abundance of the grant going to waste because enterprising farmers, stock raisers, and miners had yet to take control of the land and reap its resources. In their minds, the area was the perfect location to develop a Mexican hacienda. The two men were particularly concerned with the underdevelopment of New Mexico and the way it had suffered under Spanish colonial rule. They wrote, "Of all the departments of the republic, with the exception of the Californias, New Mexico is one of the most backward in intelligence, industry, [and] manufactories." The two men believed that this was an opportune time to develop the grant's resources, which would allow them to trade with New Mexico's interior towns along the Rio Grande. They also pointed out that the grant's natural resources, such as "the fertility of the soil, containing within its bosom rich and precious metals, which, up to this time, are useless for the want of enterprising men, who will convert them to the advantage of other men," could be developed for trade with larger markets such as the thriving Chihuahua Trail trade with Mexico and the emerging Santa Fe Trail trade with the United States. Beaubien and Miranda, forward-thinking entrepreneurs, were eager to exploit the grant's resources and begin competing in the larger market economy that waited at the threshold of New Mexico as the Santa Fe Trail trade began picking up.[30]

The two men were not only interested in making money for themselves as hacienda owners and trail traders; they also assured Armijo that their ownership would have economic benefits that would spread across the region. They viewed "idleness as the mother of vice" and wanted to bring the land under their private ownership so that they could induce their fellow New Mexicans to migrate across the mountains, form communities, and become industrious farmers, ranchers, and miners on the new land grant. What was not clear, however, was who in particular would migrate to work the land, and what their legal status would be. Would they be viewed by Beaubien and Miranda as small individual landowners, as sharecroppers, as wage laborers who worked for cash, or as *peones* who would have an economic and social relationship to the *patrones* that would not be based on a cash economy? Beaubien and Miranda themselves were not entirely clear about who would live and work on the grant, but they wrote about settling their own large families there and employing the "hands of individuals who would work" the property. Although they made no specific reference to settling or hiring colonists and workers, their intended enterprise obviously required settled labor beyond that of their immediate families if their frontier enterprise was to succeed. These details were important because the grant's intended use determined how much acreage Armijo, under Mexican law, could give the two men. If the grant was only for their personal use, then the acreage was limited to eleven leagues (about 97,000 acres) for each grantee. If, however, they intended to settle families, build communities, and develop the grant, then Armijo could give them unlimited acreage.[31]

These important legal details did not seem to concern either Governor Armijo or Beaubien and Miranda, as the three men were close friends. Beaubien was a French Canadian who had migrated to Taos through the fur trade and his connections to the St. Vrain family. He had married María Paula Lobato, a local, prominent, and wealthy Hispana, and for fourteen years had made his home in Taos, where he was a politically, economically, and socially leading citizen.[32] Guadalupe Miranda had even stronger ties to Governor Armijo as he was Armijo's collector of customs for New Mexico, a coveted and important job because the customs fees were integral to the New Mexican government's financial solvency. It was also rumored that a large portion of Armijo's wealth came from the money he skimmed from the customs collection.[33]

Their close connections through government business and financial dealings had probably allowed the three men to discuss the purpose of the land grant and its economic potential prior to Beaubien and Miranda's petition. Because of these ties, no one on either side of the transaction felt the need to specifically delineate the legal terms of the grant. Therefore, within a matter of days, Armijo granted his friends' request without much fanfare and without revealing the exact legal status of the grant. Armijo wrote, "In view of the request of the petitioners, and what they state therein being apparent, this government, in conformity with law, has been proper to grant and donate to the individuals subscribed, the land therein expressed, in order that they may make the proper use of it, which the law allows."[34]

Political events, however, prevented Beaubien and Miranda from taking immediate possession of the grant. In June 1841 the Republic of Texas crossed the international border and invaded New Mexico, claiming that Texas's western boundary extended to the Rio Grande, encompassing the major New Mexican cities of Santa Fe and Taos. Although the invasion was quickly rebuffed, and the filibusters were jailed and punished by Armijo, anti-foreign sentiment swept across New Mexico.[35] Critics of the grant, including Father Antonio José Martínez, suspected the political loyalty of everyone who was not a native New Mexican, and Martínez suspected Beaubien in particular because he was French by birth and was known to be friendly with American traders and trappers. In 1817 Martínez had left his family and village in New Mexico to attend the Tridentine seminary in Durango, Mexico. There he studied for the priesthood amid the height of the fervent nationalism that swept the Mexican countryside, and which would eventually culminate in Mexico wresting its independence from the Spanish crown. It was here that Father Martínez became imbued with a liberal political philosophy that championed the Mexican poor against foreigners and the rich. Martínez became an ardent Mexican nationalist, liberal, and advocate; this philosophy carried over into his career as a local parish priest near Taos, New Mexico.[36]

Although Martínez tried to stop Beaubien and Miranda from taking possession of the grant, by 1843 the public fear of foreigners had died down. So, Beaubien and Miranda asked Don Cornelio Vigil, justice of the peace, to officially transfer the land to them. On February 22, 1843, Vigil, Beaubien, and Miranda ventured out from Santa Fe and Taos east across the Sangre de Cristos to survey the land, erect mounds that would mark the boundaries of their property, and convey it to the petitioners. No mention was ever made of the Jicarillas who already lived in the area, and the three men marked the territory as if there were no competing claims to the land. In the Spanish and Mexican tradition of conveying property, the three men walked the perimeter of the grant, which would have been hundreds of miles, leaving behind five cairns to mark the boundaries where natural geographic markers were unavailable. Vigil then made a map of the land grant depicting various natural topographic features such as mountains and rivers, as well as the five markers (see map 3). While Vigil used straight lines to convey the extent of the grant, in reality the boundaries were based on the area's natural topography. Vigil's mapping reveals an intermediary step between the Jicarilla mental map of the property encompassed by the four rivers and the U.S. surveyor general's map, based on the grid system, which would eventually be acknowledged as showing the grant's legal boundaries. While the Mexicans grantees and grantors accepted and embraced the natural limits of the land parcel, they also placed artificial boundaries to mark the private property.

The Mexican government, based on Spanish custom, also had a formal ceremony for taking possession of private land. Justice of the Peace Vigil went with Beaubien and Miranda into the land and "took them by the hand, walked with them, caused them to throw earth, pull up weeds and show other evidences of possession." These acts signified the taking of land as symbols of the grantees' work and improvement of the grant. If "idleness was the mother of vice," then this performance of work signified their ability and desire to possess the land and develop its full potential. Vigil, after asking Beaubien and Miranda to take formal possession, then gave the two men the "perfect and personal possession asked for by them in order that it may answer as a sufficient title for them, their children, and successors."[37]

American lawyers and historians have since speculated as to whether or not this conveyance from Vigil to the two grantees actually took place; the historical evidence does leave open the question of the validity of the ceremony. For instance, on February 22, 1843, the day that they supposedly took possession, Beaubien and Miranda were not in the vicinity and therefore could not have participated. Even if they left Taos on February 23, we know that they were back in Taos within a week because on March 2, 1843, they signed notarized documents that conveyed interests in the grant to both Governor Armijo and their friend Charles Bent. Given the distance between the markers (hundreds of miles), the fact that two of the

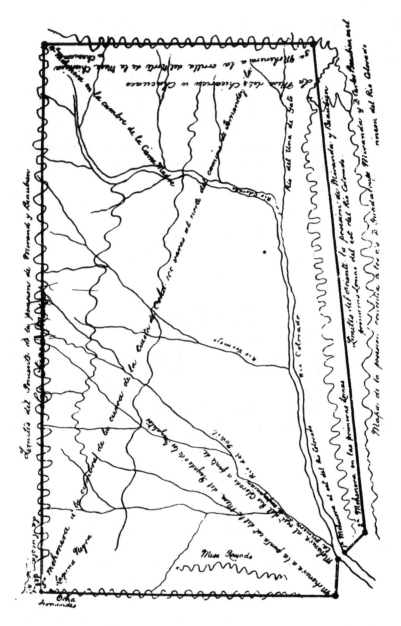

Map 3. Cornelio Vigil map of the Beaubien/Miranda Land Grant. From U.S. Department of Justice Papers, *U.S. v. Maxwell Land Grant Company*, Complaint 72100, RG 267, NA, WDC, Exhibits.

cairns were in the heart of the Sangre de Cristo Mountains, and the time of year—dead of winter—it seems almost impossible that the investiture of the land took place as they said it did and with all of the appropriate pomp and circumstance.[38] This was only one of the irregularities that lawyers would later point to in attempting to invalidate the grant's boundaries. The imprecise language in both the Beaubien/Miranda petition for the land grant and Armijo's conveyance coupled with the questions surrounding the ceremony all laid the foundation for later charges of corruption in Governor Armijo's grant to Beaubien and Miranda.

Within two weeks of the alleged conveyance, Father Martínez lodged another and more effective objection. This time he was concerned with the grant's vast size. First, although Beaubien denied it, Martínez made public the fact that Charles Bent, an American, had been given a share of the grant.[39] Father Martínez pointed out that Governor Armijo had no authority to convey land to foreigners. Ever since Texas had wrested its independence from Mexico in 1836, the Mexican government had been particularly careful about giving land to outsiders. Bent's interest in the grant, argued Martínez, should make the whole transaction null and void. Martínez challenged Bent because he viewed Bent as an Anglo interloper and his primary public enemy. Three years later Martínez would be accused of instigating the Taos Rebellion against the newly installed U.S. government, in which the then-governor Bent and Carlos Beaubien's son Narcisco were murdered by a group of Hispanos and Pueblo Indians from Taos.[40]

In opposing the land grant in 1843, Martínez also pointed out that both the Pueblo tribes of the upper Rio Grande Valley and the Plains tribes, particularly the Jicarillas, used the land as a hunting ground. He also reminded Governor Armijo that Hispano villagers from the *río arriba* area of the Rio Grande used the area within the grant as a commons for grazing livestock in the summer. Martínez feared that placing such a large tract of land in private hands would leave Indians and Hispanos without a livelihood. A great champion of the poorer inhabitants of the province, Martínez opposed such large private land grants in principle because they deprived the local people of common grazing land and, consequently, their means of survival. He feared that once entrepreneurs like Beaubien, Miranda, or Bent controlled the land, they would put it to commercial use and shun the local subsistence use that the Pueblos and Hispanos depended upon. Martínez launched the first formal legal conflict over the meaning of property as the usufructuary practices of the Jicarillas and the communal practices of the Hispanos collided with the nascent market capitalism of these entrepreneurs.

Furthermore, Martínez's opposition to the Beaubien/Miranda Land Grant played itself out before a backdrop of fears about Anglo encroachment in New Mexico. Just about the time that Vigil finally conveyed the land to Beaubien and Miranda, Josiah Gregg published *Commerce of the Prairies,* an account of the value of the Santa Fe Trail trade between the United States and New Mexico, which encouraged increased trade across the trail.[41] Martínez and his followers believed they would not necessarily benefit from the trade, and in fact feared they would be taken advantage of by the Americans. Martínez left New Mexico immediately after the conveyance to Beaubien and Miranda and traveled to Durango, Mexico, where he successfully petitioned for the recision of the grant. The recently appointed New Mexico provincial governor, Don Mariano Chávez, who replaced Armijo and did not share the former governor's friendliness toward foreigners, nor his policy of granting such large land parcels, abided by the Durango government's injunction. Chávez issued a proclamation that prevented Beaubien and Miranda from using their land in any way until the New Mexican assembly could meet and decide the true ownership of the land. After a year of waiting, the New Mexico assembly finally concluded that Martínez's petition was based on false information and therefore did not impede the rights of Beaubien and Miranda in any way. On April 18, 1844, by order of the provincial assembly and the new acting governor, Don Felipe Seña, Don Cornelio Vigil reinstated Beaubien and Miranda's land title.[42] This first conflict over the conveyance and ownership of the Maxwell Land Grant ended only four years before the province of New Mexico was turned over to the American forces as a result of the Treaty of Guadalupe Hidalgo, which ended the U.S.–Mexican War. The process of defining property rights and ushering in market capitalism that Armijo had begun by issuing such a large land grant would continue under the U.S. legal and economic system. But for the next fifty years, charges of patronage, absentee landlordism, and unjust claims would cloud title to the land.

In the midst of all this political confusion and military occupation, Beaubien and Miranda managed to hold on to the land grant, and under the supervision of Beaubien's son-in-law, Lucien B. Maxwell, they began settling the eastern frontier of New Mexico. In recognition of these new settlements, in April 1844 New Mexico governor Seña appointed Carlos Beaubien the justice of the peace for the new communities along the Poñil and Cimarron Rivers.[43] Miranda, however, never took a day-to-day interest in the grant and remained a silent partner. The Beaubien family, through the work of Maxwell, first established a small community at

Rayado, which eventually served as the headquarters of the land grant, where they sold grain and meat, and offered accommodations to those traveling along the Santa Fe Trail. After the U.S.–Mexican War and after New Mexico had become a U.S. possession, the community at Rayado also supplied goods and services to the nearby U.S. military posts and Indian agencies.

Establishing communities on the land grant, however, was not an easy task, and the settlers faced problems from both the harsh high plains environment and raids from Plains Indians who eyed the growing stock herds with envy. For the first few years many of the settlers annually retreated to Taos during the winter months but would return the following spring and continue to build their community along the riverbanks. Rayado's development followed a pattern of development similar to other Mexican frontier settlements. These communities, which followed Spanish law and custom of development, had three elements considered integral to the community's survival: the plaza for living, the *vara* strips of land for agriculture, and the commons for hunting, gathering, and grazing.

The Hispano settlers also located themselves on different sections of the grant depending on the type of work they were doing. During the day families worked their strips of land, which were away from their homes, but in the evening they returned to the plaza. Ideally, the families built the plazas in a square with their homes, made from adobe bricks, along the perimeter. They would make only one gate for access so that they could secure their children and livestock within the confines of the plaza and away from hostile Indians or intrusive Anglos. Doors and windows opened only into the plaza square: there was no access in or out of the plaza except through these main gates. Although Rayado was not quite as fortified, the natural environment of the bluffs provided adequate protection as the plaza at Rayado sat in a lowlands bowl, with a river running through the town.[44]

Thin land strips (*varas*) that touched the small rivers at perpendicular points allowed each family fair and equal access to water and complemented life within the plazas. This land use pattern also allowed for very dense development with about ten to twenty agricultural plots on each acre, which was essential in terms of using the limited water resources wisely as well as for protection from intruders. Each *vara* strip ranged in width from twenty to five hundred *varas* (one *vara* is equal to a man's step, or about one yard) and could be as long as ten miles, depending on the topography. During part of the year, the families could divert the river at will because the river flow was substantial and the plots small enough that no farmer could overburden these three rivers. On smaller irrigation canals, which usually flowed along the back sections of the *vara* strips, however, a ditch system *(acequia)* with an elected *mayordomo* would have been necessary to regulate the flow of water equitably.[45] These small plots could sustain a family by growing vegetables for family use and some feed for the livestock and horses. Some of the larger *varas* were probably used exclusively for commercial use so that the feed could be sold to outsiders.

The settlers on the land grant would have also depended on the vast area beyond the bounds of the plaza and the agricultural areas for their survival. Most land grants, such as the Sangre de Cristo, had certain areas officially established as the commons. On the Beaubien/Miranda grant, however, there appears to have been no official designation of a particular place as a commons. Nevertheless, Maxwell allowed all of the settlers to graze cattle and sheep, hunt, and gather foodstuffs and herbs from the plains that surrounded the Rayado settlement. Although the Hispanos maintained permanent homes, introduced livestock, and engaged in more intensive agriculture, in many ways their land use pattern mimicked the Jicarilla pattern of diverse use of the environment. This communal pattern of homes built around the plaza, combined with the commons and their thin irregular plots of agricultural land, allowed the Hispanos to make a living for themselves as well as pay rent to Beaubien, and later to Maxwell.[46]

Though it is difficult to know who exactly was living and working on the land grant, they were probably working-class Mexican citizens who might have owned small parcels of private property or a share in a community grant before they moved across the mountains. Once they crossed over to the new land grant, however, their property relationships became more complex and less clear. First, these settlers came to have a responsibility, both financially and socially, to the *patrón*, Beaubien, but probably maintained a closer relationship to Maxwell, who would come to dominate eastern New Mexico's emerging economy. There were very few private property owners within the confines of the land grant, and most workers lived there on a sharecropping basis, as day laborer, or in a *peón/patrón* relationship. Second, the complexity of property relationships was due in a large part to the changing political structure as Americans began moving into the area. While Father Martínez continued to protest these changing labor and property relationships on the grant, his objections were quickly set aside as all New Mexicans now had to face the threat from American invasion.[47]

Once Hispano migration onto the land grant started, the middle ground that had been characterized by no single ethnic group dominating the region began to break down, and a number of confrontations between the new settlers and the more established Jicarilla Apaches broke out. The Jicarillas' migratory patterns, as well as the off-and-on-again nature of Hispano settlement, allowed for more and more contact, which often ended in violence and depredations on both sides. One of the largest problems that U.S. Indian Agent Calhoun faced was controlling the sale and traffic of liquor from "lower-class" Mexicans to the Jicarillas. Public leaders such as Beaubien believed that the liquor made the Indians rebellious and violent.[48]

Although the Jicarillas would later come to see Lucien B. Maxwell as an ally and friend, Maxwell's first encounter with the Jicarillas ended violently. On June 1, 1848, Maxwell was traveling toward Taos along the Santa Fe Trail with a large load of goods he had received in trade from the Plains Indians—eighty horses and mules, and six hundred deer skins. At the confluence of the Greenhorn and Arkansas Rivers in southeastern Colorado, the Jicarilla Apaches attacked him (see map 4). He made a successful retreat to Bent's Fort with only a loss of some twenty horses and mules. At the fort he met up with a party of thirteen U.S. traders who were also on their way to Taos. He joined them as the group left the fort and made their way south the following week. Despite their precautions, about two hundred Jicarillas attacked the party and took all of their animals. The Indians, however, were "not satisfied with this" and drove the traders from their camp, leaving them with no food or shelter. Maxwell and his group had to make their way on foot across the mountains to Taos. The Jicarillas killed three men and wounded Maxwell and seven others.[49]

Although Maxwell and the Jicarillas had clashed, over the years the Indians came to perceive him as an ally against the U.S. government. By the mid-1860s, the Jicarillas faced starvation and the loss of their homeland as their hunting lands were encroached upon by Hispano and Anglo settlers. Rather than blaming Maxwell for the difficult times that had befallen them, they instead turned to him for food, work, and advice in dealing with the U.S. government agents and other Anglos, which he provided. Maxwell acted as a cultural, economic, and social broker between the Jicarillas and the U.S. government, which wanted them removed from the area. In 1866, Indian Agent William F. Arny formalized Maxwell's position as *patrón* to the Jicarillas and made him the local Indian agent at the Cimarron agency. Maxwell was then able to hand out rations of wheat, meat, and blankets, all at the federal government's expense. Thus he received the benefits of acting as the *patrón* to the Jicarillas without actually giving them anything personally or allying with them formally. Instead Maxwell used the largesse of the U.S. federal government to maintain his personal and mutually beneficial relationship with the Jicarillas.[50]

### THE U.S. MILITARY AND SECURING THE SANTA FE TRAIL

The Jicarillas' relative isolation became more and more threatened as traders traveled across their territory on the Santa Fe Trail. As the value of the trail trade increased, and after the U.S. occupation of New Mexico, the new government in New Mexico became determined to subdue any hostile Indians on its eastern frontier and protect the trail because of its important military and commercial functions. Calhoun was particularly concerned about the violence of the Indians toward travelers, and he warned Col. Edwin V. Summers about becoming too complacent with the Jicarillas. Calhoun wanted them subdued and militarily removed from the area surrounding the trail.[51] U.S. / Jicarilla relations were tense from the beginning, but after the end of the U.S.–Mexican War, when the army stepped up its efforts to subdue all of the Indians, relations became violent and vicious. Col. George A. McCall, who had conducted an inspection of the territory, declared that the Jicarillas were among the most troublesome Indians and that they would "continue to rob and murder our citizens until they are exterminated. I know of no means that could be employed to reclaim them."[52]

In the wake of that proclamation, the army had placed a detachment at Rayado in order to protect the crops, stock, and community in August 1849. Capt. Henry Judd, commander of the U.S. troops near Las Vegas, exercised his authority over the new territory and demanded that a group of Jicarillas and their leaders, who were trading with Hispanos and the Mescalero Apaches in Las Vegas, "come into his Quarters, and form a treaty with the government of the United States." The "treaty" called for the Jicarillas to submit to the authority of Commander Judd and to bring in and surrender their weapons. The Jicarillas, angered and dismayed by the captain's demand, fled Las Vegas to return to their lodges on the outskirts of town. Under Judd's orders, the troops immediately mounted and pursued the Jicarillas.[53]

During their retreat one of the Jicarillas turned and shot an arrow, wounding Lt. Ambrose E. Burnside in the hand.[54] The cavalry returned fire with their guns, killing fourteen Jicarillas. (Three of the dead "were afterwards brought into town and burned," probably as a warning to others who would thwart U.S. rule.) The Jicarillas, however, did not stop to engage the cavalry in a battle, but instead "continued running in every direction— crying in Spanish 'Why are the Americans killing us?' Others of them replied, 'Quien sabe (Who knows)?'" In the aftermath of the skirmish, the army took seven Jicarillas hostage: five women, one of whom was the daughter of the Jicarilla chief Lobo, a boy, and a young man. The young man made his escape that night, but the army imprisoned the others for almost a year before they set them free. One Anglo observer noted that "the Indians did not dream of being attacked by the troops as they supposed they were at peace with the Americans—and they looked upon this affair as treachery [and] determined on having revenge."[55] Although the Jicarillas had never been entirely comfortable with the Spanish, French, or Mexicans on the periphery of their homeland, they had managed to avoid most direct violent confrontation and had maintained their autonomy and distance from European encroachers. On the other hand, the swiftness and violence with which the U.S. Cavalry reacted to the Jicarillas foreshadowed the new era of violence that would follow, and the Jicarillas quickly learned to distrust the Americans: whatever middle ground that might have existed just after the U.S.–Mexican War had vanished.

The Jicarillas' revenge followed just months later in the autumn of 1849. Dr. J. M. White and his traveling party—Mrs. White, their daughter Virginia, an African American slave couple, two Mexicans, and the wagon master, Mr. Calloway—met their deaths along the Cimarron cutoff of the Santa Fe Trail (see map 4). Because the White party had been in such a hurry to get to Santa Fe, they had left the wagon train led by Captain F. X. Aubry just before its arrival at Bent's Fort in Colorado. Even though Aubry and others had warned them against taking the Cimarron cutoff, White chose to take the shorter but more dangerous route to Santa Fe. On October 23, a group of "Jicarillas and Utahs [Utes] who had concealed themselves behind crude breast-works that they had been [*sic*] thrown up, formed of loose stones, by the side of the road" ambushed the White party about seventy miles from Barclay's Fort in New Mexico Territory at a place known as Wagon Mound or the Point of Rocks. The Indians killed all of the men in the party immediately, and they took Mrs. White, Virginia, and the slave woman as prisoners.[56]

The news of the ambush made national headlines, and a ransom was offered for the captives. The capture of the women became an overwhelming concern to the U.S. military and to Indian Agent Calhoun. Relatively few women traveled along the Santa Fe Trail in the early years after the war, and the U.S. government and New Mexico boosters were interested in seeing this number increase in the hope that the presence of women would encourage settlements and establish "civilization." The capture of Mrs. White and her daughter, in particular, gave fodder to eastern newspapers who questioned the ability of the U.S. government to protect the trail and the women who might venture into New Mexico. Indeed, the violence against the women called into question the very manliness of the army and

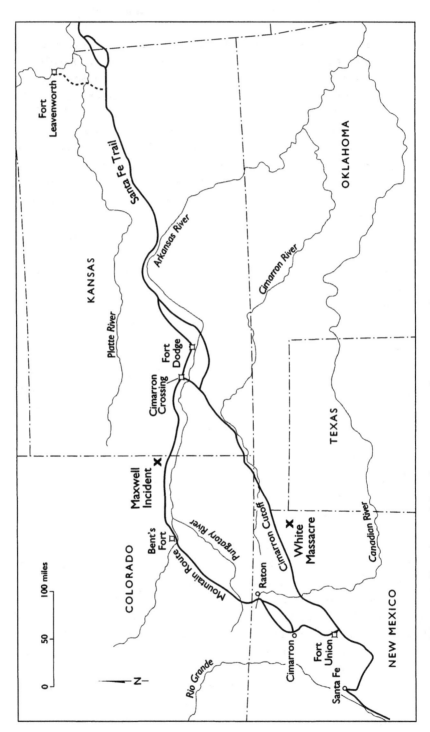

Map 4. Sites of the Maxwell incident and the White massacre on the Santa Fe Trail.

the Indian agency and made people question their ability to control the Indians' supposed desires for revenge, violence, and rape. Calhoun voiced his own concern as he spoke of the "impotency" of his office to find the women, and his hope that "if the two captives are not to be liberated, it is to be hoped they are dead."[57]

When the news reached the army in Las Vegas, Captain Judd ordered Sergeant Henry Swartwout and twenty men to go east across the plains, find the site of the massacre, and subdue the Jicarillas. They took with them Chief Lobo's daughter (the woman captured earlier in Las Vegas), hoping that she might lead them to the Jicarillas and be exchanged for Mrs. White and the other women. As the party encamped for the first evening, the Jicarilla woman asked if she could walk to the top of the ridge. Swartwout gave her permission to go, and she sat on the ridge wailing until morning. In the morning, however, she appeared calmer, and Swartwout ordered her into the wagon so that they could continue on their search for the Jicarillas. The woman, however, refused, and grabbed a butcher knife that lay nearby. She attacked the teamster who had been trying to coax her into the wagon, and "the teamster in trying to make the escape stumbled and fell, when another man seeing his danger knocked the woman down with his fist." She then turned on the other man, who escaped her frenzied attack. She managed, however, to stab two nearby mules, which later died. Upset at the confusion, Sergeant Swartwout ordered her shot immediately. Sergeant Mortimer complied, pulling a pistol out of his holster and killing her. Without another mention of the incident, the party continued to search in vain for Mrs. White, but ultimately returned to Las Vegas, unable to find any of the Jicarillas.[58]

At about the same time, after news of the White massacre reached Taos, Major William N. Grier, with a company of soldiers and a party of sixty or seventy Hispano volunteers, crossed the Sangre de Cristo Mountains to pursue the Jicarillas. With Kit Carson as their tracker and guide, the band of searchers traversed over two hundred miles of the plains, following the trail of the Jicarillas and their prisoners. They finally discovered a small Jicarilla village of "about forty warriors with a large number of women and children and over one hundred head of loose stock" in a canyon of the Red River. Rather than heeding Carson's advice—attack immediately and surprise the quiet village—Major Grier waited for a mountain howitzer to arrive from the rear of their caravan. This allowed two Jicarilla scouts to spot them, warn the village, and take shots at the army.[59]

The extra time also allowed the Jicarilla villagers to take flight. After the howitzer arrived, the army and volunteers charged. They pursued the

Jicarillas for six miles but were unable to overtake the whole group. They killed a number of Jicarillas, but Major Grier had to accept the skirmish as a defeat. He returned to the original site of the Indian village only to find the warm bodies of the captured women from the White party with arrows through their hearts.[60] That night, as the group of dejected men prepared for bed, they heard noises. Puzzled by the small squeaks, they suspected an animal of some kind in the brush. Upon further examination, however, they found an Indian child of about eight months strapped to a board. His scared and fleeing mother had somehow left him behind or had hidden him in the brush to be recovered later. William Grier wrote, "An old gruff soldier stepped up and said: 'Let me have the brat.' He picked up a heavy stone, tied it to the board, dashed the babe and all into the water, and in a moment no trace of it was left." Before throwing the baby into the water he merely said, "'You're a little feller now, but will make a big Injun bye and bye. I only wish I had more to treat the same way.'"[61]

As this early brutality on both sides indicates, within the first year of the United States' official arrival into New Mexico, Jicarilla-Anglo relations were at a critical level from which they would never recover.[62] Although relatively little information about early contact between the Spanish, Mexicans, and Americans and the Jicarillas exists, if we compare the Ulibarrí account of the Spanish encounter with the Jicarillas in 1705 and the Grier account of U.S.–Jicarilla relations in 1849, the contrast is stark. While the Spaniards were eager to incorporate the Jicarillas into their empire and subdue them through trade, religion, and diplomacy, the U.S. Army's first attempts to deal with the Jicarillas relied on intimidation and warfare. Although the violence would ebb and flow, the two sides never reached a repose or a place of mutual accommodation on New Mexico's eastern plains.

Within the first ten years of the Beaubien/Miranda Land Grant's existence a number of people died and hundreds were displaced as Jicarillas, Mexicans, and Americans all jockeyed for control of the region. Each group had competing claims, different boundaries, and unique mental territories that defined not only their homes, but also the kind of life they could enjoy. This first decade of the grant's existence offered a prelude to events that would ensue throughout the rest of the century. Different people (Anglo and European investors, in particular) with different claims would come to the land grant, and with them they would bring the power of the U.S. government, law, and military. They would also bring with them the power of market capitalism, which, through the railroad and the development of a national market, would transform not only the meaning of property on the land grant, but also the lives of all those who lived, worked, and invested in the territory. But all of this dramatic change was still two decades away. First, the grant's inhabitants would have to come to terms with the economy and social structure that Lucien B. Maxwell would impose on the grant that came to bear his name.

# 2 Regulating Land, Labor, and Bodies

*Mexican Married Women, Peones, and the Remains of Feudalism*

A native of Kaskasia, Ill. A fur trader and trapper, who by
industry; good fortune and trading became sole owner, in 1864 of
the largest single tract of land owned by any one individual in the
United States.

> Epitaph on Lucien B. Maxwell's grave

A woman, on marrying, parts with many of her civil rights, and
amongst the rights alienated by the conjugal association is that of
appearing generally in court as plaintiff or defendant, alone or
without consent of her husband.

> *Chaves v. McKnight and Gutieres*, January 1857

When Col. Stephen Watts Kearny led the U.S. Army of the West into
Santa Fe in 1846, he was not merely conquering a Mexican province for the
U.S. government. Kearny was also leading a moral crusade against what
some U.S. political leaders, such as John C. Calhoun, regarded as a despotic
and feudalistic system of government and property.[1] The editor of the
*Boston Times* summed up their mood best when he wrote,

> The "conquest" which carries peace into a land where the sword has
> always been the sole arbiter, . . . which institutes the reign of law
> where license has existed for a generation . . . must necessarily be a
> great blessing to the conquered. It is a work worthy of a great people,
> of a people who are about to regenerate the world by asserting the
> supremacy of humanity over the accidents of birth and fortune.[2]

These U.S. supporters of the war with Mexico justified the conflict, in
part, as a way to free, if not re-create or regenerate, what would become
the American Southwest from the Old World mire of debt-peonage labor,
hacienda aristocracy, and the Catholic religion. Mexican War advocates
believed that the U.S. had a moral obligation, indeed a Manifest Destiny, to
replace Mexican feudalism and the *patrón/peón* relationship with small

farms and free yeomen of the United States. To these Americans, the U.S.–Mexican War was just one more instance of the liberalization that was sweeping the world in the late 1840s, culminating in 1848 with the Frankfurt Assembly, the barricades of Paris and Dresden, and the Hungarian uprising.[3] Even the less violent changes in land systems, such as the Great Mahele in Hawai'i and the passage of the first Married Women's Property Acts in the United States, seemed to herald a new era of liberal property regimes.[4]

These proponents of the U.S.–Mexican War were correct in noticing the enormous differences between the systems of land tenure dominant in Mexico and the United States, at least north of the Mason-Dixon line. The Spanish and, after 1821, Mexican governments had distributed huge land parcels through royal or executive grants to particular individuals or communities favored by the crown, president, or provincial governors. These grant recipients were then expected to settle families on their estates in order to create a buffer zone of protection from encroaching foreign powers and hostile Indians. This system had its origins in the Spanish Reconquest and *encomienda* of the late fifteenth century, under which the king rewarded loyal men who had proven their military valor against the Moors with huge estates. By contrast, U.S. law distributed lands owned by the federal government through auction to the general public for standardized prices and, later, through uniform systems of possession and patent under the Homestead Act. This contrast in land distribution practices meant that Kearny was replacing, or at least overlaying, Mexican land law with a very different system. Such a collision of property regimes led to enormous uncertainty among people who held their property under the Spanish/Mexican system of royal or executive grant. Former Mexican citizens who were now incorporated into the United States feared that the U.S. government would confiscate their land, throw it into the public domain, and open it to U.S. settlers.

The Treaty of Guadalupe Hidalgo, which ended the U.S.–Mexican War in 1848, provided Mexican landowners with only limited legal protection. The original treaty contained Article 10, which clearly recognized the property rights that former Mexican citizens had enjoyed under Mexican law, guaranteeing that U.S. courts would be obliged to enforce their rights. But the U.S. Congress refused to ratify Article 10 because many congressmen had justified the war as a way to free Mexican *peones* from the domination of the hacienda system and the *patrón*.[5] If the U.S. recognized the property rights of Mexican citizens and thereby dominated the economic fortunes of the *peones*, then Congress's goal of eliminating feudalism and debt peonage would fail. Some congressmen argued that by ratifying Article 10 they would be undermining the republican ideals of equality and individualism that had justified the war in the first place.[6] Ironically, while Congress's failure to ratify Article 10 did dispossess large Mexican landowners, particularly the Californios, the failure of Article 10 also hurt small landholders who held land through community grants.[7]

Thus Kearny's occupation of New Mexico threw land titles into confusion, causing leading landowners such as Guadalupe Miranda to sell to people such as Lucien B. Maxwell, who were willing to speculate on the validity of these Mexican land grants under U.S. law.[8] The concern over the validity of land titles was the direct result of irreconcilable differences between the two property regimes. It was also the result of U.S. ideological hostility to what Americans saw as Mexican feudalism and the hierarchy of landowners over landless *peones*. Yet there was a deep irony in this American reluctance to recognize Mexican systems of land tenure. In refusing to enforce rights defined by Mexican law, U.S. courts ultimately relegated other members of Mexican society, married women, to the state of "feudalistic dependence" from which U.S. law was supposedly liberating Mexican *peones*. While U.S. lawmakers were quick to point out the inequalities inherent in the hacienda system, they turned a blind eye to analogous sources of hierarchy and subordination in the United States: enslavement of African Americans and unequal treatment of women. More specifically, Anglo-American law, and especially the law of coverture—which allowed husbands to control their wives' property, barring its sale, lease, or bequest without the husband's signature—was just beginning to be reformed in the United States. Mexican law denied husbands such extensive power over their wives, because the civil law on which Mexican law was based lacked any substantial rule of coverture. Under Mexican law, a married woman could own, sell, lease, and bequeath her property without her husband's signature. By refusing to recognize Mexican practices, U.S. courts stripped Mexican married women of these rights, re-creating them as common-law dependents of the husband, master of the household.

This chapter looks at how the uncertainty surrounding land title after the U.S. conquest of New Mexico aided Lucien B. Maxwell in acquiring his vast estate. Contrary to Maxwell's epitaph, he did not obtain this land through "industry, good fortune, and trading" alone. Rather, he acquired the grant by marrying María de la Luz Beaubien, who was the daughter of the wealthy and prominent Carlos Beaubien, one of the original owners of the Beaubien/Miranda Land Grant. Maxwell obtained the core of his vast estate as the result of a dynastic alliance in the Mexican feudal tradition. He was not unambiguously the "sole owner" of the Maxwell Land Grant because his wife was co-owner of the parcel with the right to control its disposition. In fact, the doctrine of coverture may have aided Maxwell's property acquisition, for it gave Maxwell's sisters-in-law an enormous incentive to sell their holdings to him and thus avoid the legal consequences of the new U.S. property regime.[9]

The irony of this legal transformation was that it was facilitated by U.S. lawmakers' fear of peonage and, more generally, feudalistic subordination. The New Mexican system of peonage and *patrón* domination persisted after 1848 in New Mexico despite the efforts of U.S. courts to eradicate it. Lucien Maxwell continued as the *patrón* of his hacienda until he and Luz sold the grant in 1869. As feudal overlord, he owned slaves, dispensed justice among his tenants, and ruled his estate through quasi-familial relationships rather than through contractual formalities, which he disdained.[10] In short, U.S, law did not eradicate the feudalism of the *patrón/peón* system during the two decades of Maxwell's tenure. But U.S. law did install the Anglo-American feudal regime of coverture. The conquest of 1848 did not represent a radical break with the hierarchy of the hacienda system, but rather a perfection of it: the law preserved the informal quasi-familial control of *patrón* over *peón* and extended this control to the *patrón's* wife and other female relatives.

## LUCIEN B. MAXWELL'S RISE TO PROMINENCE

After the U.S. victory over Mexico in 1848 and the U.S. occupation of New Mexico, Carlos Beaubien and Guadalupe Miranda became concerned about the status of their property holdings, particularly the extensive grant they had received from Governor Manuel Armijo in 1841. The two grantees, however, dealt with the changes quite differently. Miranda sold his claims and share to Lucien and Luz Maxwell soon after the Americans arrived. Miranda, a Mexican loyalist, saw no future for himself in the new territory of the United States. After Santa Fe's fall to Kearny's troops, Miranda fled over the border with Governor Armijo to Mexico, where he remained.[11] The Beaubien family, however, took over Miranda's shares, remained on the grant, and attempted to perfect their title to the full extent of the grant's boundaries. Carlos Beaubien died before the U.S. government gave the final patent to the land grant, but his family—particularly his son-in-law, Lucien B. Maxwell—carried on the enterprise.

In 1848, while Mexicans hurried to establish their property rights, the enterprising Lucien Bonaparte Maxwell profited from this confusion by speculating that Mexican property rights and land grants would be recognized by the United States under the Treaty of Guadalupe Hidalgo.[12] Through his marital connections, Maxwell eventually gained control of the entire grant. As a result of his property acquisition, Maxwell was probably the richest man in all of New Mexico Territory during his lifetime, and he ran very profitable mining, ranching, and farming enterprises. These typical western American businesses, however, were not based on his own individual effort or even on that of his family. Instead, they depended on his use of feudalistic practices reminiscent of Mexican haciendas, such as peonage labor and sharecropping-type relationships between himself and his tenants.[13] His persona as a benevolent yet often violent *patrón*, a huge hacienda owner, a wild gambler, and a generous friend has taken on legendary proportions. Overblown tales of his opulent residence and overbearing personality—along with stories that Billy the Kid died at the hands of Pat Garrett within the Maxwell home—have taken Maxwell beyond the pale of respectable history and into the annals of the mythic Wild West.[14]

The romantic mystique that surrounds Maxwell's life stems in part from his early career as a trapper and trader. Maxwell epitomized the ideal of male daring that dominated the contemporary accounts of the early Western "frontier." Prior to settling in Taos, Maxwell had worked as a hunter for three of John C. Frémont's explorations of the trans-Mississippi West. Frémont led Kit Carson, possibly Maxwell, and others to help incite the Bear Flag Rebellion, which began the process of expelling the Mexican government from California and bringing American rule to the West Coast. During Maxwell's earlier travels with Frémont and Carson, he passed through the trading hamlet of Taos, New Mexico, where the financial opportunities of the region captivated him. During one of these visits, his uncle, the successful fur trader Ceran St. Vrain, introduced him to Carlos Beaubien, the man who would most influence the course of Maxwell's life.[15] Between Maxwell's exploits with Carson and Frémont, he returned to Taos. While settling himself into the community, he courted and then, in 1844, married the thirteen-year-old María de la Luz Beaubien, one of Carlos Beaubien's six children.[16] Beaubien, himself a French-Canadian turned Mexican trader, was by this time one of the most prominent citizens in colonial New Mexico. He owned shares of a number of Mexican land grants, including large portions of the Beaubien/Miranda and Sangre de Cristo grants. Through the thinnest of connections, Maxwell had managed to make an excellent marriage, which brought with it social mobility and financial opportunity through his wife's family.

Intermarriage between *ricas*, unmarried women from wealthy families, and outsiders such as Maxwell occurred frequently on the Mexican-American frontier and played a significant role in acculturating foreigners into New Mexican society.[17] In fact, Luz Beaubien's father, Charles, a French-Canadian, had married María Paula Lobato, daughter of a wealthy Taos landowner, in 1827, taking on Mexican citizenship and changing his name to Carlos. Whether to establish trading alliances or to acquire property, through intermarriage Anglos allied themselves with prominent families, thus uniting the outside Anglo world with the local Hispano culture.[18] Given Luz's young age at the time of her marriage to Maxwell, it seems unlikely that she had much say in the matter or much experience with which to judge the wisdom of such a match. Beaubien probably arranged what he perceived to be a workable and profitable union between his daughter and the ambitious outsider.

Between 1844, the year of their marriage, and 1848, when the couple moved away from Taos to set up their own home, Luz remained with her family while Maxwell came and went between expeditions with Frémont. At the age of eighteen, Luz left her family to begin a new life as one of the original inhabitants of the Rayado settlement, which Beaubien and Maxwell had decided would be the best location from which to operate the Beaubien/Miranda estate. In founding the settlement, Kit Carson, one of the Maxwells' fellow settlers, wrote, "We [Maxwell and Carson] felt that we had been leading a roving life long enough and that now, if ever, was the time to make a home for ourselves and children. We were getting old and could not expect much longer to continue to be able to gain a livelihood as we had been doing for many years."[19] By 1851, almost twenty families (Anglo, Hispano, and Indian) were living in the Rayado settlement and working on Maxwell's system of shares, wherein the settlers, and in many cases the *peones*, promised to pay half of the harvest to Beaubien as rent, with Maxwell acting as the middleman.[20] Luz's sisters, Eleanor Beaubien Trujillo and Petra Beaubien Abreu, and their husbands also moved permanently to the settlement. The extended Beaubien family profited from the newly arrived U.S. Army post at Rayado, which rented quartering for soldiers and stables for horses, and purchased food for the troops and feed for the mounts, from the Beaubiens and Maxwell, who was not above charging monopoly prices to the U.S. government. Maxwell quickly earned a reputation as a shrewd businessman, but from his standpoint this was not enough. Most of the profits he earned went directly into the pocket of his father-in-law while he remained merely the foreman of the Rayado ranch.[21]

After their success at establishing the community at Rayado, the Maxwells decided to go out on their own and move away from the Beaubien family. Their years in Rayado probably convinced the Maxwells that working the land grant was a lucrative venture, and they began acquiring sections of the grant as their own private property. In 1857 the Maxwells purchased from Luz's parents, Carlos and Paula Beaubien, a twenty-two-square-mile tract of land north of Rayado—Cimarron—which sat at the mouth of a canyon that led to Taos and abutted the Cimarron River. Here they established their new home and ranch headquarters. With this small but ideally located piece of property, they were well on their way to building a small empire on the plains east of the Sangre de Cristo Mountains.[22]

Between 1858 and 1867, the Maxwells expanded their enterprises and eventually inherited or purchased all of the Beaubien/Miranda grant. In 1858 they bought Guadalupe Miranda's half of the grant for $2,745. Miranda's son, who stayed in New Mexico, brokered the deal, but it was not until ten years later that Miranda actually signed over a warranty deed to the couple. Only when the Maxwells prepared to sell the grant to English investors a decade later did they think it wise to record this transaction with the county clerk. They knew that their previous arrangement with Miranda, based on their word and a handshake, would not prove their claim to the investors or the courts.[23] In fact, Maxwell had a reputation for not wanting to sign legal documents, believing that his reputation and his word were enough to secure business transactions. He often became angry when people asked him to sign notarized documents. Melvin W. Mills, a lawyer who worked for Maxwell, remembered a particular incident:

> He never wanted to do business in a business way, but preferred to take another's word, and never wanted to write anything. At one time I went down to Cimarron from Elizabethtown to get him to extend a bond that he had made to Chaffee, Gauley, and others and he got mad because I wanted him to sign the extension on the back of the paper, and, he threw the paper and his cigar that he always carried in his mouth into the fireplace.[24]

Maxwell later found, however, that he had to revise his business practices as he became more involved with the American and European world of markets and entrepreneurs.

Maxwell found it difficult to move in this impersonal world because his wealth and power had been derived from the more traditional alliances provided by marriage and family. For example, the Maxwells acquired the remaining shares of the grant when Carlos Beaubien died in February 1864, leaving his estate to his six children as undivided interests in the grant.[25] Beaubien held interests in a number of grants, but his claim in the Beaubien/Miranda grant was his largest asset. As was common practice when a Mexican father passed property to his heirs, Beaubien bequeathed his interest to all of his children, male and female, in equal shares. All gained equal opportunity to develop and live on the grant. How they used their property was entirely up to them. In Beaubien's mind, his daughters (with their husbands) had full autonomy to do what they wished with the land.[26] But the Beaubien heirs chose to sell their interests to the Maxwells.

Over the next five years, after Beaubien's death and the acquisition of Luz Beaubien Maxwell's inherited share, the Maxwells purchased the other five undivided shares from her siblings. Only months after Beaubien's death, the Maxwells purchased Teodora Beaubien Mueller's share for $500, and Juana Beaubien Clouthier's for $3,500. We can speculate that Teodora and Juana were the first to sell because they lived the farthest from the grant: both had married Anglo businessmen, not ranchers, and both permanently resided in Taos. While Frederick Mueller, Teodora's husband, acted as the executor of Beaubien's estate, he apparently had no interest in acquiring any of the real property for his business ventures.[27]

A few months later, on July 20, 1864, the Maxwells purchased Eleanor Beaubien Trujillo's interest in the grant for $3,000. Although Eleanor and her husband, Vidal, signed the deed, Eleanor may have been willing to sell because she was in the midst of marital troubles that would soon end in divorce.[28] Given the law of coverture, Eleanor probably feared that her husband, who was living with another woman, might gain control over her property. By taking cash from the Maxwells in exchange for her real property interest, she could retain legal control over this significant asset: cash was considered by the courts to be personal property and not subject to the coverture laws. The Trujillo divorce was a messy and ugly case involving Vidal's infidelity with numerous women and his squandering of Eleanor's property. In the end, however, Eleanor Beaubien had little to fear. Judge Kirby Benedict was so disgusted by Vidal's behavior and his failure to appear in court that he awarded all marital assets, which were quite substantial and which were for the most part her dotal property, to Eleanor. As we shall see, Eleanor Beaubien was lucky; most women marrying or divorcing in New Mexico Territory at the time did not fair as well in the legal system.

Over the next four years the Maxwells acquired the remaining portions of the grant. First, in 1866, Maxwell quieted a claim to the Beaubien/Miranda grant from the heirs of Charles Bent.[29] Then, two years passed before the Maxwells acquired another share from Petra Beaubien Abreu for

$3,500. The Abreu family by this time had established their own large ranch and home at the original Rayado settlement and had been purchasing property in that area.[30] In fact, the Maxwells paid Petra cash and traded some of their property around Rayado for her interest in the grant.[31] Finally, just months before they sold the grant to English investors, the Maxwells purchased the last share from Paul Beaubien, the youngest of Carlos Beaubien's heirs, for $3,500.[32] But long before the Maxwells had legally acquired clear title to all of the grant, they were living within the confines of the grant and working the land as a hacienda, exercising practical possession before they acquired formal title.

It is important to reflect on how Maxwell acquired his property. Maxwell has come to epitomize the diligent frontiersman who conquered the American West by making a large expanse of land economically profitable. Yet he did not acquire the land through the mythical attributes that have come to be associated with these so-called "pioneers": diligence, industry, and individual effort. Rather, Maxwell acquired his wealth through such Old World tactics as marriage, inheritance, and peonage. He also benefited from the change in government, capitalizing on the uncertainty that his sisters-in-law faced with regard to their own property holdings. And there was much for these women to be confused about as they negotiated their economic and social position in New Mexico Territory.

## LUZ BEAUBIEN MAXWELL AS PROPERTY OWNER

Historians of the Maxwell Land Grant and biographers of Lucien B. Maxwell have generally dismissed the presence of María de la Luz Beaubien Maxwell. With a single sentence about her marriage to Maxwell, she disappears into the background of the Maxwell mansion, estate, and business.[33] These biographies suggest that Maxwell envisioned himself the domineering *patrón* and may not have appreciated Luz in her role of co-entrepreneur in their estate. Luz also had a large family and household, which would have kept her occupied and apart from the affairs of the outside world.[34] Furthermore, Luz spoke no English during her years on the land grant and probably did not read or write. Consequently, she may have felt ill at ease dealing with the many Santa Fe traders who passed through their home. Visitors to the Maxwell ranch often commented that they never saw women in the public spaces of the mansion (evening meals were served by young men), and Luz Maxwell rarely mingled with her husband's guests.[35]

Nevertheless, historians cannot so easily dismiss the role of Luz Beaubien Maxwell. Historical evidence indicates that Luz was a successful businesswoman both during and after her husband's lifetime. After Lucien and Luz sold the bulk of their propertied estate in 1869, they continued to sell other parcels of property jointly. In some cases, however, only Maxwell's signature appears on deeds. These variations in their transactions suggest that Luz had influence over some aspects of their financial affairs, while Maxwell kept other dealings separate.[36] One might even surmise that the transactions for which Lucien cosigned were for Luz's property, and that he cosigned only because U.S. law required his consent in his wife's business transactions. Furthermore, twenty years after Lucien's death, court documents show that Luz owned her own cattle business, the partnership of Maxwell and Brazil, which ran more than two thousand head of cattle on her property on the Fort Union Reservation.[37] Luz was not a quiet and passive *doña* of the Maxwell hacienda, but an active and integral part of New Mexico's cattle industry.

Likewise, upon the sale of the whole estate to an English syndicate in 1869, Luz's signature again appears on the documents, indicating that she was the co-owner and coseller of the property. In fact, despite the grandiose claims of historians and the epitaph on his grave, Lucien B. Maxwell was not the largest landowner in all of America: he shared that title with his wife. Whether or not Luz played an active role in running the estate will remain a mystery to historians. Nevertheless, as a Mexican woman she retained the ability to own and dispose of her property. Her legal situation when the grant was conveyed was far better than the one that women—Anglo, Indian, or Hispano—would face on the estate over the next twenty years.

Luz Maxwell's signing of her name was no trivial act: it signified a vast difference between the restrictive Anglo-American system and the relative autonomy women enjoyed under the Spanish-Mexican legal regime. As a title company report noted later, Luz Maxwell's signatures on these documents make sense only as an effort to comply with Mexican law and, in particular, civil property law.[38] Compared to the claims of American husbands, Mexican husbands' claims were limited to property that their wives brought into marriage through dower, inheritance, or purchase. Prior to the U.S. conquest of New Mexico, women frequently willed property to their heirs independently, made contracts with persons outside of their family, often without the signature of their husbands, and in general disposed of their property as they chose. Doña Gertrudes Barcelo of Santa Fe is just one of the more prominent examples. As a married woman she owned property, made loans, sold real estate, and made her own will—all without the consent of her husband.[39] While most New Mexican women were not as wealthy or powerful as Barcelo, they nevertheless faced fewer legal impediments to a commercial role in New Mexican society.[40]

Luz Maxwell's signature, under Mexican civil law, was a crucial detail in legal transactions disposing of the Maxwell estate. Since she had inherited a share of the grant from her father, and since she and her husband had acquired other shares, she shared control over such transactions, at least to the extent that Mexican law governed them. Thus she played an important legal and social role in acquiring property from her family both through inheritance from her father and by purchase from her siblings. By stark contrast, Lucien Maxwell came to New Mexico with very little capital and no real social standing. Had he not married Luz, he would have found it difficult to generate business dealings with the wealthy and influential Beaubien and Miranda families. Absent his marriage to a *rica*, he was an outsider, and a cash-poor one at that.

Luz Maxwell's legal autonomy, however, depended on whether Mexican or U.S. law applied to the land grant when the Maxwells acquired title. Under the common law prevalent in the United States, her signature would have been superfluous: a paranoid lawyer probably would have asked for it, but it was unnecessary to complete a transaction. The U.S. property system into which Mexican women entered after the Treaty of Guadalupe Hidalgo in 1848 provided them with few protections.[41] When the United States acquired other civil law countries such as Spanish Florida and French Louisiana in the early part of the nineteenth century, the government made few provisions to clarify women's property rights under U.S. law.[42] So how specifically Mexican women's rights would be incorporated in all the territories covered by the Treaty of Guadalupe Hidalgo remained unclear in 1848.

During the 1840s, two contradictory impulses ran through American society: liberalization of married women's status and anti-Mexican sentiment. Although since 1839 various states had been passing Married Women's Property Acts, which in theory gave more property rights to married women, the law of coverture remained quite powerful. Moreover, the decade between the passage of these first acts and the end of the U.S.–Mexican War also marked the pinnacle of anti-Mexican sentiment, which applauded the triumph of liberalism and democracy over the despotism of Mexico. Though the irony provoked no comment at the time, the Married Women's Property Acts were promoting the kind of legal equality that Mexican law already took for granted. So while the status of American women, at least in theory, appeared to be improving throughout the nineteenth century, the status of Mexican women who now found themselves living under U.S. rule declined.

A female American citizen in the middle of the nineteenth century could expect to have very little control over the property she brought into marriage as dower, through inheritance, or through contract. She, unlike Mexican married women, could not make a will on her own property unless her husband gave his consent in writing to the court. If she contracted for goods and services, and then her husband decided not to release the necessary funds, she could not be held accountable for the financial transaction. According to the doctrine of coverture, merchants should know better than to contract with a married woman.[43] In short, American women in the nineteenth century retained almost no control over their property and had to rely on their husbands to take proper care of their assets. Perhaps Luz Maxwell and her sisters realized the constrained legal situation and made strategic decisions to preserve their wealth and status in the new territory of the United States.

CONQUEST AND LEGAL TRANSFORMATION IN NEW MEXICO

While the rest of the United States was liberalizing through Married Women's Property Acts, legislation and court cases from New Mexico's early territorial period were instituting coverture as the prescribed law for the newly conquered population.[44] For example, territorial legislation in 1852 explicitly stated that women could engage in property transactions only if their husbands cosigned the contract.[45] Furthermore, one of the earliest territorial cases involving the rights of married women made it quite explicit that coverture was the law. In 1857, Mariana Martínez brought before the Territorial Supreme Court a complaint against her husband, Tomás Lucero. Martínez and Lucero had been legally married for seven years but had separated amicably. They did not seek a legal separation from the local government, and they had not filed for divorce. Nevertheless, Lucero and Martínez had moved in with other partners, and Tom Lucero even had two children by his current live-in partner. Martínez sued Lucero because he was using and "wasting" the dowry she had brought to the marriage on maintaining his new family.

The territorial court disagreed, however, with Mariana's assessment of her marital situation. According to the law, Mariana Martínez and Tomás Lucero were still legally husband and wife, and thus she could "not during the conjugal association, recover from her husband her separate dotal property, or resume the administration thereof. . . . The administration of the dotal property, whether appraised or not, belongs exclusively to the husband during the existence of the marriage."[46] The court went on to say that Martínez could recover control over her dotal property only if "the husband abandons or deserts his wife, or where he refuses to maintain her, or where, by reason of insolvency, he is unable to afford suitable maintenance for her." But Mariana had not made such a case against her husband. She had simply asked to take back the property that was hers, and which, she believed, he had no right to use for the benefit of his new partner and family. The court also stated that since Mariana had left the marriage voluntarily, her act was "subversive to the true policy of the matrimonial law, and destructive of the best interests of society." Therefore she had no legal claim to her dotal property.

The territorial court punished Mariana Martínez but not her husband, Tomás Lucero, for the act of adultery. The court went on, "Where the wife has eloped and is living in a state of adultery, they [courts] withhold all countenance to such grossly immoral conduct, and they will leave the wife to bear as she may the ordinary results of her own infamous abandonment of duty." Using phrases such as "derelict in her conjugal obligations" and "sullied by the unrefuted charge of guilt," the Territorial Supreme Court of New Mexico made her responsible for the failed marriage. Furthermore, the court punished her by protecting her estranged husband's right to use her property to maintain his new family. She, on the other hand, was left with none of the money or property that she had brought into the marriage. As a married woman under U.S. common law, Martínez possessed no legal ability to control her property.

Law, however, is often a double-edged sword, and sometimes coverture could actually work to a woman's benefit. Take the case of Manuela Antonia Chávez, who was the daughter of Francisco Chávez, one of the wealthiest men in territorial New Mexico. She came into her marriage with more than $30,000 in property and assets. Her husband, José María Gutiérrez, had made a number of bad business deals while they were married and had used her dotal property to secure the transactions. In this particular case, Manuela sued both her husband and the man to whom he owed money, William S. McKnight, for the return of her property. McKnight had been trying to foreclose on her home and ranch in order to pay off the money that Gutiérrez owed him. The court first stated that "according to the civil law, a woman, on marrying, parts with many of her civil rights, and amongst the rights alienated by the conjugal association is that of appearing generally in court as plaintiff or defendant, alone or without consent of her husband." This policy limited women's rights when compared with their more liberal rights to appear in judicial and ecclesiastical proceedings during New Mexico's colonial period.[47] Yet in this particular case, where the husband had allegedly injured the wife's property, officers of the court ruled that they were obliged to protect her right to be heard and to sue for the return of her property.[48]

The court went on to define what it meant by dotal property and what it took to be the meaning of a dowry: "[I]ts legitimate purposes was to conduce to their conjugal contentment—to secure their comfort, to protect them from want, to enable them to provide amply for their family, and to promote their general property and happiness." While dotal property came under the control of the husband, he nevertheless had an obligation to use it in the best interests of his family and wife. The court further noted that Gutiérrez stood as a defendant because he had indeed squandered Chávez's property by "improvidently using her dotal property, by applying it to purposes foreign from those for which it was placed in his hands; by making it liable for securityship." The court ruled that McKnight could not take Chávez's dotal property as payment for her husband's debt, and that Gutiérrez would have to find other means for making payment. Although married women could not control their property, their husbands did have an obligation to protect it and use it wisely. When accusations of adultery were absent, the court seemed more willing to protect the women against the waste of their husbands. Manuela Chávez's class position as the daughter of one of the wealthiest and most influential men in the territory more than likely helped her maintain a respectable reputation and made the court take her claims seriously.

Many women attempted to avoid the burdens placed on them by coverture laws. In 1854 or 1855, Quirina Baca and her husband, Filomeno Gallegos, separated by signing an articles of agreement letter, which was notarized. Because they were Catholic, they did not seek a legal or ecclesiastical divorce. Gallegos renounced all his marital rights to the property his wife had brought into the marriage as dower or had later acquired as part of their community property. Gallegos further renounced all his rights as a married man to any property his wife might acquire in the future, and he wrote that she should have such property for her sole and separate use, subject to her sole control, and that she should in every way act as a *femme sole*, an unmarried woman. Baca assumed her maiden name and began engaging in business transactions and purchasing property.

In 1867, Baca purchased El Bajado Rancho in Santa Ana County. She then sold an undivided half interest in her property and entered into a partnership with J. L. Collins to run a stage agency, government forage agency, and general hotel. In 1869, probably because Collins had become ill, they settled accounts associated with their partnership. Baca owed Collins $1,871 as a result of their agreement. At the time of his death she still owed him that sum. Baca, however, did not have enough cash to pay the debt, so she signed a mortgage against her property in order to cover the debt. In this case before the Territorial Supreme Court, Collins's heirs sued for the money she owed their father.[49]

The court ruled that Collins's heirs could not collect on the debt that Baca owed to their father because married women could not execute mortgages without the written consent of their husbands. Therefore, the mortgage Baca signed to secure her debt to Collins was legally void even "though at the time of its execution she was living apart from her husband under an agreement with him and she was to have the entire management and disposal of her property."[50] Baca's legal husband had not signed any of the papers; consequently, there was no legally binding contract. She owed Collins's heirs nothing. Although in the last two cases, the law of coverture actually benefited these specific married women, the purpose of the law was to limit married women's legal rights by protecting them from abusive husbands and unscrupulous businessmen. In short, coverture protected women from making bad decisions and placed them in a subordinated relationship to their husbands.

In 1873 the New Mexico territorial legislature liberalized marital property law somewhat. The new law allowed a woman who had been abandoned by her husband for one year to use their marital property and act as a single woman. But the woman had to prove, through sworn affidavits, that her husband had abandoned her and had left the territory. If her husband had not left the territory, then a wife's only option was to use the courts to force her husband to support her and their children in an appropriate manner with the very money she had brought into the marriage. In 1887 the territorial legislature again reiterated its commitment to coverture by passing a law stating that in any civil case brought by a married woman or against a married woman, her husband had to be "joined as a party with her unless he be a non-resident of the territory or unless they shall be living apart from each other."[51] From a legal point of view, then, affluent Mexican women had every reason to be skeptical about their ability to control property as the U.S. legal regime was gradually, but securely, being locked into place after 1848.

In studying the language and metaphors that the courts used to define and subordinate the status of Mexican married women, connections emerge between the imperialism we have come to associate with European expansion and the U.S. experience in bringing these formerly Mexican territories under its control. Anne McClintock, in *Imperial Leather*, illuminates the role constructions of race and gender played in Europeans' views of their imperialist expansion into Africa and Southeast Asia at the end of the nineteenth century. McClintock points out that European conquerors —from the Portuguese trader José da Silvestre, who saw women's breasts imbedded in the landscape, to advertisers for Pears' Soap, who wanted to emasculate the conquered people they sought to cleanse—all felt compelled to gender the conquered landscape and peoples as feminine, empty vessels passively awaiting filling.[52]

In much the same way, the U.S. government and proponents of Mexico's annexation found it necessary to feminize the newly conquered Mexican population. For example, Sen. Sidney Breese from Illinois stated, "The Indian population [of Mexico], numbering about four million, are reputed to be very gentle and quiet in their disposition, apt to learn, and willing to improve, and, if not possessed of all their manlier virtues, have at least those which fully ensure their cheerful acquiescence to our control and rapid advancement under it."[53] In feminizing the Mexican population, the political rhetoric also emphasized America's manliness in conquering a subordinated nation. *The New York Herald* spoke of America's need to act "manfully" in dealing with Mexico and pointed out that California, in particular, possessed wealthy and virtuous heiresses who awaited Yankee dominance.[54] In fact, a number of newspapers alluded to intermarriage and the property acquisition that would inevitably occur. One Philadelphian wrote, "Our Yankee young fellows and the pretty señoritas will do the rest of the annexation, and Mexico will soon be Anglo-Saxonized, and prepared for the confederacy."[55] So by feminizing Mexico, conquering the territory, and taking over women and their property, Americans would prepare this new area to become a part of the United States. Of course, this manly rhetoric also symbolized Americans' desire to conquer subordinate peoples and attain their Manifest Destiny of controlling North America.

Furthermore, the men responsible for implementing U.S. common law often benefited from the change in property regimes because they were familiar with the new system and used that knowledge to their advantage. For example, Stephen B. Elkins, a prominent Missourian turned New Mexican lawyer, successfully represented Quirina Baca against the Collins heirs. Elkins, who later in his career would serve as a lawyer for the Maxwell Land Grant Company, as territorial attorney general, and as the U.S. congressional delegate, had a reputation for taking cases that he knew he could win and from which he could make a substantial profit. In manipulating the system of coverture, he ironically preserved Baca's estate by proving that she was incapable of managing her affairs. The case also directly benefited him monetarily and professionally as he gained a reputation as someone who could negotiate the new U.S. legal system. But his negotiation inevitably came at a price to his Mexican clients.[56]

These changing legal conditions may have played a significant role in the decision that the Beaubien women made in disposing of their propertied interest; however, their social and economic position, as well as the location of the grant, may also explain their actions. The Maxwell Land Grant, on the eastern side of the 13,000-foot Sangre de Cristo Mountains, was far away from Santa Fe and Taos. These geographic barriers made the property difficult to work and also economically risky. Except for sporadic stops along the Santa Fe Trail such as Raton, Las Vegas, and Rayado, few permanent settlements existed in eastern New Mexico during the mid-nineteenth century. By the 1860s only the Maxwells, two of the Beaubien sisters and their families, and a handful of other families had made permanent homes on the eastern slope of the Sangre de Cristos. Even the settlers who came to work the land for the Maxwells tended to migrate back across the Sangre de Cristos into the Rio Grande Valley once cold weather appeared. So while the people in these settlements had access to the Santa Fe Trail trade, they remained isolated from the urban centers of New Mexico's culture, politics, and trade in the towns of Santa Fe and Taos.

In addition to the problems associated with its isolation, people also questioned the extent of the grant's boundaries. The Maxwells paid less than $50,000 for property that came to be known as the largest estate in the United States. The various heirs and claimants to the land grant sold at below-market prices because of pending litigation and questions surrounding the grant's validity and limits. Throughout the 1860s and 1870s, these questions remained unanswered. Although William Pelham, the surveyor general of New Mexico, had approved the grant, and the U.S. Congress confirmed it in 1860, neither Pelham nor Congress ever specified the exact acreage, but instead relied on complicated and confusing descriptions and surveys. People familiar with Maxwell and the estate speculated that the grant extended anywhere from 160,000 to 2,000,000 acres.[57]

Furthermore, local custom and familial exchanges offered no clarification of the grant's exact boundaries. All the conveyances between the Maxwells and the Beaubiens, Miranda, and the Bent heirs had been transferred as shares of the grant with no mention of exact acreage. Also, during their tenure, the Maxwells never erected any fences to mark property boundaries. Indeed, there seemed to be no good economic reason to do so. The Maxwells had no neighbors who might encroach on their property, and fences, which had to be made of wood, would have been prohibitively expensive on this high plains landscape. No one, from Beaubien and Miranda to their heirs and final owners, Lucien and Luz Maxwell, knew the grant's exact boundaries. During the Maxwells' tenure on the grant, however, the boundaries made little difference as they went about their business of building a home, a family, and a ranching business in the heart of what would later be patented by the U.S. Congress as a 1.7-million-acre estate.[58]

Yet pending litigation, isolation, and uncertainty over acreage and validity of title do not exhaust the reasons why the Beaubien sisters may have had to sell their property for such a low price. Another sort of uncertainty, and perhaps the most decisive reason, concerned which legal regime governed the land grant. If U.S. law applied, the Beaubien sisters would not have retained control over the estate at all: their husbands would have had legal control over the land. Their right to use the land in any manner they thought proper would have been worthless if conflict ever arose between the sisters and their respective spouses. This would have been particularly true for Eleanor Beaubien Trujillo, whose marriage ended in divorce and who may have taken a lesson from the experiences of women like Mariana Martínez. The sisters may have sold as a rational reaction to the likelihood that U.S. law had already stripped them of the rights they were waiving with quitclaim deeds to the Maxwells. While the women could hold cash as their own personal property, they could not hold land. Luz Maxwell, on the other hand, benefited from her sisters' strategic decisions only because she maintained a solid marriage to Lucien. Maxwell, however, suffered the unfortunate circumstance of dying relatively early in life in 1875, leaving Luz a wealthy widow. After Maxwell's death, Luz was free to act as a *femme sole*, or single woman, and run her own cattle business.

## PEONAGE IN NEW MEXICO

Why was the U.S. government not particularly interested in protecting the property rights of Mexican married women? The failure to recognize the wide variety of property rights under Mexican law was due in part to U.S. lawmakers' deep disdain for what they understood to be the hierarchical, aristocratic, and feudalistic hacienda system of land tenure in Mexico. Ironically, these were the same congressional leaders who had fewer problems justifying the continued existence of slavery, as well as women's lower political and economic status. Members of Congress had ratified the Treaty of Guadalupe Hidalgo, which legally protected the rights of Mexican citizens, but at the request of President James K. Polk, they had also refused to ratify Article 10, which specifically guaranteed the property rights of Mexican citizens.[59] Polk and Congress did not wish to give Mexican citizens the right to perfect their titles under Mexican law, and instead assured the Mexican negotiators that land grants would be protected under U.S. law. Moreover, many congressmen did not want to give unequivocal recognition to the property rights of feudal landlords who held vast estates in Texas, New Mexico, and California. They considered such extensive land parcels inimical to the Jeffersonian ideals of equality and individualism that they imagined to be the foundation of U.S. property law. Maxwell and his estate seemed to be the perfect example of what they feared most. Indeed, Anglo visitors coming down the Santa Fe Trail rarely failed to comment on Maxwell's paternalistic, and sometimes harsh, rule over his baronial estate.[60]

The irony, however, was that congressional refusal to recognize Mexican property law relegated Mexican women to precisely the state of feudalistic dependence from which they intended to rescue Mexican *peones* on hacienda estates. This is to say that as a matter of plain legal description, the position of women under U.S. law and *peones* under the rule of the *patrón* were similar. Neither held clear title to property. Neither married women in the United States nor *peones* in New Mexico could use or dispose of the land they inhabited as they chose. This similar legal status, however, does not mean that Mexican married women and *peones* were ever conscious of their common subordination, let alone that they united to resist it. But the situation in New Mexico bore a peculiar resemblance to the antebellum American South, where White women and African American slaves lived under the dominant rule of the master but never joined to overthrow such paternalism.[61]

To better understand the parallel relationships between married women and the *patrón*, and *peones* and the *patrón*, we must look more closely at the *patrón* and *peón* relationship on the New Mexican frontier. The modified hacienda system was part and parcel of the Mexican grant system through which *patrones* like Maxwell held title to land. The *patrón* took on the obligation of settling families on the grant, which was usually in a frontier location, as a condition of receiving enhanced acreage. In effect, the Mexican government intended *patrones* (and, in the case of Texas, the empresarios) to be the leaders, overlords, and *alcaldes* of their communities in addition to fulfilling their responsibilities as private property owners. Of course, in practice *patrones* did not rule as dictators but as feudal magnates who used incentives and force only when necessary to motivate their *peones* or the settlers they had induced to come to the frontier. While the *patrón's* tenants had no formal legal rights recorded in any deed, they did possess a set of circumstances and informal customs that limited the discretion of the legal owner, and which informally protected their interests. The *patrón* was, in effect, head of an extended family—an informal, closely knit association. While the rhetoric of familial association may seem exaggerated, Maxwell at least respected the duties of the *patrón* insofar as he did not evict his tenants without cause.[62]

Why was the U.S. government willing to tolerate this type of paternalism in the American South's slave society but unwilling to adopt the New Mexico peonage system, which it viewed as immoral, for incorporation into the U.S. legal and property system? Congress held divergent opinions about the two regions. The antebellum Congress worked under the assumption, which was slowly changing, that the American South consisted of sovereign states that, under the Constitution, allowed their citizens the right to possess slaves. On the other hand, the land and people conquered as a result of the U.S.–Mexican War, and those of the American West in general, were not sovereign states but were directly governed by Congress through the territorial system. The region's citizens had few independently granted constitutional rights, much less the right to own human property. The West was a conquered territory that could be molded to fit the congressional notions of a just and moral society. Congress therefore believed that it could dictate the West's property regime.[63] More important, this problem of unfree labor would reappear in Congress at the end of the Civil War. Thus Congress, through the territorial system, dealt with peonage as a rehearsal for the issues that arose after Emancipation and during Reconstruction.[64]

When the United States took control of New Mexico, the debt-peonage system that provided the workforce for large ranches and farms like the Maxwell grant concerned the federal government. Congressmen were troubled by a land tenure system that placed so much land in the hands of a few owners and left a whole class of workers to fend for themselves against hacienda owners. The problems associated with *peones* and *patrones* were of particular concern in New Mexico, because the institution persisted long after U.S. occupation. In 1857, the Territorial Supreme Court first took up the issue of peonage in the case of *Mariana Jaramillo v. José de la Cruz Romero*.[65] Mariana, a young girl of thirteen or so, ran away from her *patrón*, José de la Cruz, for reasons not outlined in the case. Romero sued

Mariana and her father, claiming that she still owed him $51.75 in cash or services on her debt. The justices ruled that since Mariana was a minor (they also believed that, given her young age, the debt was actually her father's), Romero could not force her to repay the debt and hold her in servitude. Although this was a clear-cut case, the Territorial Supreme Court took the opportunity to examine the history of debt peonage in the region and tried to make sense of where this labor relationship might fit into the U.S. legal system.

The court devoted numerous pages to discussing the institution of peonage and found it an amorphous commercial relationship that had no clear institutional set of norms that regulated labor practices. The court wrote, "We have been unable to find any law creating and defining the duties and rights, the civil and domestic relations under the specific denomination of peon." [66] Even after conducting its own legal research, the court found few laws that regulated the practice of people selling their labor and personhood to a *patrón*.[67] The court concluded that in the absence of any clear, historically specific legal description, the *peón/patrón* relationship would be best viewed by the U.S. government and territorial officials as a contract in which both parties willingly engaged in the exchange of labor for credit or cash—free labor. For the court, the most important element of the contract was "the consent of the parties [which] was invariably the foundation upon which a servant became bound to service."[68] The court also noted that the relationship went beyond economics since it was based on the "personal interests" of parties who chose to live in close proximity to one another and shared cultural and social ties as well. For example, the *patrón* often acted as a *padrino*, or godfather, to children being baptized or young couples getting married. Moreover, *peones*, servants, and even Indian slaves often lived within the familial household.[69]

Nevertheless, although the court viewed the relationship as socially beneficial and economically lucrative, it still found ties between *peón* and *patrón* wanting; the court felt the relationship was basically uneven and despotic. Legal opinions mimicked contemporary rhetoric that criticized the hierarchy of Mexican cultural, social, and economic institutions; anti-Mexican sentiment reverberates throughout the opinion. For example, the court wrote that this case "called to mind a period under a former government in this country when no degree of tolerable certainty existed in judicial forms, proceedings, and decisions, and when the laws and their just benefits were so often set aside or crushed under foot by prejudice, corruption, or passion—by interest, power, and despotism."[70] The court detested the Mexican legal regime, with its odd labor, social, and property practices. Yet, ironically, they did not seem interested in eradicating peonage.[71]

The court's main concern was how to label, codify, and then regulate the practice of debt peonage within the U.S. legal system. This type of servant/master relationship, while possessing many similarities to southern slavery, still held as one of its basic tenets the right to freely choose one's *patrón*. The court, and indeed U.S. lawmakers, had difficulty eradicating peonage even after the Civil War and passage of the Thirteenth Amendment.[72] One change the New Mexico territorial legislature made in 1852, however, was to take away from the *patrón* the legal right to punish *peones*. Instead, legislators gave that function to the local authorities and courts, who would treat it as a public matter. Moreover, the court eradicated the use of corporal punishment, which had been the *patrón's* prerogative, and instead mandated imprisonment as the only method of punishment, which was to be determined by the courts, not by the *patrón*.[73] By agreeing to view the *patrón/peón* relationship as a contractual relationship between two "equal" and willing partners, the court deftly avoided the thorny issues that would have arisen if comparisons to slavery were made too closely. But as the facts of this case make perfectly clear, abuses occurred that put this type of labor relationship beyond the realm of a free labor relationship between equals.

Significantly, these debt-peonage cases more often than not involved the abuse of a woman or girl. On one side of New Mexican society, women like the Beaubien sisters could own property and control economic assets, but many, many more women lived and worked under the control of the upper classes. For example, in 1852 the court heard another peonage case that involved similar allegations of abuse in the *patrón/peón* relationship. Marcelina Bustamento sued Juana Analla to have Juana's daughter, Catalina, returned to Bustamento's service. When Analla found out that Catalina, who was also Bustamento's stepdaughter, lived in the house as a servant, she retrieved her daughter from the household. The court documents tell the story of how Catalina came to be placed in such an ambiguous household situation in the first place. Years earlier, Juana Analla had been the servant/*peón* of Carpio Bustamento, Marcelina's husband. While in his service, Juana Analla had given birth to two of his "natural" (illegitimate) children. She eventually left his service but still owed him $145 on her debt. Upon her departure, Bustamento "forgave" $45, and she in turn left her two children with him so that he might "maintain them as a legitimate father" would. Although the court case does not say specifically, we can speculate that domestic conflict had broken out between Bustamento, his wife, and Analla, who was probably forced through both economic circumstances and fatherly coercion to give up her children to her master/lover. Carpio Bustamento, upon Juana Analla's departure, then gave his natural daughter, Catalina, to his legal wife, Marcelina, as a servant for her household use. Marcelina Bustamento never claimed that she raised the girl as a daughter in her household. She simply demanded the return of her servant as payment of the mother's debt. The court found the whole situation appalling, returned Catalina to her natural mother, and ruled that children and their labor could not be used to settle debts between adult *peones* and their *patrones*.

While court officials rightly stopped the abuses that came before them, even the two cases involving Catalina Bustamento and Mariana Jaramillo, young female children, reveal the kind of abuses that took place within the debt-peonage system. There were probably many other such situations that escaped the scrutiny of both local authorities and the court system. Moreover, these two cases came to the court's attention only because the *patrón* or mistress believed that he or she had unfairly lost service due to him or her and sought legal relief. We have no evidence of *peones* using the courts to punish unfair or abusive *patrones*, which illustrates the skewed power relations between classes in territorial New Mexico, where not everyone stood as equals under the law. The court, even with such evidence of abuse, did not seek to eradicate the entire labor system but instead contented itself with simply punishing its abuses and regulating its practices.

### LABOR RELATIONS ON THE MAXWELL LAND GRANT

Maxwell inhabited the legal arena in which the U.S. government sanctioned the *patrón*/*peón* relationship. Indeed, he created a world of intimate and complex labor relations with his settlers who came freely, *peones* who worked the land, and Indian slaves he owned. Through his enterprises at Rayado and later at Cimarron he attracted and settled hundreds of settlers and *peones* who worked on his land and paid him rent through in-kind payments such as crops and livestock. Maxwell also had Native American servants who were probably slaves captured during the myriad Indian wars that raged on this frontier during the late nineteenth century. Indeed, one of his closest associates, Kit Carson, was known for his role in leading campaigns against Indians and taking captured Indian children into his home. These captured Indians were often used as slaves in New Mexican households and thus were incorporated into this frontier world.[74] In 1860 the Maxwells had three Indian servants living in their household. By 1870 the Maxwell household had fifteen servants, including seven Indians under the age of fifteen.[75]

One of their servants, Deluvina Maxwell, illustrates one end of the labor spectrum—New Mexico's Indian slave trade. Deluvina, a Navajo child, was taken from her home near Canyon de Chelley after a raid by Ute Indians in which her entire family—father, mother, and three brothers—was massacred. Maxwell purchased the seven-year-old Deluvina from the Utes, with whom he had friendly trading relationships, as a present for Luz Maxwell. Deluvina worked as a household servant for the Maxwells most of her life, until she died in Albuquerque in the 1930s.[76] Deluvina comes to our historical attention because of her supposed connection to New Mexico's most infamous outlaw, Billy the Kid. By some accounts, Paulita Maxwell (Lucien and Luz's daughter) was the reason Billy the Kid was hanging around the Maxwell estate when Pat Garrett shot him.[77] Deluvina, Paulita's servant, was very attached to Billy and aided the lovers' attempts to see each other despite the Maxwell family's objections. Deluvina supposedly attacked Garrett when she found out it was him who shot the Kid.

Yet the devotion of Deluvina to Billy the Kid and his forbidden relationship with Maxwell's daughter overshadow the real drama of Deluvina's life. Here was a woman who as a child watched the brutal murder of her family, was taken captive, and sold to a *patrón* in a foreign land—all of this under the benign neglect of the U.S. government, which could not control the Indian wars, the Mexican and Anglo slave traders, or the trade among the various Indian groups. She inhabited a world where she was a captive slave who had little control over her life, much less any property she could ever hope to own. Although most of Maxwell's *peones* did not live in such an extreme state of servitude, Deluvina's life illustrates the extent to which the *patrón* system could operate under U.S. laws while avoiding the label of slavery. Also, unlike the South, where a clearer line, based on race, existed between master and servant, in New Mexico unclear boundaries separated the *patrón* and his or her *peones*, slaves, and workers. It is even difficult to give full descriptions of the various people who worked on the Maxwell estate because workers were not easily categorized as slave or free, *peón* or contract laborer, settler or sharecropper. Maxwell probably liked the ambiguity of these labor relations, as he consistently placed himself in the middle of all economic transactions on the estate.

Maxwell comfortably played the complex role of *patrón*. While these labor relationships seem complicated and multifaceted to historians, for Maxwell his role was relatively similar whether he was dealing with his sisters-in-law, wife, slaves, *peones*, workers, lessees, or business associates. He was the leader of an insular community that depended on him to negotiate with the outside world, which was rapidly moving toward the Maxwell estate: he was the conduit through which most of the cash flowed on the grant.

When Maxwell broke away from his father-in-law's business and estate at Rayado, he strategically picked the site of Cimarron for his new home because it sat at the crossroads of the Santa Fe Trail and the mouth of Taos Canyon, which led directly across the Continental Divide to Taos. Maxwell hoped to redirect some of the trade away from Santa Fe, through Cimarron, and direct it west to the upper portion of the Rio Grande Valley. He possibly aspired to work as a middleman between traders anxious to sell their goods on the eastern side of the divide and return east for another load, and the communities of the upper Rio Grande, which were eager to acquire more eastern goods than they could acquire through Santa Fe. By contacts with emerging markets for agricultural and ranching goods supplying the army posts and the Jicarilla Indian agency, for example, Maxwell created a flourishing business. His newly acquired wealth was something he never tired of showing off to those who stopped in Cimarron.

The Maxwells were known throughout the West for their opulent mansion (by nineteenth-century frontier standards) and exceptional hospitality at Cimarron. Many travelers crossing the Santa Fe Trail hurried eagerly toward the Maxwell home for an appetizing meal, luxurious accommodations, and an evening of gambling with Lucien. The Maxwells hosted everyone who came to their home, and it was said that Lucien never accepted payment for food, drink, or accommodations. One visitor described the estate as a sort of "barbaric splendor, akin to that of the nobles of England at the time of the Norman Conquest." Another guest remembered seeing as many as fifty people sit down to a dinner of beef and mutton. And William Ryus recalled that the Maxwells set their tables with solid silver serving dishes and cutlery, and tablecloths made of the finest woven floss. Clearly the Maxwells' enterprises had been lucrative since they apparently had the cash to purchase these luxury items from the trail trade. Maxwell's opulent lifestyle and carefree attitude toward money became legendary; visitors told of gold and silver coins carelessly placed in a chest of drawers in plain view, of high-stakes gaming, and of incredible generosity. Maxwell typified the *patrón* who gave freely to his *peones* and friends. In return, he expected respect from everyone, timely payments from his renters, and loyalty from his friends and business associates. He punished severely those who did not comply.[78]

One visitor, Henry Inman, reported that although most of Maxwell's settlers were *peones*, Maxwell was "not a hard governor, and his people really loved him, as he was their friend and adviser."[79] Inman, a southerner, comfortably accepted the antebellum plantation system and saw many similarities in the way Maxwell ran the estate. Inman's observation also points out the close and intense relationship between the *patrón* and *peón:* a relationship that in day-to-day life was remarkably similar to the kinds of paternalism evident in the American South at the time.[80] This similarity was probably not lost on those in Congress who were anxious to contain the extension of slavery and do away with the legacy of the large Mexican land grants.

One long-time Maxwell employee, Calvin Jones, also compared the Maxwell estate with plantations in the South. But Jones did not find the hacienda a pleasant or inviting place. Jones recalled an incident when a Mexican servant did something that displeased Maxwell, who in response took a plank and whipped the man with it. Jones also remembered, "I knew him to tie up one man, a Mexican, and shave off the side of his head close to the skin with a butcher knife, then he struck him fifteen or twenty lashes with a cowhide, and told him if he ever caught him on the place again, he would kill him." Apparently the man did not take Maxwell seriously. He returned a decade later, and Maxwell shot him to death, without repercussions from the U.S. legal system.[81]

The relationship between Lucien B. Maxwell and the Hispanos, almost five hundred by some estimates, who migrated west from the Rio Grande Valley, was really a modernized Mexican hacienda system suited to New Mexico's frontier conditions. The *patrón/peón* bond between Maxwell and individual Hispanos and Jicarillas was a personal and informal relationship between dominant and subordinate persons involving nontransferable rights and duties for both. Regardless of the kind of intimacy suggested by friendship or *compadrazgo,* the tie between Maxwell and his *peones* remained mainly a financial one that was an especially lucrative one for Maxwell. The 1860 census taker noted that Maxwell owned $25,000 in real estate and $39,000 in real property. By 1868 the Maxwells had an annual income of $50,000 and were one of the wealthier families in the territory. A visitor in 1870 estimated that although many of Maxwell's tenants had left their farms to take up mining on Baldy Mountain after gold was discovered, Maxwell still collected more than 100,000 bushels of wheat, corn, and oats as rent.[82]

The Maxwell hacienda ran not as its feudal predecessors had in Mexico, but in a more modern incarnation that could adjust to market forces and combine the labor of the hacienda with the emerging capitalist markets in the area.[83] Immanuel Wallerstein and other scholars of colonial relationships suggest that these "large, so-called self-sufficient haciendas" on the frontier should not be viewed as arcane remnants of feudalism, but as modern economic units capable of adjusting to modern market forces. The Maxwell estate, through ranching, farming, and trade, went beyond the subsistence-based economy of the Jicarilla Apaches, who had been the only other land users in the area prior to the grant's establishment. The workers on Maxwell's hacienda produced surplus commodities for the nascent market economy created by the presence of the U.S. Army, the Indian agency, and the arrival of the Santa Fe Trail trade.

Despite the intrusion of the market into the workings of the estate, Maxwell maintained the informal economic obligations on his estate by personal ties rather than by legal contracts or state enforcement. The grant was much too extensive for Maxwell to manage single-handedly, so he allowed Mexican settlers to hold plots of land on which they built homes and farms. In turn, these settlers paid "rent" to Maxwell in grain, cattle, wool, or sheep, which he then traded to outside markets. Although not as strong as U.S. homesteaders' rights, squatters did have rights to their small parcels. In fact, Maxwell carried out the original intention of the Beaubien and Miranda grant by acting as a Mexican empresario who took a large grant of land and agreed to settle it for the Mexican government. He developed the land, brought settlers onto the estate, and created a stable economy for the migrants. Social and economic relations on the Maxwell grant were inherently unequal in terms of power, but the system was mutually beneficial because the settlers improved the land, and Maxwell protected their homes and farms from Comanche and Kiowa raids on their livestock, as well as from the Anglo settlers moving into New Mexico.

As *patrón*, Maxwell was the legal owner of his estate: in theory he could have evicted all five hundred settlers and reserved the land for his personal use. This scenario was, of course, impractical given the immense size of his holdings: no individual could work that much land. In practice, Maxwell was constrained by informal norms that limited his discretion and gave settlers "squatter's rights" that he could manipulate in his favor, but not eliminate. When Maxwell's successor, the Maxwell Land Grant Company, attempted to assert its legal claim to the grant in fee simple and absolute without encumbrances placed on the land by these Hispano settlers, it was soon driven into bankruptcy by their resistance. The settlers expected adherence to the unwritten norms developed by Maxwell over the years. More important, these settlers expected to be treated as individuals who had a specific and unique relationship with the property owner. The Maxwell Land Grant Company's gravest mistake was in treating the settlers as an undifferentiated group. It was because company agents treated the settlers as an indistinguishable mass that the settlers eventually developed a type of class consciousness that allowed them to overcome their differences and band together against the company.

Prior to the company's arrival, Maxwell had maintained a complex and fluid set of individual property relationships with his settlers. There was nothing simple or clear-cut about the way Maxwell ran his estate. He had assembled one of the largest pieces of private property in the United States through deft negotiations with his wife's family. He also ran one of the most tangled and ambiguous labor systems of the mid-nineteenth century. So when outsiders came into New Mexico and tried to organize the estate and the enterprise along the lines of established U.S. business and legal practices, the match was far from perfect.

## THE MAXWELLS SELL THE GRANT

Living conditions across the grant changed dramatically when soldiers from Fort Union discovered gold on Baldy Mountain in 1866. Within a few months the grant was flooded with prospectors who hoped they had found another California gold boom. One man remarked that the new diggings were "as rich as any yet 'struck' on the North American continent." Soon more than fifteen mining companies had sprung up within the boundaries of the grant, and some of them began taking water from local creeks for hydraulic mining. By May 1867, the miners had established a government with rules for staking claims, and the mining community of Elizabethtown appeared almost overnight, becoming the second largest town on the Maxwell Land Grant.[84]

In the first two years after the discoveries, Maxwell profited handsomely from the boom. Not only did he set up diggings of his own, but he also sold claims to miners on his land.[85] His best profits, however, came from selling goods to eastern miners who passed through Cimarron on their way up the canyon. He also successfully invested in ditches, sawmills, smelters, and roads, which only enhanced the profitability of the mining district in those early years. While the Maxwells were spectacularly wealthy by nineteenth-century New Mexican standards, in early 1869 they suffered financial losses from speculations that went awry as the mining boom slowed. For example, Maxwell wasted a considerable sum of money trying to build a ditch to bring water down from the Sangre de Cristos to the placer mines near Elizabethtown. The ditch was poorly constructed and never delivered the promised water.[86]

Maxwell, who was really more of a *patrón* than an entrepreneur and businessman, felt comfortable with his life as a rancher and farmer and eventually backed away from these capitalistic ventures. The complications of the gold discovery and the increasing population on the grant convinced the Maxwells that it was time to sell and retire to a home back in Rayado. Maxwell told two men, "I am tired of this place, from the Indians and the new-comers on the land." He offered to sell to the two men everything he owned, including the livestock and the mines, for $200,000. The would-be purchasers, however, declined, believing the land was not worth Maxwell's asking price.[87] However, investors outside of New Mexico believed the estate was worth four times Maxwell's estimate. By early 1869, the Maxwells had begun negotiating with these outside investors. Ironically, Lucien and Luz Maxwell were motivated to sell by many of the same factors that had forced their family members to sell to them: a changing legal regime, a new economy, and outside market pressures.

Maxwell's strange enterprise was ethically ambiguous. The control of the grant by a single member of a dominant racial caste made it similar to the slave-based plantation system of the antebellum South, and even more similar to the sharecropping system that developed after the Civil War. Yet the antebellum South is not an exact analogy. The Maxwell estate, with its localized landholding by settlers and *peones* as well as the in-kind rent payments, supported a unique culture of small-scale Hispano farming. This arrangement allowed residents a degree of economic autonomy that later developments on the grant would largely eliminate. Maxwell's estate has been characterized by historians as either benevolent *patronismo* or magnate tyranny. Most likely it was a mixture of both, and Maxwell probably saw no contradiction in the dual role he played.

Aside from its ambiguous ethical character, Maxwell's estate had peculiar economic foundations. It was a massive enterprise involving hundreds of tenants and thousands of transactions among Anglo miners, Hispano farmers, and Jicarilla clients. Yet this complicated and sizable enterprise lacked precise and formal legal definition. The informality of the Mexican legal regime governing the land had two characteristics. First, the grant's external boundaries were only crudely delineated: even the Maxwells had only the vaguest conception of the extent of their holdings. Their legal rights to the property were defined by usage and custom rather than by specifically recorded boundaries. Second, the internal rights and obligations between the occupants of the grant and Maxwell were unclearly defined. The occupants acknowledged that they owed Maxwell some sort of payment, but the basis of calculation for payments was not clearly defined by any written contract or deed. Thus Maxwell's internal relations with his tenants and his external relations with the rest of the world possessed an informality curious for an enterprise of such size.

This informality is less mystifying when one considers that the workers on the grant were local and had ties to the Maxwells. Furthermore, Maxwell's enterprise demanded little capital investment; he did not exploit national and international credit markets to develop the grant's resources. Aside from his failed attempts to engage in capital-intensive mining, Maxwell did not invest much in equipment or infrastructure. He did not need to define the precise boundaries of the grant because he never found it necessary to secure loans from international and national lenders or investors. As we shall see, the Maxwell Land Grant Company tried to develop the grant more intensively and therefore needed to attract money from the world credit markets. Such credit would not be forthcoming until a clearly defined system of landholding replaced the informal system of operating the grant.

This hacienda or *patrón* system was disrupted when the Maxwells sold the grant to European investors in 1869. In its place, the company's managers established the U.S. system of partition and sale as well as the institution of private property. It was virtually impossible for the Hispano settlers to adapt to the new regime and remain as ranchers or farmers, much less as property holders on the grant. The U.S. legal system could not incorporate the informal property regime that had evolved under Mexican law, and consequently the *peones* and settlers lost what few property rights they had established under Maxwell.

The problems that *peones* and married women faced during this early history of the Maxwell Land Grant grew out of the U.S. legal system's inability to accommodate different labor and property regimes. Consequently, Mexican land tenure, which encouraged intimate relations between *patrón* and *peón*, and married women's property rights were not preserved in their original form or with the original set of reciprocal obligations. U.S. lawmakers failed to see the economic and social functions that Mexican land grants and property systems had served and were deeply offended by the notion of haciendas and feudalism existing on U.S. soil. By replacing Mexican with U.S. land law, however, Congress encouraged the creation of a *patrón* system, not for Hispano *peones*, but for Mexican married women. Women's legal position in the United States was analogous to the position of the *peón* in the *patrón* system: a theoretically benevolent and familial dependence that meant to protect those deemed incapable of participating in the property regime.

Ironically, the United States law that regulated married women's property was more feudal and paternal than the Mexican law it replaced. While they remained under Mexican law, and later after the Americans moved in —under New Mexican custom—the Beaubien sisters were quite autonomous and free to deal with the *patrón* as they chose, at least in terms of property relations. Luz Maxwell's name appears on many documents, although under U.S. law that was unnecessary. Moreover, the Beaubien heirs sold to Maxwell at their convenience: Maxwell does not appear to have pushed any of them into giving up their property. Under U.S. law, and particularly as a result of coverture laws, however, the Beaubien sisters could not necessarily expect to enjoy the same rights that they had exercised earlier in their lives.

In the end, the power of market capitalism—which demanded of its participants a knowledge of markets, bonds, stocks, and interest—as well as the uncertainty of their legal status as married women under the U.S. regime, proved overwhelming for the Beaubien sisters. For them it was easier to sell their land (with their husbands' names included) to the Maxwells and move on to other enterprises. All continued to be prominent citizens of New Mexico and to engage in ranching and farming enterprises within the confines of early territorial society. Luz Maxwell, along with her son and brother-in-law, was named executor of Lucien's estate upon his death and continued to run a profitable enterprise from her home in Rayado; with Maxwell gone, she could act as a *femme sole* and make her own business transactions.

This western example of the gendered workings of the law reminds historians to take region seriously as a category of analysis.[88] While women's legal historians have typically told progressive stories that detail the rise of women from the patriarchal family of the eighteenth century to the individual property holder of the twentieth, in this case the typical tale does not ring true. The story for Mexican American women is a declensionist tale, a loss of autonomy as individuals capable of contracting and holding property became wards of their husbands, on whom they were legally dependent.

This transformation in property and legal regimes brought drastic changes to both the *peones* and women owners on the grant. Both suffered, but for opposite reasons. The *peones* lost because their informal property rights as squatters or tenants, recognized and enforced by the *patrón*, had no equivalent in U.S. law and consequently could not be recognized: they lost their land and livelihood. The Beaubien/Maxwell women also suffered under the U.S. system, but they lost because the very formal property rights that had been recognized under Mexican civil law were called into question. Now women had to rely on the informal communal property system established for them by U.S. law: coverture. They now had to rely on the good will of their husbands (their *patrones*) to protect their interests. In the end, both *peones* and Mexican women suffered loss of property and livelihood because their old Mexican property rights would not be incorporated into and recognized by the new system of law.

Figure 1. Lucien B. Maxwell (left) with Charles F. Holly and Judge John Watts, 1869. This photo was taken after they had completed the deal to sell the land grant to the London consortium of investors. Courtesy of the Arthur Johnson Memorial Library, Raton, New Mexico, and reproduced by permission of the Center for Southwest Research General Library, University of New Mexico, negative no. 2000–13–0009.

Figure 2. Emblem embossed on the Maxwell Land Grant stock certificates. Note the abundance that surrounds the voluptuous young woman. Reproduced by permission of the Center for Southwest Research General Library, University of New Mexico, negative no. 000–147–0126.

Figure 3. Maxwell Land Grant Company office, Raton, New Mexico, ca. 1890. Reproduced by permission of the Center for Southwest Research General Library, University of New Mexico, negative no. 000–147–0096.

Figure 4.   Deluvina Maxwell with Ida Harris Custer to her left, ca. 1930. After
her capture and sale to Lucien B. Maxwell, Deluvina lived with the Maxwells
until her death. Courtesy Museum of New Mexico, Palace of the Governors,
negative no. 58751.

Figure 5.    Jicarilla man and woman; photo taken at the Abiquiu, New Mexico, Indian Agency by the Wheeler Survey in 1874. Frank McNitt Collection, reproduced courtesy of the New Mexico State Records Center and Archives, no. 5754.

Figure 6. WPA painting, ca. 1930s, of the Maxwell Estate depicting Maxwell, Kit Carson, and María de la Luz Beaubien in front of their "mansion" in 1865. Artist Manville Chapman painted this mural for the Shuler Theater in Raton. WPA Collection, reproduced courtesy of the New Mexico State Records Center and Archives, no. 5360.

Figure 7. Charles Berninghaus's painting "Old Maxwell House" shows the Cimarron, New Mexico, home ca. 1930s. WPA Collection, reproduced courtesy of the New Mexico State Records Center and Archives, no. 5373.

Figure 8. Train station at Cimarron, New Mexico, ca. 1890s. The railroad transformed the economy of the Maxwell Land Grant by the mid-1880s. Reproduced by permission of the Center for Southwest Research General Library, University of New Mexico, negative no. 000–147–0056.

Figure 9. Hispano and Anglo men with a company surveyor building a section of the Vermejo Ditch, which was to irrigate the heart of the land grant, 1891. Reproduced by permission of the Center for Southwest Research General Library, University of New Mexico, negative no. 000–147–0137.

Figure 10. Cattle roundup for the Maxwell Land Grant and Cattle Company, 1887. Reproduced by permission of the Center for Southwest Research General Library, University of New Mexico, negative no. 000–147–0021.

Figure 11.  Thomas O. Boggs (shown ca. 1880s), a Maxwell Company land agent, was consistently frustrated by his inability to come to a settlement with the settlers on the land grant. Reproduced courtesy of the Philmont Museum, Cimarron, New Mexico.

Figure 12.    The Stonewall Valley (shown ca. 1916) in Colorado was home to
the Russell family and others who persistently resisted the Maxwell Company's
attempts to remove them from their homes. Photograph by Ernst Roth, Sr.
Courtesy Museum of New Mexico, Palace of the Governors, negative no. 85757.

Figure 13.   One of the few existing photos of María de la Luz Beaubien Maxwell, ca. 1890s. Courtesy of the Arthur Johnson Memorial Library, Raton, New Mexico, and reproduced by permission of the Center for Southwest Research General Library, University of New Mexico, negative no. 2000–013–0008.

Figure 14.   Teodora Beaubien Mueller with child, ca. 1890s. She was one of the first Beaubien women to sell to the Maxwells. Courtesy of the Arthur Johnson Memorial Library, Raton, New Mexico, and reproduced by permission of the Center for Southwest Research General Library, University of New Mexico, negative no. 2000–013–0010.

Figure 15. Juana Beaubien Clouthier with family, ca. 1890s. She sold her share in the Beaubien/Miranda Land Grant very early to the Maxwells. Courtesy of the Arthur Johnson Memorial Library, Raton, New Mexico, and reproduced by permission of the Center for Southwest Research General Library, University of New Mexico, negative no. 2000–013–0005.

Figure 16.   Eleanor Beaubien and Vidal Trujillo on their wedding day, ca. 1890s. The couple would later divorce amid rumors of his adultery. Courtesy of the Arthur Johnson Memorial Library, Raton, New Mexico, and reproduced by permission of the Center for Southwest Research General Library, University of New Mexico, negative no. 2000–013–0002.

Figure 17.   Pablo Beaubien, ca. 1890s, the only surviving son of María Paula Lobato and Carlos Beaubien. Courtesy of the Arthur Johnson Memorial Library, Raton, New Mexico, and reproduced by permission of the Center for Southwest Research General Library, University of New Mexico, negative no. 2000–013–0003.

Figure 18.   Painting of María Paula Lobato Beaubien, 1811–64 (shown ca. 1850s). The portrait hangs in the Philips Mansion at the Philmont Boy Scout Ranch. Reproduced courtesy of the Center for Southwest Research General Library, University of New Mexico.

Figure 19.   Petra Beaubien Abreu, ca. 1890s, who helped the Maxwells settle and later remained at Rayado, New Mexico. Reproduced courtesy of the Center for Southwest Research General Library, University of New Mexico.

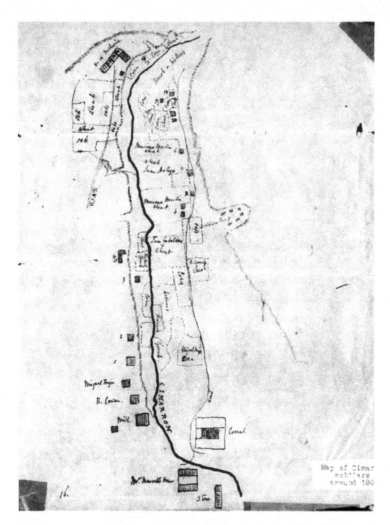

Figure 20. Map of Cimarron, New Mexico, 1865. Note how the farms and property abut the Cimarron River and are relatively small. This land use pattern would deeply disturb the company's managers as they tried to rid the landscape of the strips in favor of the grid. Reproduced by permission of the Center for Southwest Research General Library, University of New Mexico.

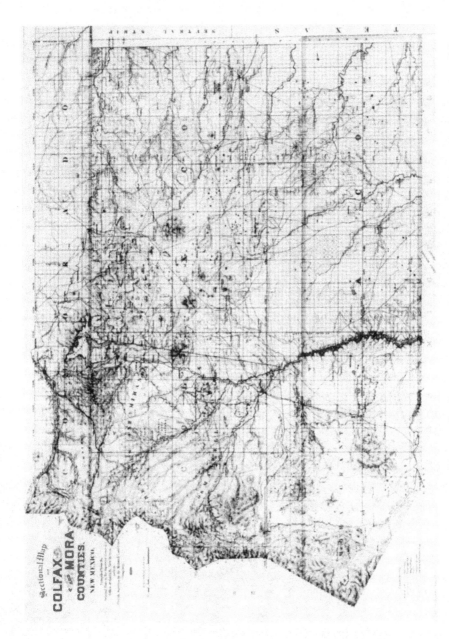

Figure 21. Surveyor's sectional map of Colfax and Mora Counties, 1889. Note how the grid is imposed on top of the topographical features of the map. Courtesy of the author.

Figure 22.   View of the Cimarron River valley, 1995. Reproduced by permission of the estate of Frederick D. Montoya.

Figure 23.   Ruins of Elizabethtown, New Mexico, 1995. Reproduced by permission of the estate of Frederick D. Montoya.

Figure 24.   The remains of Colorado Fuel and Iron in Cokedale, Colorado, 1995.
Reproduced by permission of the estate of Frederick D. Montoya.

Figure 25.   Rayado, New Mexico, site of the original settlement of the Beaubien
and Maxwell families (ca. 1930s). Reproduced courtesy of the Philmont Museum,
Cimarron, New Mexico.

# 3  From Hacienda to Colony

He [Largo, a Jicarilla leader] hoped his grandchildren would
when they grew up to be men and women, have so improved the
opportunities offered them, that they would be able to live like
white people and have at least sufficient education to transact their
own business.

Thomas Dolan, "Report of Council Proceedings
with Jicarilla Apache Indians," 1873

The traditional relationship between *patrón* and *peón* ended when Lucien
Bonaparte Maxwell and his wife, María de la Luz Beaubien Maxwell, sold
their vast estate in northern New Mexico to European investors in 1869.
Their sale to the Maxwell Land Grant and Railway Company produced a
transformation of property relations that were, at least for the people living on the land grant, as radical and far-reaching as the legal revolution ef-
fected by the 1848 conquest of New Mexico. The sale confronted the various inhabitants of the land grant—Jicarilla Apaches, Hispano farmers and
laborers, and Anglo miners—with a novel concept of property: the fee
simple absolute. This type of private property, unlike their prior property
relationships with the Maxwells, was defined by a clear, unencumbered
title that could be marketed in the international centers of Amsterdam,
London, and New York.

The reciprocal obligations between the Maxwells and those living on the
grant had been based on local norms and routines that were not recorded in
any legal document. By contrast, the newly created Maxwell Land Grant
and Railway Company, through its agents in New Mexico, enforced private
property rights based on formally recorded documents interpreted according to nationally uniform legal norms laid down by the U.S. Congress and
the Supreme Court. This transformation of the legal and, consequently, the
social regime was predictable. The company's investors and agents wanted
to increase the productivity of the grant's immense natural resources and
integrate the estate's potential wealth into the market that lay to the east in
Chicago and St. Louis. Such an increase in productivity required capital secured by formal, marketable title: a title recognized throughout the world
of international credit markets from the Netherlands to New York. Local
customs and oral promises in New Mexico could not provide such security.

78

The company therefore spent the next twenty years working to replace the old world of the Maxwell estate with a new property regime.

The sale from the Maxwells to the company highlighted not only the change in ownership but, more significantly, the new owners' different notion of property, which was based on their intention to integrate the grant's resources into the market economy. Although Maxwell had acted as a middleman between the grant's *peones* and the larger markets, he never made massive capital investments in the land, preferring to reap more modest rents from his tenants' labor and limited improvements. Maxwell's few attempts to engage in larger capitalized developments, such as the Moreno Ditch, had ended in financial disaster. His laborers, whether farmers or stockmen, worked the land to its potential, but with little manipulation in terms of creating canals, plowing large fields, digging mines, or creating immense herds of cattle or sheep, all of which would have demanded large capital outlays. The company's shareholders and bondholders, on the other hand, had only one purpose in mind: to maximize the return on their investment in the grant. Few company owners ever visited the grant, and with the exception of one or two men, none ever intended to live on the grant or work the land themselves. Because the grant was a pure investment for the distant owners, it became company agent John Collinson's job to begin quickly making the grant's farming, ranching, and mining resources pay dividends to the shareholders and bondholders in the East and Europe.

This chapter describes how this new concept of property rested on ideas—myths, actually—about the American West. In particular, it examines the mythic belief that the West was an expanse of unsettled, unsocialized, natural wilderness waiting to be converted to the use of national capitalist markets. This myth underlay U.S. territorial policy, the promotional literature of bonds salesman, and the politics of title surveys in the American West. But this concept of land came into direct conflict with the different land regimes that had thrived under the patronage of Lucien B. Maxwell: informal and personal relations between the *patrón* and different sets of clients in which each party owed the *patrón* an ill-defined, but workable, set of services and payments in return for informally defined rights to use the land. Such a regime was utterly unmarketable in international capital markets: it was too local, customary, and ad hoc to secure bonds for intense capital development such as irrigation canals, large-scale mining, or industrial cattle ranching. The Maxwell Land Grant and Railway Company therefore ignored the reciprocal obligations and property relationships between Maxwell and his clients that had defined Maxwell's tenure on the land grant.

Yet, in ignoring the actual property relations that were already in place, the company also inspired conflicts with the land's actual possessors that the company could not win without the armed force of the federal government. When government troops were used against the Jicarilla Apaches, the company was able to oust the prior inhabitants. Indeed, because the federal government was willing to take responsibility for the Indians, the U.S. representatives negotiated with the tribe's leaders to remove them, at least in theory, to a piece of property of equal value. However, when the federal government refused to back the company against Anglo miners and Hispano farmers, the company could not enforce its conception of property against settler resistance. By refusing to take responsibility for these prior grant inhabitants, the U.S. government forced the Anglos and Hispanos to defend themselves against the company. Indeed, the company's intransigent assertion of absolute dominion over the land inspired massive, organized resistance, something Maxwell himself had never faced.

The company's unsuccessful efforts to impose its will can usefully be compared to other attempts by nineteenth-century capitalists to assert the concept of fee simple absolute title against complex usufructuary rights of non-European stakeholders—for instance, the liberalization of communal title in El Salvador or the Great Mahele in Hawai'i. Unlike these efforts to expropriate inhabitants in the name of economic development, the Maxwell Land Grant Company's effort was at least initially unsuccessful. The specific reasons for this failure, which are explored in this chapter, show how the history of the American West is remarkably similar to, yet still distinct from, other imperial and colonial ventures where capitalists were attempting to displace precapitalist land-tenure systems with their more "liberal" forms of holding property.

## THE MYTH OF THE UNSETTLED AMERICAN WEST

Both the world market and the U.S. government had an attitude and policy regarding the American West that were rooted in one fundamental misconception, that the West was unsettled nature. This is not to say that private entrepreneurs and government officials regarded the West as uninhabited. To the contrary: they realized that incorporating the West into U.S. and world markets would involve removing Indians from the land and placing them on reservations. But because they regarded Indians as impermanent, nomadic tribes, their presence did not challenge the dominant conception of Western land as unsettled. True, Indians occupied land, but to government officials and prospective land purchasers, they did not appropriate it by imposing on it rules for exclusive possession, capital improvement, or permanent occupation.[1] By displacing the Indians, the government would not be taking private property as the U.S. government understood the term; they would simply be eliminating a "savage" obstacle to the land's best appropriation by society.

Thus the American West presented a blank slate on which the U.S. government and private pioneers could draw their own conception of private property. The founding document of U.S. westward expansion, the Northwest Ordinance, reflected the assumption that the West could be carved into parcels, townships, and sections without regard to any preexisting customs, rules of ownership, or even natural geography, all of which might frustrate the imposition of geometrically pristine lines and squares on the landscape of the Enlightenment imagination of the new American Republic.[2] The use of a simple grid also ensured that the parcels would not have overlapping boundaries, which meant they could be sold to buyers on the world market such as land companies and immigrants.[3] Likewise, the fundamental assumption of Congress and the Polk administration during the period of Mexican annexation was that by annexing only the northern third of the Mexican Republic, the U.S. government would largely avoid its settled portions. In a speech after U.S. troops had taken Mexico City, Senator John C. Calhoun noted, "Our Army has ever since held all that it is desirable to hold—that portion whose population is sparse, and on that account the more desirable to be held. For I hold it in reference to this war a fundamental principle, that when we receive territorial indemnity, it shall be unoccupied territory [north of El Paso]."[4] Senator Lewis Cass of Michigan expressed similar notions about an empty northern Mexico: "We do not want the people of Mexico, either as citizens or subject. All we want is a portion of territory which they nominally hold, generally uninhabited, or, where inhabited at all, sparsely so, and with a population which would soon recede, or identify itself with ours."[5] Widespread fear by legislators such as Calhoun and other proponents of extending U.S. jurisdiction over alien settled populations deterred Congress from annexing all of Mexico, to the frustration of the most ambitious imperialists in the Democratic Party, such as Jefferson Davis and Sam Houston. The fundamental premise of Manifest Destiny was that the United States would never have to absorb populations with a religion, language, race, or concept of property different from those of the mostly White, Protestant men the Eastern states sent westward to conquer the continent.

To be sure, some U.S. policymakers had their doubts about absorbing even the more sparsely settled portions of the Mexican Republic. Most of these doubts about incorporation rested on Americans' racialized ideas about the inferiority of Mexicans. Newspapers across the country, led by young men such as John L. Sullivan, the newspaper editor who coined the phrase "Manifest Destiny," clearly saw Americans as a superior race destined to overtake any Indians and Mexicans who crossed their path. The *New York Evening Post* declared that "the Mexicans are Aboriginal Indians, and they must share the destiny of their race," which was presumably to be removed, killed, and pushed aside by American society.[6] John C. Calhoun, before the Senate, made the point quite explicit:

> I know further, sir, that we have never dreamt of incorporating into our Union any but the Caucasian race—the free white race. To incorporate Mexico, would be the very first instance of the kind of incorporating an Indian race; for more than half of the Mexicans are Indians, and the other is composed chiefly of mixed tribes. I protest against such a union as that! Ours, sir, is the government of a white race.[7]

Others were not as concerned with the lower racial status of the Mexicans, but nevertheless complained about incorporating such an inferior system of law—in particular, property law—into the United States. Waddy Thompson, an American diplomat who had spent time in Mexico, complained specifically about the land grant system that was already in place in the conquered territory:

> It is not the country of a savage people whose lands are held in common, but a country in which grants have been made for three hundred and twenty-five years, many of them two and three hundred miles square; nothing paid for these grants when they were made, and no taxes upon the lands afterwards; it is all private property, and we shall get no public domain which will pay the cost of surveying it.

Thompson at least realized that the land was not empty and already had a well-established system of government and property; he nevertheless worried about the inferiority of the Mexican system and the poor citizens it had created. He continued, "We shall get no land, but will add a large population, alien to us in feeling, education, race, and religion—a people unaccustomed to work, and accustomed to insubordination and resistance to law, and an expense of government who will be ten times as great as the revenue derived from them."[8]

Despite the misgivings of many Americans, the United States ended the U.S.–Mexican War with the signing and ratification of the Treaty of Guadalupe Hidalgo and began the process of incorporating this newly acquired territory into the body politic of the United States.[9] The United

States' territorial system established a political relationship that put the federal government at the center and the new territories of New Mexico and California on a tether at the periphery, dependent on the federal government for financial assistance, laws, and government officials. New Mexicans, of course, had previous experience as an outpost of a distant and central government. The rule of both Spain and Mexico had been haphazard and weak, but apparent nevertheless.[10] The United States also possessed a long and successful history of incorporating new and distant territory into their political sphere of influence. The Northwest Ordinance of 1787 had provided specific rules and guidelines for bringing new territory into the fold of the federal government.[11] The new territory's residents were simply expected to follow the established pattern of the Midwestern states that had come before them in order to place themselves on an equal footing with the other states.

New Mexico, however, possessed a unique legal, social, and economic history that made fitting into such a mold difficult. Prior to 1848 and the U.S.–Mexican War, the United States possessed little experience incorporating new territories that held such a settled and well-established population. The U.S. experiences with Spanish Florida and French Louisiana in the earlier part of the century provided some guidance to the federal government in dealing with the Mexican territory, which was physically more distant and unknown to Eastern policymakers.[12] New Mexico in 1848 could be reached only after a long and treacherous horse or wagon ride on the Santa Fe Trail. Trade was growing but was still limited, with few direct and regular communications between Santa Fe and St. Louis, much less with Washington, D.C. The vast geographic distance made it difficult for the federal government to staff the territory with the proper officials and establish an efficient government. As a result, New Mexico remained under military control until 1850, well after the end of the war and the signing of the treaty.

The relative isolation of distant New Mexico also made it difficult to find Eastern politicians who would be willing to travel to, much less settle and work in, the new territory. The early history of territorial New Mexico is filled with apocryphal stories of wayward politicians who rebelled against the Republican Party and were exiled to New Mexico. Not only was New Mexico geographically remote, but early visitors also labeled it an uncivilized, exotic, and backwards place where the people suffered because of their inferior race. Early territorial officials such as W. W. H. Davis, who wrote *El Gringo*, set the standard for reporting and interpreting New Mexico's racial composition for the rest of the United States and prospective territorial officials.[13] The result was a long string of reluctant, if not racist, territorial officials throughout the rest of the late nineteenth century. From Gov. Lew Wallace, who wrote *Ben Hur* during his tenure, to L. Bradford Prince, who sought social status and political prominence in accepting the position as territorial governor, the territorial history of New Mexico is littered with stories of corrupt officials. These men rarely had any desire to govern New Mexico, and the politically corrupt and bureaucratically over-burdened territorial system allowed New Mexico to languish in territorial status for sixty-one years.[14]

The attitude of private capitalists mirrored the assumptions of the propagandists of Manifest Destiny. The essential premise of European investment was that the West was unappropriated, undeveloped, abundant wilderness, ready for purchase and development by outsiders. Although not as obvious as its political incorporation through the territorial system, the incorporation of New Mexico's economy into the financial world of the United States may have had an even more profound effect on the grant's inhabitants at the end of the nineteenth century. The outcome of the Civil War and Reconstruction assured that the North would dominate the nation economically and that Northern interests would control the West's abundant natural resources. After the Civil War, businessmen and politicians began integrating the U.S. economy such that all of the nation's regions came together in a national economy dominated by an industrial and urban center in the northern tier of states between Boston and Washington, D.C., in the East and Chicago and St. Louis in the Midwest.[15] This industrial core, with its growing and compact population centers, demanded the raw materials necessary for manufacturing goods, processing food, and transporting natural resources and the finished products between regions. Consequently, the South and West began to supply the demands of this emerging industrial center through such "gateway" cities as San Francisco, Chicago, St. Louis, New Orleans, and, later, places such as Los Angeles and Denver. Eastern manufacturing and financial interests integrated the Western economy into the Eastern markets and eventually dominated the American West.

Perhaps the most dramatic agent of incorporation was the railroad and its spread across the entire North American continent, linking Eastern markets with Western resources. The first transcontinental railroad in 1869 incorporated the Northern states and united the West with the Northeast to create a dominant "North" over the Western and Southern regions. The Atchison, Topeka, and Santa Fe reached the Maxwell grant in 1877 and completed the grant's consolidation into the economy of the eastern United

States—a process that had begun in the first half of the century with the opening of the Santa Fe Trail trade. The railroad brought the demands of the market to the doorsteps of the Maxwell grant inhabitants. St. Louis merchants now became interested in importing New Mexican cattle and sheep to their markets. Chicago merchants wanted grain, and the railroad itself wanted the grant's timber for rail ties to construct rail lines farther west and south. The arrival of the railroad transformed Indian, Hispano, and Anglo relationships with one another, the company's agents, and perhaps most profoundly, the landscape. As a direct result of the railroad's arrival and its opening of the available markets to the grant's inhabitants, the grant was irretrievably pulled into the United States' sphere of economic dominance.[16]

On the Maxwell Land Grant, a shift from the *patronismo* practiced by Maxwell to a more direct relationship with the market economy came about as a result of the grant's incorporation into the larger national and world markets. Earlier, workers' informal relationships between themselves (as *peones*) and the *patrón* (Maxwell), who acted as the buffer between their labor and their integration into markets, had epitomized labor relations. Once Maxwell and others like him departed, these *peones*, and agricultural workers in general, had to interact with the market directly by selling their labor and purchasing goods from organizations, whose owners were rarely visible or physically present in New Mexico, with the cash they now earned. This fundamental shift in the relationship between production and consumption affected all the grant's residents as they struggled to adjust to these changes.

Changes in labor and the economy, however, would not have been possible without the flow of liquid capital into the American West. One very simple fact helped produce this flow: few European investors obtained accurate information about, much less ever saw, the West and the projects in which they invested. In reading the promotional literature of the Maxwell Land Grant Company in the nineteenth century, one is struck by the apparent abundance of the landscapes depicted by the promoters. The advertisements, which appeared in English and Dutch newspapers as well as in the company's promotional materials, speak of the estate's fertile agricultural land (implying, of course, a stable and flowing water source) and the suitability of the grant for cattle ranching. One particular promotional piece, published in Dutch, quoted at length from W. W. Griffin's field notes about "gorgeous pasture, exquisite soil, abundant and splendid grass, as well as continually streaming water."[17] The promoters and bondsellers of the grant did not, however, publish such important facts as the average rainfall or the average monthly temperature during the winter months. Perhaps even the real facts would not have dissuaded European investors from their enterprise; the myth of the bounteous West may have been too strong to be undone by such gloomy statistics.

Bond salesmen's boosterism misled investors on two accounts. Easterners and Europeans possessed an overinflated vision of the West's, and particularly the Maxwell Land Grant's, economic potential. These misconceptions are not surprising given the type of information potential investors would have had the most access to: promotional brochures from the bond salesmen themselves, popular travel literature about the West, and investment brochures from railroads, which were interested in settling the area along their expensive railroads. All portrayed the West as the land of opportunity and abundance. For example, one Maxwell Land Grant Company brochure exclaimed, "With all of its particular qualities and elements of the property, it must, when capital is linked with advanced efforts, lead to the unavoidable result, that this will become one of the most pleasant private properties in America."[18] These images were probably particularly alluring to Europeans who found it difficult but appealing to imagine the West's wide open spaces. The grant was relatively rich in terms of timber, grazing lands, and later coal, but it never matched the over-inflated expectations of investors. This constant collision between people's imagined ideas about the grant and the harsh reality of actually developing it caused the most conflicts between European management and the agents living on the grant.

Second, bond salesmen and promoters, particularly Harry Whigham of the Maxwell Company, misled European investors into thinking that the grant had no human inhabitants. The promotional literature rarely mentions Native Americans and never mentions the hundreds of Mexican Americans living on the grant. W. W. Griffin, the company's first surveyor, only mentioned seeing one group of Mexican farmers in the Purgatory Valley, and he noted that the area had "come to support a sizable population but could easily support ten times more people, even under the inadequate farming techniques still popular with the Mexicans."[19] Consequently, investors and managers did not consider how much it would cost in terms of time, effort, and cash to rid the grant of its inhabitants. The myth of an empty West, and particularly an empty Maxwell Land Grant, combined with the myth of a bountiful Western landscape created a set of European investors and managers entirely unprepared for the realities and difficulties of making such an investment. Bitterness and disappointment were common feelings of those unfortunate enough to get involved with the Maxwell Land Grant and Railway Company during the company's first decade of existence.

The legal complications over property rights to the land grant and its resources left perhaps the most enduring legacy of the Maxwell grant's incorporation into U.S. politics and economics. All of the actors involved with the grant had different conceptions about property and their particular rights to the grant. The Jicarilla Apaches knew they "owned" and used the entire expanse of the grant and had only allowed Maxwell to use the grant in cooperation with them. Hispanos knew they had property rights derived from their tenure under the Maxwells to their homes, the fields they tilled, and the land on which they grazed their sheep and cattle. Anglo settlers knew they possessed homestead rights granted by the U.S. government. And finally, the company knew it had rights to the land purchased from the Maxwells. The conflicts that took place over the next thirty years all centered around how people understood their own property rights and how they acted to protect those rights, which eventually resulted in litigation, political struggles, and even armed resistance.

## CONFRONTING THE WORLD OF THE MAXWELL ESTATE

The sale of the grant by the Maxwells to the investors organized as the Maxwell Land Grant and Railway Company set in motion all of the tensions between the European investors, whether in London or Amsterdam, and the individuals, whether Native American, Hispano, or Anglo, in northern New Mexico. With the sale passed any hope of a hybrid organization based on the hacienda system that might incorporate itself and its economy into the market. In its place a new type of corporate farming and ranching, to which the existing inhabitants would have to adapt, emerged in this northeastern corner of New Mexico.

The Maxwells' relative financial success in running the grant attracted the attention of investors from Europe and New York. Many distant investors had already eagerly ventured into Western land development and thought they could make even more money than Maxwell using the proper management techniques for the farms, herds, and mines.[20] Also, the recent discovery of gold on Baldy Mountain and the somewhat overzealous proclamations of the mine district's worth by boosters attracted all kinds of speculators, particularly ones who could not visit the area personally and ascertain for themselves the land's true value. The Maxwells, who were getting older and who were probably ready to move away from the burdens imposed on them by managing the property (particularly after the discovery of gold), welcomed outside interests and engaged in various negotiations for the sale of the land. No single investor within the territory possessed enough personal wealth or the access to capital to purchase the grant, so in April 1869 Luz and Lucien Maxwell gave Colorado Senator Jerome B. Chaffee, who was also a well-known and highly skilled businessman, the option to purchase or find purchasers for the land grant within the year.[21]

Chaffee had made his reputation as a Colorado politician, mine owner, and one of the West's most prominent businessmen and speculators. He had investments in nearly a hundred gold and silver mines across the West and, with his accumulated wealth, had established the First National Bank of Denver in 1864. Through his banking enterprise he possessed connections with financiers in New York and Europe, whom he was always eager to entice into investments in land, mines, and cattle operations. Closer to home, he had financial ties to Santa Fe and New Mexico since many businessmen in the Western states looked to Denver first for financing. It was probably through these connections that Chaffee became aware of the Maxwells and their desire to sell the estate.[22] In this peripheral economy, where capital was difficult to raise, Chaffee filled an important role as a financial mediator who had the connections to link the excess capital of the eastern United States with the underdeveloped resources of the West.

On the western frontier of post–Civil War America, available and low-interest capital remained difficult to find. For example, in 1870, when the Maxwells were negotiating to sell the grant, short-term interest rates in London were 3.1 percent, while they were 7.25 percent in New York, 9.1 percent in New Mexico and Colorado, and 19.65 percent in California.[23] Thus the West, and New Mexico in particular, enticed European investors who were anxious to find a profitable investment in which to place their capital. In fact, entrepreneurs such as William Blackmore from London and Wilson Waddingham from Amsterdam made it their entire business to travel the West looking for investments that they could sell to potential investors back in Europe.[24] By contrast, New Mexican businessmen found it nearly impossible to raise the amount of money needed to invest in large-scale agricultural, ranching, or mining development.

Because of the vastly disparate amounts of capital available, the late nineteenth century marked the steady integration of the West's resources, economy, and labor into the national and international markets of capital investment, farm products, lumber, and energy resources. In the case of purchasing and developing the Maxwell estate, even New York investors could not find enough money at the right price, and Chaffee had to turn to London investor John Collinson to finance the transaction.[25] By enlisting the financial aid of outside investors such as Chaffee and Collinson, Maxwell completely shed his role as an Old World *patrón*. Although over the years Maxwell had slowly moved his enterprise into the market economy growing around him and had acted as a broker between the estate's *peones* and the purchasers of goods on the outside, he still clung to the hacienda system with all its social and economic implications. With this sale, however, Maxwell now embraced a market economy based on the sale of shares and bonds to finance debt, rather than the less abstract world of gold, silver, and real property as security for transactions.

Maxwell's move into the world market and his sale of the grant in its entirety placed new limitations and restrictions on how he ran his enterprise. For the most part, Maxwell had been fairly relaxed about how he delineated his property rights. As long as the tenants paid their customary rents, he seemed relatively satisfied. There appears to be no instance of Maxwell ever marking his boundaries or disputing with neighbors over land and property rights. This informal system, however, did not provide the security demanded by investors who might want to trade this land on the open market. Potential outside investors required a clear accounting of Maxwell's land, as well as an accurate map of the grant's boundaries. Furthermore, the distance between investors in Europe and the land grant in the West required easily verifiable assurance as to the accuracy of these boundaries. Investors were unlikely to travel out to New Mexico to see their property and instead relied on public documents and maps to understand the extent of their investments.

Before they marketed the land to European investors, Maxwell, Chaffee, and their business acquaintance, the surveyor general of New Mexico, Thomas Rush Spencer, enlisted W. W. Griffin, a local surveyor, to privately survey the Maxwell estate. Surveyor General Spencer, a federally appointed territorial official, apparently saw no conflict of interest in aiding friends and speculating in land sales while directing the New Mexico surveyor general's office. This willingness to use his public office for personal profit was entirely consistent with tradition. Government surveyors routinely traded on their inside information about the quality of the public domain.[26] Congress had created the office of the surveyor general to clarify the boundaries and ownership of the Mexican and Spanish land grants in New Mexico, and had entrusted the surveyor general with the very difficult and delicate task of defining and securing former Mexican citizens' individual and community property rights.[27] Then, after all property owners had made their claims and established their rights, the remaining lands would be put into the public domain and opened up to settlement by American citizens. The Department of the Interior, which had authority over the surveyor general, intended for this process to run quickly and smoothly so that New Mexico's lands could be incorporated into the federal system. Surveyor General Spencer, however, had business dealings that conflicted directly with his duties, and critics, including the radical Republican George Julian, were quick to point to the corruption in the New Mexican system.[28]

The survey, as directed by Chaffee and Maxwell, supposedly followed the boundaries described in the 1841 conveyance from Mexican governor Manuel Armijo to Carlos Beaubien and Guadalupe Miranda. In the end, Griffin's private survey revealed that the grant encompassed almost two million acres in the territory of New Mexico as well as a portion in the state of Colorado. Although unofficial and entirely paid for by Maxwell and Chaffee, in promotional material the company made reference to Griffin as an "Inspector, certified by the United States" and implied that the estate had been officially mapped.[29] Even at this early stage, the sellers recognized the ambiguity of the boundaries laid out by the Mexican documents giving the land to Beaubien and Miranda. Maxwell and Chaffee therefore made this land venture as profitable as possible by extending the grant's boundaries to the documents' most generous interpretation. In return for Griffin's moonlighting survey, Chaffee and Maxwell not only paid him for his work but also gave him twenty shares of stock in the Maxwell Land Grant and Railway Company. Later, after Maxwell had invested his money in the newly formed First National Bank of Santa Fe, he also gave Griffin a job as a bookkeeper and teller.[30] Griffin's relatively fluid move from government official to private businessman was not unique but, in fact, fairly typical of territorial officials who used their government office as a means to finding other, more lucrative employment.[31]

Simultaneous with commissioning the survey, Chaffee went to work securing the grant's extended boundaries through his political connections in Washington, D.C. Chaffee successfully lobbied against House Bill 740, which had been introduced in Congress at the request of the Secretary of the Interior, who sought to limit former Mexican land grants to individuals to eleven leagues.[32] The act sought to limit all Mexican land grants that were in the process of confirmation in California, New Mexico, Texas, and other Western states. Land reformers such as George Julian and others wanted the boundaries to encompass only a reasonable acreage for an individual, regardless of what the boundaries had been under the Mexican government. In the case of the Maxwell grant, the law would have limited it to 97,000 acres, as opposed to the 2,000,000 that Griffin had surveyed and Chaffee and Maxwell claimed when trying to sell the property. The bill died, and Congress never placed any restrictions on the extent of private land grants when they were transferred from Mexican to U.S. law. From Chaffee's perspective it was imperative that the grant's acreage not be limited in any way as he needed as much land as possible in order to make a healthy profit. Although he escaped the threat from Congress, he and the Maxwell Land Grant Company would soon face a similar challenge from the Department of the Interior.

Chaffee, concerned about the validity of the survey in the eyes of the federal government, wanted to have the Department of the Interior recognize the Griffin survey as the official survey and secure the boundaries around the grant. In particular, he did not want the Department of the Interior to commission its own survey independently. Chaffee pressured J. S. Wilson, commissioner of the General Land Office, who was under the secretary of the interior, to make Griffin's survey the authoritative mapping of the grant. Chaffee assumed this was merely a pro forma request as Griffin was already employed as a surveyor for the New Mexico surveyor general. He asked Wilson to write him only if "there is any doubt about his [Griffin] surveying the Grant" or if "there is to be any great delay about it. I would be very thankful if you will notify me." [33] Just as Beaubien and Miranda had used their influence with the Mexican government to attain the grant, here Chaffee used his access to both the executive and congressional branches of the U.S. government to ensure the maximum extension of the grant's boundaries. Because of Chaffee's ability to extend the boundaries through his manipulation and influence of local and federal officials, he guaranteed that the sale would go smoothly regardless of how specious his and Maxwell's claim to the acreage. Moreover, the English purchasers and bondholders, who were too remote in terms of both geography and access to information to grasp the sellers' duplicity or question the boundaries of the investment, remained unaware of their investment's tenuous underpinnings. The land transaction proceeded as scheduled.

In January 1870, the Maxwells made out a deed to John Collinson, a well-known English investor, and a joint-stock company doing business as the Maxwell Land Grant and Railway Company for "two million acres more or less," and sold it for $1.35 million, or a mere 85 cents an acre.[34] Collinson owned the majority (35,563) of the 50,000 shares of the company, with other well-known European and Eastern investors, Wilson Waddingham, W. A. Bell, and W. J. Palmer, accounting for another 12,000 shares. Local businessmen R. H. Longwill, Miguel A. Otero, and Stephen B. Elkins, who were probably eager to expand their business opportunities with one of the largest transactions and potentially one of the largest companies ever to come to New Mexico, purchased the few remaining shares. Collinson and his board then issued bonds that they guaranteed at a 7 percent return, payable every six months, to other smaller investors across Europe and the United States. Bonds sold in 1870 would be redeemed at par on July 1, 1895, payable in either London in pound sterling or Rotterdam in Dutch guilders. Collinson sold most of the bonds on the Amsterdam and London bond markets.[35]

Collinson told bondholders that the proceeds would be used to have the estate "surveyed, subdivided and sold at reasonable rates to actual settlers, and the valuable mineral deposits energetically and scientifically developed and worked."[36] The language in Collinson's advertisement warrants discussion on two points. First, he promised to sell the land to "actual settlers," implying that he either did not know about the hundreds of Jicarillas, Mexican American farmers, or Anglo miners already living and working on the grant, or that he was ignoring their existence. Second, Collinson clearly revealed the differences between the Maxwells' perception of the property as a hacienda and his own market-oriented ideas about property ownership and his intentions to develop the grant's resources efficiently.

In assuring the legality of the sale between the Maxwells and the European investors, Surveyor General Spencer, Maxwell's and Chaffee's earlier business ally, enlisted William Pile, New Mexico territorial governor, and Territorial Supreme Court Justice John S. Watts to file in Santa Fe for the incorporation of the company to do business in a U.S. territory. Since New Mexico had no law specifically authorizing foreigners to own land, three prominent New Mexico politicians acted as the nominal owners of the company and finalized the sale because Collinson and his financial backers, as foreigners, could not. Within three weeks the Maxwell Land Grant and Railway Company had gained approval from the territorial legislature to begin operations. Given the stature of the men who pushed for the incorporation, this final step was a mere formality, and the investors began doing business. The company planned to build a railroad and engage in large-scale stock raising, timber cutting, and mining on their newly acquired acreage.[37]

Within months, however, the company faced financial ruin. Secretary of the Interior Jacob D. Cox became concerned when House Bill 740 failed.

Cox, a reform-minded bureaucrat, believed in the public domain and thought the homestead system remained the best method of distributing property to U.S. citizens. In response to Congress's failure to limit Mexican and Spanish land grants, Cox decided to take executive action through the Department of the Interior by limiting all Spanish and Mexican individual land claims to 11 leagues per applicant. Furthermore, in the specific case of the Maxwell Land Grant, Secretary Cox ruled that the original conveyance from Governor Armijo to Beaubien and Miranda had been an individual grant to the two men (not an empresario grant of unlimited acreage), and therefore the two men, under Mexican law, could have received only 22 leagues or 97,000 acres.[38] Secretary Cox wrote, "There can be no hesitation to determine that it was the purpose and intent of Congress to confirm to Beaubien and Miranda to an extent not greater than 11 square leagues to each claimant."[39] The ruling left the newly formed company, which depended on extracting the natural resources from the extended grant for profit and financial survival, near the brink of bankruptcy.

The company's New Mexico agents nevertheless continued to survey and plat various portions of the two million acres, hoping for a reprieve engineered by their advocates in Washington. They had reason to be hopeful when Cox left office, but the new secretary of the interior, Columbus Delano, refused to reverse his predecessor and alter the 22-square-league standard. Secretary Delano told the company to choose the 97,000 acres it wanted included in the patent, and the rest would be open as public domain and be available to homesteaders eager to come to New Mexico.[40]

The company's stockholders, troubled by the ruling and its implications for their investments, drafted a letter from their offices in Amsterdam to the secretary of the interior, asking, "[H]ow could the government lay hands on private property, recognized as such by law? . . . European capital has already experienced many disappointments by American enterprises, and in what measure the Netherlands have suffered thereby is sufficiently well known." The directors went on to inform the secretary that "if the confidence of foreign capital for the enterprises of your country is ever to be restored, and for the development of your country that confidence cannot durably be missed, then it is assuredly a first requisite, that the Government itself should show that it respects and protects individual rights."[41] The letter reveals the extensive relationship between European investors and American enterprises, and shows the pressure that the company felt to secure those investments. The letter reminded the secretary of the interior about the importance of European capital and the role that the federal government should continue to play in securing that capital. Only with the threat of withdrawing all of their capital from the American West did the Maxwell Company's European investors feel they could manipulate the uncooperative U.S. government into protecting the interests of core merchants and land speculators. Moreover, this conflict between the U.S. federal government and the European investors revealed their competing ideas about property. Policymakers such as Cox, Julian, and Delano wanted to protect the rights of the small farmer by protecting the public domain and opening it up to these industrious republican immigrants. On the other hand, the European investors also had a clear sense of private property, but it was a private property that benefited the large-scale capital investor and did not care a bit about the individual landholder.

These land reformers, such as George W. Julian and Secretaries Cox and Delano, came out of the radical Republican tradition that favored the rights of an individual to own property, which in turn would pave the way for a moral and prosperous democracy. They saw the company's agents as corrupting the idea of individual property rights, and their requests as an attack on the homestead system, and they refused to submit to the company's threats. George W. Julian, in his *North American Review* article on the process of confirming these Mexican land grants, expressed the moral outrage these reformers felt. Julian wrote of land grant owners, "They believed in the gospel of 'devil take the hindmost.' To rob a man of his home is a crime, second only to murder; and to rob the nation of its public domain, and thus abridge the opportunity of landless men to acquire homes, is not only a crime against society, but a cruel mockery of the poor."[42] Although Julian's rhetoric was about protecting the poor, he referred only to Anglo-Americans who would have been moving to New Mexico to find homesteads. Julian had no sympathy for the workers who had earlier inhabited these land grants and were also losing their property rights to these corporations. Nevertheless, despite its limitations, their rhetoric about property rights and creating homes was not merely an economic or political issue but also a moral one for these governmental reformers.

For the next seven years, until 1878, the Department of Interior's personnel tried to persuade the company's agents to choose the 22 square leagues they preferred and to accept the judgment made by the Department of the Interior. The company, however, unwilling to recognize the U.S. government claim that the majority of their holdings were now a part of the public domain, refused to abide by the Department of Interior's dictates.[43] The company simply could not financially afford to accept the judgment without a legal battle. The early decisions by Secretaries Cox and Delano marked the genesis of all the legal conflict on the Maxwell Land Grant as U.S. homesteaders and Hispano settlers flocked to the area to settle on what they believed to be free and open public domain.[44]

Even though the company's managers stalled and refused to choose the 97,000 acres, the General Land Office did not wait for them to make up their minds and instead opened parts of the grant as public domain and sold homesteads under the rules of the 1862 Homestead Act. The government team of surveyors faced the difficulty of surveying the treacherous landscape and trying to decide what was private or public property within the grant's claimed acreage. The commissioner of the General Land Office, S. S. Burdett, fretted that the grant was virtually impossible to survey because of "many points being 10,000 to 12,000 feet and canyons hundreds of feet deep impassable for miles." He also worried that all of these geographical factors might mean that no one would do the job and surveyors would "recoil from contracting for it." Nevertheless, the government managed to get parts of the grant surveyed, and they issued homestead patents, many with final deeds. As homesteaders began moving into the territory, they came into direct conflict with the company's agents, who were not willing to let them settle the land despite homestead papers from the U.S. government.

Furthermore, in 1877 J. A. Williamson instructed the surveyor general of New Mexico that his surveyors were to "avoid establishing any part of the northern boundary" of the Maxwell Land Grant as this was under investigation and litigation. Rather, the surveyors were to confine their activities to the foothills of the Chicauco Mountains, and at the base of the foothills run a straight line; under no circumstances were they to move any farther north across the Purgatory River, which was in Colorado.[45] It was under these directions that the Colorado portion of the Maxwell Land Grant was set aside as public domain. Secretary Williamson, tired of waiting for the Maxwell Company's agent to choose its 97,000 acres, made a decision and closed the northern portion off to the company and placed it instead in the public domain. Homesteaders, like Richard Russell, received free and clear titles. What Russell and the federal government did not count on was the company's ability to overcome these bureaucratic threats and secure the extended boundaries of the grant. The legal havoc that the Department of the Interior created through this policy of survey and settling land before titles were entirely clear would come back to haunt them in the following decade, pitting homestead claims against company land claims. Eventually homesteaders and long-time Hispano residents, along with the soon-to-be removed Indians, would lose their property to the more powerful Maxwell Company.[46]

JICARILLAS, MINERS, AND HISPANOS:
THREE PROPERTY CONFLICTS ON THE MAXWELL LAND GRANT

These controversies over the boundaries of the grant, most of which took place in boardrooms and government offices in Washington, D.C., New York City, London, and Amsterdam, eventually came into direct conflict with the actual inhabitants of the grant—the Jicarilla Apaches, Anglo miners, and Hispano settlers—and intruded into their lives in very tangible ways. There were three ambiguous types of property regimes that Maxwell had used, which the company now had to confront: (1) the extent of the Jicarilla Apaches' right to live within the grant's boundaries; (2) the property rights of miners who had purchased from Maxwell the right to mine within his property; (3) the property rights of Hispanos living there, working the land and raising livestock. The company, in contrast to Maxwell, possessed other ideas about how the land should be managed, and consequently decided how, and even if, the prior inhabitants would continue to live on the grant. Instead of adopting Maxwell's *patrón* system, the company pursued a rigid scheme for making Indians and those people that they called "squatters" recognize company property rights. The company believed that only through a strict recognition of private property rights could it make a profitable return on its investment. While Maxwell had respected, more or less, the Jicarillas and Hispanos living and working on the vast estate, the company ended this relaxed attitude toward the recognition of property rights, usufructuary or otherwise. Moreover, the federal government never recognized the rights of the Jicarillas or the Mexicano settlers to live legitimately within the boundaries of the land grant. In short, Maxwell's sale of the land marked the end of individual economic relationships between those living on the grant and the grant's owners.

The sale and the change of policy on the grant altered the living patterns and economic foundations not only of the Jicarillas of northern New Mexico but also the Utes of southern Colorado. Indian Agent W. F. Arny wrote the Department of the Interior that "the sale of the grant by Maxwell [has produced] much discontent among the Utes and Jicarilla Apache Indians who also claim the grant and say they only allowed Maxwell to have it because he was their friend." [47] Arny believed that Maxwell had an informal, unwritten agreement with the Jicarillas in which he allowed them to live on the grant and maintain their traditional way of living through hunting and some agriculture. In exchange, the relatively sedentary Jicarillas acted as a buffer against outside encroachments from the Plains Indian groups who found Maxwell's ever-increasing stock holdings enticing. The Jicarillas obviously never "sold" the land to Maxwell, but early in their relationship allowed Maxwell the use of it for grazing his livestock. Over the years Maxwell probably gradually gained control over more and more of the land. This arrangement would have been consistent with Jicarilla property systems of communally held land: they allocated usufructuary rights and not fee simple absolute rights to Maxwell, whom they viewed as an important ally in their increasingly changing world. It seems improbable that the Jicarillas would give Maxwell property rights that would allow for the sale of their economic base without their consent.

The sale of the grant to an anonymous set of international investors, who did not understand or adapt to the delicate balance between the various inhabitants on the grant, threatened to incite hostilities between the Jicarillas and the incoming company. Maxwell, personally, had exercised a considerable amount of sway over the Jicarillas. He advanced beef and flour rations during food shortages, at his own expense if necessary, to prevent the Jicarillas from raiding and stealing livestock from the Hispano settlers on the grant. Thus Maxwell kept the peace, even if an uneasy one at times. Indian Agent Arny feared, correctly, that the company would not maintain this practice, thus compelling the Jicarillas and Utes around the Indian agency at Cimarron to become violent and attack company agents and settlers.[48] Shortly after the company had taken control of the grant, a Jicarilla named San Francisco attempted to break into the company store at Cimarron, where a clerk shot him to death. The Jicarillas expressed their fury at both the death and the food shortage that had driven San Francisco to steal food by demanding that the company open the store and distribute food freely to the hungry families. Arny attempted to bring the situation to a peaceful close, but eventually had to call up from Fort Union the Eighth Cavalry Regiment, who stationed themselves in Cimarron until the Jicarillas dispersed from the town. The Cavalry temporarily defused the situation, but Arny, pushed by the company's directors, realized that the Jicarillas had to be removed if the company continued to encourage settlement within Jicarilla territory.[49]

For the next several years, the Jicarillas lived an even more nomadic life as they constantly tried to escape the scrutiny of federal officials, who sought to round them up and remove them to a new home that would be acceptable to the Jicarillas. In June of 1873, New Mexico Indian Superintendent L. Edwin Dudley told the Jicarillas that the lands they had been living on were now the property of the company and that the government had no control over the hostile Anglos who were rapidly settling the area. He informed the Jicarillas that the federal government could only protect and feed them if they agreed to move south to the Mescalero Apache Reservation, where land would be assigned to them and their rations doubled.[50] The Jicarillas found this move, and what amounted to a bribe in exchange for giving up their homeland, entirely unacceptable. If they had to leave, which they did not want to do, then they insisted on having their own reservation.

Unlike the company and the accompanying international market that now influenced the area, the Jicarillas did not view land as a fungible good: they believed their homeland confined within the grant's boundaries held unique qualities that matched their particular economic, social, and religious needs. Consequently, the Jicarillas remained unwilling to exchange their homeland for a reservation. The negotiations between the Jicarillas, the federal government, and the company for the removal of the Jicarillas to another location illuminate how ideas about property and ownership often collide with one another. The Jicarillas' worldview, in which land was a spiritual as well as an economic good, could not be accommodated within the capitalistic and private property regime of the company and the federal government. Anglos in the territory reacted unsympathetically to the plight of the displaced Jicarillas and viewed them as an unnecessary drain on the lagging territorial economy. The editor of the *Las Vegas (New Mexico) Gazette* complained about the proposal to give the Jicarillas their own reservation and wrote, "They have hunted and fished along the mountain streams and eaten government beef until they have lost all energy and are too lazy and helpless to do anything."[51] The emerging market economy had failed to incorporate the Jicarillas into the changing world, and now non-Indians found it difficult to understand Jicarilla land use and actions. Recently arrived Euro-Americans saw no tragedy in the loss of land the Jicarillas faced. The most enlightened of the newcomers advocated removal to a remote area where they could be forgotten and left to fend for themselves.

The U.S. government pursued the policy of removal, and Dudley could find no way to keep the Jicarillas on even a small part of their traditional land. When offered a reservation some 150 miles west of Cimarron, at the headwaters of the San Juan River, the Jicarillas reluctantly agreed and moved west to their new home near Tierra Amarilla, New Mexico. The federal government, however, had to remove the Jicarillas from their new home when Anglo miners discovered valuable ore deposits and people swarmed the reservation. The Jicarillas then took it upon themselves to move back across the Sangre de Cristo range to their original home at Cimarron. For the next several years they eluded company and Indian agents as they attempted to maintain their homes on their traditional land. When in 1873 the new commissioner of Indian Affairs, E. P. Smith, finally authorized Thomas Dolan to find the Jicarillas a new reservation, the tribe was scattered all across northern New Mexico between Cimarron and Tierra Amarilla (see map 2).

Dolan had a difficult time convincing the various factions of the Jicarillas that they needed to make a treaty with the federal government and come onto reservation lands near Dulce, New Mexico. When he first attempted to meet with the Jicarillas at Cimarron, they told him that they had no authority to make treaties and he would have to talk with the group camped near Tierra Amarilla. Was this the truth or a stalling tactic? Either way, Dolan got nowhere in Cimarron and in the dead of winter crossed the Sangre de Cristos and worked his way into the San Juan Mountains looking for the Jicarillas. When he arrived in Tierra Amarilla, he found that the group had dispersed, and he waited patiently for days for the group of tribal elders to answer his summons. He wrote to Commissioner Smith, "They listened attentively, through the reading [of the proposed treaty], frequently expressing their approbation. After I had concluded reading the Article of Agreement, as I expected, many of them positively refused to have anything to do with it, stating that the government had no right to take them from the home, which they had occupied for so many years."[52] But, after days of negotiations and gift giving on the part of Dolan, the Jicarillas finally agreed to the treaty.

As Dolan returned to Cimarron, he was met by a group of Moache Utes who agreed to share their Indian agency with the Jicarillas and to have the tribe as their new neighbors. All seemed to be going well for Dolan, except now he had to convince the Jicarillas still at Cimarron that the Jicarillas in Tierra Amarilla had agreed to removal and that they too would have to move west and join the rest of their people. José Largo and San Pablo, leaders of the Cimarron Jicarillas, were suspicious of Dolan's credentials and authority to negotiate treaties and told him that they wanted to wait until spring, when the government would send a more reliable agent. Dolan, however, convinced them that unless they signed the agreement now, they would not have government rations to sustain them through the coming winter and their people would suffer.

Both men finally agreed, but not without hesitation. Dolan wrote of Largo's apprehensions, "But still there were many things connected with the agreement, which he was not able to fully comprehend. The paper was so very long, and contained so many things, that it was hard for a man as old as himself, who could not read, to remember all that it contained. He wanted to know more about that part referring to farms and schools and becoming civilized." Dolan patiently explained the document and the provisions for farm implements, schooling, and rations. Finally, Largo "said it was good, and that he hoped his grandchildren would when they grew up to be men and women, have so improved the opportunities offered them, that they would be able to live like white people and have at least sufficient education to transact their own business."[53]

In this twelve-page report from Dolan to Commissioner Smith, this is the only place where we get any sense of the Jicarillas' voice and opinion of the treaty. But what did Largo mean when he said that he wanted his grandchildren to "live like white people"? Dolan interpreted these words as the triumph of assimilation over tribalism, and Largo's acquiescence to the inevitability of assimilation. But the words can be read in a different way as well. Here Largo, a tired and defeated man who had finally given in to the federal government and agreed to remove his people from their homeland, hoped that in the "white" world they would find the tools to "transact their own business" by mastering the legal concepts of property, title, and exclusive possession which had eluded him and by which he was now trapped. These are sad and moving words from a man whose only hope lay in the better world he hoped future generations would find in the rapidly changing world of northern New Mexico.

With the end of his speech, Largo agreed to sign the document. Of the end of the treaty transaction Dolan wrote, "One more question, he said, 'How many people do you want to sign this paper?' I replied, 'Yourself, San Pablo, and all of your principal men.' He replied, 'It is not necessary to have many names—San Pablo, myself—the Captains and a few of the young men are enough. I am ready to sign the paper.' Whereupon the Articles of Agreement were duly signed and attested."[54] This brief exchange between Dolan and Largo illuminates the collision between the Jicarilla world of oral agreements and community governance and the U.S. world of treaty making and removal. The Jicarillas possessed no formal mechanism for recognizing the treaty, and like Maxwell's earlier dealings with them, relied on custom, their word, and their influence within their community to uphold the deal. Dolan, however, would have to return the agreement to the secretary of the interior, who would shepherd the treaty through Congress, and then the president would sign the bill removing the Jicarillas from the grant. Removal would not occur until four years later, in 1877, when President Grover Cleveland set aside a reservation for them, and the federal government provided them with a permanent home on their present-day reservation near Dulce, New Mexico.[55]

Their removal to a completely alien spiritually and physically unappealing environment made the Jicarillas the first inhabitants to experience the loss of their homes at the hands of the inflexible Maxwell Land Grant Company, homesteaders, and government officials. On the other hand, at least the federal government acknowledged that they had a responsibility to the Jicarillas and owed them some form of compensation for the loss of the property. Later, when the company needed to evict Hispanos and Anglos from the grant, the federal government—for a variety of complex reasons rooted in ideas about conquest, race, and incorporation—would not be as willing to involve themselves in that removal process.

For the company, the federal government's removal of the Jicarillas from the grant turned out to be the easiest phase of clearing the land of its prior inhabitants. Because the company's agents had the direct aid of the federal government, territorial officials, and local law enforcement agencies, any threat that the Jicarillas might pose to company control over the grant's resources had been quickly diluted by the power of the federal presence on the grant. The problems that the company encountered with Hispano settlers and Anglo miners and homesteaders, however, were not so easily solved. The federal government adamantly refused to have any part in removing the Hispanos and Anglos, both of whom the company deemed unacceptable inhabitants of the grant.

Unable to wield influence over the federal government, the company's agents instead had to use their own resources to ensure the removal of the unwanted settlers and miners from within the confines of the grant. For example, the company took out advertisements in local papers asserting their property rights. One notice stated, "The Maxwell Land Grant and Railway Company hereby warns all persons from cutting hay without permission on their [company] property." Perhaps it did not occur to the company agents that most of the people on the land who would be in the business of cutting hay and harvesting crops could not read Spanish, much less English. Even those literate in English would have found it difficult to understand the company's demand that farmers not harvest what they believed to be their own crops. As far as the settlers were concerned, the earlier set of relationships established by Maxwell for the harvesting, sale of the product, and rent paid need not necessarily change. The company found it difficult to convince the settlers that they needed to stop their old patterns of subsistence and in-kind payments and adapt to the new labor and cash economy imposed by the company. Instead of adapting itself to the hacienda system and *patronismo* already established by Maxwell, the company intended to hire outside laborers (from where is unclear) to harvest the crops, load them on wagons, and carry them to the nearest train depot, in La Junta, Colorado, bound for St. Louis or Kansas City.[56] The plans for the development of the grant and company, which were drawn up in the headquarters in New York City, deemed it too expensive, inefficient, and backwards to continue Maxwell's patterns. Instead the company's directors, without ever actually experiencing a growing and harvesting season on the grant, insisted on streamlining the grant's administration through the imposition of the system of production associated with a market economy.

The company's directors in New York and agents on the grant were particularly concerned with evicting the miners working the gold fields near Elizabethtown. The farming and ranching aspects of the grant only held potential wealth, but the mining endeavors promised immediate returns to the company's coffers if it could quickly take control of gold output. The company, through posted circulars, warned resisting miners that its property rights were not open to negotiation: the company owned all mining claims regardless of miners' prior arrangements with Maxwell. Under the new company policies the grant manager, John Collinson, gave notice that all miners and settlers had to come down from the mountains into Cimarron and sign documents recognizing the company's claims.[57] The miners could then continue their business after they had agreed to give a generous percentage to the company. The new policy led to open hostilities with the miners immediately after the company's agents posted the asserted claims. On October 27, 1870, only months after the company had taken possession of the grant, the miners rioted and started a fire that threatened to burn down the entire hamlet of Elizabethtown. Like earlier incidents with the Jicarillas, this uprising also prompted Collinson to call for troops. Once again, troops from Fort Union headed north to calm tensions and prevent violence on the grant. Anglo and Hispano miners, however, proved more difficult to subdue. The government could not simply march them off to a distant reservation, but instead had to negotiate for a peaceful settlement. The standoff between the restless miners and the troops continued almost six months, until in April 1871 an armed mob seized company property.

The violent outbreak required New Mexico territorial governor William A. Pile—coincidentally the man who only a year earlier had applied for the company's incorporation papers in New Mexico Territory—to become officially involved in the conflict. Pile's willingness to involve himself revealed that through the use of financial entanglements and incentives, Maxwell Company officials were able to gain assistance from local territorial officials and elites who were anxious to profit from the territory's new financial ventures. But even the local officials' ability to control the settlers' movements and violence was limited, and often they could not contain the problem. Without the power of the federal government and, in particular, the ability to call out the army and use force, the company was limited in what actions it could take against the settlers.

Besides sending in more troops, Pile said he would pardon the miners only if they would lay down their arms and recognize the company's property rights. If not, he warned, "in that case they will be held guilty of continued violence and will be dealt with to the utmost extremity and severity authorized by law."[58] Pile's concern lay not with the plight of the miners, who felt that the company had wrongly evicted them, but with the financially failing company in which he had a personal and financial interest. Pile's influence even stretched beyond what he could do within his own jurisdiction. He wrote to his friend Hamilton Fish, secretary of state, asking him to influence Secretary Delano in the Interior Department to get the Griffin survey completed and a patent issued before real trouble broke out on the grant. He told Fish that within the "claimed boundaries of the tract of land there are a large number of families living, some under lease-holds given by Mr. L. B. Maxwell, the former owner, and others under what it known in this country as 'Squatters Title.'" Pile also described that there "are also within the claimed boundaries of this estate large and valuable mineral deposits. Many persons holding mining claims under leases and by locations under the U.S. Mining law." Pile pointed out that as long as the government continued to treat parts of the grant as public domain, then miners would continually make seemingly valid mining claims on company property. Pile concluded that "difficulties are continually arising between these persons and the managers and employees of the company."[59] The only solution Pile could see was securing the company's claim to the grant. Only a final drawing of the boundaries with a clear title would solve the conflicts between the current inhabitants and what Pile perceived to be the rightful owners of the grant.

The miners, not easily swayed from their point of view despite government intervention, continued to claim ownership to the lands on which they lived and worked. An Elizabethtown newspaper described the situation under which most miners had leased their land: "[Maxwell] was liberal in his dealings and requirements—indeed many were under personal obligations to him for assistance, and most of our leading men were his friends. So not wishing to make issue with a man who had shown himself so generous, and not pausing to inquire into the rights of the matter, the miners acknowledged Maxwell's claims and accepted his terms."[60] Under

this casual system of economic and proprietorial arrangements on Maxwell's estate, which not coincidentally were very similar to the Jicarillas' relationships with Maxwell, there had been no need to explicitly and formally assign rights: each party came to a satisfactory agreement that would
meet the needs of Maxwell and the miner. Maxwell acted as *patrón* to the
miners, who were indebted to him for money and favors. Maxwell provided
the raw materials of land and natural resources while the men and their
families provided the necessary labor to extract worth from the grant. All
of these mutual obligations between miners and Maxwell created a free-
form, sometimes inequitable, but workable system of property rights. One
could characterize this loosely organized system as what Robert Ellickson
has termed a "land regime—amalgams of law and custom," or a system of
informal norms as well as formal rules.[61]

The company, however, delineated property rights in a more specific and
formal manner, and the miners felt unsure about what specific claims they
had to the land after its purchase by the company. The "squatters" living
around Elizabethtown remained convinced, however, that they at least possessed the right to stay in their homes and work their mining claims without the obligation of paying rent to the new company. The editor of the
*Railway Press and Telegraph* (with a masthead that read, "A Tribune for
the People—The World is Governed TOO Much") wrote of the company,
"Let the owners of this grant have an official survey made to obtain a
patent, and show us that we are on their lands—if they can—but until
they do this we will assert that we are not their tenants and will utterly disregard their demands and disown their pretensions."[62] The miners possessed well-established claims and believed that they had settled equitably
with Maxwell and that the company had the responsibility of proving otherwise. The miners were the first settlers to launch a rhetorical, if not legal, attack that questioned the extent and legality of the company's claims
to land and placed the burden of proof on the company to specify who
owned which particular piece of the grant. This rhetorical move revealed
the miners not as the unsophisticated ruffians often associated with the
mythic miner of the Western frontier but as legally savvy individuals. The
mostly Anglo Eastern miners, aware of their rights as citizens, were unwilling to quietly go away in the face of company opposition.

The *Railway Press and Telegraph's* rhetoric and slogan—"The World
is Governed TOO Much"—harkened back to Jacksonian democratic ideals.
These settlers believed that they had the right to use their property, whether
for mining, farming, or ranching, unencumbered by government or corporate intervention. In the tradition of the same populist libertarian philoso-

phy that had guided earlier Jacksonians, these settlers and miners feared the power of elites to rule over them and to take away their property and livelihood, and they rebelled against any authority that seemingly impinged on their rights as landowners.

To make matters worse, there was no face-to-face relationship or personal rapport between the managers of the company and the miners. Unlike Maxwell, Collinson, who believed that the title he held from Maxwell should speak volumes to the unruly miners, was not likely to sit down and negotiate personally with the miners. Consequently, a deep mutual hatred began growing. A few days after Collinson's stated deadline to the miners to appear before the company to sign leases for their mining rights, the paper supported the miners' protestations and criticized the "high-mightiness" of Collinson. The editor wrote, "How are you miners on the 'eject'? Are you prepared to vacate and abandon your claims and improvements on the dictation of this high flyer? Or do you think you have as good a right to your own property as somebody else has, [even] if said somebody did pay over a million dollars on speculation for the ghost of a fictitious title to it."[63] The bitter class critique from the miners may have shocked Collinson. The distant company, and even the trustees in Santa Fe, had not anticipated the venomous resistance from the Jicarillas, the miners, or the small-scale farmers. Instead, they naively assumed that no one would notice or object to the sale of such a large piece of land, even though it was home to many more people than just the Maxwells and their family.

During the 1870s the Jicarillas and the miners were not the only inhabitants who came under attack from the company. On the more remote portions of the grant, small farmers and ranchers, mostly Hispano, who had been living undisturbed for years began to feel the outside pressure of the company's policies as their land use patterns, based on barter and community, were overwhelmed by the imposition of a market economy and a grid for defining property boundaries, as well as the sale of the land parcels. As discussed in chapter 1, during Maxwell's tenure the Hispanos had migrated across the Sangre de Cristo Mountains to farm and ranch along the valleys of the Vermejo, Poñil, Purgatory, and Cimarron Rivers (see map 5.) The land use pattern revealed an efficient use of the area's limited water resources while also demonstrating the community's desire to give relatively equal access to all the families. This allocation of natural resources, combined with Hispano life centered around the plazas, made for a communitarian-based society. When the company took over, however, they found the Hispanos' use of the thin strips of land along the rivers to be inefficient and immediately began "reclaiming" the land so that they

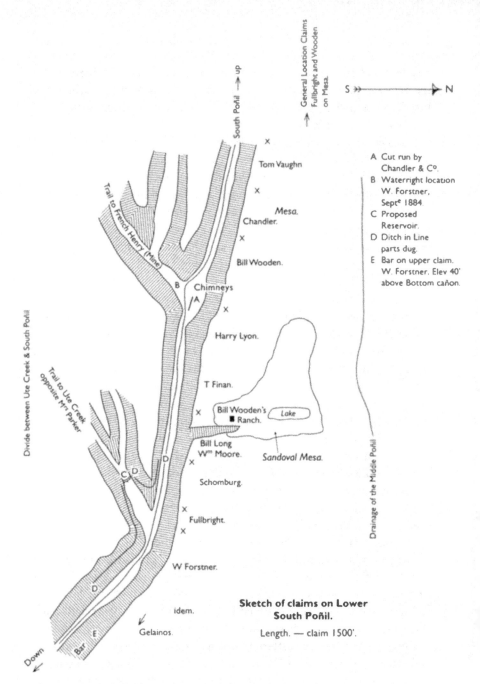

Map 5.   Property claims on the Poñil River, ca. 1885. The cross-hatching near the river represents the area where the Hispano settlers had their claims. The names to the right of the river represent Anglo claims. Map reproduced from a hand sketch in Maxwell Land Grant and Railway Company Papers, Archive 147, Zimmerman Library, Special Collections, University of New Mexico, Albuquerque; labels spelled as in original sketch.

could build a system of dams and irrigation canals that could deliver water to other parcels of land not near the waterways. The company's agents put a higher value on plots of land that could be individually irrigated. In short, they wanted to reclaim the land for use in the market system, no matter what the cost to the community ethic and economy.

The company's managers found the Hispano plazas and plots irregular and cumbersome as well as incompatible with defining marketable titles. The company wanted to survey the land and make the property lines within the boundaries of the grant conform to the U.S. system of sections and townships, and they planned to sell the land to interested farmers and ranchers in 160-acre increments. In their brochures and through their agents who traveled through the Midwest and Northeast, the company promised "improved" land that would have working irrigation systems in place by the time immigrants came to settle. Technically the prior settlers or "squatters" could purchase one of these newly drawn plots, but few did. First, only a few had enough cash to purchase such a large parcel of land, and second and perhaps more important, the company discouraged them, preferring to see them leave the grant altogether. Consequently, the company's local agents began filing ejection suits in district court in Cimarron to get the squatters off the land. As soon as the court entered judgments against settlers, the company would enlist the local sheriff, assuming he was sympathetic to the company, to evict them.

In response to the company's ejection suits, Anglo and Hispano settlers on the grant formed squatters clubs and anti-grant leagues. They held a mass meeting on March 30, 1873, during which the participants agreed to protect their homes and property rights, with guns if necessary.[64] As a result of the settlers' solidarity, armed conflicts between grant agents and anti-grant settlers began just two months later. During this early period of violence on the grant it is important to take note of the interethnic cooperation between Anglos and Mexicans. For a brief time, both groups seemed to overlook their differences, whether they were ethnic, religious, or cultural, and instead banded together again the common enemy—the company. All this would change, however, over the next few years as the violence on the grant continued to escalate, culminating in 1875 in the Colfax County "War."

## ETHNIC DIVISIONS AND THE COLFAX COUNTY "WAR"

The Colfax County "War," which Professor Howard Lamar rightly labeled "a tortuous sequence of events," really was not a war at all. The "war" acquired that term as local participants and their descendants retold the story of the violent skirmishes that engulfed the land grant for those few months of 1875.[65] Nevertheless, the violence touches on two fundamental issues surrounding the arrival of the Maxwell Land Grant Company in northern New Mexico. First, the events illustrate the violence that had begun to permeate life on the grant as the hostility continually grew between the company's agents and the settlers. Men working for the company constantly complained that the settlers and miners harassed them as they tried to complete work on irrigation and fencing projects across the grant. However, the violence by the mid-1870s was taking on a different characteristic as well. Issues around what constituted an anti-grant position and a pro-company stance became more complicated because of race and class. As new settlers, mostly Anglo, began to take an active interest in economic and political activities, the old alliances among settlers, miners, farmers, and ranchers—regardless of religion, race, or class—against the company became strained and broke apart during the so-called war.[66] One legacy of the violence was that Anglos and Hispanos became suspicious of each other, and as Anglos gained more power on the grant, they, as well as company and territorial officials, came to view the Mexican American settlers as outsiders, labeling them "squatters." Landlessness, then, became associated with ethnicity: either as "Indians" who could be removed or as "Mexicans" who did not deserve American land and property rights.

These emerging racial conflicts suggest the second issue that the violence exposed: the influence of outside (read: Anglo) businessmen and politicians—particularly the Santa Fe Ring—on the affairs of the grant's settlers. The territorial system, which allowed for corrupt officials to oversee the governing of Western territories, failed the citizens on the grant miserably. Not only did settlers come under attack from the hostile company, but the government, through territorial officials, helped the company gain control of the grant. The Santa Fe Ring, arguably the most influential group involved in the economic, political, and social development of the territory, was "a set of lawyers, politicians, and businessmen who united to run the territory and to make money out of this particular region."[67] Like other post–Civil War machines, the Ring relied on national Republican Party and governmental patronage to keep it functioning. Much like New York's Tammany Hall, the Ring used a spoils system to influence territorial legislators, judges, and federal government appointees in order to implement the development-oriented programs of the Ring's members. Rather than relying on industrial manufacturing as its instrument for profit, which was typical of Eastern machines, the Santa Fe Ring relied on land. The Maxwell Land Grant possessed the dubious honor of being the largest in a series of land grabs perpetrated by the Ring's members.⁶⁸

Although the Santa Fe Ring depended on national party patronage to ensure its success, it was most successful at manipulating local political and economic situations. Lawyers Stephen B. Elkins and Thomas B. Catron, both investors in the Maxwell Land Grant Company, maintained law offices in Santa Fe that often served as the informal headquarters of the Ring's activities. While Catron served as the U.S. attorney general, he also carried on his law practice, which specialized in clearing Mexican and Spanish land titles so that they could be approved by the U.S. General Land Office. Since most of his clients were poor, Spanish-speaking Hispanos who could not afford his services, Catron agreed to clear their titles in exchange for a percentage of the land grant. By 1894 Catron held interests in seventy-five land grants, owned nearly two million acres, and acted as the attorney for the owners of another four million acres. One of the Elkins & Catron law office's most prominent clients was the Maxwell Land Grant Company, and each partner would at some point have a significant financial interest in the enterprise.⁶⁹ This local legal, governmental, and mercantile elite, as represented by Elkins, Catron, Pile, and Chaffee, was able to apply enough economic, political, and legal pressure to influence the outcome of the settler/Maxwell Company conflict on the grant.

In the early 1870s the Santa Fe Ring mirrored many of the political and economic trends that were thriving in Gilded Age America, which was not surprising since most of New Mexico's political elite had come from the East and had learned the political ropes within the Republican Party's spoils system.⁷⁰ The Ring's members tied themselves to federal politics by aiding the election of Jerome B. Chaffee of Colorado and Stephen B. Elkins of New Mexico as delegates to Congress, both of whom became owners and administrators of the Maxwell Land Grant Company. Chaffee, of course, had been the driving force behind putting together the investors for the Maxwells, and together, Elkins and Chaffee used their governmental positions and influence to ensure that Congress would indeed patent the land grant for two million acres, and that the company would soon turn a profit. In short, Catron, Chaffee, and Elkins were Gilded Age Republican spoilsmen in the tradition of Jay Gould and James Fiske, and the success or the failure of the Maxwell Land Grant Company depended on these Ring members' ability to secure the grant's title and financial position. For a significant interest in the company, all of these men used their social and political influence as well as their government positions to ensure the enterprise's success. As New Mexico, the grant, and the Mexican Americans became politically incorporated into the political and economic life of the United States, New Mexico's Hispanos continued to lose control over their land, their economic livelihood, and, in many cases, their own safety. The skirmishes in Colfax Country, however, were merely a preview of the violence that came to mark the lives of all the people on the grant for the next twenty years.

The violence in Colfax County began on September 14, 1875, with the murder of Reverend Franklin J. Tolby, a Methodist minister who had openly and vigorously attacked the Santa Fe Ring and its members' involvement with the Maxwell Land Grant Company. Tolby had been writing open letters to the *New York Sun* about the corruption of territorial officials and their influence on the grant's inhabitants.[71] A passerby found Tolby's body about twenty miles outside of Cimarron on the road to Elizabethtown. Robbery had not been the motive; all of Tolby's personal belongings remained intact, and his horse stood tethered to a tree six hundred yards away. For several weeks rumors circulated about the identity of the criminal. The Reverend O. P. McMains, a good friend and fellow minister of Tolby's, began investigating the murder on his own because he did not trust local officials, who were friendly to the company and the Santa Fe Ring. After about a month, McMains began to suspect a local Hispano, Cruz Vega, who worked as a laborer at odd jobs around the grant. Vega had been hired by the local postal contractor, Florencio Donaghue, for just one day, September 14th (the day of Tolby's death), to carry the mail between Cimarron and Elizabethtown. This circumstantial evidence, combined with McMains's prejudice that Hispanos on the grant acted as stooges for grant officials and government leaders sympathetic to the Santa Fe Ring, convinced McMains that he should confront Vega personally with his suspicions.

McMains led a group of six Anglo men to meet Vega, who had been tricked into arriving at an open field on the evening of October 30, 1875. In order to scare Vega, the men strung a noose around his neck and the other end of the rope over a tree. They then asked him who had employed him to kill Tolby. Vega confessed to aiding in the murder of Tolby, but only after the men had tortured and beaten him severely. He said that Manuel Cardenas had actually killed Tolby. Both had been hired by Vega's uncle, Francisco "Pancho" Griego, and Florencio Donaghue, Ring supporters and mail contractors, to kill Tolby, who apparently had evidence of fraud against Griego and Donaghue and had threatened to go public with the information.

McMains later claimed that he left the scene after Vega had been tortured but was still alive, convinced that Vega had told the truth. McMains believed that both Vega and Cardenas had acted merely as the front men for the Santa Fe Ring, whose members were eager to see the Maxwell Land Grant Company succeed and for the settler troubles to dissipate. Getting rid of Tolby would remove one of the grant's most active opposition leaders and perhaps warn others about what could happen if they did not fall in line. While McMains believed that Vega and Cardenas should be punished by the law for Tolby's death, he claimed that he was more interested in exposing the conspiracy and discrediting the Santa Fe Ring. McMains said that before he left the tree where the six men held Vega, he told the mob to let Vega go as he was not the real criminal. McMains said he departed under the assumption that the men would do as he had asked. The men, however, did not comply with the minister's directions, and the six men, after beating and torturing Vega, shot him dead and hung him from a pole for his supposed hand in Tolby's murder.[72] There is always the unspoken possibility that given the rising racialized tensions on the grant, they killed Vega to terrorize the local Hispanos. Why the group lynched Vega remains unclear, but the fact that a Catholic Mexican had murdered a Protestant Anglo minister, no matter what the political motivations, placed Vega outside the bounds of civilized society and made him lynchable and punishable by mob rule.[73] Vega's ethnicity as well as his crime prevented him from benefiting from the United States' fair and "blind" legal system.

As Hispanos and Anglos clashed over who should be blamed and held accountable for Tolby's and Vega's deaths, the "war" gained ethnic overtones. Anglos, particularly new arrivals who were settling homesteads, felt that Hispanos such as Vega and Cardenas had acted as agents of the Ring because they had no property and were dependent on wage labor. Like earlier Jeffersonian agrarianists, these Anglo homesteaders believed that Hispanos posed a threat to their newly formed community because they were landless or worked only small holdings and therefore could be persuaded by outsiders such as the Santa Fe Ring to work against new settlers on the grant. Because Hispanos had no access to making an independent living, they would always be suspect as being in collusion with outside capitalists and contending political forces.

Hispanos, on the other hand, had their own analysis for the set of problems resulting from company control and the influence of the Santa Fe Ring. They were slowly losing their lands to the company and also were not succeeding within the new market economy. These local Hispanos seemed unlikely to ally with those responsible for the economic decline. Hispanos on the grant believed that Vega's murder was nothing more than a racially motivated lynching by Anglos against one of their own for a crime that he may or may not have committed, but which certainly had not been his idea. Vega had nothing to personally gain from the death of the minister, and they believed that he had lost his life at the hands of a lynch mob, who wrongly blamed local Hispanos for the economic strife.

Two nights later, at the Saint James Hotel in Cimarron, the violence continued when Griego, whom Vega had identified as the man who had hired him, accused R. C. (Clay) Allison of being the leader of the mob who killed Cruz Vega, Griego's nephew. Allison, a Vermejo rancher with a violent reputation, had been a strong supporter of Tolby and did not appreciate the suggestion: he shot Griego three times and left him dead, slumped over his unfinished drink.[74] The killing of the second Hispano brought tensions to a boiling point. Hispanos resented Anglo implications about their collusion with the Ring and felt like scapegoats for the grant's myriad problems. They also protested that the sheriff, a Santa Fe Ring sympathizer, had done little to find and arrest the murderers of Vega and Griego.

The sheriff, however, had no problems finding and arresting the Hispanos involved in the violence. A week later, the sheriff arrested Manuel Cardenas, the man Vega had named as his accomplice while the mob had tortured him. Cardenas confirmed Vega's version of the events and told the sheriff that Melvin W. Mills, the lawyer for the Maxwell Land Grant Company, and the county probate judge, Dr. Robert Longwill, the Colfax County representative of the Santa Fe Ring, had hired him and Vega, through Griego and Donaghue, to kill the Methodist minister Tolby.

Griego had a long and close association with Longwill and Mills. Two years earlier Griego had murdered two soldiers who had been playing cards with him at the Saint James Hotel in Cimarron. He had fled the county but came back and turned himself in to Mills, then justice of the peace. At that same time, Elkins, Longwill, and Mills were running for public office in the territory, and Mills cut a deal with Griego, promising him "that if [he] and his friend, C. Lara, would use all their influence with the Mexicans in favor of the ticket of Elkins and Longwill, Griego should not suffer." Griego and Lara agreed, but only reluctantly since they had both been vocal opponents of the Ring and the company. As a result of Mills's coercion, they carried on a political relationship with the Ring members, which culminated with Mills hiring Vega and Cardenas to kill Tolby for the Ring. In return, when court opened the following session, Lara was appointed interpreter to the grand jury and the charges against Griego were dismissed.[75]

News of Cardenas's confession spread quickly across the grant and stirred more fears, anger, and racial suspicions. Longwill, fearing he could not get a fair trial in Colfax County—or worse, that he might be lynched before getting a trial at all—fled immediately across the Sangre de Cristos to Santa Fe, closely followed by a posse led by Clay Allison, who saw himself as the avenger for Tolby's death. Fortunately for Longwill, he had enough of a head start on Allison that he managed to escape the wrath of the mob. Cardenas was not so lucky and lost his life in his prison cell the very night of his arrest—shot by an unknown gunman. Finally, the sheriff placed Mills and Donaghue into protective custody at Cimarron. For the third time since the Maxwell Land Grant Company had taken over the grant, a cavalry detachment from nearby Fort Union was sent by territorial governor Samuel B. Axtell to keep the peace.

In Santa Fe, Longwill and his friends from the Ring convinced Axtell that they could not get fair trials on the Maxwell Land Grant, and in January of 1876 the governor attached Colfax to Taos County, a Ring stronghold, for administrative and judicial purposes. The grand jury in Taos, not surprisingly, dropped all charges against Longwill and Mills for the murder of Tolby because of lack of evidence. They did, however, indict O. P. McMains and fourteen others for the murder of Cruz Vega. The verdict—guilty of murder in the fifth degree—was, however, later overturned because of legal technicalities.[76]

Two years after Tolby's murder, the fallout from the violence in Colfax County had ended. An uneasy calm settled over the grant, but life would never be the same because Anglos and Hispanos had come to view each other with mutual suspicion. The collusion of Vega, Griego, and Lara with local Santa Fe Ring associates only lent credence to the feelings that Mexicans were suspect because of their landlessness and dependency on the local political machine. Moreover, Governor Axtell and the territorial legislature did not immediately return the courts and administrative offices back to Colfax County. The act of removing the courts to Taos left a bitter taste in settlers' mouths because they knew that the Taos courts remained under the Ring's full control. Not only did the court's move provide a safe environment for Longwill and Mills, but it forced everyone in Colfax County having governmental business to trek across the mountains, sometimes in the dead of winter, to conduct any legal and contractual business. The Maxwell Land Grant Company took advantage of the long distance and its access to resources and saw this as the perfect opportunity to begin ejection suits in full force against all "illegal" squatters within the confines of the grant.[77]

## THE MAXWELL COMPANY'S
## LEGAL AND FINANCIAL PROBLEMS

By the mid-1870s the company, never on particularly stable financial ground to begin with, began to feel the financial pressures of running such a large endeavor. The problems with the settlers began to cause serious financial problems for two reasons. First, although the company agents willingly purchased improvements from the settlers or sold the settlers the parcels of land they lived on, it was expensive in terms of both time and cash to finish such transactions. Furthermore, the company's directors and agents had never counted on such expenditures. Second, the bad publicity generated from the continuing violence on the grant and the questions surrounding the validity of the grant's expanded boundary made it difficult to lure investors who would provide cash for daily operations. The bad publicity also made it difficult to find wealthier Anglo and European settlers who would purchase 160-acre plots at the going market price. So, partly as a result of the violence and the ensuing instability on the grant, and also of the Panic of 1873, which had sent financial markets across the country into a downspin, the company faced serious financial troubles. In June 1873, two years before overt violence erupted on the grant, the company had not been able to meet its financial obligations and did not make an expected bond payment. By the summer of 1875 the company's financial situation was even worse, with their stock worth only five cents on the dollar, and in July the company declared bankruptcy. To make matters worse, the territory of New Mexico's district court issued a demand for back taxes from 1873, 1874, and 1875, a total of $12,500 plus interest, which the company was unable to pay.[78]

Finally, in December of 1876 the territorial government sold the company at public auction in order to cover the back taxes owed to New Mexico. In an interesting turn of events, M. W. Mills, who months earlier had just narrowly escaped the violence in Colfax County, purchased the grant, acting as a middleman for Thomas B. Catron. Mills paid $16,500 for the company at auction and then sold it to Catron the following July for $20,000. Perhaps the local mercantile elite, led by Catron, saw this as an opportunity to make their way into the larger cattle and grain markets that the company had begun to establish. Or perhaps Catron was merely working as a middleman who would hold the company safe until the owners could redeem the company. It is difficult to say which is true, but both explanations reveal the importance of the connections between local political and economic elites with outside officials and investors. New Mexico territorial law, however, allowed the company's directors a period of redemption, and they were able to reorganize and wrest control of the company and its property back from Catron. They purchased his shares for $20,961.85.[79]

It was becoming clear to company officials that unless they could legally secure their boundaries, they would continue to have troubles with the squatters and with attracting investors. The company's best chance of succeeding now rested with the U.S. Supreme Court. In *Tameling v. Interstate Land Company*, the court had overruled an earlier decision by Secretary Jacob D. Cox that had limited Spanish and Mexican land grants to only 22 square leagues.[80] Thus the company had good reason to believe that it could finally receive a patent from Congress that would entitle it to the two million acres it claimed. Only with these enlarged and legally secure boundaries could it hope to make the estate a profitable enterprise.

Stephen B. Elkins, the congressional delegate, who was looking after his own and Catron's interests in the company, was the first to act on the *Tameling* decision. In June 1877 he sent a letter to the Interior Department asking that the original survey commissioned by Maxwell and Chaffee and conducted by Deputy Surveyor General Griffin be reinstated as marking the grant's true boundaries. The commissioner of the General Land Office, J. A. Williamson, refused this proposition, saying that "Mr. Griffin acted under authority of private and interested parties in the execution of the survey at their cost . . . and hence I refrain from acceding [sic] to your proposal in the matter of the survey."[81]

Elkins, not easily discouraged, asked Williamson to issue a contract that commissioned a new survey. Elkins further suggested that Griffin's old field notes and plats be used as a guide for the government-sponsored survey. Elkins realized that the old plats would guide the new survey along the extended boundaries of 1.7 million acres. Williamson agreed to a new survey, and on June 28, 1877, he wrote to the surveyor general of New Mexico, Henry M. Atkinson, instructing him to "select a capable and disinterested deputy who had no connection or business transaction referable to the interest of the owners of the grant, . . . so that the deputies may be free from any bias or undue influence in the lawful execution of the survey."[82] Despite Williamson's well-intentioned advice, Atkinson, a member of the Ring and friend of Elkins and Catron, contracted Elkins's brother, John T. Elkins, to complete the Maxwell Land Grant survey.

Whether Commissioner Williamson knew of Atkinson's political connections and corrupt endeavors in New Mexico is not clear, but he had good reason to suspect Atkinson's motives. The Santa Fe Ring had lobbied the Department of the Interior for the appointment of H. M. Atkinson to the post of surveyor general of New Mexico. Jerome B. Chaffee sent an ominous endorsement to the department: "Our friends and the men in New Mexico want H. M. Atkinson. Don't fail to appoint him."[83] Clearly, Atkinson owed favors to Chaffee, Elkins, and other members of the Ring, and he reciprocated by making sure that the survey would turn out as they planned. Just days after Atkinson appointed John T. Elkins and Walter G. Marmon to conduct the survey, the party traveled out to the northeastern corner of the state to mark the boundaries. Stephen Elkins went along to watch. By the beginning of 1877 the two surveyors had completed the survey and transferred the plats back to Washington for patent approval by the Department of the Interior and Congress.

From the very beginning of the survey, controversy and accusations of fraud clouded its validity. Because the survey had been conducted during the dead of winter and often at altitudes over 10,000 feet, some suggested that the survey team had never left Santa Fe. Richard Russell even wrote accusingly that perhaps the lines were drawn and discussed over a beer in a Santa Fe tavern.[84] Others made more substantive claims and complained to the Department of the Interior about the wrongly drawn boundaries. U.S. homesteader Benjamin Houx, protesting Elkins's presence, wrote that "at the time of the starting said recent survey the Secretary of the company [Pels] claiming to own said grant and an attorney of said Company [Elkins] were on the ground and through their influence the survey was wrongly started."[85]

In June 1878 Surveyor General Atkinson wrote to Williamson saying that he wanted to forward the plats, but there were so many complaints that he feared the boundaries would be questioned. He nevertheless assured the commissioner that the protestations in no way reflected that quality of the survey but were merely political accusations. He further pleaded that Elkins and Marmon be paid their salary as promised. By 1879 a review by the Department of the Interior had to be suspended because every section of the survey had been questioned by a deluge of letters from settlers who were complaining to the General Land Office. Williamson wrote back to Atkinson informing him of the suspension and directed him to examine the situation; if an error had been made by Elkins and Marmon, he was to direct them "back into the field and correct the survey."[86]

Although Williamson probably did not realize it, he was colluding in the fraud that Elkins, Atkinson, and other company members committed in order to extend the grant's boundaries. Atkinson did send Elkins and Marmon back into the field, and—not surprisingly—they found that their original boundaries were the true ends of the Maxwell Land Grant. In May of 1879

Interior Secretary Carl Schurz issued a patent for the company's entire claim as established by the Elkins/Marmon survey.[87] Because of the company's ability to form a beneficial relationship with territorial officials, its prospects began to rise. The key to the company's success in controlling and profiting from the grant was its ability to control the federal and territorial government bureaucracy. What the settlers in their battle with the company, and many historians who look at world-systems theory, have not accounted for, however, was the self-interest of local government officials. By allying themselves with Eastern bureaucrats and European capital, men like Catron, Elkins, and Atkinson not only assisted in controlling the land grant but also provided a large financial and political benefit to themselves.

## COMPARISONS TO OTHER LAND DISPOSSESSIONS

The switch from family-owned and -operated hacienda to corporate enterprise was not unique to the Maxwell Land Grant or even to New Mexico. The changes on the grant merely illustrate trends that occurred across all of the American West and in many other parts of the world during the latter part of the nineteenth century. From Central America to the Pacific Islands to South Africa, investors and developers from England and the Netherlands exploited the natural resources and native populations of these peripheral economies throughout the nineteenth and into the twentieth centuries. In fact, the outstretched arm of capitalism and the market economy had been incorporating subsistence economies on distant peripheries since the sixteenth century.[88]

Moreover, the method of incorporation and land dispossession followed a similar path regardless of the time period or location. Businessmen seeking maximum returns from their property investments transformed the nature of their land entitlement by regulating the recognition process and enforcement regimes. This transformation had two aspects. First, investors replaced unwritten local custom and quite complex usufructuary rights with formally recorded interests and clear boundaries demarcating private property. These newly recorded entitlements almost always excluded the prior local and informal rights that inhabitants had been living under before European investment and presence. Second, investors transferred authority to interpret and enforce these newly created entitlements from local (native) officials to the national courts and legislature, where investors had greater influence than the people they were displacing. In the case of the Maxwell Land Grant, the company's officials removed the power to determine property rights from the local *alcalde* to the U.S. Supreme Court, the executive branch, and Congress. In short, investors preferred authoritative arenas geographically and culturally remote from the land and its inhabitants. Local interests and customs only interfered with investors' interest in creating titles that were marketable anywhere and to anyone. Investors, in short, sought to eliminate dependence on space-bound customary norms and translate their titles into terms that a world market could understand.

Other places in the American West experienced similar incorporations into the world market, resulting in native inhabitants losing their land to European and Eastern U.S. interests. The transformation of south Texas into the winter garden of the United States could not have occurred without the influx of capital and Anglo farmers and ranchers into the area in the late nineteenth century. Their move into the border area foreshadowed Mexican Americans' loss of land and their transformation from property owners to wage laborers.[89] Furthermore, Native Americans across all of North America since the first arrival of Euro-Americans, whether Spanish, French, Russian, or English, saw their economies disrupted and their lands taken as these newly arrived adventurers searched for mineral, agricultural, and ranching wealth, all of which required massive capital investment based on a formal and clear title to the land.[90]

One particularly interesting comparison with the Maxwell Land Grant is the case of land dispossession of native Hawaiians during the Great Mahele (division of lands) of the 1840s. As with the case of the Maxwell grant, the impetus for the Great Mahele came from an overseas investment project, this one by Ladd & Company, a British land development enterprise formed as a joint stock company. The investors negotiated a secret contract with King Kaukikeaouli in November 1841 for division and cultivation of Hawai'i's excess lands, those not held by the king or his chiefs. Ladd & Company eventually established a subsidiary called the Royal Community of the Sandwich Islands that publicized Hawaiian land availability to Europeans and settled immigrants to the islands. This first foreign land development effort in Hawai'i eventually failed for many of the same reasons as the Maxwell Company would later fail: lack of capital, resistance from local inhabitants, and lack of knowledge about the landscape. Ladd & Company's experience, however, did establish a pattern that would eventually be known as the Great Mahele.[91]

Local Hawaiian chiefs owned all lands in the form of *ahupuaas*, which were pie-shaped parcels that extended and widened from their points at the top of the inland mountains to the ocean front. Workers and peasants could move from parcel to parcel somewhat freely, but only the local chiefs actually owned the land. Because of pressure from missionaries, who were interested in seeing the peasants become stable, immobile farmers, and pressure from businessmen, who were interested in developing the vast land resources of Hawai'i, a Board of Land Commissioners was created by statute in 1846. The commission worked on dividing the lands for nine years. The king, through negotiations and coercion, eventually gave up most of his rights to the lands of the kingdom, except for certain estates, "crown lands," which were reserved to the reigning monarch for his private use. Chiefs could take out fee simple title to land they had previously held in fief. Commoners could buy small lots or *kuleanas* in fee simple as well. Everyone had to have their land surveyed, which turned out to be a problem. Because a clear, shared definition of a *kuleana* was lacking, land acreage varied from island to island. Furthermore, petitioners had to pay a commutation fee to the Hawaiian government in order to perfect title, which amounted to one-third of the land's unimproved value. The fee could be paid in land or in cash, but since cash was rare on the islands, most Hawaiians ended up losing land in order to pay their commutation fees. Furthermore, many chiefs paid their fees in land, and this land eventually became a large part of Hawai'i's public lands.

After 1850 the constitutional monarchy and the legislature agreed to allow foreigners to purchase lands under the same conditions granted to native Hawaiians. Europeans and Americans who were already living on the islands immediately acted, unlike the native Hawaiians, who were slow to embrace this land reform measure. As with the later U.S. homestead system, the Great Mahele was complicated in terms of dealing with the bureaucracy in order to establish a proper claim to land. It was also expensive because of filing and commutation fees. The end result of the Great Mahele proved economically and culturally disastrous for native Hawaiians. While 1.5 million acres had been set aside for the "crown lands" and "government lands," the native tenant farmers only received 30,000 acres for their needs. Furthermore, because commoners, who had suffered from the burdens of paying tribute to chiefs, were now free to leave the land, many of them sold their perfected titles to eager foreigners and moved along. By the end of the century, foreigners owned four acres for every acre a native Hawaiian owned.[92]

These examples of property loss and dispossession of native peoples suggest the larger connections of the Maxwell Land Grant story to other places and times. Although the characters, geographic regions, and specific circumstances differ, these historical instances from south Texas to Hawai'i to northern New Mexico tell the story of invasion, incorporation, and, eventually, dispossession. American Western historians, until recently with the work of William Robbins, William Cronon, Patricia Limerick, and David Montejano, have been reluctant to engage these broader connections.[93] Since Frederick Jackson Turner's "Significance of the Frontier," in which he argued that the frontier had created a democratic American character, the West's historians have been pointing to the uniqueness of the American Western experience rather than to its connections with the rest of the post-colonial world.[94] Nevertheless, these dramatic events on the Maxwell Land Grant, which have provided the rich material for myth making and tales of male violence, also provide evidence to challenge notions of American Western exceptionalism. The events leading up to the Colfax County "War" and the violence that pervaded the 1880s ask historians to reflect on trends and developments across the rest of the Americas and developing world during this time period and to search for connections and explanations for this violence, land loss, and incorporation.

At the close of the 1870s, on the grant itself the charges of fraud and the fear of a changing world never really subsided. The legitimacy of the Elkins/Marmon survey was at the root of all the litigation that was to take place during the 1880s. The settlers continued to complain, and the accusations were only further fueled by the inherent hatred between the company and the anti-grant settlers. The company, moreover, could not solve any of its difficulties: lack of new settlers, lack of investors, and settler resistance. The company continued to lose money throughout the rest of the decade, and once again, in 1880, the company was put on the auction block after it was unable to pay $4.3 million of interest to the first bondholders. The company also owed $1,835 in interest on a second bond issue they had made to help with operating expenses. Their highest costs had come from buying out some settlers and, through expensive legal proceedings, ejecting others who would not compromise with the company. In the 1880 purchase, a consortium of Dutch bondholders who had been investing in the land grant company took over the management and began to directly control the day-to-day workings of the grant. They named Harry Whigham, a knowledgeable New York financier, as receiver in charge of the operations of the troubled land grant company. Whigham would answer directly to the directors and carry out their desires to finally see a profit on their investments.[95] For the first time in more than ten years, prospects finally looked bright for the European investors of the Maxwell Land Grant Company. However, the decade of the 1880s would be no better, as the company would face legal barriers and violent battles that threatened to bankrupt it and make the enterprise, in the final analysis, a failure.

# 4 Prejudice, Confrontation, and Resistance

## Taking Control of the Grant

Somos hijos de la tierra.
López brothers et al. to President
Grover Cleveland, November 19, 1887

The aggressions of said company are becoming unbearable and
must be remedied. And as we ask but a lawfull remedy which is
certainly within your power to grant and therefore your duty to.
Richard D. Russell to T. J. Anderson,
General Land Office, June 3, 1888

[Dutch] emigration is therefore so much desired, because every
man that we locate there has a vote and becomes a Grant man, a
peaceable industrious laborer.
M. P. Pels to Amsterdam Committee, August 30, 1887

The close of the 1870s brought an end to the Colfax County troubles, a
patent from Congress, and the sale of the company to a new set of directors. It looked as if stability might finally settle across the Maxwell Land
Grant. The decade of the 1880s, however, brought little relief to the belea-
guered company or the weary settlers. The company consistently faced financial failure as the Hispano and Anglo settlers continually resisted every
move that the company made to bring the land under its control. Although
the company did finally secure title to the entire 1.7 million acres through
the Supreme Court, it came at a cost of thousands of dollars in legal fees
and a prolonged legal struggle that left its title unclear while it litigated.
Furthermore, the lawsuit gave hope to the struggling settlers, who awaited
relief from the courts. Although this was a difficult decade for the company,
by the end of the 1880s it had subdued the most violent conflict between
the company and settlers, which left two men dead and settler resistance
severely weakened.

The Maxwell Land Grant Company's owners had spent most of the 1870s
using their influence to fix problems external to the grant itself. They had

influenced congressmen, federally appointed officials, and financiers in an effort to secure clear rights to the property they believed rightfully belonged solely to them. Yet they had never managed to make real profits on the enterprise. In 1880 the Dutch investors took control of the company, hoping to bring themselves financial solvency. Now, with the Elkins/Marmon survey complete and accepted (at least for the time being), a patent issued from Congress, and the arrival of the new management team, the newly organized corporation turned its attention to the problems within the grant's boundaries. While the corporation technically had control of the grant on paper, now it had to gain actual control of the land and the people who lived there. The company's managers, particularly Harry Whigham, the company's new receiver and assistant secretary, believed they would finally make a profit on their New Mexico enterprise.

### EARLY FAILURES AT CONTROLLING THE GRANT

Whigham, however, had not learned from the company's earlier mishandling of the Elizabethtown riots, the Colfax County incident, and Jicarilla uprisings. Instead, he pursued transgressors of the company's property rights even more aggressively, regardless of the settlers' reactions. The problem with unwanted Hispano and Anglo settlers had become progressively worse during the last decade. The company managers' efforts to secure their legal rights from Congress had left them little time to pursue the local problem of ridding the grant of these inhabitants.[1] In 1878, just prior to congressional approval of the grant's boundaries, 2,500 uninvited persons lived on town lots, mining claims, and "jumped" ranches and farms. Because of these extralegal settlers who paid no rents, the company had generated a yearly average profit of only $6,000 since its start a decade earlier.[2] This policy of forcing the settlers to bend to the company's will only exacerbated tensions on the grant, and the settlers prepared themselves to battle the company.

By May 1880 the Dutch bondholders had become so dismayed by the company's consistently dismal performance that they organized a buyout of the English and American investors. They purchased the company's first and second mortgages for $1.1 million. The men reorganized the corporation under Dutch law and elected a new set of reputable directors from Amsterdam, London, and America, including George Pullman—a director in name only—who never attended one board meeting. Nevertheless, his reputation lent stature to the fledgling company. The new directors also elected a whole new group of company officers, including Frank Sherwin, a New York businessman, as president. They charged Sherwin with bringing financial solvency to the company and profits to the foreign bondholders—not an easy task given the company's financial shape. To make sure that Sherwin did his job, the directors elected as vice president W. F. Ziegelaars, a Dutch investor who would have the Dutch interests foremost in his mind as he oversaw the American management team. Harry Whigham, as assistant secretary, would be responsible for the day-to-day operations of the company and answer directly to Sherwin. The outside trustees for the company included Chicago entrepreneur Cyrus McCormick, who, like Pullman, acted mostly as a figurehead.[3]

During their first two meetings the board of directors immediately issued 12 million Dutch guilders' worth of forty-year bonds which would bear no more than 7 percent annum to their holders. They also stipulated that interest payments could total only 75 percent of the company's profits. As the numbers below reveal, the people who purchased these bonds rarely saw 7 percent interest on their investment and were lucky to receive any dividend from the company in a given year. The directors also discussed and then accepted Frank Sherwin's detailed report about his plans to bring high profits through methods of "exploitation and development" of the grant's resources.[4] During the first two years, business moved along smoothly, if slowly, and the board of directors seemed content now that they had direct control over the Maxwell enterprise. Profits, however, did not pick up, and the company remained financially unstable.

By the mid-1880s the company's financial situation still had not improved significantly. In 1880 the company garnered only $643 from rents collected from the cattle grazing, farming, and mining enterprises. Each year was a little better: in 1881 they collected $2,196; in 1882, $3,521; in 1883, $6,116. But this income certainly could not float a company that had issued hundreds of thousands of dollars in stocks and bonds to investors. The poor profits came because the coal miners, farmers, and cattlemen who had been living and working on the grant were unwilling to make deals with Whigham and pay rent to the company. Serious opposition both in terms of violence and legal action grew as these prior inhabitants became convinced that they had a legal claim to keep their property and not pay rent to the company. Not until well after the 1888 battle at Stonewall Valley, the last bit of organized resistance to the company, would the company's profits rise substantially.[5]

As the financially dismal years ticked by, Frank Sherwin became more concerned with the settler problems, the consequent dismal financial performance, and, perhaps more importantly, the future of his job. In a series

of letters to Harry Whigham in March 1882, just two years after the reor-
ganization, Sherwin asked Whigham to help him deceive the board of directors. Sherwin, fearing that the contents of these letters would leak to the
public and drive down the company's stock, devised an elaborate secret code
for telegrams sent between Whigham in New Mexico and Sherwin, who
was in London trying to sell more bonds to raise cash for operations.
Sherwin also directed Whigham to redo the accounting books to make the
company's financial situation look more favorable to the Dutch board of directors and to potential European investors in London and Amsterdam.
Sherwin desperately needed good news from America to keep the price of
the stocks and bonds inflated and to acquire new investors. Furthermore,
Sherwin told Whigham that in his report for the board of directors meeting the following month he was only to report the positive aspects of the
grant's business. Whigham was to send any news of problems directly to
Sherwin in code or in personal mail addressed to him in London, far away
from the Dutch directors.[6]

Whigham, however, came under competing pressure from the board of
directors directly because they had not yet received his reports and the annual meeting was just weeks away.[7] In an effort to comply with Sherwin's
requests, it was taking Whigham longer to supply the necessary documentation. Whigham was also failing to manage the grant efficiently. Another
officer of the company wrote to Sherwin complaining that Whigham was
derelict in his duties as he was failing to sign important coal and cattle contracts that would bring the company significant monies.[8] Whigham seemed
to have almost no control over the day-to-day operations of the New Mexican enterprise. There was very little money coming in from the grant, and
the stocks and bonds were slowly but steadily losing ground in European
markets. Sherwin's increased demands to help him deceive the directors
only further taxed his abilities. Nevertheless, Sherwin and Whigham managed to get through the annual meeting with limited questioning and held
onto their jobs for three more years. By early 1885, however, the Dutch
board of directors began to get suspicious. W. F. Ziegelaars, formerly the
vice president but now the newly elected chairman of the board, wrote to
Whigham that his reports were to come directly to Ziegelaars and not to
Sherwin, who was on his way out of the company. The board of directors
also sent a trusted Dutch businessman, M. P. Pels, out to New Mexico to
look over the financial books.[9] What Pels found when he arrived in Cimarron shocked him and the rest of the investors: the company was financially
destitute. Much to the surprise of the Dutch board of directors, within
three months of Pels's visit, the Maxwell Land Grant Company had to file

for bankruptcy because it was almost £1 million in debt. Moreover, Sherwin had lost his job, and Whigham had earned himself the reputation of being utterly incompetent.

What had really whittled away the company's resources was the trouble they were having in settling with the grant's inhabitants. There were also new conflicts with homesteaders who had settled on the grant believing it to be a part of the public domain. The Department of the Interior had opened up sections of the grant to settlement, and in 1880 there were at least 107 homestead entries within the Maxwell Land Grant's boundaries. Of these, more than half (65) belonged to Hispanos who had adapted to the U.S. land tenure system and applied for homesteads. Hispanos' plots, however, rarely followed the surveyor's plat line. Although they would apply for the full homestead of 160 continuous acres, the descriptions of their plots were complex and often crossed two or three quarter sections.[10] The grant's Hispanos had combined two worlds: their own historical land patterns, which followed the contours of the land, with the scientifically engineered lines of the surveyor's plat. How the Hispanos, or the Anglos, for that matter, came to the grant or how they adapted to the prevailing land system was, of course, of no concern to the company's managers.

What did concern the company's managers was the lawsuit that the federal government had filed against the Maxwell Company for infringing on the public domain of Colorado. The government claimed that the northern boundary of the land grant should not have gone beyond the New Mexico/ Colorado line and therefore that land belonged to the public domain of the state of Colorado. Moreover, because of all the confusion during the 1870s, the U.S. General Land Office had issued final land patents to more than a hundred families living on the grant who could challenge the company's property claims with one of the most sacred of U.S. property institutions —the homestead. From a legal point of view, only the homestead holders on the Colorado portion would be affected. Yet settlers all across the grant felt encouraged by the suit and stepped up resistance. During Pels's early tenure, through the mid-1880s, few settlers came to terms with the company as all were willing to wait and see what the outcome of the suit would be and how the company would react. They had good reason to feel encouraged as the lawsuit continued to drag on, eventually ending with the Supreme Court's jurisdiction in *United States v. Maxwell Land Grant Company* in 1887.

Three years after the Dutch investors had taken direct control and the company and bondholders had invested significant monies in the enterprise, none of them had very much to show for their efforts. The grant was still overrun with hundreds of nonpaying tenants. The company may have been mismanaged by Sherwin and Whigham, but the directors became aware of how trying it could be to run an enterprise thousands of miles away in a foreign country that they had never visited. Yet, despite all indications that this was not a profitable enterprise, the Dutch investors did not give up. More importantly, they never seemed to grasp the real problem. In reading the correspondence between the Dutch directors and Whigham, it is clear that they misunderstood the quality of the landscape and the attitudes of the people. The directors continued to envision the land grant as W. W. Griffin had described it for the company a decade earlier: as a lush, abundant landscape teeming with cattle, flowing rivers, and rich mines. This, as Harry Whigham kept trying to tell them, was simply not an accurate picture. The Maxwell Land Grant, while rich in natural resources, required immense amounts of work to acquire those resources. The grant was also filled with people hostile to the company's burgeoning cattle, farming, and mining enterprises, which were beginning to encroach upon the limited water supply and available fertile lands. What would the directors have thought if they could have stepped off the train at Cimarron and seen the arid, almost bleak world of the Maxwell Land Grant? What would they have said about the hundreds of families trying to make their homes and livelihoods on such a harsh landscape? Maybe they would have at least known enough to keep their money and go back home richer for the direct knowledge of actually seeing the land they were trying to develop.

THE ARRIVAL OF DUTCH MANAGEMENT: M. P. PELS

When Marinus Petrus Pels arrived in February 1885 to look at the company's financial records, the enterprise was in utter disarray. To make matters worse, the old issue of the company's title was again being raised by the Atchison, Topeka, and Santa Fe Railway. The railroad company, which was currently building a line across the grant between Trinidad and Las Vegas, New Mexico, was suing the company because they wanted indemnity for the money they were putting into the railroad in the event that the company's title turned out to be imperfect.[11] Because of the current litigation between the State of Colorado and the Maxwell Company, they acted cautiously. The railroad's lawsuit, however, was the last blow for the Maxwell Company stock, as potential investors became increasingly scared off from the enterprise.

Pels never went back to the Netherlands permanently. The board of directors elected him the new general manager of the Maxwell Land Grant, and Pels settled his family—a wife, three daughters, and a son—in Denver. He began to manage the affairs of the Maxwell estate from his office there, with frequent trips to Cimarron—more than three hundred miles south of Denver.[12] Pels, a Dutchman, had worked for the East India Company, the trading company of Dummler & Company, for which he had managed properties and businesses abroad with great financial success. He had also worked as consul for the United States to Batavia, Java, and brought years of experience in managing colonial possessions. The managers believed that the New Mexico property simply needed someone experienced with managing peripheral enterprises, and Pels seemed more than prepared for his new job in northern New Mexico.

During the latter half of the nineteenth century and well into the twentieth, the Dutch had a worldwide reputation for being excellent colonial administrators. Europeans marveled that such a small country could maintain such a successful overseas empire, stretching from Indonesia to Africa. European businessmen became captivated by J. W. B. Money's 1861 book, *Java, or How to Manage a Colony,* which extolled the positive aspects of Dutch colonization practices. In particular, people believed that Dutch success was based on their efforts to understand local customs and engage in a "cultural synthesis," which melded the necessities of the local economy and society with the capitalist goals of the Dutch entrepreneurs.[13] Through intimate knowledge and experience with local economies and leaders, the Dutch had made Java into a rich colonial enterprise that provided 20 to 30 percent of the Netherlands' income during the latter part of the nineteenth century.[14] Certainly, Pels, who had worked in Java, would have been familiar with the success of Dutch colonial practices, and he brought this knowledge to his new colonial post. The longer Pels managed the Maxwell Land Grant, the more he came to view it as similar to other Dutch colonial enterprises, and he used lessons learned from Java to manipulate the grant's settlers as he attempted to move the enterprise into the world market. In the eyes of Pels and the other company managers, there were important similarities between a colonial possession in East India and a colonial possession in northern New Mexico and the American West. Both were distant enterprises for profit, and both possessed difficult problems with native inhabitants. Where Americans saw homesteaders and even squatters as rugged individuals moving onto the frontier to create a new democratic society, European investors saw troublesome interlopers invading their imperial enterprise. To the Dutch directors there was little difference between a rebellious Zulu or Indonesian chieftain and the American squatters—all were native opponents to their transnational and capitalist endeavors.

As Pels took over the grant's day-to-day operations, it seemed to calm the Dutch investors for a while. In June 1885, the Amsterdam committee wrote a letter to its bond and stock holders to tell them of the impending changes. The letter alluded to prior problems with mismanagement and the failure to come to terms with the rebellious settlers, but promised that with Pels's arrival the grant would soon be under control and profits would return shortly. The letter also reminded the investors that despite these financial setbacks the grant still held immense value. "The value of the property itself is beyond all question. Its special adaptedness for grazing land to meet the requirements of great Cattle Companies, and its wealth in Coal, Timber and precious metals justify a high estimate of its value, if it were only free from the engagements, encumbrances, and lawsuits." [15] Those important, but impossible, words—"if only." The company's Amsterdam directors convinced themselves that there was nothing inherently wrong with the enterprise, and that if only they had the right management, if only they could settle the lawsuits, and if only they could get rid of the settlers, then they would have a profitable enterprise. But as the 1880s rolled along, those "if onlys" would become increasingly difficult obstacles to overcome.

Pels, determined to bring financial solvency to the grant's owners, began a direct effort aimed at removing the settlers from the grant. First, he attempted to clearly mark and fence the grant's boundaries. Second, he stepped up efforts to attain ejection suits from the district court against rebellious squatters and persuade local sheriffs to enforce the law. Third, he began selling land at the market price of $1.50 per acre, with the company providing 7 percent financing, to those willing to settle permanently and abide by company rules. Fourth, he purchased the improvements—homes, barns, fences, ditches—and livestock from those settlers unwilling to buy land from the company, but who would willingly move off the grant. Finally, he commissioned an extralegal county assessment from the Las Animas County assessor, D. F. Wilkens, to determine exactly how many settlers lived on the grant and how much they owned. This last action proved to be one of the most valuable tools available to Pels as he vigorously pursued settler removal.

All of Pels's strategies for wresting control of the grant away from the squatters and settlers reflected the company manager's desire to clearly define property rights and consequently cement the company's domination over the people, the land, and its resources. In a report to the committee in Amsterdam, which was now responsible for overseeing the grant, Pels reiterated the company's policy: "Our idea has always been to fence the grant; to expel all cattle not belonging there; to buy the cattle from the squatters;

and to sell to the squatters the land they now occupy . . . or to lease the land to them for farming." [16] These tactics, moreover, meant to open the way for the company's ultimate goal: the land's resettlement by sympathetic Dutch immigrants.

The company's managers envisioned a large estate where they would have complete control over the laborers, products, and management of the grant. They also hoped to build an infrastructure to support town development and to attract more investment by the Atchison, Topeka, and Santa Fe and other railroads so that goods produced on the grant could be shipped easily to Eastern markets.[17] Because of the company's serious financial trouble at the beginning of the 1880s, it became essential for the company to exact rent payments, leases, or deeds from the existing inhabitants. Pels, however, soon realized that the squatters were, for the most part, poor subsistence farmers who would never be able to raise enough cash to purchase homestead-sized (160-acre) farms and ranches from the company directly. The ones who did have large parcels had used the liberal terms of the homestead system to acquire their land. The company therefore began a program to eliminate, rather than negotiate with, the current inhabitants. After they were gone, the company hoped to replace them with new settlers, preferably Dutch, whom they were encouraging to migrate.

The company's managers preferred Dutch immigrants because they would be new to America, unable to speak English, and therefore entirely dependent on the company. This would have been a welcome change for the managers, who were tired of dealing with uncooperative, even hostile, Anglos and Hispanos. In a letter from Pels to Frank Springer, the company's lawyer, Pels noted: "When we buy improvements it is desirable to locate settlers theon [sic] as quickly as possible as otherwise some new men may jump them." [18] When the company made progress by purchasing a squatter's improvements and removing him from the grant, Pels did not want the ranch taken over by another Anglo or Hispano squatter who quickly moved onto, or "jumped," the abandoned ranch and used it as his own. Pels feared leaving the purchased ranches unattended, and he wanted them settled with his own group of sympathetic Dutch immigrants. "Emigration is therefore so much desired," he wrote, "because every man that we locate there has a vote and becomes a Grant man, a peaceable industrious laborer." [19] Pels and the other managers brought their prejudices with them and consistently compared the lazy Americans and Mexicans to their hardworking and honest countrymen.

The settlers on the grant, however, opposed Dutch immigration and perceived it as a threat to their continued residence. One group of settlers went so far as to warn Dutch immigrants against coming to northern New Mexico. In a letter reprinted in Dutch newspapers, one writer, who used the initials L. H., warned Dutch immigrants not to come "to a country where life is in danger, where terror prevails, where the company's agents are burned in effigy, and absent themselves when a campaign is on." Not only would the Dutch colonists' lives constantly be in danger because of the anti-company and anti-foreign sentiment that pervaded the land grant, but the letter also cautioned would-be immigrants about the inhospitable environment. One-half of all the company's cattle died in the first year, and the highly touted irrigation system was archaic and rarely filled with water. Although it is impossible to measure the success of such an appeal, the New Mexican and Coloradan settlers took matters into their own hands, directly warning Dutch immigrants that their lives would be difficult as they struggled to make a home in the midst of a inhospitable environment and hostile neighbors.[20]

Pels believed the only way his Dutch immigration plan would work was if he could first purge the grant of the existing settlers, particularly the Hispanos in the northern mountains. Pels wrote to Mr. C. Lohman, the New York Maxwell Land Grant Company agent in charge of Dutch immigration, that he should come to New Mexico and Colorado and scout out the most appropriate portions of the grant for settlements, particularly the Stonewall Valley.[21] On that same day Pels also corresponded with the committee in Amsterdam, telling them that the New Mexico agents eagerly awaited the arrival of the Dutch immigrants. He wrote of grant agent Jan Van Houghten's success: "Since he has been there he has fired out of the beautiful Ventero [Vermejo] Valley many Mexicans; and by his energy you may rely upon it not one Mexican will be permitted to settle upon that estate." Pels believed he held the upper hand in ejecting the settlers. He continued to urge their replacement with European immigrants, writing, "I should not hesitate to recommend immigration, though for the first time not to exceed six or eight families, to be increased later, when we have fired out more of these Mexicans, as will be the case very soon." Pels boldly concluded, "They [the squatters] are already so afraid of the things above their heads that the land plowed and seeded this year is one-third less than last year; and this time we are going to push matters with the squatters, and will have our own way pretty quick."[22] Ironically, the removal of these settlers lowered grain and feed production and limited the expansion of the company's cattle operation, all of which lowered the company's profits. Nevertheless, these short-term losses were worth the cost to Pels if it meant ridding himself of the settler problem. Even Pels's term "firing out" conjured up the idea of burning out or driving out unwanted animals from the valleys and forests.

Pels's second strategy for taking control was through ejection proceedings. During the 1880s the company pursued settler removal through the territorial, district, and county courts. As early as 1882, New Mexico Territorial Supreme Court Judge L. Bradford Prince took the side of the company and evicted Hispanos from their homes. Against Juan Aragón he ruled, "Now therefore we command you that without delay you cause said Maxwell Land Grant Company and Railroad to have possession of the lands . . . within sixty days from the receipt of the writ."[23] However, attaining an ejection from a sympathetic territorial supreme court and actually removing the settlers were two entirely different matters. Both the company and the local courts found it difficult to persuade local law enforcement officers to serve notice and then enforce the ejection suits by physically removing families from their homes. For example, when Raton sheriff A. C. Wallace was supposed to remove O. P. McMains and his family from their home and sell their possessions, he backed down. Although he did go through the motions of holding a sale, none of the two hundred onlookers would bid on the McMains' property. Rather than confront what he regarded as a hostile "mob" and incite a riot, Wallace left without removing McMains.[24] The difficulty that the company faced in enforcing its legal rights and the settlers' unwillingness to give up or negotiate resulted in a stalemate.

## FAILED COMPROMISES AND NEGOTIATIONS

The settlers' recalcitrance combined with the pending litigation stressed the company's financial situation, which became so severe that Pels and Whigham decided that they had to negotiate with the feuding settlers. First, in March 1886, representatives from the two sides agreed that the company would halt ejection suits against the squatters as long as the case was pending in the federal courts. Second, the two sides agreed that if the suit was found in favor of the company, then the squatters would agree to pay rent to the company. The agreement read, "The spirit of this proposition is that everything shall remain as it is now with the settlers until the final decision of the said suit, but settlers may if they choose fence lands they now occupy not to exceed one hundred and sixty acres in one tract." The agreement, signed by ten Anglo and two Hispano representatives as well as by Harry Whigham, indicated cross-ethnic support to end hostilities on the grant. The company directors in Amsterdam, however, refused to approve the agreement, saying that since the suit applied only to the Colorado portion of the grant, the local company managers (Whigham and Pels) had no business making compromises with the rest of the grant's inhabitants.[25]

The Amsterdam committee, whose main goal was profits, could not see the wisdom in such a compromise; all they saw were short-term losses. Pels and Whigham, however, had to deal with the day-to-day problems and were more willing to make compromises with the settlers. This was only the first of many conflicts between the New Mexico managers and the Amsterdam committee. While both sets of managers wanted to make the enterprise run smoothly and profitably, each side had different ideas about how to accomplish the goal. This early attempt at negotiation was a single, passing instance. Never again would there be such an opportunity for the company and the settlers to work out a compromise. The Amsterdam committee's stringent attitude led the settlers and squatters to distrust the company's managers and fear removal, and eventually culminated in violence on the northern section of the grant.

After the failed compromise Pels resumed his policy of removing any unwanted inhabitants with even greater vigor, but now he tried negotiation and compromise as well as legal solutions. In addition to the ejection suits, Pels methodically pursued his task through the third and fourth strategies: selling land to the squatters or purchasing their improvements if they agreed to leave the grant. While these approaches forced the settlers to recognize and accept the company's legal right to the grant, both policies also took into account that the squatters, as Pels labeled them, had been living on the land and would continue doing so as this was their home. The new policies also recognized that the settlers had made improvements for which the company ought to compensate them. Pels, however, quickly came to understand the daunting task he faced. Realizing that the company's unpopularity damaged his credibility with the settlers, Pels tried to mitigate such attitudes by using a more personal approach.

In 1887, just prior to the battle in the Stonewall Valley, Pels stepped up his efforts. He not only feared that violence would erupt soon, but he also believed that the U.S. Supreme Court would return an unfavorable decision in the pending lawsuit.[26] He wrote to the managers in Amsterdam about his plans: "We deal first with the most influential settlers, and go personally to visit all the others, which is quite a job, but is the best plan to follow." Although his plans were extremely costly in terms of both time and money, Pels believed this was the only way to remove the squatters without bad publicity and violence. Personal visitations, however, often took their toll in terms of manpower and frustration. Only a month earlier, Pels had complained to Harry Whigham, "It is true that you speak of 'negotiating' with settlers, but you will clearly see that it is a super human task to 'negotiate' with 540 settlers. You cannot ask these people individually whether they would like to sell." [27] Nevertheless, despite his complaints, Pels persevered and attempted to deal personally with all of the settlers. After only a few years of living on the grant, Pels began to understand the importance of recognizing the reciprocal and personal nature of business relationships. Although Pels was no Maxwell, he did attempt to take on the persona of a benevolent manager willing to make deals with squatters or settlers and plead their case to the distant corporation. Pels was also using the successful Dutch tactic of "cultural synthesis" by emulating and taking on the role of *patrón* and middleman.

Pels's hard work sometimes paid off with some settlers giving in to the company's demands. In general, Anglos tended to negotiate more freely, as company agents tended to value their improvements more favorably than those made by Hispanos. The company agents also tended to give Anglos better interest rates and payment schedules. For example, J. A. Todd, who held a ranch on the Colorado portion, quickly agreed to purchase his ranch outright and recognize the company's rights because they had given him such favorable terms.[28] Others, such as E. J. Randolf and his wife, not only agreed to recognize the company's rights and purchase their land, but also went to work for the company as day laborers, herding stock and digging irrigation ditch systems. In fact, some settlers, mostly Anglos, willingly took the side of the company and curried favor with Whigham and Pels. Edward Twitty, who had a fairly large cattle operation with 250 head, so ingratiated himself to Whigham that it was not difficult to see through his motives. Twitty wrote Whigham, "Such conduct [settler resistance] is deserving of the utmost contempt and will ultimately bring disaster upon themselves. I am sorry to hear of this state of affairs because it reflects upon the character and jeopardizes the interest of others on the range." [29] In the face of these "sellouts," tensions started mounting as settlers began taking sides instead of presenting a united front as they had when the company first arrived. A decade earlier, during the Colfax County skirmish, the anti-grant faction feared Hispano collusion with the company, but by the late 1880s the grant's Hispanos were among the grant's most vocal opponents.

The company's prejudicial treatment of Hispanos left them few alternatives, while Anglo settlers had more room to maneuver with the company's agents.

The narrative of resistance and compromise most often has been presented as a contest mainly between men and the company, with women rarely appearing as independent actors. While few women wrote directly to the company's managers asking for relief or to make a business proposition, some did seek to preserve their homes and families despite the "principles" at hand. Even though her husband worked as an anti-grant leader, Mrs. C. B. Ladd, whose family ran five thousand head of sheep in the Vermejo Valley, wanted to purchase land from the company. Her husband's own turn against the company had come recently as he had been one of the representatives who had negotiated the settlement with Pels and Whigham a year earlier. Mrs. Ladd's purchase was to be on her own account, and she insisted to Whigham that her husband not know, as he would have opposed the transaction. Mrs. Ladd, fearing that eventually they would lose their land to the company and be left homeless, wanted to secure a home that would not be affected by the outcome of the lawsuit. Using her own money, Mrs. Ladd would purchase the land for the family's resettlement if that became necessary.[30] As a woman with independent means, Ladd willingly went behind her husband's back to ensure the family's financial stability.

Another woman, Mrs. L. R. Thomas, was left in dire straits when her husband was murdered in a land grant skirmish. Lacking the money to purchase her homestead outright from the company, she asked Whigham for mercy and leniency as she tried to make a living off the land. She was willing to settle with the company because she had few options, and she wanted Whigham to offer her generous terms for payments. She, however, was not beyond criticizing the company and chided him about the exorbitantly high prices that he charged for the land. She said, "When I wanted to sell it to Mormons I could not get over 100 dollars for it," and Whigham wanted her to pay almost twice that amount. Both of these women, as well as Marian Russell, who later legally fought the company all the way to the Supreme Court, sought to maintain their families' homesteads and keep their homes secure. Abstract principles of resistance held little appeal to these women, who knew what the consequences of ejection and homelessness could be for them in this desolate landscape.[31]

Authors such as Anne Hyde and Annette Kolodny have discussed how women often had more realistic perceptions of the landscape they encountered in the American West. While men tended to be overly optimistic about the land's potential and overly enthusiastic about the trip west, women often focused on the hard work and sacrifice it would take to get to the West and make the land profitable. Tamsen Donner, who was worried about the land's harshness as they left the main trail for the infamous Hastings Cutoff, was probably the wisest member of the Donner party.[32] This same cautious attitude appears in other examples as well. Although there are no recorded instances of women appearing at any of the violent encounters between the company and the settlers, in a number of cases women made compromises with Pels and Whigham. Arguably women could see beyond the conflict to what the future held for their families in this atmosphere of escalating hostility.

With men, however, Pels's strategy of talking individually with the settlers met with little success. Most resisted the company's attempts to have them peacefully leave the grant or purchase their ranches and farms. One particularly volatile anti-grant leader, F. B. Chaplan from Stonewall, refused even to respect the company's desire to negotiate with the settlers. Pels became disgusted with Chaplan's attitude and wrote him,

> I sent you word that I could be found at home this forenoon, and my messenger informs me that your reply was a very impolite one. I respect old age; I know that your case is a hard one; I have extended a friendly hand towards you in face of the action of the government in olden times; but the Maxwell company insists to be recognized, . . . and I wish to be treated as a gentleman.[33]

Chaplan, however, never acquiesced to Pels's requests, never acted politely to company agents, and the following year was one of the anti-grant leaders at the Stonewall Valley confrontation.

By the summer of 1887 the future looked particularly gloomy for Pels. The settlers knew of the case pending before the U.S. Supreme Court, and they held out hope that the final decision would bring them relief from the company's incessant demands. Pels seems to have sensed the violence that was to follow within the year. On July 18, 1887, he wrote a long letter to the committee in Amsterdam, complaining about the status of his projects on the grant. The settlers refused to lease grazing land for only a year because they felt it would take them that long just to round up and count their stock. Some were willing to lease for five years, but Pels refused because he wanted the land cleared of the settlers' cattle so that the company could take control of the range as soon as possible. Most of the settlers felt that the rent of fifty cents per head was too expensive, and they refused to sign agreements with Pels. Moreover, settlers such as Chaplan began using violence against the company agents. Pels complained, "When I went there [the Maxwell estate] everything was in a state of disturbance; people were fully ready to fight anyhow, and when Mr. Whigham went up to the settlers at the river Vermejo, he was awaited there by a body of armed men who intended to hold him up to have an explanation." [34] Pels feared that the surliness and stubbornness of the inhabitants would finally lead to a violent confrontation.

After Pels voiced his concerns to the committee, he became anxious and almost paranoid about the settlers' movements and actions. The settlers had whittled away at Pels's patience and forbearance, and as the stalemate between the two sides dragged on, Pels became openly hostile to the settlers. To his agent in the Stonewall Valley area, Henry Bowlden, he cautioned, "I do not believe that these people are so well satisfied with the way I dealt with them as you supposed. My informations are [sic] rather to the contrary, and I am prepared for some trickery. I do not expect any recognition of the liberal way in which I treated them." By early autumn of 1887, Pels feared that the settlers were not merely unhappy, but also ready to openly revolt. He wrote to his agent in Cimarron, J. D. Dawson, "Advises [sic] from the grant show that there is a source of organized conspiracy, and that the people mean war. If they want war they can have it. It seems that it is no good to be kind and conciliatory to people, but they prefer to throw in their own window glasses." [35] Despite the awkward metaphor, Pels believed that he had acted in good faith with the settlers, but he never truly understood the settlers' position. He did not understand that for them his "negotiations" were not merely business deals. Instead Pels's demands, as they saw them, involved the well-being of their families and in many instances meant either leaving the land they had lived on for generations or paying for something that they had always believed belonged to them.

Although Pels could not understand the complexity of their resistance, he did not deny its effectiveness in preventing the company from controlling the grant. He continued, "If this feeling prevails and the excitement extends, I think it would be foolishness to buy any cattle at all since every man on the grant will steal or kill the cattle belonging to my company, at least in the mountains." [36] By ignoring Pels's entreaties to negotiate and using guerrilla tactics such as killing company livestock and attacking company agents, the settlers had effectively brought the company's business to a standstill. During the mid-1880s the company conducted very little business in terms of settling new immigrants, removing squatters, or selling stocks and bonds. The settlers' effective tactics had cost the company dearly. In the face of these problems, Pels had to devise other strategies to surmount the obstacles to his dream of a Dutch colony.

In 1887 Pels initiated a new tactic aimed at getting the squatters to finally negotiate their removal or purchase their land. Instead of treating the settlers and squatters as one coherent group, Pels began to talk about them in terms of their differences. More importantly, Pels began to treat the settlers differently based on their status as property owners and their ethnicity. In fact, by the end of the century Pels's policy became imbedded in the cultural and social landscape of the grant as propertylessness became directly tied to Mexican-ness. Pels pursued a divide-and-conquer strategy by trying to keep the Anglos and Hispanos from working together. Thomas O. Boggs, a company agent under Pels, visited the Anglo settlements alone, while Jesús Silva, a squatter who had earlier settled his property dispute with the company, visited the Hispano communities. As Pels noted, "He being a Mexican the Americans will pay but little attention to him." If, however, the Anglos saw Boggs visiting the Hispano settlers, then they would know something was going on. Under Harry Whigham's supervision, Boggs and Silva pursued this tactic of dealing with the "Mexicans" and "Americans" separately. Whigham planned a meeting of the Vermejo Hispanos for December 10, 1887, and wanted Silva to make sure that the "leading Mexicans of the upper Vermejo come down to Pedro Chávez's at whose house we will hold the meeting." Whigham also cautioned Silva to remain as anonymous as possible: "I want you to keep there amongst the Poñil Mexicans. I want you to work the matter quietly, I would prefer not to have any American present at the meeting." The conference apparently brought no satisfactory solution because within two weeks Boggs complained of his treatment by the Mexicans: "I get a good deal of abuse but I can stand it as I generally talk them out of the most of it and leave them friendly."[37]

The settlers, however, also met within their own ethnic communities in an effort to take action against the company's influence. The Hispanos were particularly active in terms of seeking redress from the federal government. Boggs reported, "I hear there was a large meeting on the Poñil a few days ago getting up a petition to Congress and there will be one in the upper Vermejo in a few days for the same purpose." Mexican Americans found their own leadership and pursued their own legal course of action quite separate from Anglo agitators such as the Reverend O. P. McMains, who since the Reverend Tolby's death and the Colfax County "War" had been publicly confronting the company.[38] Boggs went on, "I find by inquiring, that one Tenduro Vigil is an influential man in that part and is a Mexican lawyer. I will visit him this trip as he sent word to me to be sure and call on him."[39] The Hispano settlers, who were sure that they were not getting a fair deal from the company, sought relief from Congress, the secretary of the interior, and even the president himself.

On November 19, 1887, Ignacio López and five other Hispano men wrote to President Grover Cleveland asking him for help. They told Cleveland that two-thirds of the one thousand families on the grant were "Hijos de la Tierra" (Children of the Land), or Mexicans, who had lived and owned property on the grant "for eleven years and up." They asked Cleveland to personally write and tell them their legal rights with regard to the grant, believing that once Cleveland knew about their plight, he would assure them of their place on the land. They hoped that armed with a letter from the president, they could then persuade the company's agents to leave them alone. Hispanos were not helpless or passive in their attempts to secure their rights: they knew enough to petition the government directly for clarification and not rely solely on the company's interpretation of their rights. They were, however, naive to believe that relief might come directly from the government, particularly the president of the United States.[40]

## CHARTING ANGLO/HISPANO ECONOMIC DISPARITY

Despite their appeals to the federal government, Hispano settlers still had to negotiate directly with company agents who were prejudiced against them and saw no reason for them to remain on the grant. Although Pels and Whigham wanted all Hispano squatters and settlers off the grant, they were unwilling to pay what the Hispanos thought they deserved for the improvements they had made to their land. Whigham wrote Boggs, "You know as well as I that whatever improvements the Mexicans put on are of very little use to us or to anybody acquiring their property later." The company agents did not like aesthetically or understand environmentally the value of the Hispanos' adobe structures, both homes and barns. Instead the company's agents preferred the wood, A-frame structures erected by the Anglos. Consequently, the agents tended to place greater value on Anglo improvements and paid higher prices for them (see table 1). After cautioning Boggs about the low value of Hispano improvements, Whigham left Boggs to "determine in every case whether such improvement will have any permanent value to us."[41] But while "permanent value" seemed perfectly obvious and indisputable to Boggs and Whigham, the Hispanos had entirely different notions about what was valuable. In most cases, Boggs assigned low assessments to Hispano property and made insulting cash offers to the owners.

Table 1. Maxwell Land Grant Company's Valuation of Settlers' Property
on the Grant, 1887

|  | Anglo | Hispano | Total |
|---|---|---|---|
| Number of settlers | 256 | 296 | 552 |
| Settlers with assessed property | 179 | 249 | 428 |
| Average years of tenure | 2.79 | 6.68 | 4.74 |
| Total value of improvements | $75,852 | $40,497 | $116,349 |
| Average value | $424 | $163 | $294 |
| Average acres farmed | 33.34 | 39.41 | 36.38 |
| Average acres irrigated | 21.85 | 41.57 | 31.71 |
| Average number of cattle | 308 | 10 | 159 |
| Average number of sheep | 34 | 38 | 36 |
| Average yards of fence | 1,646 | 458 | 1,052 |

SOURCE:  Settlers Book, March 1887, item 149.5, Maxwell Land Grant Company Papers.

By analyzing the Settlers Book, which was the company's private record of each and every settler's holdings, it appears that the company valued fencing more than any other type of improvement. Although Hispanos possessed larger farms on average, lived on them longer (thus making more improvements), and tended to irrigate more acres, they received on average about one-third the evaluation that Anglos received from the company (see table 1). In most of the other categories—such as types of crops and the number of goats and sheep—no pattern emerged regarding ownership and ethnicity. The three variables, however, that do account for a discrepancy in valuations between the two ethnic groups are: (1) acres fenced, (2) yards of fence, and (3) number of cattle. Anglos had more than four times the number of acres fenced (an average of 88.21 acres versus 21.13) and almost four times as much fencing (an average of 1645.96 yards versus 457.81). Anglos, on average, also tended to have over thirty times the number of cattle that Hispanos had (308 versus 10).[42]

One explanation for the discrepancies can be found by comparing how the groups used land and viewed property rights. The company and its agents placed a premium on fencing, the most visible indication of private property. Only a fence can accurately mark the difference between land that looks remarkably similar, but which possesses different owners. For a company that was absolutely consumed by legally marking and protecting its perimeter, and surveying and selling square plots within the grant, fencing was obviously the most valuable improvement that a settler could make.

Hispanos, on the other hand, possessed the historical perspective of living under a different property regime that valued communal property. They had shared plazas, which served as a common square for public functions during the day and a place for grazing livestock at night. They shared the region's limited water resources by farming *varas* (long strips of land along a river) rather than abiding by survey-created squares. As a group, they also had probably lived on, or at least knew of, community land grants dating back to the period of Mexican government. For the most part, they viewed fences as unnecessary given the communal way they had used property. Furthermore, fences were considered wasteful in an environment that possessed relatively few trees.[43]

This difference between conceptions of private property not only explains the discrepancies in the company's improvement valuations, but also helps to explain overall economic disparity in terms of who was participating in the market economy. While Anglos and Hispanos possessed nearly the same number of sheep, Anglos had thirty times the number of cattle (an average of 308 to compared to 10 for Hispanos). While Anglos became enmeshed in the growing cattle market created by the Maxwell Company, Hispanos tended to keep cattle more for subsistence. Ten cattle would allow a family to keep a small herd for their personal use, barter with their neighbors, and perhaps allow them to sell one or two cows a year. Such small herds, however, probably precluded them from engaging in the cattle market full-time. Anglos, on the other hand, were already taking advantage of their proximity to the railroad and their ability to supply distant markets in Chicago, St. Louis, and Kansas City.[44]

The Maxwell Land Grant Cattle Company, a subsidiary of the parent company, was run for most of the 1880s by the company's lawyer Frank Springer. The cattle company sold separate bonds and shares and was run as a separate enterprise that, for the most part, did much better financially than the parent corporation. Consequently, Springer spent a considerable amount of time negotiating with the company's directors over who controlled the profits. The Dutch directors were eagerly selling cattle company bonds and stocks on the European market, but were slow to send the proceeds to Springer, who needed the cash to purchase more cattle as well as to pay off debt he had incurred from previous purchases. Springer, like Pels, faced the problems associated with running such an extended enterprise and spent most of his time haggling for funds from the Dutch corporation. Springer's other main concern was running the day-to-day operations of

Table 2. Maxwell Land Grant Company's Valuation of Settlers' Property on
the Vermejo River, 1887

|                             | Anglo    | Hispano | Total    |
| --------------------------- | -------- | ------- | -------- |
| Number of settlers          | 33       | 66      | 99       |
| Total value of improvements | $15,375  | $9,325  | $24,700  |
| Average value               | $466     | $141    | $304     |
| Average acres farmed        | 51       | 37      | 44       |
| Average acres irrigated     | 49       | 38      | 44       |
| Average yards fenced        | 3,083    | 770     | 1,927    |
| Average number of cattle    | 157      | 38      | 98       |

SOURCE: Settlers Book, March 1887, item 149.5, Maxwell Land Grant Company Papers.

the cattle business. When he wasn't struggling to find cash, he was busy negotiating good rates from the railroad so that he could ship the cattle east.
Springer not only sold the company's cattle but also acted as a broker to
other ranchers on the grant who used the Maxwell Cattle Company as an
agent for the sale of their livestock.[45]

Economic discrepancies based on ethnicity, as indicated by the cattle example, remain the same even if we control for location on the grant. By the
1880s Anglos were beginning to occupy the most fertile and valuable portions of the grant, while Hispanos were occupying fewer and fewer acres.
Nevertheless, in a number of grant locations, such as Vermejo Park, Poñil
Park, and the Stonewall Valley, Hispanos maintained strongholds. In the
Vermejo area, we see that the pattern of economic disparity remains the
same, although the differences are somewhat less dramatic (see table 2).
The Vermejo, which is today one of the homes of media mogul Ted Turner,
was one of the most fertile areas on the grant and sits just at the foot of the
Sangre de Cristo Mountains. Although it is now home to Turner's buffalo
ranch, it was one of the most valuable cattle grazing areas in New Mexico
well into the twentieth century. According to company records, the value
of improvements for Anglos in the Vermejo was on average more than
three times the value of improvements made by their Hispano neighbors
(an average of $466 versus $141). Despite the fact that both groups shared
an equally valuable land resource base, the decisive factor again was the
amount of fencing (an average of 3,083 yards for Anglos versus 770 for
Hispanos) and the number of cattle (an average of 157 for Anglos versus 38
per Hispano family). Although these Hispanos lived in one of the most

fertile areas of the grant, ran three times more cattle than their Hispano counterparts on the rest of the grant, and lived in what would eventually become one of the prime cattle-producing areas, they still did not engage in large-scale ranching.

The reason for discrepancies between Anglo and Hispano participation in the Maxwell Company's cattle industry can be explained in terms of who had access to cash and land. Cattle ranching required capital to purchase or produce a herd. Because the company did not run a *partido* system of loaning livestock to individuals, as Maxwell did, the only way a local rancher could acquire a herd was through outright purchase of livestock, which took cash, or increasing the herd through births, which took large parcels of land with exceptionally good feed. Furthermore, given company prejudice toward the Hispanos, it was unlikely that they could acquire favorable credit terms on which to make livestock purchases, and few other sources could loan such large amounts of money. Although Hispanos tended to live along the rich river bottoms, as indicated by the fact that they had more irrigated acres, they still possessed, on average, smaller landholdings. The land use pattern that had begun when they settled under Maxwell's tutelage maintained itself well into the 1880s. While this pattern worked well for a family that was farming and ranching only to meet subsistence and barter demands, it did not allow for the flexibility of engaging in the market. For them to enter the market, they would need more land, and for more land, they needed cash or credit to purchase it from the company.

Here it is interesting to compare the Maxwell Company with Frank Bond and his company, which was located on the western side of the Sangre de Cristo Mountains in the Española Valley. Bond ran a modified *partido* system in which he loaned sheep out to local Hispano shepherds throughout New Mexico and into the San Luis Valley of southern Colorado. The shepherds agreed to terms about how many sheep to return at the of the contract, which could run anywhere from one to five years. For example, a shepherd might agree to take 100 sheep and return 150 at the end of two seasons. Any surplus livestock (over the 150) belonged to the Hispano shepherd free and clear, but if there was a shortfall, he would be indebted to Bond. The shepherd bore the entire risk—including bad weather, poor feed, and disease—of the enterprise. Furthermore, Bond also controlled access to the local railroad, the Chili line, and consequently to the outside wool market. Most of the wool produced in the region was bought and sold through his mercantile store in Española. The store also sold basic goods and allowed purchases on credit, which was essential to the region's cash-poor Hispanos.[46]

Bond's financially successful amalgamation of the market economy with the old Hispano practices of *partido* and *patronismo* should have been a lesson for the fledgling Maxwell Company. Bond became a successful businessman because he understood the way Hispanos in the region had done business prior to the arrival of larger capitalist markets. He adapted his own enterprise to fit in with existing ways of doing business, and because of his access to the outside world, he was able to control the emerging markets. Bond's flexibility, compared with the intransigence of the Maxwell Company, reveals how much its inflexibility cost the company's coffers. The settlers and squatters had obviously been willing to negotiate with Pels in the early days, but as the company's failure to adapt to their new environment became apparent, the stalemate continued. The stalemate also led to immense amounts of hostility, which played out in term of ethnic differences that eventually led to violence.

Despite the cultural gulfs separating Anglo from Hispano and settler from manager, Harry Whigham and M. P. Pels thought they had been more than generous. Whigham believed the squatters had lived there for "many years, paying nothing for farming, grazing, etc., and paying no taxes at all, and we have the right to some income from those lands at last." Whigham remained ignorant and saw no prejudice in his condescending attitude when he wrote to Boggs, "You can allow the privilege of keeping a few head of goats, burros, milk cows, horses and oxen on their places, provided they run them within their fence and not outside." The company slowly encroached upon the land of the Hispanos, who depended on small parcels and a few head of livestock for their livelihood. After this "fencing-in," it was only a matter of time before the company exacted a lease from them or removed them from the grant. Whigham concluded his letter to Boggs, "If they follow on your instruction and become thrifty farmers who want to do some good work in the future, and bring in some profit to the company instead of following their usual and indifferent ways," then they would be allowed to stay on the grant and continue paying rent.[47]

## THE COMPANY TAKES MORE AGGRESSIVE ACTION

Since the personal appeals of Pels, Whigham, and Boggs did not move the majority of the settlers and, in most cases, only further antagonized the squatters and settlers, Pels turned to more-insidious methods to ensure compliance or outright removal. Pels was the first manager to realize that if he acted more like a *patrón* and less like a corporate manager, then he might make progress with the settlers. Pels instituted a plan that allowed the squatters to lease their land for five years at below-market rates and pay rent much as they had done under Maxwell; some were allowed to pay in-kind rather than in cash. Unknown to the settlers, however, Pels's plan was designed to evict them in the long run. First, by signing a lease with the company, the squatter implicitly recognized the right of the company to own the land and initiate leases, therefore making it difficult for the lessee at the end of the five years to claim ownership of the land. Second, the company had no intention of renewing the lease once it expired, and the un-suspecting lessees would be removed with no hope of legal recourse against the company. In case the squatter was unsure about embracing Pels's offer, the company enhanced the temptation to sign a lease by offering low rent, in some cases actually lower than what they had been paying to Maxwell.[48]

The company also discouraged permanent settlement by selling only large plots that conformed to the surveyor's township lines on the plat ap-proved by Congress. Whigham wrote to Boggs, "We are not, however, in-clined to sell to every Mexican a patch of five, six, ten or twenty acres, as he is occupying now, and mostly laid out in an irregular line or form." Whigham pointed out that the company adamantly refused to recognize the pattern of prior land ownership and would force the squatters to com-ply with the new land regime. He continued, "If a few people want to buy we will send up our surveyor to run the township lines, and they have then to buy the land in sections of forty, sixty or more acres, laid out in regular blocks as above described."[49] By Whigham's standards this was a generous offer. He was willing to let them purchase an increment smaller than the standard 160-acre homestead, but he would not go lower than 40 acres, which was beyond the financial means of most Hispanos in the area. The Hispanos who had lived on the grant under Maxwell's tenure had estab-lished their farms and homes along the various rivers and water sources with an eye toward irrigating the farms with relative ease and little in-vestment for infrastructure. They also tended to cultivate only enough land to meet the subsistence needs of their family as well as their payment to Maxwell, and they did not want to move onto a surveyed lot that was most likely a good distance away from the river.

These settlements, which were based on Maxwell's hacienda model, were far too haphazard for the company managers' tastes, which demanded the surveyor's geometrical pattern to better keep track of land ownership and rentals. Company policy reflected the belief that this land venture would profit only if the inhabitants lived in specific squares with specific delineated rights. But the company's intransigence threatened its financial solvency, as it aggravated the settlers and induced them to act just as stubbornly. The company, too concerned with immediate profits and ensuring its legal rights, failed to see that in the long run the settler resistance cost time and profits. This standoff merely paved the way for future violence on the grant.

The company agents' prejudice against the squatters never allowed them to consider a less rigid course, and they specifically singled out Hispanos as lazy and poor tenants. One company report noted, "With a few exceptions Mexicans cultivate the valleys. Modern methods of tilling the land conducted by more active white people, would no doubt increase the yield."[50] The agents saw the Hispanos' subsistence farming and lack of infrastructure as somehow indicative of their work ethic and moral character. They also had no desire to incorporate the prior settlers into their enterprise and stubbornly intended on replacing them as soon as possible with "more active white people." This, however, was not going to be easy, as Hispano settlers would not move easily. Boggs commented that "the hard headedness of the people is beyond all comprehension." He simply could not understand why, in the face of the company's determination to run them off, they simply would not go away. Instead, the Hispanos constantly harassed him as he went about company business. While they were not menacing, he still found their threats unsettling. He wrote, "No one to my knowledge has made any threats or troubled me in any way only in slang Spanish words but this does not hurt."[51]

The company agents also feared what they perceived as the clannishness of the Hispanos and realized that they would fight to keep the company from putting new settlers on their land. One agent complained "of the secret [Mexican] organizations which deligate [sic] and designate men to shut off water, destroy ditches, and fences, steal horses and cattle, and commit continuous injury in such an extent that some of the best men had to leave and abandon their ranches."[52] A few years before Las Gorras Blancas, the white-capped night riders who cut fences and burned railroad property, even rode through the area, Hispanos were already organizing guerrilla-type activities to keep Anglo interlopers at bay. Moreover, the company's agents viewed the Hispano squatters as a dangerous horde. They rarely dealt with them on individual terms and instead wanted to run them off the grant as a group. The agents were anxious to be rid of the Hispanos rather than sell land to them and hope that they would turn into the thrifty, industrious grant farmers the company desired. Their fear, in the end, made them incapable of coming to a peaceful settlement.

Company prejudice was not reserved solely for the Hispanos. Although not quite as severely, the company also criticized Anglo settlers. Pels wrote,

"Nearly 2/3rds of the squatters on the Grant are Confederate Missourians, old bushwackers, lazy farmers, spending their time in sitting on the fence smoking a corn-cob and cursing the grant." In some ways Pels regarded the Anglos, particularly the ones from the Eastern states, as particularly difficult because many of them held homestead patents or, at the very least, understood enough about their property rights to make Pels's job more difficult. In the end, of course, Pels hoped to eliminate both the Hispanos and Anglos and replace them with European immigrant farmers. He continued, "I now think if I could get rid of this element, . . . this would be a very desirable move and give room to have their places filled by industrious new farmers. It would thus create a new and better element on the grant."[53] Twenty years later, however, the Maxwell Land Grant Company ironically would tout the grant's multicultural nature in its promotional literature: "Though coming from various states in the Union, different parts of Europe and Mexico, together with the native population, its inhabitants are yet as homogeneous a class of people as can be found anywhere between the Atlantic and Pacific Oceans, they being industrious, thrifty, and progressive."[54] In the late 1880s, the company's agents would have never used words such as "thrifty and progressive" to describe either the Anglos or the Hispanos. They and the directors continued to dream of an unattainable Dutch colony in northern New Mexico filled with European farmers who would work for the company and neither complain nor ask for private property rights. The Dutch colony, however, was doomed to fail given the recalcitrance of both sides and their failure to negotiate.

What hurt Pels's negotiations most was the distance between the Amsterdam management, who made policy without a clear understanding of the situation, and New Mexico, where the actual problems with settler resistance occurred. More than once Pels had convinced settlers to recognize the company's rights, move off the grant, and sell their livestock and improvements, only to have his efforts impeded by the financiers in Amsterdam. One particular instance in 1887 probably sent the settlers over the edge and forced them to directly confront the company. Pels had convinced a very large group of settlers to sell their cattle herds to the company. Chutes were built, and the ranchers had begun the difficult task of rounding up the stock from the open range. Quite unexpectedly, however, the Amsterdam committee sent a telegram to Pels telling him to delay purchases until the directors had considered the matter further. Angry and frustrated, Pels warned the committee that a "lost opportunity never comes back. Sherwin had splendid opportunities too, but he also lost them." This was a bold reference for Pels, who had been called in to replace the incompetent Sherwin, and revealed that he, too, was beginning to understand the difficulty of running the grant with the Amsterdam committee controlling the finances. Finally, after two months' delay, the committee wired Pels $50,000 for the purchases.[55] The effort was too little, too late, however, as Pels needed six times that amount to purchase all the cattle he had contracted for with the settlers. Sent away angry and bitter at Pels's unkept promises, the settlers became even more recalcitrant. From the settlers' point of view, it was obvious that there was just no dealing with the company or with Pels. They had little choice but to quietly move off the grant with little hope of receiving any cash payment from Pels—or they could fight.

Just prior to the Stonewall Valley violence, Pels became particularly concerned with the lack of coordination among the Amsterdam committee, the board of trustees in New York, and the grant managers in Cimarron, New Mexico. He demanded that the Amsterdam committee give him a freer hand in dealing with the problems of the grant: "You must approve beforehand all I do, and can discharge me if I don't do it well, but I must be able to act when once there—Trustees or not—these are no times to be afraid of burning our hands in cold water."[56] Pels did not wait for their answer and took matters into his own hands as he negotiated with the few willing settlers, but the board of trustees and the Amsterdam committee later rebuked Pels for handling the situation on his own.

Pels subsequently wrote a letter explaining the difficulties of managing such a situation: "I will be glad as always to see you on the Grant," implying, of course, that he had never seen them on the grant and that they should have more trust in his firsthand knowledge. He went on, "Whereas I am informing you of everything that is going on here in the matter of the settler trouble. I should wish very much that you should have outlined to me what steps you intend to make in this matter, as it is most desirable to act harmoniously, especially as it is impossible to give you the whole history of the settlers in writing this being a most complicated business."[57] Pels felt that he was doing the best he could given the difficult situation, and that the least they could do was back him up in his decisions. In these few sentences Pels outlined the major problems with running any enterprise on the periphery from the comfortable distance of New York or Amsterdam. Pels, Whigham, and Boggs believed that they had done everything humanly possible to find a peaceful solution to the settlers' complaints. The three recognized that the situation was very volatile and that the angry settlers and uneasy company agents were on the brink of war. The directors and trustees, most of whom had never set foot on the grant, thought differently, however, and sought to impose their own ideas about how company affairs should be administered. Given that the local grant agents were just beginning to understand the ethnic, social, and political dynamics of the grant, it was no surprise that outsiders were even less sympathetic to the grant agents' difficult position, much less to the settlers' desperate situation.

The same squabbling and lack of policy coordination between the company and its local managers that had disrupted the stability of the settlers and squatters also negatively affected the company's financial welfare. In that same letter to the board of trustees, Pels informed them that a large sale had fallen through because of investor concerns over the instability of the grant's future. Pels wrote, "The St. Louis parties who have been considering the purchase of the Vermejo lands write me under date of the 11th to say that owing to the many difficulties that appear to attend investment on the Maxwell Grant having reference to the land, they do not think it advisable to continue negotiations further."[58] Although the company had never thrived financially, by 1888 it was in such serious turmoil that bankruptcy was often mentioned. The constant efforts to visit and negotiate with settlers had been a drain on the company's finances and had taken its toll. Also, the Supreme Court had just heard arguments on both sides of *U.S. v. Maxwell Land Grant* and would soon decide the grant's boundaries once and for all. Thus all efforts at negotiation on the grant came to a virtual standstill. In such a transnational enterprise, where the European directors constantly battled directly with its colonial managers and indirectly with the colonials themselves for control over the periphery's natural resources, the cost of that struggle in terms of lives, money, and lost opportunities was borne, even if unequally, by both sides. While the company suffered financial setbacks and losses, the grant's inhabitants bore the majority of the costs in the company's attempts to take control.

Pels's renewed efforts at filing ejection suits only further fueled the flames of resistance. On the Colorado portion of the grant, the company's managers were particularly interested in ridding the grant of the long-time resident Hispanos. In the first part of 1887, the company sued twenty-three people for ejection; of these, sixteen were Hispanos from the South Fork of the Las Animas River and the San Francisco Valley, both of which had been centers of resistance to the company's policies.[59] The company's managers also wanted to rid this same Colorado portion of the anti-grant leaders and filed ejection suits in the Third District Court of Colorado against F. B. Chaplan, Richard D. Russell, and José Luis Torres. Of Chaplan and Russell, Pels complained that he had treated them fairly, but they were "for Colorado what McMains is for New Mexico, one of the leaders, and have to be managed with a firm hand." Pels feared Torres because he was one of the

Hispanos with the most land, and Hispanos looked to him for leadership. In the case against Russell, the company sued for possession of the land, three thousand dollars in damages, back rent from April 1868, and a temporary injunction against further improving his land.[60] It was a suit that left little room for compromise.

Although the Maxwell Land Grant lay within two different political boundaries, the state of Colorado and the territory of New Mexico, the inhabitants and company managers thought of it as one unit and virtually ignored the political or legal significance of the boundary. For example, although the Supreme Court case affected only the Colorado portion of the grant, company agents and settlers acted as if it would determine boundaries for the whole grant. Furthermore, violence on one portion of the grant did not mean it was an isolated incident, but usually reflected unrest throughout the grant. Here was a case where outsiders could easily mark theoretically significant political lines, but where the day-to-day inhabitants ignored such marks and instead saw the space as a culturally, socially, and environmentally cohesive place. Thus when tensions began to mount on the northern (Colorado) portion of the grant, they reflected the very local problems but also indicated the future unrest that would sweep across the land grant.

The company's managers, exasperated with the situation, were tired of chasing after the settlers to make them accept the company's position. Harry Whigham declared his ultimatum to T. O. Boggs at the end of 1887: "They [the settlers] have to settle in writing before January first, and any man who has not come in by that time will be proceeded against in court." Whigham, weary of hearing the settlers' excuses, did not believe their declarations of poverty. Settlers often claimed they were cash poor and could not purchase their land. While this was probably true to some extent, they also intentionally exaggerated their financial situation to put off the agents. Whigham continued, "They have had plenty of time to make up their minds, and when they can collect money to pay McMains they do not seem to be so very poor after all. As to buying their lands, we do not object to this and will make the payments as reasonable as possible." Whigham's letter revealed his exhaustion and the company's inability to continue losing time and money. In the last months before the Stonewall Valley violence, he even softened his position and showed some willingness to compromise on terms and create payment plans, at 7 percent interest, acceptable to the settlers.[61]

Even the more flexible terms, however, could not persuade some of the settlers, such as F. B. Chaplan, to vacate their claims. Others, however, had settled with Pels and Whigham only to have the company's directors cancel their contracts. In the case of Richard Russell, the directors became concerned over the amount of money Pels wanted to pay Russell for his large ranch, and they canceled the contract. In March 1888 the company again filed suit against Chaplan and Russell. Pels, however, took a new tactic in trying to divide the settlers. Pels instructed the lawyers to use settlers who had made their peace with the company as witnesses to testify against the troublemakers who still refused to recognize the company's claims. In the cases against Chaplan and Russell, the company called E. J. Randolf, another Stonewall Valley resident who was now working for the company, to testify that the land did not belong to either Chaplan or Russell but was the sole property of the company. What legal effect Randolf's testimony had is unclear, but Randolf's appearance indicated the divisions that were beginning to arise within the settlers' ranks. After his testimony, Randolf and his family found living in the valley difficult, if not dangerous. By the end of the summer their lives had been threatened by masked men and their house had been burned down, setting off the Stonewall Valley battle.[62]

The company's directors also decided to supplement judicial remedies with their political clout. They asked Colorado governor Alva Adams for a change of venue in the ejection suits, complaining that the Trinidad newspaper, the *Daily Citizen*, and many citizens were so prejudiced against the company that it could not receive a fair trial in Trinidad. The petition claimed "that there are a number of settlers on said grant who are industriously circulating reports prejudicial to the plaintiff and denouncing the plaintiff as an avaricious and unjust corporation and that it is attempting to rob the settler of the land upon said grant." The petition concluded that no jury could be found who was not prejudiced against the company, and therefore the suits had to be removed to another jurisdiction. Governor Adams agreed and had suits moved to Denver, which meant settlers had to travel more than three hundred miles to defend themselves against the company. Governor Adams's interest, however, was more than gubernatorial: he had recently purchased interest in a syndicate that ran a resort at the Pooler Hotel in Stonewall, Colorado. He, too, may have been anxious to remove the settlers and make a profit on his new investment.[63]

## LOCAL INFLUENCE, LOCAL CORRUPTION

The settlers and squatters had to face not only the company's threats by traveling back and forth to Denver for court hearings, but also the company's influence within the local bureaucracies. In the early months of 1887, Harry Whigham took up the final strategy the company would use to remove the settlers. He hired D. F. Wilkens, the Las Animas County assessor, to traverse the Colorado portion of the Maxwell Land Grant and personally report back to him the dollar value of improvements as well as the number of cattle, sheep, and horses that the various settlers and squatters possessed. Wilkens conducted his survey under the pretext of official county work, but he was paid directly by Whigham, and the results were solely for the use of the Maxwell Land Grant Company in its efforts to purchase the settlers' improvements.[64] Whigham had finally resorted to bribing Wilkens, a government employee, because the settlers had been refusing to let grant agents onto their property and shooting at any of them who dared.

Wilkens, like the company's agents, also encountered suspicion and hostility among the settlers as he made his survey of the homesteads. In addition to his constant complaining about the weather and the disagreeable conditions under which he worked, Wilkens wrote to Whigham, "I have had some difficulty with some of the Mexicans as well as with some of the Americans. I must say that I have been treated very shabby in some places. . . . Half of the people would not invite me into their houses. Have had to do the best that I could . . . but never the less [sic] I have obtained the information sought." Apparently, the Colorado settlers suspected that Wilkens was not merely working for the county assessor and were unwilling to let him survey their property. Wilkens realized their suspicions and warned Whigham that everyone on the northern portion of the grant "damns the grant, and every body [sic] that works for it."[65]

Despite the settlers' unwillingness to cooperate, Wilkens managed to obtain the information he needed. He enclosed a survey of the houses he covered with a list of the monetary value of the improvements and the number of cattle, horses, goats, and sheep. Wilkens also told Whigham, "You will doubtless be surprised at the no. of cattle and horses that pastured on the grant without paying revenue for the same."[66] Clearly Wilkens realized the intentions of the company's managers and how they planned to use the information he provided. Wilkens willingly and diligently pursued his task of spying for the Maxwell Land Grant Company under cover of his appointed office. Wilkens's assessments, however, probably did not accurately reveal the true value of the inhabitants' homes because few would answer his assessor's survey. He was forced to resort to intelligent guessing. He wrote to Whigham,

> I have [sic] hard work to get other homes. But have managed to get
> them all. By a little strategy I see what they have got, in the way of
> improvements, and place my value on it. Have to get the amount of
> farming land by guess, there is not one man so far that would give

the amount of stock. I have given up trying to get any account of them.[67]

Settler resistance was not always violent or even active. Merely refusing to assist the government's or grant company's investigation was an effective strategy. Wilkens complained to Whigham that the rumor of Wilkens's fraudulent assessment "has spread all down the river." He asked Whigham if and how he should proceed. Wilkens feared for his life as "mobs" came to greet him as he went about his surveying of the homesteads. He also continued to complain that no one would board him for the evening, and he was forced to sleep outside, sometimes in the rain. Wilkens howled most about the Hispanos of the northern portion of the grant and the vehemence with which they defended their homes and property. "It was the Archuleta family and their neighbors that wanted to assault me. Had I shone [sic] weakness they would have done so. They all demand to see my Commission for doing this work, I tell them that it is none of their business about my authority."[68] This clearly was not the answer that was going to get him out of trouble with the settlers. Now they knew for certain that he was working for the company and warned everyone to not cooperate with him.

In April 1887, Wilkens, tired and feeling that he had completed his work, wrote his last letter to Whigham stating the conditions for exchanging the information: "Should I be out of town when you come? Mr. Bright will be in the office and will give you the information desired. You can talk to Bright with confidence about any matter that may come up." Apparently Wilkens and Whigham wanted the relationship kept secret, or at the very least they did not want people to see them together. Aside from the settler problems, the other problem that plagued the company's financial situation was its lack of cash flow, and the biggest drain was the property taxes. Whigham, however, had been working on this problem as well. In the same letter Wilkens assured Whigham that he had attempted to fix the company's tax assessment at a lower rate: "The County Attorney and the Board desire me to assess the company in ten thousand acres of coal land at $5 per acre, the Stonewall and South Fork Land at $2.50 per acre, and the balance at $1.25. So you can see about how they feel. I may possibly fool them somewhat, when the time comes."[69] Wilkens's coziness with Whigham therefore benefited the company doubly. First, his information about the value of the settlers' improvements aided the company in its acquisitions. Second, by misinforming the local government about the value of the company's assets, the company could expect a lower tax bill. This would have been a welcome break for a company that had already been sold for back taxes once and had a limited cash flow. The company's collusion (through Whigham) with the local county government (through Wilkens) assured that it would receive an edge in its fight to expel the existing settlers.

## OPTIONS CLOSE AND TEMPERS FLARE

As the year wore on, the situation on the grant became more intense as a settlement seemed impossible and violence inevitable. Richard Russell was particularly desperate to see an end to the troubles. His failed negotiations with Pels had left him few options, and he did not want to lose his very valuable ranch and homestead. In March he wrote the secretary of the interior asking for relief. Russell portrayed the company as the encroacher onto the land of persecuted people who were helpless against such a large corporation, which harassed the settlers with impunity. Russell, however, also blamed the Department of the Interior for allowing the company to run roughshod over the public domain. Russell rightly pointed out that the General Land Office, through malfeasance or negligence, had allowed the company to survey and settle the Colorado portion of "the Maxwell tract without authority of the law." Russell believed that the San Francisco and Stonewall Valleys were "ten miles to the north of the land described in their deed" that Congress had used to patent the grant. The company simply had no business in this area, and, to make matters worse, they were establishing a resort at Stonewall. Russell went on to say that the company wrongfully possessed this land and had been "denuding the county of timber and using the proceeds to persecute the people." [70]

Two months later, Russell complained again to government officials in Washington and sought an unbiased examination of the situation. He wrote to T. J. Anderson, the assistant land commissioner, complaining once again about the Elkins/Marmon survey: "There are included in this survey 300,000 acres of government lands and my homested [sic] I well understand is also included." He complained that the issues surrounding the legality and extent of the survey should have been cleared up years ago because people had been living on these government-issued homesteads as if they were part of the public domain.

> I have put in 22 years to acquire this land [and] am now well advanced in years and have a large family. And if this is a reform administration and willing to undo the work of those who were in collusion with the land thieves they will investigate and find whether I have spoken truth. Send an honest agent and I will convince him beyond a doubt that what I assert is true.[71]

The General Land Office neither listened nor acted on Russell's plea, and a month later he was again writing to them for relief. He complained of what he saw as a "vast conspiracy organized in Santa Fe to rob the government of land." Russell, frustrated with the corruption and never-ending battle against the company, closed his last letter ever to the government: "The aggressions of said company are becoming unbearable and must be remedied. And as we ask but a lawfull [sic] remedy which is certainly within your power to grant and therefore your duty to."[72] Relief never came from the government for Russell and the other grant inhabitants, and as they sat and impatiently waited, tempers began to flare. Finally, Russell and the other settlers took matters into their own hands.

The situation became particularly volatile in the summer of 1888 when the company sold five thousand acres and the Pooler Hotel to twenty-four investors, including Colorado governor Alva Adams. They planned to open a resort that would offer a year-round retreat for fishing and hunting in the Stonewall Valley, and the sale required the immediate removal of the settlers and their livestock. A year earlier, despite the foot-dragging of the committee in Amsterdam, Pels had managed to buy cattle from several of the Stonewall settlers at twenty dollars per head. Prices in the spring of 1888 had fallen dramatically, however, and now Pels was willing to pay only fifteen dollars per head, with the calves included. This seeming unfairness further enraged the Colorado inhabitants, who again refused to deal with the company. Pels and Whigham, however, were anxious to see the resort open, and they took a "take it or leave it" attitude with the settlers. Pels was willing to bring the full weight of the company's influence and the law to bear against the settlers if they did not cooperate this time.[73]

Completely frustrated by the pressures from the new investors and the simultaneous lack of progress in dealing with the settlers, Pels wrote another agent about Boggs's incompetence: "I am afraid that Tom Boggs' trip to the Moreno Valley will cost us more than all the hay is worth. He is absolutely of no use, and has not the slightest ideas of the value of money, and draws checks like a drought horse. This is why I wrote him that he had to quit by the end of this month."[74] As far as Pels was concerned, he was tired of negotiating with the settlers and was ready to take more drastic steps. Just one week before the Stonewall Valley incident, Pels wrote to M. W. Mills, a company lawyer, telling him of the most recent troubles on the grant. The settlers had been cutting fences and "property and life of men who [were] in sympathy with grant [were] no longer safe." Settlers such as Russell and the López family had been begging for relief from

Washington, D.C. Pels felt that their most recent actions were meant to cause so much havoc that federal troops would have to be called onto the grant, therefore calling attention to the plight of these inhabitants.[75]

Pels wholeheartedly opposed calling in federal troops to bring a final conclusion to the settlers' resistance. He continued, "I pretend to have the right to travel unmolested over the grant; I cannot do so now, and unless protected by the court, I shall see that I will protect myself." Pels believed that the government could not be counted on to protect the company's rights, and he offered another solution: "We have money enough at our disposal, and I can get from Chicago five hundred to a thousand reliable well armed and trained men within three days time, and if bloodshed should follow, nobody else but the courts and the government will be to blame." Pels proposed hiring Pinkerton agents to "protect our property, to prevent our cattle from being killed, our houses and other property from being burnt, or other depredations committed to our property and that of our friends."[76] On August 16, 1888, just days before the Stonewall Valley battle, Thomas O'Neil rode into Stonewall looking for Cox or Russell in the hopes of "jumping" a company ranch for himself and his family. But Mr. O'Neil was not who he said he was, nor did he have a family: although Pels did not hire an army of Pinkerton agents, he did hire one.[77]

On the eve of the Stonewall Valley conflict, August 24, 1888, Pels wrote from Denver to his agent in Trinidad, "I have seen Mr. Hill, U.S. Marshall, this morning, and he will send up [to Stonewall] an energetic man to serve ejectment papers. He says that he is not afraid of that settlers movement, and if any trouble should arise he will go up there himself and find men enough without any assistance of the militia or troops to bring those settlers to terms, especially the white ones." The next day, probably as the skirmish in front of the Pooler Hotel was just beginning, Pels continued his letter:

> It is true that the expense will be large, but still we have to fight it out now within the limits of the law. Of course we will be resisted, and then it is a matter for the Sheriff, or if necessary for the government to take this matter up and see that the law is enforced. Even if those men are masked they will speak and it will not be dificult [sic] to detect the American leader amongst them which you know as well as I.[78]

Pels was willing to risk a violent confrontation with the settlers, which would then be a criminal matter the local authorities would have to deal with, whether they wanted to or not.

Pels had every reason to believe that the Trinidad sheriff, W. T. Burns, and the Las Animas County government supported the company 100 percent. On August 24, 1888, the day before fighting broke out, he wrote to the board of trustees in New York, "I found the sheriff there [Trinidad] a very good man, an intimate friend of Holdsworth [a company lawyer], and fully determined to do justice and if necessary to appeal to the Governor of Colorado." The sheriff, under the direction of Pels, would send six men, who were "excellent shots," to serve the ejection notices to the recalcitrant Colorado inhabitants in Stonewall. Pels also noted that the deputies "have been tried before when there were troubles in the mines of the Colorado Fuel and Iron Company."[79] Pels had also been assured by R. B. Holdsworth, the company agent in Trinidad, that the sheriff was reliable. That same day Holdsworth wrote to Pels, "I have just seen the deputy under sheriff Taylor, (Sheriff Burns is in Kansas City) and he also is a personal friend of mine, he has the warrants and says he will fetch his men at any cost. It pays to be on good terms with the officers and have them indebted to you for political favors, (of course don't mention this)."[80] The company had pursued the same policy of cajoling and bribing local law enforcement officials that it had used with the surveyors and county assessors. This time, however, the effect was more dramatic—and fatal—as the company and settlers clashed for the last time. Pels was determined to be rid of Chaplan, Russell, Torres, and other Colorado troublemakers one way or another, and he knowingly sent armed men to confront the settlers.

# 5 The Law of the Land
## U.S. v. Maxwell Land Grant Company

Why, after almost thirty years of covert resistance and subtle accommodation, were the settlers willing to confront the company agents at the Pooler Hotel on the morning of August 25, 1888? The settlers' unorganized opposition, pitted against the company's intransigence, had led to rising tempers and increased frustration, but conceivably the standoff could have continued for years without a decisive victory for either side. In the two decades since the company had taken over the land grant, neither group had been able to expel the other from the grant, and neither had ever gained a truly decisive advantage. The company continued to maintain financial solvency despite costly settler resistance, bankruptcy, and poor profits. The settlers, on the other hand, managed to live, if not thrive, on the grant despite the company's repeated covert and overt efforts to get rid of them.

Ironically, the event that finally brought the two groups into violent confrontation with each other arose out of an context entirely different than the one they had been living in on the grant. On April 18, 1887, a year before the battle at Stonewall, the U.S. Supreme Court handed down its decision in the matter of *U.S. v. Maxwell Land Grant and Railway Company*. The decision confirmed conclusively that the Maxwell Company possessed the legal right to 1.7 million acres of land in Colorado and New Mexico. With this legal affirmation of their property rights from the nation's highest court, the company's managers had the legal right to do with the land what they chose, but this legal right was a long way from their possessing the day-to-day right to use the land. Thus, in the year between the Supreme Court decision and the Stonewall battle, Pels and Whigham stepped up their efforts to remove the settlers. The company now had the law behind them, and there was no need to compromise or negotiate with the settlers.

This final decision came after five years of litigation that had begun in August 1882, when the U.S. government filed a lawsuit in federal district court seeking a declaratory judgment that the Maxwell Land Grant did not extend north of Colorado's southern boundary. Although the settlers followed the litigation with interest, the federal government's motive in filing this lawsuit was unrelated to the interests of the New Mexico settlers. The government simply wanted to ensure that the company's boundaries did not extend beyond the Colorado/New Mexico border, and that the contested territory in Colorado remained within the federal public domain. But the lawsuit provoked the most articulate and ambitious effort in the Court's history to reconcile Mexican and U.S. ideologies regarding land.

Following the district court's judgment in favor of the company, the federal government appealed to the U.S. Supreme Court, which issued another opinion in favor of the company that provided a detailed and revealing account of how Mexican law would be translated into American doctrine. The Court's opinion in *U.S. v. Maxwell Land Grant Company* was not completely coherent; indeed, it was self-contradictory. But its contradictions exposed deep divisions in not only the Court's own precedents, but also in the American conception of the public domain. These divisions went to the heart of the U.S. understanding of property and attempted to deal with the question of how the U.S. courts could enforce the Mexican conception of land law without undermining the republican system of property. In trying to resolve this dilemma, the Court papered over the contradictions inherent in U.S. land policy with a bewildering variety of legal doctrines—as if abstract legal reasoning could bridge the deep ideological cleft in the American mind-set. But in its efforts to integrate American and Mexican law, the Court created a hybrid that ideally suited the requirements of world capital. Indeed, the Court's legal reasoning facilitated the expansion of market capitalism into the American Southwest.

This chapter breaks away from the story of the day-to-day struggles to control the Maxwell grant and its resources; this narrative shift is necessary in order to understand the legal background against which all of this violence, resistance, and removal took place. Without the power and authority of the law, the company's agents and resistant settlers would have been locked in a protracted and relatively equal battle. The Supreme Court decision, however, gave the company the necessary tools and power finally to oust the settlers. Furthermore, it is not sufficient to look at the *Maxwell* decision as an isolated case as it pertains to advancing the narrative of this story. Instead, this chapter contextualizes the *Maxwell* decision within American legal history and jurisprudence about property in much the same way that I have attempted to contextualize the colonization and violence of the Maxwell Land Grant within larger historical trends at the end of the nineteenth century. The *Maxwell* decision indicates the complex and difficult task the U.S. judiciary faced as it attempted to translate Mexican property law in general into U.S. property jurisprudence, as well as the specific problem of incorporating the Maxwell Land Grant into the American and New Mexican property system.

## OVERVIEW OF *U.S. V. MAXWELL*

The Court's analysis is of most immediate relevance to us because the Court laid out a legal argument that revealed its perplexity about how to integrate Mexican law into the U.S. property system. The Court's confusion appeared in the way it defined the issues presented by the government's case. The U.S. government made two arguments about why the Maxwell Land Grant Company's land could not include the territory north of the Colorado/New Mexico boundary. First, the U.S. government argued that, under Mexican law, the grant to Beaubien and Miranda was an individual grant and therefore could be no larger than 11 leagues or 97,000 acres. They argued that since, under the Treaty of Guadalupe Hidalgo, the United States had agreed to honor Mexican grants only to the extent that they were valid under Mexican law, Congress could not have intended to confirm a grant that included over a million acres, 265,000 acres of which lay to the north of the state/territorial boundary. Second, the U.S. government argued that the company's 1879 patent was based on a fraudulent survey performed by a surveyor with economic ties to the company. By addressing these two issues in *Maxwell*, the court clarified fifty years of jurisprudence about how Spanish and Mexican land grants would be incorporated into U.S. law.

Justice Miller's resolution of these issues highlighted the degree to which he wished to avoid any reliance on Mexican law and instead base the validity of the Maxwell grant on the independent 1860 act of Congress that confirmed the grant's title and gave ownership to Beaubien and Miranda. First, Justice Miller spent four pages analyzing the laws of Mexico and their application to the Beaubien/Miranda grant. He concluded that, contrary to the U.S. position, Beaubien and Miranda were entitled to 1.7 million acres of land because the Mexican government had conferred on them an empresario grant, a type of grant that was not subject to the 22-league limit. (The merits of this position will be explored at length later in this chapter.) Justice Miller, however, in the next section backed away from this reasoning and decided that Mexican law was not applicable in this case. Instead, he pointed out that Congress, by law, could confirm and give away more than 22 leagues of public land if it wanted to do so. "Whether, as a matter of fact, this was a grant not limited in quantity by the Mexican decree of 1824 . . . it is not necessary to decide," wrote Justice Miller, because if "Congress, acting in its sovereign capacity upon the question of the validity of the grant, chose to treat it as valid for the boundaries given to it by the Mexican governor, it is not for the judicial power to controvert their power to do so."[1] In short, Beaubien and Miranda derived their land grant from the "sovereign" Congress, not from the Republic of Mexico. In attributing this invention to Congress, Miller ignored the historical context that Congress had never before handed out such a large parcel of land to an individual, and that such an action would have gone against the very principles Congress held regarding the distribution of lands as embodied in the Homestead Act.

Why did Justice Miller assume that Congress meant to confirm 1.7 million acres rather than 97,000 acres? The statute was simply entitled "An act to confirm certain private land claims in the territory of New Mexico." The whole purpose of the law was to validate claims rooted in Mexican law, not to give away land *de novo* with new grants. Moreover, the statute was completely silent about the acreage covered by the Beaubien/Miranda Land Grant. This claim was listed with thirteen other land grants that were to be confirmed "as recommended by the surveyor-general of the territory, and in his letter to the commissioner of the general land office."[2] But in 1860, the surveyor general of New Mexico had not yet surveyed the Beaubien/Miranda claim. The first survey—the private survey paid for by Maxwell and completed by W. W. Griffin—was not completed until 1869. There was nothing on the face of the 1860 statute expressly stating that Congress intended to confirm a grant of more than 22 leagues. To support his conclusion that the statute confirmed a larger tract, Justice Miller cited only one piece of evidence. In the 1860 confirmation, Congress had explicitly limited two of the claims listed in the statute to 5 and 11 square leagues, respectively. By failing to impose a similar limit on the Beaubien/Miranda grant, Miller argued, Congress must have intended implicitly to confirm the entire 1.7-million-acre claim without qualification. In reality Congress was confirming what the surveyor general had determined about the quality and extent of the Beaubien/Miranda grant, and he had not yet measured or located the boundaries. Miller's inference was thin evidence for such a far-reaching conclusion. Congress's purpose would be better inferred from the Mexican land laws that defined the claims being confirmed than from congressional silence in the 1860 statute.

The Court's complete abandonment of Mexican law became more clear four years after *U.S. v. Maxwell,* when the Court issued its opinion in *Interstate Land Company v. Maxwell Land Grant Company.*[3] The Interstate Land Company claimed title to 60 million acres located in Las Animas County in southeastern Colorado. Much of Interstate's land was encompassed by the Maxwell grant's boundaries. The Interstate Land Company's claim was based on an 1832 empresario grant from the governor of Coahuila y Tejas to José Manuel Royuela and Joseph Charles Beale.[4] The delicious irony of the case was that it cast the Maxwell Land Grant Company in the role that had been played previously by the U.S. government in the earlier *Maxwell* case. In order to defend its title, the Maxwell Company had to argue with a straight face that empresario grants did not create enforceable property rights under U.S. law—an ironic argument coming from the confirmed holder of 1.7 million acres of the Beaubien/Miranda Land Grant.

The Court agreed with the Maxwell Company's lawyer Frank Springer and rejected the Interstate Land Company's claim. Empresario grants, according to the Court, were *conditional* grants: the Mexican government granted them to the empresario only on the condition that he colonize the land by settling families on it. But neither the empresarios, Royuela and Beale, nor the Interstate Land Company had met this condition. According to the Court, the grantee "could not have been put in possession of any specific portion of [the claimed tract] without first establishing a colony of at least 100 families. As that was confessedly not done by him, no rights of property were acquired."[5] This resolution in *Interstate* raised an obvious question about the Maxwell Land Grant Company's title: if empresario grants were valid only to the extent that the empresario fulfilled the stated conditions and settled families on the grant, then how could the Maxwell Land Grant Company's claims be valid when the company was busily trying to evict its settlers from the land? Surely, the company's claim, based on the 1841 grant to Beaubien and Miranda, was no better than the 1832 grant to Royuela and Beale.

The Court neatly avoided this problem by pointing out that the Maxwell Company's claim was based not only on an empresario grant authorized by the Mexican government, but also on property rights granted to them by Congress. The Court stated that the Maxwell Company's title "was not rested solely upon the fact that the grant was generally understood to be an empresario grant but upon the proposition that the action of Congress in confirming it was made to Beaubien and Miranda . . . without any qualification of limitation as to its extent."[6] Mexican law seemed to drop out of the case. In the Court's final analysis, the Maxwell Company derived its title entirely from the 1860 statute. But this interpretation of Congress's action went against American notions about the public domain and the creation of a liberal republic.

Thus the Court incorporated Mexican law into U.S. law simply by having the latter engulf the former. Rather than attempting to translate the Mexican conception of property into American terms, the Court abolished Mexican property law altogether and substituted U.S. statutes in its place. But this legal maneuver hardly puts the confusion to rest. For the question still remains: Why did the Court choose to ignore Mexican law? After all, the documents related to the Maxwell grant and available to the Court hardly required such a result. The 1860 statute confirmed Mexican law and was not necessarily supposed to create new rights protected by the U.S. government. The whole point of the statute was to protect the expectations of property holders under Mexican law as required by the Treaty of Guadalupe Hidalgo. Why, then, disregard Mexican law and disguise the whole transaction as a *de novo* grant by Congress, free from the cultural context of Mexico with its tradition and norms of landownership?

To answer this question, we need to look beyond the litigation over the Maxwell Land Grant to the larger ideological struggle over the American public domain. The implicit distrust of Mexican land law in the *Maxwell* and *Interstate* decisions reflects a deeper and more widespread anxiety among U.S. lawmakers and courts about whether the "feudal" land regime of Mexico could be incorporated into the "republican" system of landed property to which Americans aspired. To Americans, the Mexican grant system seemed rooted in the arbitrary and lawless discretion of individual governors to bestow huge tracts of land on individual speculators, creating communities governed by feudal magnates, such as Maxwell. Many judges and lawyers believed that such a regime could not be squared with American notions of impartial government by laws or with republican equality.

By contrast, American law distributed land according to stated legal principles such as the Homestead Act and geometric specifications such as the grid, under which every citizen, in theory, had an equal opportunity to acquire a parcel to support his or her household. The apparent incongruity of the Mexican and American land regimes caused Congress and the courts to incorporate Mexican land law into the American system only tentatively, with ambiguous treaty provisions and confused, judicially crafted doctrines. This hesitancy to embrace Mexican law, however, actually led to a result far less egalitarian than the regime required by Mexican law. In the end, the fear of the "feudal" regime allegedly created by Mexican law caused U.S. courts to strip Hispano settlers of those rights provided by the Mexican empresario system while giving them nothing in return.

IDEOLOGICAL CONFLICTS OVER THE PUBLIC DOMAIN:
"REPUBLICAN" VERSUS "FEUDAL" PROPERTY

To understand the depth of the conflict between U.S. property law and Hispano-Mexican land law, it is important to have an overview of the way Mexican land law worked prior to the Treaty of Guadalupe Hidalgo in 1848. The Regulations for the Colonization of the Territories, passed on November 21, 1828, by the reform government of Guadalupe Victoria, provided the bureaucratic apparatus for the distribution and settlement of land along Mexico's northern frontier. The colonization law gave territorial governors the power to distribute three types of land grants to either foreigners or citizens: community, individual, and empresario grants. In New Mexico, governors usually bestowed community grants to Hispano villages or Indian pueblos that wished to gain legal security for customary lands or to go out onto the frontier and establish a satellite community. For example, the village of Pícuris, New Mexico, was founded by a group interested in leaving Taos to form an independent community farther east on the frontier in order to take advantage of trading opportunities with the eastern Apache Indian tribes. These grants were rather successful, and by 1848, the year of New Mexico's U.S. occupation, there were over sixty community grants in New Mexico.

While community grants often benefited a larger number of people and fostered community building, individual grants were the most commonly allocated type of land grant. Mexican governors distributed land to favored individuals with few stipulations attached to the grants, much like the earlier Spanish *encomiendas* had been distributed. The only limitation was that an individual grant was limited to eleven leagues (one league equals two and a half square miles), including one irrigable league, four temporal (meaning land needing only rainfall to produce crops), and six of rangeland.[7] In reality, however, these specific guidelines were rarely followed, and grantees were usually given rough approximations of eleven leagues. The individual grantees, such as Beaubien and Miranda, would petition the governor for the particular piece of land desired, which was usually in an unsettled portion of the province but which had a reputation for being fertile. The governor would then grant the land with little personal consideration on his part about the specific geographic traits or economic potential of the land encompassed. The burden for determining the land's worth fell entirely to the grantee, as the governor took little responsibility in deciding which lands should be cultivated and settled. In New Mexico, for example, the government infrastructure and bureaucracy were so weak that rarely did a surveyor appear to mark clear boundaries or take inventory of the land's exact resources.

Finally, governors could exceed the eleven-league limit by bestowing grants on an empresario or contractor who agreed to settle families on parcels near Mexico's northern border. According to Mexico's colonization law, empresarios had to settle two hundred families and establish a Mexican colony equipped with a militia as a condition of their grant. Failure to comply with these terms resulted in the empresario losing the land and any profits derived from land sales. In return for undertaking such colonization, however, the empresario also reaped rich rewards: there was no limit on the size of the grant, and the Mexican government exempted foreign empresarios from paying "tithes, excises, nor any other tax, under whatever name it may be" for the first six years of their tenure.[8] Empresario grants could contain millions of acres of land: the grant to Beale and Royuela, for instance, encompassed sixty million acres.

The Mexican government took a huge gamble when it enticed foreigners to colonize its northern frontier. It was a bet it lost in Texas as Anglos poured across the border under the empresario system and in 1836 declared their independence from the country that had so hospitably welcomed them. New Mexico, however, was an entirely different place from Texas, with its own unique position in the Mexican federation. Given its geography, New Mexico was far more isolated from foreign encroachment and did not come under immediate, direct threat of Anglo invasion until the 1840s. Despite the failed Texas invasion in 1836, New Mexico's governors remained relatively confident about the security of their borders and continued to grant large land tracts. Governor Armijo, in particular, although fairly suspicious of foreigners, carefully oversaw the distribution of land within his province. When a foreigner asked for land, as in the case of Carlos Beaubien, Armijo granted the parcel only if a native New Mexican was a partner in the venture. In this case, Guadalupe Miranda was Armijo's trusted collector of customs and had made a career of taxing foreigners and treating them with suspicion.

It is easy to see how sharply Mexican land law diverged from U.S. law. In particular, Mexican land law was deeply alien to the U.S. practice of land distribution in three respects. First, Mexican land law tended to bestow enormous personal discretion on territorial governors to give land to individuals or communities according to their political predilection. The first article of the colonization law provided that "political chiefs" or governors of each territory could "grant the public lands of their respective territories to land contractors, families, private persons, Mexicans or foreigners who may apply for the purpose of cultivated them or living upon them."[9] The law provided no real guidelines under which grants were to be made, nor did it provide much procedural restraint: governors could effectively distribute millions of acres at will. To be sure, some procedural restrictions were placed on empresario grants, including approval by the provincial congress. But most provincial governors had enormous influence over provincial politics, so these barriers were often more apparent than real.

Second, Mexican law tended to distribute land in immense parcels. Even the individual grants, which were *limited* to 11 leagues, were enormous compared to the typical parcel distributed by the U.S. government—the homestead of 160 acres, which was a quarter section. Eleven square leagues equaled 97,000 acres or 27.5 square miles, which was three-quarters of a township (36 square miles, as defined by the Northwest Ordinance). In effect, the Mexican government typically handed out the equivalent of a town to an individual rather than parcels capable of being managed by a single household.

Finally, Mexican law privileged the interests of the state rather than the interests of individual households. In particular, Mexican land distribution focused almost obsessively on the formation of tight-knit communities for the purpose of national defense and border control. Empresario and community grants were expressly designed to create frontier communities to ward off foreign and Indian encroachments. Even individual grants were allocated to individuals in consideration for extraordinary service to the state, often in relation to national defense. This custom of using land distribution to fund border protection and reward military service had ancient roots in the Spanish history of the reconquest of the Iberian peninsula. The system of land grants set up by the 1824 colonization law was the theoretical descendant of this essential military system of land subsidies for prominent and faithful citizens.

It would be difficult to imagine a system of land distribution more at odds with the presuppositions of American land law than the Mexican grant system. The three defining aspects of that system—executive discretion, enormous parcels, and an emphasis on community formation and border control—were diametrically opposed to American customs and practices of land distribution. More important, this tension between the two regimes did not arise solely from conflict with U.S. law but also from conflict with U.S. ideology. As a general matter, American land policy was heavily influenced by what might be called the "republican" ideology of landed equality. The essence of this ideology was that the American republic could remain a democracy of equal citizens only so long as citizens maintained their independence through ownership of productive resources such as land.[10]

The aspiration, therefore, was to divide up the public domain among citizens so that each household would control a parcel sufficiently large to support that household economically, but sufficiently small so that the household could manage the land independently. The 1862 Homestead Act was merely the pinnacle of the U.S. government's attempts to transfer government-owned property to individuals. Ever since the Northwest Ordinance of 1787, when Congress attempted to meet its shortage of funds through sales of the United States' ceded Western territories, there had been established policies to help settle the Western states.[11] The common methods that drove the distribution of lands were homesteading, squatting, public auction, allocations to veterans of wars, surveying of townships, and eventually the extension of credit to would-be buyers.[12]

This orderly distribution of land depended on dividing the landscape itself so that equal parcels could be distributed to individuals. Probably in no other aspect of land law were the differences between Spanish/Mexican and American law more apparent than in the surveying of the Western lands. As discussed in chapter 3, Hispano settlers tended to choose five- to twenty-acre plots that best met their subsistence needs, usually long, narrow plots abutting a stream. The Hispanos' small plots, and even the Maxwell Land Grant's boundaries, followed the area's natural geography: rivers, mountain ranges, and natural barriers such as deserts often marked the most environmentally suitable limits. This seemingly haphazard pattern of settlement struck Americans, who were used to the grid pattern both within their city plans and even in the open spaces of the American West, as a disorderly and improper way to settle land. According to cultural geographer John Stilgoe, who described the grid as the best representation of "Enlightenment optimism" that meant to establish an American national order on the land, "the grid objectified national, not regional, order, and no one wondered at rural space marked by urban rectilinearity."[13] That is, no one wondered if they were Anglo American and came from the East. Hispanos and Native Americans, however, who had their own ways of ordering their local and regional world, wondered at the seeming stupidity of regulating a landscape without regard to natural geography.

Republican politicians, such as Thomas Jefferson and Albert Gallatin, struggled to design a system of land distribution that would ensure that independent citizens would have access to land for productive use. This goal led republicans to oppose systems of land distribution that gave wealthy speculators or land companies special access to large tracts of land. But it also led republicans to distrust squatters who did nothing more than engage in subsistence farming without investing effort in improving the land to create an enterprise capable of producing a surplus above the household's needs. Mere squatters who made no such improvement were hardly the thrifty, diligent, enterprising citizens who would maintain their independence. Rather, people who espoused this republican ideology tended to view subsistence farmers as indolent and barbaric, "nearly related to an Indian, the scum and refuse of the continent."[14] Even the Dutch managers on the Maxwell grant, Pels in particular, embraced this Jeffersonian ideology, with their talk of lazy, unprogressive Mexicans and bushwhacking Missourians who had nothing better to do than smoke their corncob pipes while sitting on their potentially productive landscape.

A complete incorporation of the Mexican land grant system seemed to nineteenth-century lawmakers like an attack on the core ideal of republican government. Consider, first, the enormous discretion of Mexican governors, such as Armijo, to hand out huge parcels of land defined by the petitioner seeking the grant. U.S. land policy had, from its inception in the Land Ordinances of 1784 and 1785, adopted an entirely different system in which the federal government tightly controlled the definition of the parcels according to obsessively geometric specifications.[15] The U.S. government relied upon its own survey, defined by the grid, prior to distribution to private persons, and not on the ad hoc notions and natural boundaries that defined Mexican property. The U.S. system had some obvious costs: for one thing, it eliminated the capacity of grantees, squatters, or speculators to custom-tailor a parcel to the contours of land and water. However, the grid system also served some fundamental goals of U.S. land policy, including minimizing the possibility of overlapping parcels and thereby allowing land to be bought and sold on an international market.[16] The grid system also could guarantee a certain degree of impartiality in land distribution: the land allocation systems—auction, preemption, bounty warrants, or homestead—would in principle be equally accessible to all so long as the definition and description of lots were established and available in publicly accessible places.

## INCORPORATING MEXICAN LAW
## THROUGH TREATY AND STATUTE

After 1848 the U.S. government attempted to resolve the tensions and incorporate Mexican law into the U.S. property regime in two ways: by upholding treaty obligations and by creating administrative structures to adjudicate claims to Mexican lands. First, under the Treaty of Guadalupe Hidalgo the United States had promised to protect the property rights of Mexican citizens once they had been incorporated. Article 10 of the treaty specifically addressed the issue of land grants and assured Mexican citizens that their property rights and the way they viewed property would be protected under the new regime. The text reads, in part, "All grants of land made by the Mexican government, and remaining for the future within the limits of the United States, shall be respected as valid, to the same extent that the same grants would be valid, if the said territories had remained within the limits of Mexico."[17] The Mexican government realized that thousands of Mexican citizens in California, New Mexico, and Arizona did not yet hold clear and free titles to their land because of Mexican land law requirements and the slow-moving bureaucracy. It may have also realized that there were *peones* and settlers on empresario grants who held a kind of land title that might not be readily recognized or understood in the United States. The Mexican negotiators hoped that by specifically delineating the property rights of Mexican citizens in the treaty, property rights would be protected by the U.S. government and court system in the same way as if the former citizens were still a part of Mexico.

While the Mexican government saw protection for its citizens in Article 10, the U.S. government saw an intrusion into its legal system. Consequently, President James K. Polk, Secretary of State James Buchanan, and the Senate rejected the provision and ratified the Treaty of Guadalupe Hidalgo without Article 10. As justification for the Senate's actions, Secretary of State Buchanan explained to the Mexican delegation that "it is our glory that no human power exists in this country which can deprive the individual of his property without his consent and transfer it to another." Buchanan's statement was supposed to assure the Mexican minister that those with valid titles would be able to "maintain their claims before our [U.S.] courts of justice."[18] But Buchanan's assurances ignored the fundamental differences between the two land systems and what each viewed as a valid title to private property.

Part of U.S. efforts to placate the Mexican government on this matter was the addition of the Protocol of Querétaro, which was to clarify the U.S.

government's support of fair adjudication of land grant claims.[19] By replacing the Treaty of Guadalupe Hidalgo's Article 10 with the protocol, however, the U.S. government replaced enforcement of Mexico's positive and particular land law with enforcement of only generalized "property rights," unattached to any particular time or place. While property holders under Mexican land law were, according to the protocol, entitled to enforcement of their "legitimate title," there was no clear understanding or specific recognition of what such title entailed exactly. Subsuming this conflict under the general and seemingly uncontroversial protection of "property," which was implicitly identical everywhere, merely hid the inherent cultural divisions between U.S. and Mexican property law. It also ignored the fundamental tensions already present within U.S. property law. The late-nineteenth-century U.S. courts were, of course, thoroughly familiar with land entitlement based on such general principles.[20] However, the Supreme Court's isolation of the Maxwell Land Grant's title away from Mexico's specific legal regime, and the purposes underlying that regime, had devastating consequences for the grant's occupants. The Court's reasoning and decision, based on general principles of property rather than on the specific context of the land grant, stripped the Maxwell Land Grant's prior inhabitants of the protections that would have been afforded to them by the underlying purpose and condition of the empresario grant.[21]

The Court's and federal government officials' anxieties about preserving Mexican property rights were similar to the anxieties Americans felt about accommodating Mexicans in their practice of Catholicism and incorporating them into the fold of U.S. citizenship. As discussed in chapter 3, there had been considerable discussion over just how Mexicans should be incorporated into the United States, and the results were unjust in the eyes of most former Mexican citizens. Article 9 of the Treaty of Guadalupe Hidalgo promised U.S. citizenship and free exercise of the Catholic religion to the recently conquered Mexicans. The original text had two paragraphs protecting their religious freedom. Mexicans who wanted to stay within U.S. boundaries feared the prevalent anti-Catholic bias, and the Mexican government sought to protect its Catholic inhabitants from such prejudice. The text specifically protected the practice of Catholicism, the property of Catholics, both private and ecclesiastical, and the freedom of movement and communication between Catholics in Mexico and the United States.[22] The article seemed relatively straightforward and uncontroversial since it merely echoed the rights protected by the First Amendment. The U.S. Senate, however, deleted this detailed protection during the ratification process and replaced those words with the phrase, "and in the mean time shall be . . . secured in the free exercise of their religion without restriction."[23] The U.S. government felt that it had done an adequate job of protecting the religious rights of the citizens who had been brought in as U.S. citizens after the acquisition of Florida and Louisiana, and saw no need to delineate the specifics of that protection for Mexican citizens.

More importantly for the purposes of analyzing the Maxwell Land Grant case, the change in the text of Article 9 made former Mexicans' legal status as full citizens uncertain. The original text read that the new territories acquired by the United States "shall be incorporated into the Union of the United States, and admitted as soon as possible, according to the principles of the Federal Constitution, to the enjoyment of all the rights of citizens of the United States."[24] The treaty's language implied that Mexicans would be brought into the fold of U.S. citizenship quickly with no questions asked about their former status. However, after the Senate revised and ratified the treaty, the text read that these Mexican citizens "shall be incorporated into the Union of the United States and be admitted, at the proper time (to be judged of by the Congress of the United States), to the enjoyment of all the rights of citizens of the United States according to the principles of the Constitution."[25]

By rewriting Article 9, the Senate made the promise of U.S. citizenship for these former Mexican citizens based on something more political than the U.S. Constitution. Instead, citizenship depended on the whim and desires of Congress to confer it on these newly acquired citizens. Without this constitutional protection, former Mexican citizens suffered prejudice from the very beginning in 1848. When the U.S. government brought Mexican citizens into the United States, the government, whether Congress or appointed officials, treated Mexican Americans as second-class citizens of the Union. It was no coincidence that New Mexico had the longest territorial period, sixty-four years, of any state in the Union. Only Puerto Rico, another U.S. colonial possession with a majority Latino population, can claim a longer territorial period. By placing Mexican citizens at the mercy of Congress, the treaty established a legacy of congressional neglect of Mexican citizens.

These tensions between the federal government and formerly Mexican citizens, which began as a result of the treaty, continued for decades with very little resolution about the ways and means of incorporating Mexican citizens and their property into the United States. The second way that Congress attempted to deal with tensions between Mexican and U.S. law was by passing statutes and establishing bureaucratic offices to deal with the day-to-day problems of adjudicating claims to formerly Mexican land. But, just as Congress had done with the treaty, it managed to sidestep direct responsibility for adjudicating the conflicts over the meaning and use of the public domain and the tension between Mexican and U.S. property law when it passed the 1860 law that gave a patent to the Beaubien/Miranda Land Grant. Instead of taking it upon itself to deal with the inherent tensions between Mexican land grants, the U.S. public domain, and private property rights, Congress assigned that problem to the Office of the Surveyor General of New Mexico, which was created in 1857. This system of administrative review of all Mexican land grants allowed for the surveyor general to make a recommendation about the validity of the grants, and then for Congress to confirm the grant. Consequently, the surveyor general had full responsibility for deciding the boundaries and nature of land grants, but he was not always an impartial judge of the validity of grants' boundaries. Furthermore, Congress seems to have taken a hands-off approach regarding his decisions and rarely reviewed or overturned them.

By the time the *Maxwell* case was decided, the power of the surveyor general of New Mexico over such matters had already become an established precedent as a result of *Tameling v. U.S. Freehold and Immigration Company*.[26] This case dealt with the Sangre de Cristo grant in southern Colorado, which had also belonged to Carlos Beaubien. A parcel that had been severed from it was known as the Costilla estate, and John C. Tameling, a U.S. citizen, had homesteaded on a portion of it, believing it to be outside of the boundaries of the Mexican land grant and within the public domain of Colorado. The Freehold Company, which now controlled the Sangre de Cristo grant and, according to the company, the Costilla estate as well, sought to eject Tameling from his 160-acre homestead and have it returned to them because it was within the grant's original boundaries. Tameling argued that the Sangre de Cristo grant was an individual grant, and that its boundaries exceeded the 11-league limit on individual grants. Tameling maintained that the company had no right to a larger parcel of land, and therefore his homestead was off their legal property.[27] This case asked the Supreme Court to review the Interior Department's policy on setting the 11-league limit, which had so infuriated the Maxwell Company's directors.

In this 1876 case, the Supreme Court held that Spanish and Mexican land grants could exceed the 11-league limit established by Secretary of the Interior Jacob D. Cox in 1869. The Court went on to say that the secretary of the interior also did not have the authority to arbitrate the boundaries of Mexican land grants. The Court held that since the surveyor general of

New Mexico had marked the boundaries of the grant, and since Congress had confirmed those boundaries on June 21, 1860, then the boundaries established by the surveyor general and approved by Congress were the true and legal boundaries. Furthermore, the Court held that by confirming the boundaries, Congress made a grant *de novo* (new), which was essentially a quitclaim deed on the part of the U.S. government to these land grants, and now the grants were protected by U.S., and not just Mexican, law.[28]

The Court therefore made the surveyor general and Congress the legal arbiters of Mexican land grant boundaries, and noted that neither the executive nor judicial branch possessed the authority to review congressional approval of land grants. Justice Davis asked in the *Tameling* case whether or not Congress's vote to confirm the Sangre de Cristo grant extended the boundaries of the claim. The Court avoided answering the question by saying, "This [statute] was a matter for the consideration of Congress; and we deem ourselves concluded by that action of that body."[29] So if Congress extended the boundaries, even if it was in violation of Mexican land law and the Treaty of Guadalupe Hidalgo, the Court decided that it was not in the position to question Congress's authority to do so. The Court simply took itself out of the position of having to adjudicate the complicated issues surrounding these land grants, because "no jurisdiction over such claims in New Mexico was conferred upon the courts." The Court pointed out that "the surveyor-general, in the exercise of the authority with which he was invested, decides them [boundaries of land grants] in the first instance," and his actions are overseen by Congress. Justice Davis thus concluded that "the final action on each claim reserved to Congress, is, of course, conclusive, and therefore not subject to review in this or any other forum."[30] In *Tameling,* the Supreme Court placed solutions of land grant boundaries squarely within the province of U.S. politics and outside the realm of Mexican rules of property.

The *Tameling* decision, moreover, construed Congress's 1860 statute, which confirmed more than a dozen New Mexican land grants, including the Beaubien/Miranda Land Grant, incredibly broadly. The Court argued that the 1860 statute, in effect, replaced the complex Mexican grant regime with an American version of the grant system and remade the grants into a legal hybrid of the two regimes. The 1860 congressional enactment made further reference to Mexican land law unnecessary. The surveyor general marked the boundaries, and Congress confirmed title to this delineated parcel in fee simple absolute to the owners. Although both the survey and confirmation were intended to enforce property rights originating in Mexican land law, the limits imposed on such title by Mexican land law, aside from the physical limits of size, were simply ignored by Congress and, therefore, by the Court.

## EARLIER U.S. EXPERIENCE WITH TRANSLATING
## AND INCORPORATING FOREIGN PROPERTY

As indicated by the *Tameling* case, the *Maxwell* case was not the first time that the U.S. Supreme Court had dealt with the issues surrounding the incorporation of foreign property regimes into the U.S. property system. In fact, since the 1830s the Court's docket had contained litigation surrounding how Spanish and French land grants, attained as a result of the Louisiana Purchase and the Adams-Onis Treaty, should be understood and respected by U.S. courts. Over the half century between the earliest cases of the 1830s and the *Maxwell* case, the Court had devised an incredibly complex doctrine that revealed its uncertainty about how to reconcile republican ideals of individual property holding with the rights that were already attached to these large parcels of land.

Given the confusion of both Congress and the executive branch in dealing with land grants, the judiciary was left to figure out how to integrate the Hispano-Mexican system of grants into the American system of property. Unlike the political branches, the judiciary had little capability to pass the buck: if given jurisdiction over a question, the lower courts were legally obliged to decide it, and the courts were generally expected to provide an account of their reasons in an opinion. As the United States expanded westward, incorporating territory formerly governed by French, Spanish, and Mexican law, the Court was confronted with dozens of land grant claims. The various treaties incorporating these territories, from the 1794 Jay Treaty to the 1848 Treaty of Guadalupe Hidalgo, invariably provided that the United States would respect the property rights of the inhabitants of the territory being annexed. The Court therefore developed an elaborate jurisprudence to deal with the land grant cases that it decided prior to the *Maxwell* litigation.

These cases posed a dilemma for the Court. On one hand, under the leadership of Chief Justice John Marshall and Justice Joseph Story the Court had developed a jurisprudence and a legal culture that gave extraordinary protection to "vested rights" of property.[31] As Justice Story stated, "It seems to be the general opinion, fortified by a strong current of judicial opinion, that since the American revolution no state government can be presumed to possess the transcendental sovereignty, to take away vested rights of property."[32] Moreover, Chief Justice Marshall's 1810 opinion in

*Fletcher v. Peck* constituted, perhaps, the best articulation of this property theory of vested rights; speaking for a unanimous Court, he argued that the legislature's recision of the grant was invalid under "general principles which are common to free institutions"—in particular, the "great principles of justice" that "when absolute rights have vested under [a] contract, a repeal of the law . . . cannot divest [those rights]."[33] Justice Johnson's concurrence contained a more colorful phrase: once property was "vested in the individual," it became "intimately blended with his existence, as essentially so as the blood that circulates through his system."[34] No matter how corrupt, the initial grant of land to a person therefore bound all future legislatures to respecting those property rights.

Nonetheless, this jurisprudence enforcing vested rights was controversial. By protecting such rights, the Court necessarily restricted the power of Congress, a democratically elected legislature, to tinker with property, specifically foreign land grants, and make property generally available to the public. As the *Maxwell* case demonstrated, to the extent that the Court enforced the claims of these land companies and other grantees, it necessarily removed such land from the public domain and therefore from settlement by the public. Contemporary legal theorists were acutely aware that the right to retain property and the right of the landless to acquire new property would inevitably conflict.[35] Moreover, this dilemma was more than a conflict between two different classes of claimants to land: it went to the heart of the republican theory of government and property. If the holders of vested rights could remove vast tracts of land from the public domain and thereby impede the access of the landless to land, then, under the classic republican theory, the independence of the citizenry—and therefore republican equality and liberty—was in danger.

The foreign land grant cases posed this conflict in its starkest form. The claimants who held title to land grants such as the Maxwell grant demanded protection for vested rights under treaties, principles of international law, and ideas of natural justice. But opponents of these land grants argued that foreign grants conveyed no vested rights that U.S. courts should enforce. Although they made myriad objections to the enforcement of such grants, the objections shared a common characteristic: they all implicitly rested on the assumption that "property" was not a natural category that easily translated across cultures, but rather was a culturally specific category that existed in its "proper" form only in republics. Put another way, only republican property was worthy of legal protection.

Consider, for instance, the frequently made argument, as was the case in *Interstate v. Maxwell*, that Spanish and Mexican land grants, and particularly empresario grants, did not convey vested rights because such grants often had conditions about performance of tasks.[36] In the broadest sense, the strict republican could argue that *all* foreign land grants were suspect because foreign regimes did not reliably protect private citizens' rights. Since the United States was obliged to enforce grant claims only to the extent that they would be enforced by the former government, the United States would have no obligation to honor *any* land grant because a despotic government could always confiscate land without recourse. Of course, the Court rejected such a position early in its jurisprudence, noting that it would be an absurdity to argue that the United States—a republic—"succeed[ed] to the rights of his Catholic Majesty to annul the grants of his subjects" or that property rights should be "as completely at the mercy of the American government as they had been at that of the Spanish monarch."[37] But if the U.S. courts would not enforce the "corrupt" or despotic aspects of foreign regimes in American law, then the United States would have to decide which of a foreign regime's limits on a grantee's title would be enforced, and which were so contrary to the tenets of republican government that they could be safely rejected.

This proved to be a maddening effort at cultural translation because the Spanish and Mexican governments did not typically convey title to their subjects in fee simple absolute, conveniently recorded in a warranty deed. Instead, governors granted land with a wide variety of conditions, such as the grantee must perform a variety of services for the crown or republic. For instance, empresario grants required the empresario to settle two hundred families on the grant as a condition of having title to the land. Similarly, French or Spanish grants required the grantees to build such infrastructure as a sawmill, a road, or a tannery. But even individual grants contained conditions and limitations on use that were unfamiliar to American law. For instance, individual grantees sometimes received their land with the condition that they not sell or mortgage it, a restriction on alienability that, under Anglo-American legal tradition, would be unenforceable. If the Court strictly enforced the conditions, then many—perhaps most—foreign land grants would be held invalid because the annexation of land by the United States frequently made compliance with the conditions impossible or at least unnecessary.[38] Complete refusal, however, to enforce any of these grants might be seen as inconsistent with the spirit of the treaty obligations to respect the annexed population's property rights.

The Court's initial reaction to this conundrum was simply to delay decision. When confronted with the question of whether to enforce claims derived from French grants in Louisiana, Chief Justice Marshall (writing for the Court) complained that it was impossible to distinguish between vested rights and contingent rights that "were entirely dependent on the mere pleasure of those who might be in power."[39] The Spanish and French officials had been in the habit of allowing squatters to occupy government land and enforcing such squatters' rights against private intruders. But these officials never maintained that the squatters' titles would be recognized by their respective governments. Were these squatters' rights a valid claim against the United States, or not? According to Marshall, the question depended on a careful study of the political structure of Louisiana—"the edicts of the preceding governments . . . the powers given to governors . . . the powers conferred on deputy governors and other inferior officers." Unfortunately, the search for such documents had "been unavailing," and so, to the dismay of various claimants to various grants who awaited a Supreme Court precedent to clarify the matter, the Court took the case under advisement for six years.[40]

The concept of vested rights, it turned out, was culturally contingent, dependent on practices written and unwritten that could only uneasily and partially be imported into U.S. law. The degree to which the Court would enforce such practices turned as much on their perceptions of what constituted proper republican government as on the content of Mexican, Spanish, or French law. The problem, in short, was not (as Marshall suggested) a problem of inadequate legal documentation: it was a problem of ideology. Marshall himself was inclined to enforce land grants vigorously, even when their basis in foreign law seemed suspect.[41] Perhaps Marshall's willingness was related to his more general loyalty to the notion of vested rights as enunciated in *Fletcher v. Peck*—rights that Marshall maintained were "sacred" regardless of whether they were protected by any treaty.[42] After Marshall's death, however, the fate of land grant claimants before the Court was much more in doubt because the new Court, under the leadership of Chief Justice Roger Taney, had a much less passionate commitment to vested rights and a strong ideological commitment to preserving access to land.[43] Taney, an appointee of Andrew Jackson, tended to be less solicitous of vested rights than a federalist like John Marshall and more interested in protecting access to the public domain.

The Taney court needed to determine the validity of foreign grants by deciding which conditions (of the ones placed on the grants by Spain or France) the U.S. courts would recognize as legitimate conditions and thereby enforce under U.S. law. To help answer this question, the Court invoked a venerable common-law distinction drawn from the law of contingent remainders—the distinction between conditions precedent and conditions subsequent.[44] The distinction is important for explaining the Maxwell Land Grant litigation because it was precisely this distinction that was used to reject the Interstate Land Company's claim to the Maxwell Land Grant Company's land. But the Court's use of this arcane doctrine is significant for a more important reason: the Court's use of the common-law doctrine seems to have been critically influenced by the Court's theory of "just" property rights in a republic.

To illustrate the Court's desire to enforce such property rights, consider the contrast between the Court's attitude in two cases from the 1850s: *Glenn v. United States* and *Fremont v. United States.* The *Glenn* case dealt with the claims of James Clamorgan and his heirs to roughly 500,000 acres of a Spanish land grant in Missouri.[45] The land had been granted in 1796 by Colonel Delassus, the commandant of a Spanish outpost in Missouri, to Clamorgan, a St. Louis merchant, on the condition that Clamorgan settle cordage makers and hemp growers on the territory for the purpose of producing rope for Spanish vessels in Havana. Clamorgan, however, never made any investment in rope manufacturing for the Spanish monarch (nor could he after the land came under U.S. jurisdiction). In this case, the main issue was whether the conditional grant to Clamorgan, which was not completed, created any vested right to property which the United States had to protect.[46] The U.S. Supreme Court held against Clamorgan, stating that neither he nor his heirs had ever met the condition precedent to his taking title—the construction of the cordage factory. So, according to the reasoning in *Glenn*, the United States did not have to enforce this claim to such a large tract of land. In reaching this conclusion, the Court implied that enforcement of the grant would offend republican principles of land title: "To hold that an individual should have decreed to him . . . [a] domain of land more than equal to seven hundred square miles, for no better reason than that he had the ingenuity to induce a Spanish commandant to grant the concession, founded on extravagant promises, not one of which was ever complied with, would shock all sense of justice."[47] The *Glenn* case and the Court's interpretation of contingent remainders would suggest that the courts would not be sympathetic to land grants, such as the Maxwell grant, which had such unclear origins and conditions placed upon them at their inception.

Yet, *Fremont v. United States*, in which the Court enforced the grant by ignoring the condition placed upon it, produced a result that would later weigh in favor of the Maxwell Land Grant Company. In *Fremont*, John Charles Frémont, the famous (or notorious) explorer and military leader, had purchased ten square leagues (or twenty-five square miles) of land in

California from Juan Alvarado, a former provincial governor of California under the Mexican government. Alvarado had received the land from the governor of California as an individual grant pursuant to the colonization law of 1824 in consideration for his "patriotic services" and for his "personal benefit." The individual grant, however, came with a variety of conditions: Alvarado was barred from selling or mortgaging it, and he was obliged to build a house and take possession within a year of the grant. Moreover, Mexican law prohibited sales of land to anyone but Mexican citizens. Alvarado had violated the conditions barring sale (he had sold the land to Frémont after the U.S. invasion of Mexico), and he had never taken possession of the land. Did he have any vested right capable of being transferred to Frémont?

The Court, in an opinion by Chief Justice Taney, held that the grant created a valid claim even though Alvarado had failed to comply with the conditions. The Court distinguished *Fremont* from the *Glenn* case by arguing that the conditions on Alvarado's grant were conditions subsequent to the land being given to Alvarado. The Court reasoned that, unlike the grant to Clamorgan, which was for *future* services, the grant to Alvarado was a reward for his *past* services—"patriotic services" and personal benefit. The Court reasoned that although Alvarado's patriotism "cannot be regarded as a money consideration, making the transaction a purchase from the government" it nonetheless "is the acknowledgment of a just and equitable claim." [48] Since the conditions of building a home and settling were mere conditions subsequent, his noncompliance did not prevent Alvarado from holding a vested right to the land. The Court found that Alavardo was excused from building the house because compliance became impossible once the invasion of California by U.S. citizens (led, of course, by Frémont) had produced chaos in the territory.

Justice Taney pushed the law even further by arguing that Alvarado's sale of the land to Frémont did not violate the grant for a second reason. The Court argued that the conquest of California by the United States simply repealed the restrictions on the alienability of land that had been placed on Alvarado (restricting the sale of his land). The Court stated that "the Mexican municipal laws . . . might be repealed or abrogated at [the United States'] pleasure, and any Mexican law inconsistent with the rights of the United States, or its public policy, or with the rights of its citizens, were annulled by the conquest." [49] The Court noted that "there is no principle of public law which prohibits a citizen of a conquering country from purchasing property . . . in the territory thus acquired and held," and the Court inferred that any Mexican law barring such a sale violated American public policy. In particular, the Court stated that "every American citizen who was then in California had at least equal rights with the Mexicans, and any law of the Mexican nation which had subjected them to disabilities or denied to them equal privileges, were necessarily abrogated without a formal repeal."[50]

By Taney's logic and argument, once the U.S. flag was raised over the conquered territories of California and New Mexico, U.S. laws and ideologies about property prevailed over Mexican law. It is not obvious why the condition of building a cordage factory in *Glenn* was a condition precedent and therefore unenforceable, whereas the condition of building a house in *Fremont* was a condition subsequent and therefore allowed for a vested rights claim by Frémont. Much more fundamentally, it is even more unclear why Chief Justice Taney believed that the Anglo-American law of contingent remainders should be relevant at all to either case, given that the rights to land presumably vested, if at all, under Mexican civil law rather than English common law. This perplexity deepens when one considers Taney's argument that the Mexican restrictions on alienability of land were repealed by the United States' annexation of California, and this last argument seems to have left Taney in a dilemma. If annexation destroys all Mexican laws, as he argued in *Fremont*, then it ought to destroy also the Mexican laws that created the grant. But if the Treaty of Guadalupe Hidalgo preserved those Mexican land laws that defined vested rights of property, then one would think that Mexican laws barring transfer of land would also continue in force: Alvarado and Frémont needed to take the bitter with the sweet.

The impression left by Taney's opinion is simply that the Court reached for familiar Anglo-American common-law categories to translate and to choose among those aspects of Mexican law that it would enforce simply because the common law was familiar and reduced the cost of adjudication. Thus the Court refused to enforce the Mexican laws restricting the alienability of land because a familiar principle of the Anglo-American common law barred enforcement of such restrictions. Likewise, the Court was more willing to tolerate grants to individuals for their own personal benefit because such grants took the administratively straightforward form of a fee simple absolute: there was no need to inquire into whether the individual grantee had diligently pursued the public purpose with which he had been charged, because the individual had been charged with no such duties. By contrast, the whole problem with empresario grants like the *Glenn* case was that they "were evidently not intended as donations of the land, as a matter of favor to the individual" but rather were intended as efforts "to promote the settlement of the territories, and to advance [the state's] prosperity."[51] Such grants necessarily forced the Court to inquire into the future conduct of the empresario to determine how diligently the empresario pursued some state-defined goal. It was natural that Taney would want to withdraw the judiciary from engaging such an administratively burdensome task, and the doctrine of conditions precedent served this end well.

This doctrinal distinction between individual and empresario grants did not win the Court's unanimous approval. Justice Catron, author of the *Glenn* opinion, wrote a dissenting opinion in *Fremont* denouncing the distinction and arguing that because Alvarado had not met the conditions stipulated by Mexican law, Alvarado (and by extension, Frémont) lacked any vested right to the land. Catron doubted that Alvarado could have any serious expectation of owning the land since he had never taken possession of it.[52] His opinion, however, was rooted just as much in republican sympathy for the farmer pursuing small-scale preemption claims. According to Catron, Frémont's claim "presents a very grave consideration affecting preemption rights" because "California is filled up with inhabitants cultivating the valleys and best lands." These "western ploughmen" had legitimate expectations of acquiring the public domain, expectations that would be destroyed by Frémont's "floating claim," if Frémont chose land that the farmers occupied.[53] Catron had a stricter conception of what was required for a right to become vested. As did Taney, he attempted to root his argument in legal sources—in particular, in the condition that Alvarado actually build a house within a year. But his rhetoric about the "cultivators of the soil" and "western ploughmen" leaves little doubt that he derived this condition from republican traditions favoring settlers who actually used land over speculators who merely purchased it.

Catron was not alone in this sentiment. Four years later, Justice Daniels issued a blistering dissent in *Arguello v. United States*, another case in which the Court upheld an individual grant where the Mexican governor's authority to make the grant was in doubt.[54] Daniels's objection was not to the details of the majority's analysis but rather with any enforcement of grants where the governor's authority was dubious: he stated that he would have dissented in *Fremont* as well, had he been present. According to Daniels, the Court ought to presume against such grants in order to "baffle and defeat the schemes of corrupting monopoly" and "maintain and secure an equality of privilege and benefit to all citizens of the nation." To Daniels, the willingness of the Court to waive the strict requirements of Mexican law favored "the grasping and unscrupulous speculator and monopolist" at the expense of "the honest citizen of small means by whose presence and industry the improvement and wealth, and social and moral health, and advancement of the country are always sure to be promoted."[55]

Daniels's opinion is interesting because it suggests the variety of ways in which translation of Mexican property into American law could offend a republican sensibility. To Daniels, Mexico was a corrupt nation in "a state of almost incessant agitation, disorder, and revolution—controlled in rapid succession by men either themselves directly and violently seizing upon power, or becoming the instruments of those who had practiced such irregularities." The grants by Mexican governors lacked legitimacy because they "originated in practical and temporary usurpations of power . . . in defiance of the known public law." Moreover, the proof that any grant had been made could not be trusted, for it was rooted in the affidavits of dependent men whom he described as "the population of the late Spanish dominions in America—sunk in ignorance, and marked by the traits which tyranny and degradation, political and moral, naturally engender," men who would sell their testimony to the highest bidder.[56] Grants from such a system could not constitute legitimate property, and the statutes authorizing such grants ought to be strictly construed.

The racist rhetoric of Daniels's dissent can easily obscure its deeper connection to Chief Justice Taney's opinion in *Fremont* or Justice Catron's opinion in *Glenn*. In all three cases, the justices attempted to translate different aspects of Mexican property law into the American system without disrupting the republican theory on which American land distribution was supposedly based. The difference was one of degree and decorum: Catron refused to enforce empresario-style grants, and Taney refused to enforce restrictions on alienability, using the careful language of common law and vested rights, whereas Justice Daniels reached immediately for Jacksonian denunciations of monopoly and speculation. But none of the three had a culturally neutral principle by which to determine when a foreign interest in property vested. Instead, the Court arrived helter-skelter at the position that individual grants with unfulfilled conditions were generally enforceable, whereas empresario grants with unfulfilled conditions generally were not.

These judicial efforts at translation of property, however, left two great difficulties that would arise once the Court took up *Maxwell* and *Interstate*. First, what should the Court do when Congress confirmed an empresario grant that the Court would otherwise find unenforceable? Second, what should the Court do with an empresario grant in which all of the relevant conditions had been fulfilled? Were such properties sufficiently consistent with American notions of land distribution that they could be enforced by the Court? These were the questions raised by the *Maxwell Land Grant* litigation.

## ANALYSIS OF *U.S. V. MAXWELL*

How are we to understand the arguments and outcome of the *Maxwell* case in light of the preceding litigation and attempts to balance these competing property regimes? Following the precedents established in *Tameling* and *Fremont*, Justice Samuel Miller decided that the Maxwell Land Grant was an empresario grant, both under the law of Mexico and confirmed by Congress, and therefore legally entitled to the extended boundaries of 1.7 million acres. Justice Miller believed the case centered around three issues. First, he asked, did the colonization laws of Mexico, which were in force at the time the land was first granted, render the grant valid or void? Second, the Court asked, if the grant was indeed valid under Mexican law, then had a mistake been made by the surveyors such that the boundaries of the grant unjustifiably encompassed 1.7 million acres? Finally, the court investigated the charges of fraud against the Elkins/Marmon survey, which if true would have made the grant void.[57]

Miller, for the Court, first reasoned that the historical intent behind the grant suggested a presumption that the grant was an empresario grant. He wrote, "There are many things in the history of this grant to Beaubien and Miranda which would seem to indicate that it was understood by the Mexican authorities to be a grant of the class just described [empresario]."[58] Historians, however, have been reluctant to classify the Beaubien/Miranda grant as an empresario grant because that reasoning seems to justify the extended boundaries of 1.7 million acres and leaves little room for the prior inhabitants to make a worthy legal claim to property. Historians of New Mexico land grants have rightly pointed out that the Maxwell Land Grant is unlike Stephen Austin's colony in Texas, which provides the clearest example of empresario grants and their effects on settling the far northern Mexican frontier.[59]

The empresario grant to Stephen B. Austin, unlike the Beaubien/Miranda grant, was accompanied by relatively precise delineations of obligations. Moses Austin and his son, Stephen (after his father's death), were the most prominent and successful of all empresarios. In his career as an empresario, Stephen Austin settled nine hundred families and took out four empresario grants. Although the Mexican government willingly set aside the eleven-league limit, it also established guidelines the U.S. citizen had to follow (e.g., become a Mexican citizen and convert to Catholicism).[60]

By outlining Austin's obligations, the Mexican government hoped that Austin would shift his loyalty from his homeland, the United States, to his adopted country, Mexico. It was a risky assumption, but Mexico's northern frontier was in such a precarious state that this was the only solution that the Mexican government could find to prevent hostile Americans from settling Texas. For a while it had been a risk worth taking because Austin had helped the Mexican government put down the Fredonia rebellion and independence movement by Americans in the early 1830s.

According to each empresario contract, Austin was to settle two hundred families who would willingly become Mexican citizens and comply with Mexico's laws and customs. A four-step process for attaining land from the contractor was outlined. First, the settler had to petition Austin in writing saying that he (and his family if he had one) wished to be admitted as part of the colony.[61] Second, Austin sent a certificate to the settler admitting him to the colony. For example:

> El Ciudano Estévan F. Austin, Empresario, para introducir Emigrados estrangeros, en las Colonias . . . Certifico, Que _____ es uso de los colonos, que he introducido en virtud de mis contratos antes mencionados; que llego en esta colonia el día ____ de mes de _____, de año de 18 __.[62]

Third, Austin or his agent delivered to the new colonist a deed to the land that the colonist had chosen. The colonist kept one copy of the deed, while the other copy went to the land office established by Austin. Finally, the colonist signed and delivered a promissory note to Austin stipulating the terms of his mortgage.[63]

One should pause here to note the relevant characteristics of this land distribution system. First, the Mexican government conveyed to the empresario the right to sell the land within the grant's borders, either for cash or in installment payments. Moreover, the empresario was not required to hold a public auction to sell the land: the law placed no restrictions on the persons to whom the empresario could sell. In this sense, the empresario received fee simple title to the grant land. However, the Mexican government restricted the title in one crucial respect. The empresario had to reconvey title to at least two hundred individuals. The empresario, therefore, could not retain the entire estate to develop it as a single economic enterprise—a ranch or coal-mining company, for instance. Rather, he was obligated to build a community of individual landholders and occupants, and in return he could pocket the proceeds of the land sales. Was Armijo's grant to Beaubien and Miranda a grant of this sort and restricted in this way? An examination of the circumstances surrounding the conveyance suggests that it was.

When the entrepreneurs Carlos Beaubien and Guadalupe Miranda petitioned Armijo for the grant in 1841, they wrote of the "natural advantages [which] are useless for the want of enterprising men who will convert them to the advantage of other men" and asked for the land so that they could improve it by "raising sugar beets" and "establish manufactories of cotton and wool, and raising stock of every description."[64] Although they wrote about the "hands of individuals" who would work the land, they made no specific reference to how the settling or hiring of workers would occur. Nevertheless, they clearly intended to run a large enterprise that would require settled labor if the enterprise were to be successful.[65] The document, however, gives no concrete evidence as to what specific type of grant the two men intended to receive. So how was Justice Miller to interpret this document? Was the Beaubien/Miranda Land Grant made with conditions precedent; that is, did Beaubien and Miranda have to settle this frontier location in order to receive title? Or was the grant made with conditions subsequent—a grant made to the two men for faithful service to Governor Armijo and the Mexican republic on which they could build a community?

Justice Miller did not seem bothered by the vagueness of Armijo's conveyance to the two men and seemed to construe it as a condition subsequent grant. The foundations of the grant system in New Mexico were essentially based on personal, not legal, relationships. Unlike the U.S. system of public auctions and homesteads, the grant system of distributing land was based on personal connections between governmental heads and petitioners. Beaubien, and especially Miranda, were close friends of Armijo who had rendered faithful service to Armijo and to New Mexico, and it is quite possible that neither party felt the need specifically to delineate the legal terms of the grant. Although Mexican fear of Anglo encroachment in Texas had led the government to be extremely cautious and specify reciprocal legal obligations with excruciating detail, in New Mexico such precautions were unnecessary because neither Beaubien nor Miranda had any connection to a political power hostile to Mexico.[66] Within a matter of days, Armijo granted his friends' request with an equally unrevealing letter as to what type of grant he was giving or their obligations to fulfill conditions in order to make the grant valid.[67]

Moreover, the objections of Father Antonio José Martínez of Taos, who complained that the Beaubien/Miranda Land Grant encroached on Taos Pueblo lands and also limited the commons of local Mexicans, implied that this was an individual grant for the two men's personal benefit. Beaubien and Miranda, however, contradicted Martínez's claim and answered the charges in a letter to Governor Armijo that showed they viewed themselves as empresarios settling a frontier. While Martínez portrayed the grant as an enterprise run by two men for profit, Beaubien and Miranda told Armijo they were running the grant for the profit of not only themselves, but also for the government, as well as for the settlers living on the grant. They were not taking land from the Taos communities but were creating new opportunities for them. The two men complained that Martínez's injunction to delay conveying the title to them caused a loss of income because "not only does the suspension of labor on those lands injure us, for the reason of having incurred heavy expenses but also a considerable number of families and industrious men, who are willing and ready to settle upon those lands, and to who[m] we have given lands, a list of which individuals I accompany in order that your excellency, seeing the number, may determine what may be proper."[68] Moreover, Beaubien and Miranda defended their title on the grounds that they had conveyed land to "families and industrious men." This defense suggests that they regarded their title as limited by the condition precedent in all empresario grants—that the land be given away or sold to persons who would actually occupy the land. Indeed, although historians have argued that there is little evidence to corroborate this assertion, families, in letters to both the federal government and to Maxwell Company agents, claimed to have been living on the grant for two or three generations at the time of the suit in 1887.[69]

The second argument that Justice Miller used to justify the characterization of the Maxwell Land Grant as an empresario grant was the argument used in *Tameling*. In that case, the Supreme Court had reasoned that when Congress confirmed these land grants in 1860, they in essence made *de novo* (new) grants. This congressional act therefore made the land grants protected not only by Mexican treaty law, but also by U.S. laws that were better able to protect property rights. Justice Miller seemed willing to overlook the apparent contradiction of Congress giving away or granting 1.7 million acres to an individual. Furthermore, in his opinion Justice Miller went beyond the position that the Court had taken in *Tameling*. Not only was Congress the final arbiter in this matter, but, Miller argued, they had acted correctly and upheld the spirit of Mexican land law and had successfully incorporated the grant into the U.S. property system through its conveyance of it as a *de novo* grant.

In the end, Justice Miller was quite clear that the Beaubien/ Miranda grant was an empresario grant, not an individual grant. He wrote, "There is nothing in the language of the grant, nor in the petition, nor in anything connected with it, nor in the act of juridical possession, to indicate that either Governor Armijo or Beaubien and Miranda, or the officer who delivered the juridical possession to them had any ideas or conception *that the grantees were not to have all the land within the boundaries* established by that juridical possession."[70] Although Miller's reasoning was somewhat circular, he believed that the Beaubien/Miranda grant was an empresario grant by default. Miller decided that only if the language by any of the participants had indicated any limits to the boundaries would he have considered the grant to be an individual grant. Justice Miller concluded that there was no reason to question the opinion that this was an empresario grant and therefore unlimited in the amount of acreage that could have been granted by Governor Armijo. This reasoning was fair if Miller believed the surveyor general had accurately followed the boundaries marked by Vigil in 1841. And Miller had complete faith in the abilities of the Office of the Surveyor General. He wrote, "So that the surveyor general not only had the authority to determine the extent of the grant, as well as its validity, but he had the means of ascertaining it."[71]

Referring back to *Tameling*, Miller again reiterated the Court's position that disputes over land grant boundaries were to be determined by the surveyor general and confirmed by Congress. This decision in the *Maxwell* case was consistent with prior precedent as established by *Tameling* and, in fact, fairly clear-cut. Nevertheless, the fact that Justice Miller felt the need to spend more time discussing the nature of Mexican law as it applied to empresario grants suggests that even he was skeptical about the persuasiveness of this procedural argument. By delving into the history and meaning of Mexican law, Justice Miller was looking for a better way of balancing these completing claims to property.

The second issue of the case, regarding the validity of the survey, followed logically from the first issue once the Court had decided that the boundaries could extend to 1.7 million acres in theory. Now the question was whether or not the survey conveyed that much land in practice. Miller asked, "If the grant be valid, is there such a mistake in the survey on which the patent of the United States was issued as justifies the court in setting aside both patent and survey?"[72] Again the Court thought it better to defer to the expertise of the surveyor general. Miller wrote, "They knew that it was an immense tract of land, that it would be the subject of grave criticism, and they knew more about it and were better capable of forming a judgment of the correctness of that survey than this court can be."[73] Despite all the evidence of complaints from settlers on the grant, state governments, and territorial officials, the Court believed that the Office of the

Surveyor General had acted in the best interests of all of them and had determined the true boundaries. Miller nevertheless reviewed the evidence
in the record and compared Vigil's, Griffin's, and the Elkins/Marmon survey's notes to see if he could detect any mistake. In the end he concluded
that despite the complaints from "interested parties," it would be impossible to make a better survey, and therefore the validity of the Elkins/Mar-
mon survey had to be upheld. Furthermore, at the end of the section, he
again reiterated the Court's position that it was not within their jurisdiction to judge the facts: that was for the surveyor general and Congress.[74]

The Court, however, did take up the third issue since it felt that it was
within its jurisdiction to review the case and the survey specifically for indications of fraud. The State of Colorado and later the Justice Department
asked the Supreme Court to review the facts and determine if in fact fraud
had occurred when the surveys were completed. The government did not
claim that the Elkins/Marmon survey itself was corrupt. This, perhaps,
would have been a more persuasive claim, given the fact that John T. Elkins
was the brother of Stephen B. Elkins (president and shareholder of the
Maxwell Land Grant Company) and that Stephen B. Elkins had been present at the survey. Instead the government made the more difficult claim
that since the Elkins/Marmon survey was based on the Griffin survey,
which had been paid for by Maxwell, it was an influenced and fraudulent
representation of the grant's boundaries. The Court quickly dismissed this
claim, saying, "It seems impossible, in the face of these circumstances, to
assume that there was anything in the nature of fraud perpetrated in regard
to the Griffin survey and its effect upon the final survey."[75] Why the government made this more convoluted claim rather than the direct claim
against the Elkins/Marmon survey remains unclear. Justice Miller concluded, "The question of fraud . . . is not deserving of much consideration.
We are compelled to say that we do not see any satisfactory evidence of an
attempt to commit a fraud, and still less of its consummation."[76] Despite
the questions that settlers such as Richard Russell had raised about the
Elkins/Marmon survey, the Court never mentioned, much less specifically
addressed, the charges against the later survey.

## THE CONSEQUENCES OF *U.S. V. MAXWELL*

After more than a decade of legal disputes, this decision finally resolved the
Maxwell Land Grant's boundaries and gave the company the right to
legally hold 1.7 million acres. Everyone who lived on the grant—Hispano
and Anglo homesteaders and squatters, miners, and those surreptitiously

using the range—would have to give in to the company's demands to pay up or leave the grant. Yet despite the apparent resolution, the decision raises one last question for us to consider as we examine the legacy of Mexican land grants in the American Southwest, particularly with reference to the *Taylor* case. What effect did the Court's ruling that the Maxwell Land Grant was an empresario grant have on the settlers of the grant? Like the colonizers who had come to settle on Austin's grants, the Hispano settlers who had been living on the grant since the time of Lucien and Luz Maxwell presumably would have been entitled to the land that they had settled under the presumption that they, too, were colonists. If the Court really meant this grant to be an empresario grant, then the Maxwell Land Grant Company's entitlement to the land should have been burdened by these settlers' rights. Because the company was Beaubien's and Miranda's and the Maxwells' eventual successor in interest, then it also, presumably, should have shouldered the empresario's burden. The exact nature of the Maxwell settlers' rights remains unclear. In Anglo-American terms, the settlers may have held an interest in the land—say, to live in their homes to work the land—while the grantee, as trustee, might have held the real legal interest. It is also possible that the U.S. government might have simply been entitled to review the case now that the Court had clearly labeled the grant an empresario one and force the division or dissolution of the grant and turn at least part of it over to the public domain upon violation of the grant's empresario conditions. Then the Hispano squatters could have applied for their lands under the Homestead Act. Either of these findings, however, would have threatened the company's clear title and thrown the whole issue back into litigation and/or lobbying Congress and the secretary of the interior to resolve their competing claims.[77]

There may, however, be no meaningful answer to these musings on the precise legal nature of the settlers' interest. Whether the original Hispanos settlers' interest could have made an enforceable claim against the company, based on their rights as colonists, remains unclear because few surviving records provide the details of Maxwell's property system. Indeed, the empresario system was a short-lived experiment across all of Mexico's northern frontier, and the Mexican government that created the system never had to address how the conditions on the grant could be enforced. The U.S. Supreme Court translated the empresario system into Anglo-American terms by construing the grantee's rights as rights in fee simple absolute to the grant's territory with no obligations or prior claims burdening the land. In so doing, the Court followed the cue of Congress, which had rejected complete incorporation of Mexican land law into U.S. law by rejecting Article 10 of the Treaty of Guadalupe Hidalgo.

Perhaps both the Court and Congress feared that Mexican land law, including the details of the empresario system, smacked too strongly of the "feudal" hacienda system. The Court and Congress saw it as a system that conflicted directly with the U.S. ideal of land as freely alienable and completely controlled by individual owners. Anglicization of the grant therefore went hand in hand with hostility to Catholicism and suspicion of the supposed backwardness of New Mexican society. Yet the Court was unwilling to completely do away with the empresario grant, in that it allowed the custom of the extended boundaries to survive. By stripping the empresario grant of only some of its conditions, the Court effectively provided the Maxwell Land Grant Company with the power of a feudal lord without the attendant responsibilities.

Perhaps there was simply no practical way that the Court could have enforced a detailed scheme of protecting the grant's tenants without a system that would record the interests of the settlers, the conditions placed upon the grant, and the remedy that would result if the conditions were breached. No recorded system had ever existed, even under Mexican law. The grant was an informal creation from the beginning, the product of a primarily oral agreement between Armijo and Beaubien and Miranda. The incredibly vague petition and answer imply so much about the nature of the grant, but give no specific guidelines as to how the enterprise was to be run. Later, after Maxwell had taken over, the conditions on the grant were customary and rarely explicitly written in any deed. Armijo and the grantees may have understood the implied conditions. Maxwell and the settlers certainly understood, and even thrived, under their reciprocal and customary obligations. But Dutch bondholders, Congress, and the U.S. Supreme Court certainly could not, or would not, try to understand the complex relationships and incorporate them into their own systems. The process of translating the empresario grant into fee simple absolute, unencumbered by responsibilities to the land's occupants, was accomplished as soon as the land was sold to distant purchasers who would need formal definition of their entitlement in a deed. As soon as the land entered the world market, the informal understandings could not practically be given the force of law, even by the most accommodating of Supreme Courts.

*U.S. v. Maxwell Land Grant Company* and the cases preceding and following it reveal the power of government to intercede and ultimately decide the outcome of the battle between the Eastern and European capitalist developers and the Western inhabitants they were attempting to displace. Only when the U.S. government had firmly established the grant's legal boundaries was the company able to take control of the grant legally as well as physically. The *Maxwell* case, moreover, decided the outcome of the forty-year battle between two competing property systems: one characterized by the appearance of vagary and informality of land grants, and the other characterized by the very formal rules and procedures established by U.S. law and enforced by its agents. Both Anglo and Hispano settlers, like the Jicarillas before them, soon found that there was no place for the informal arrangements that were their legacy from Maxwell. The settlers reacted in the only way they believed available to them after the Supreme Court decision: they continued and even escalated their now futile, but incredibly violent, battle against the company, which eventually led to the final confrontation at the Pooler Hotel.

# 6 The Legacy of Land Grants in the American West

Thus in the beginning all the world was America.
John Locke, *The Second Treatise of Government*

The year following the Supreme Court decision, and particularly throughout the summer of 1888, opposition to the company began to gather strength on various portions of the grant. The company's managers, especially M. P. Pels, felt that the only way to bring tensions to an end was to convince the district court and the sheriff to fulfill their obligations to enforce the Supreme Court's order with ejection notices. On July 19, 1888, the Colfax County sheriff reluctantly went north from Cimarron to Vermejo Park with summonses for the illegal residents to appear in district court and face ejection proceedings. He was met, however, by armed resisters led by O. P. McMains, who cautioned him against issuing the court orders.[1] The sheriff, leery of the growing mob and fearing bloodshed, returned to town without accomplishing his duties.

The following day the sheriff managed to present an ejection notice without incident to George Blosser, who was living illegally on the outskirts of Raton, New Mexico. Luckily for the sheriff, Blosser happened to be away from home that day, and the sheriff left the ejection notice tacked to the door. Three days later, however, seventy-five armed men, again led by McMains, rode into Raton and reinstated Blosser and his family on their ranch. The crowd shouted loudly and abusively, and told the sheriff and others unsympathetic to their cause that ejections would not be tolerated. McMains warned the company representatives and local law enforcement agents, "Go and hide for the balance of the day for if our men see you again they will kill you." They also cautioned the grant managers that if they disturbed Blosser and his family again and returned to issue ejections, the grant managers "would suffer."[2] Pels realized that the situation on the grant was becoming unbearable, and he began to prepare for what he saw as an inevitable confrontation with the settlers. Feeling as if he had little support from the stingy and distant company directors, he wrote to plead with them to convince the federal government, through federal marshals, to interfere: "Has your Board no influence at all at Washington or shall you consider it after I am shot? . . . But you don't seem to care & all I have from you is an occasional telegram!"[3] The directors and the settlers remained adamant about their positions as the standoff continued, and both sides stood ready to take their chances with a violent confrontation. All Pels could do was wait and try to manage the situation as it unfolded, so he headed into Trinidad to talk with the sheriff about creating a posse that could keep the peace on the Colorado portion of the grant, where the violence seemed most likely to erupt.

It was neither coincidence nor fluke that the settlers and the company met for their last violent confrontation on the steps of the Pooler Hotel in Stonewall, Colorado. The Pooler Hotel represented everything the settlers viewed as corrupt and foreign about the Maxwell Land Grant Company. In the spring of 1888 the Maxwell Company had sold five thousand acres of land, including the Pooler Hotel and adjacent buildings, to "a group of local and state businessmen" that included Colorado governor Alva Adams. The syndicate bought the land because of its natural beauty, and they intended to create a resort for a railroad company.[4] The settlers knew of the large sale of land that had once been the farms and ranches of the Vigils, Torreses, Russells, Bells, and others who had lived and raised their families in the valley. They would not leave the valley peacefully without compensation for their improvements and years of hard work. Moreover, the businessmen proposed to make their land a resort for people perceived by the settlers as rich, idle foreign tourists. Displeased with the proposed resort, the settlers sought to stop the development through guerrilla attacks and outright violence if necessary.

The syndicate's managers had hired J. W. Llewelling to construct a large irrigation ditch that would provide water to create artificial lakes that could be stocked with fish for the tourists. Residents below the ditch resented the company taking water from the Purgatory River for what they viewed as a frivolous use. On August 24, 1888, the day before the confrontation on the steps of the Pooler Hotel, a group of armed and masked men confronted Llewelling and told him that "no man who recognized the title of the Maxwell Land Grant Company would be permitted to work or stay in that vicinity." Llewelling, not wishing to start a fight he could not possibly win, left his irrigation project and headed back to Trinidad, arriving the following morning.[5] After hearing Llewelling's report, that afternoon Sheriff Burns, concerned about the escalating violence, deputized an additional

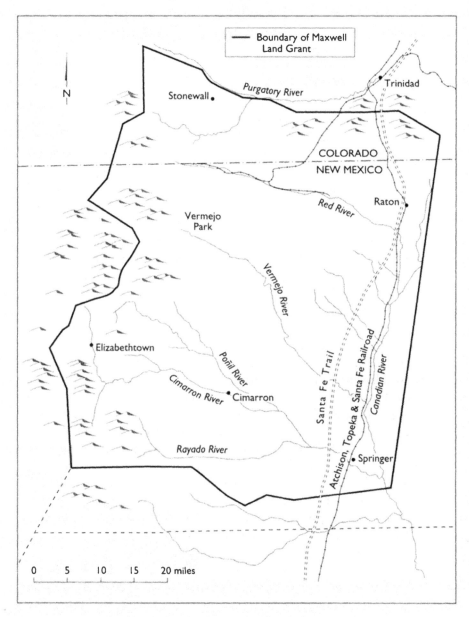

Map 6.    Maxwell Land Grant in the 1890s.

posse of twenty-five men (ten were paid by the City of Trinidad, fifteen by the Maxwell Company) to back up the posse that had left three days earlier to protect company property at Stonewall. The second party left that afternoon and headed up the Purgatory River valley to Stonewall, not realizing that they were too late to help the posse already trapped by the settlers in the Pooler Hotel.

According to later testimony by company officials, the first posse intended to ride to the Stonewall Valley only to protect company and syndicate property: they had no desire to provoke a confrontation with the settlers. The day before the posse left, however, R. B. Holdsworth, the company agent in Trinidad, had walked into C. S. Snyder's hardware store and purchased two Martin rifles, fifteen pistols, 2,075 rounds of cartridges, and one hundred loaded shells: quite a lot of ammunition for six men who had no intention of firing on anyone. The Maxwell Company paid for the supplies, and they were delivered to William D. Hunn, the leader of the posse organized to go to Stonewall. The company agents and the posse obviously expected and prepared themselves for violent resistance and intended to end it as quickly as possible.[6]

The confrontation in front of the Pooler Hotel might not have become violent if not for one man, Thomas J. O'Neil, who had arrived in Stonewall late Thursday afternoon, just a week before the confrontation. He was looking for either Richard Russell or James Cox. When O'Neil found Russell, he told him that he was interested in "jumping" a claim (illegally resettling land the company had cleared of inhabitants) and settling his family there. Russell introduced him to Cox, and both men were pleased with the new arrival's enthusiasm. Neither leader suspected O'Neil's intentions, and they invited him to stay. All three men went out to look for a claim on Saturday. O'Neil found one he liked and stayed through the weekend; he even taught the Sunday school class in Stonewall. On Monday he left, saying that he was returning to Trinidad to get his family and bring them up the canyon to settle their new claim.[7]

O'Neil was back in Stonewall by the end of the week, on August 24, with his "wife and children," whom he took to a boarding house in Stonewall. Coincidentally, just hours after O'Neil arrived, the first posse of six men rode through town and went directly to the Pooler Hotel, where they remained the rest of the evening. Russell and Cox became suspicious of O'Neil because of his arrival just ahead of the deputies, but deciding that it was of no use to worry about O'Neil at this point, they sent out the call to the rest of the grant's settlers to come to Stonewall and show their strength against the deputies.[8]

O'Neil, it turned out, was a Pinkerton agent hired by Pels to spy on the agitators in Stonewall. He had no family and no intention of jumping a claim on the grant. His appearance in the valley had been orchestrated by the managers of the Maxwell Land Grant, who felt frustrated by their inability to pursue legal means to rid the grant of the settlers. Some of the settlers' affidavits, and a newspaper article by McMains, claimed that it was O'Neil who started the gunfire on the hotel steps. McMains wrote, "O'Neil's first work was accomplished by his seemingly accidental shot which led to the firing and served as an excuse for killing 'the leader' [Richard Russell]."[9] Had O'Neil come to provoke the confrontation? It is difficult to say for sure, but the presence of a Pinkerton agent and the massive amounts of ammunition the posse carried certainly suggest that the company was prepared for a violent and, it was hoped, decisive meeting.

### THE STONEWALL VALLEY "WAR"

When Richard D. Russell woke up on August 25, 1888, he must have been uneasy about the delicate duties that awaited him in Stonewall, a short ride away. Russell was tired—tired from five years of repelling the Maxwell Land Grant Company's encroachments onto his homestead, and tired from quarreling with his neighbors, who accused him of sympathizing with the very company he opposed. Caught in the midst of this strife, Russell could barely remember the time in 1871 when he and his wife, Marian, had brought their young family from New Mexico into the Stonewall Valley.[10]

While stationed at Fort Union, New Mexico, Russell had served in the Union Army as a lieutenant during the Civil War, and for his service, the U.S. government granted him a homestead upon his discharge. The Russells chose a parcel in the secluded Stonewall Valley of southern Colorado, named for the area's dramatic rock outcroppings. It recently had been declared by the secretary of the interior to be part of the public domain and therefore open to settlement.[11] The Russell homestead, nestled against the eastern face of the Sangre de Cristo Mountains, southwest of Trinidad, possessed the benefits of fertile soil, accessible water, and natural protection from the Ute Indians, whose hunting and trading routes passed near their property. Over the preceding seventeen years, Richard and his family had planted an orchard, created an artificial lake, and built a lovely wood house.[12] Their cattle ranching and small farm provided a comfortable living for the family of eight, including four sons and two daughters. But now, it appeared that Russell and his family might lose everything for which they had worked so hard.

A year earlier, the Russells had decided to yield to the company, to let it purchase their livestock and improvements, and to move back to New Mexico. But because of their neighbors' pleas to resist the company, coupled with the inability of M. P. Pels to raise the purchase money that they had agreed upon, the Russells decided to delay abandoning their property.[13] But the growing hostility of Russell's neighbors forced his hand, convincing him that he could no longer passively wait for the company's actions to determine his fate.

Earlier in the week, a group of masked men had told the foreman in charge of the company's herds, E. J. Randolf, and his wife to get off their property, and they had threatened to hang them if they continued to support the company. The next evening, after the Randolfs had fled to Trinidad and the protection of the Las Animas County sheriff and the Maxwell Company, their home was set ablaze and burned to the ground. No one knew, or at least admitted to knowing, who had started the fire. Company agents accused the restless settlers, while the settlers accused the company of framing them for the arson to turn public opinion. The escalating violence convinced Russell that he had to act and mitigate the danger to his family and neighbors. When Russell left home the morning of August 25th to face the Maxwell agents, he went as a sympathetic, but nonviolent, anti-grant man.[14]

When Russell turned onto the main street of Stonewall, he was amazed at the number of men milling about the town. Almost a hundred settlers waited for the appearance of the sheriff's posse and grant agents who had come into town the evening before to protect grant employees and issue ejections. Russell stopped, dismounted, and talked with a fellow anti-grant leader, Sam Bell, who explained that the men were waiting for the Reverend O. P. McMains and his men from New Mexico. Ever since the Colfax County "War" in 1875, McMains had made a career of agitating against the company. Even after the announcement that the Supreme Court had ruled in favor of the Maxwell Company, McMains refused to stop his work. He was convinced that the company had no just claim to the settlers' land, which they, in good faith, had worked so diligently, believing that the land was legally their own.[15]

While Bell and Russell were talking in front of the Pooler Hotel, McMains was riding into Stonewall from the south with another hundred settlers. Encouraged by the support from the rest of the grant's settlers, Russell hoped this show of solidarity would scare away the agents before harm came to anyone. As the New Mexican settlers joined the Colorado brigade, Russell and Bell went out to talk with McMains, and discussed the recent events and what action, if any, they would take against the agents inside the hotel.[16] Company lawyer R. B. Holdsworth, Las Animas County sheriff W. T. Burns, Deputy William Hunn, and twenty-five company agents—including Pinkerton detectives, company employees, and men deputized in Trinidad—had arrived in Stonewall the day before to serve ejection notices on the settlers.

After their brief conference, Russell and McMains approached the Pooler Hotel, and McMains shouted, "You fellows want to get out of here at once. You are in the interest of the Grant and you want to hitch your mules and get out—will you do it?" Someone in the crowd, however, suggested that the anti-grant men shoot "the sons-of-bitches." Deputy Hunn then emerged from the hotel and asked Russell and McMains to wait while he went back inside to consult with the other company men.[17]

A few minutes later, Hunn walked out of the hotel and announced, "We have not molested your men nor have we done any harm about here, we are paying our board and I don't think that you people have any right to order us away." McMains warned them once again to leave, and Hunn replied, "We won't." McMains then turned to the group of gathered settlers and shouted, "Do you hear what they say?" and as he began to order the anti-grant men to surround the building, a shot rang out from the crowd. In the ensuing chaos, Russell and "Frenchy" Girardet rushed toward the hotel entrance, and McMains ordered the settlers to cover all exits. They began encircling the building, vowing not to let a man walk out free. Inside the hotel, the grant agents barricaded the bay windows with mattresses and began to shoot at the crowd. With rapid fire coming from inside the hotel, Russell stood in the midst of a deadly crossfire with his back against the front wall of the hotel, desperately trying to avoid the shots coming from the doorway and window bays. Suddenly, Girardet, who was across from Russell on the other side of the door, was hit and killed instantly.[18]

Before McMains's men could surround the Pooler, Sheriff Burns, recognizing the seriousness of the situation, had sent one of his men out the back door to Trinidad with instructions to wire Governor Alva Adams to send the Colorado state militia. Holdsworth, thinking that M. P. Pels wished to solve the problem without the publicity of state intervention, sent another runner to wire Pels from the grant office at Trinidad.[19]

Meanwhile, the shooting continued between the company men in the hotel and the settlers outside, who were barricaded behind tipped wagons and other cover. A few minutes after Girardet was killed, a bullet fired by William Hunn, who stood in the hotel window above him, struck and wounded Russell. The bullet entered his shoulder and traveled down the left side of his body before exiting from his abdomen. Lying on the porch of the hotel, he was unable to move out of the line of fire and into safety. As he lay there, he saw Rafael Valerio gunned down and shot in the head by the grant agents. The boy died almost instantly. Russell silently waited to be rescued from the firing line.[20]

The exchange of gunfire continued until about noon, when the grant agents waved a white flag and asked to talk with McMains and other anti-grant leaders. McMains agreed to the conference, and while they talked, some of the settlers carried Russell and the body of Valerio back to their respective homes. Deputy Hunn told McMains that some of his men wanted to leave, and he asked that they be allowed to do so peacefully. McMains allowed them to go. The deputy and the reverend also discussed the terms of a truce, but negotiations soon broke down, and the shooting started up again.[21]

At 4 P.M. the messengers, who had ridden the almost sixty miles from Stonewall to Trinidad, arrived in the town and gave a detailed account of the skirmish to the sheriff's office and wired the news to M. P. Pels in Denver. The sheriff's office quickly raised and deputized a posse of six men. Pels, realizing that the situation was beyond the company's control, telegraphed Governor Adams to send in the state militia, and he then hired more Pinkerton detectives as reinforcements for his men in the hotel. County Commissioners Duane D. Finch and Richens L. "Uncle Dick" Wootten argued that sending the posse up the canyon would merely be sending "canon [sic] fodder." The two men recognized that the settlers were desperate and willing to fight for their land and also knew the terrain like the backs of their hands—a decided advantage in this skirmish. Furthermore, the posse members were only men for hire and would probably run at the first instance of violence. Finch and Wootten were also afraid of escalating the skirmish into a full-fledged battle. After further debate, everyone agreed that only the two commissioners would ride up the canyon to Stonewall to assess the situation.[22]

As dusk fell, events in Stonewall quieted down. With only sporadic shooting, both sides grew tired and uneasy. As the opposing parties prepared to settle in for the night, a fire broke out in the barn next to the Pooler Hotel. The blaze spread quickly, surprising settlers who had taken refuge in and around the structure. Confusion and excitement engulfed the crowd as some fled for safety while others extinguished the fire. Inside the hotel, however, the grant agents saw their chance to escape. While the settlers scattered, the grant men ran out the back, down the gully, and up over the hills toward Trinidad. They stayed in the mountains until daybreak and then secured a wagon from a farmhouse to get back to town. The only injury was to William Hunn, who lost a thumb. Back at the hotel, the settlers eventually subdued the flames and bedded down for the night without ever noticing that the enemy had escaped.[23]

Early the next morning, just as the settlers were stirring, the two commissioners rode into the town, not knowing what to expect. They found McMains, who agreed that the commissioners would go into the hotel and talk to the grant men. A few minutes later the two men emerged with the shocking news that the grant agents were gone. Utterly confused and unsure of what to do, whom to accuse, or what to accuse them of, the commissioners rode back to Trinidad to try to untangle the situation. There were mixed reactions as the settlers returned to their homes and makeshift camps. On one hand, they felt duped because they had let the company men get away. On the other, they had stopped the ejections and had protected their families and homes, but at the expense of three of their own being shot and two killed.[24]

In the Russell home, Richard's condition worsened: he was barely alive and suffering greatly. Marian stayed at his bedside for five days until he died, and then she promised to continue their fight and protect their home.[25] Russell was buried amid charges against the government and the company for murder. The settlers wanted to avenge the three deaths, and tempers continually flared. Two days after Russell's death the settlers burned down the hotel, daring the company to do something about it, but the grant agents, fearful of the settlers' violent reactions, did not return. For the next week after the battle four hundred or five hundred settlers remained near the Stonewall Valley, three-quarters of whom were Mexicans, but no posse ever came to bother them, and the settlers' anger settled into a constant uneasiness over the next few months as they returned to the daily routines of their farms and brought in the harvest.[26]

At first glance, the settlers appeared to have won the Stonewall Valley "War" by chasing off the grant agents and postponing the practice of ejections and throwing families out of their homes. In the long run, however, the company won through intimidation and attrition. After the Stonewall Valley War, the company's claim was never again seriously challenged. The settlers either paid rent to the company or were evicted quietly from their holdings. Although there would be minor outbreaks of resistance over the next decade, the August 1888 Stonewall Valley War was the last incident of mass, organized violence against the Maxwell Land Grant Company. The company relentlessly exercised its government-granted claim to the land—the land that Jicarilla Apache and Ute Indians, Mexican settlers, and

U.S. homesteaders had inhabited "illegally" for years and, in some cases, generations.

Much to the agitation of Pels, it took the State of Colorado almost two months to bring charges against McMains and the others for conspiracy to incite a riot, arson, attempted murder of company agents, and the manslaughter of Richard Russell and Rafael Valerio.[27] This last charge was convoluted because a coroner's jury had found that Russell and Valerio had died from gunshot wounds inflicted by the deputies. Nevertheless, Pels convinced the district attorney in Trinidad, W. W. Dunbar, to bring evidence before the grand jury that implicated McMains and the other antigrant men for the manslaughter because they had incited the riot that resulted in the deaths.[28] Finally on October 3, 1888, a grand jury issued indictments, despite the fact that Dunbar thought the case weak and did not want to pursue a trial. The court issued warrants, but finding McMains became a difficult task—one for which local authorities were unwilling to risk their lives. McMains had fled across the border into New Mexico, and the local authorities did not want to incite any violence by extraditing him to Colorado. Four months later, McMains freely crossed the border into Colorado and surrendered to the authorities.[29]

As in earlier company attempts, the district attorney tried to ignite racial division among the settlers. On September 20, 1889, just weeks before McMains's trial began, Dunbar subpoenaed thirty-seven Hispanos, almost all of them from the Vermejo Valley, to testify against McMains.[30] All of these men had been on the front steps of the Pooler Hotel when the gunfire broke out, and all had led or supported the anti-grant movement against the company. The prosecution took depositions from all of the men, but in the end called none of them to testify in front of the jury. Although José Luís Torres and Justo Sandoval gave depositions for the prosecution, both eventually testified for the defendants.[31] The Hispanos refused to break ranks with the other anti-grant agitators and give testimony that the district attorney needed to convict McMains.

The trial of McMains and the others did not start until October 2, 1889, more than a year after the Stonewall Valley confrontation. In the courtroom of Judge Julius Hunter, the jury heard evidence from both sides about the nature of the skirmish and the incidents that had occurred. All of the deputies who had been sent to the Pooler to protect the syndicate's property testified about the leadership of McMains and Russell in starting the riot. E. J. Randolf, his wife, and J. W. Llewelling spoke about their fear of antigrant agitators who threatened them as they worked for the company.[32] The jury also heard from witnesses who participated in the riot against the deputies. The defense maintained that the men who went to protect the syndicate's property were only deputies nominally; in truth, it was the Maxwell Company that paid their salaries and armed them. The defense also suggested that Thomas J. O'Neil, the Pinkerton agent posing as an anti-grant man, fired the first shot, thus signaling the deputies to begin firing on the crowd. Marian Russell, the widow of Richard Russell, spoke of her husband's nonviolent nature and his desire to find a peaceful solution to the company/settler problems. The defense attorneys, Caldwell Yeaman and James Martin, were so sure of their case that they thought it unnecessary to place McMains on the stand.[33]

On October 12, 1889, ten days after the start of the trial, a jury of five Anglos and four Hispanos found O. P. McMains and his codefendants not guilty of all charges. In an era when few Mexican Americans sat on juries despite their constitutional right to do so, it is worth noting that this jury closely reflected the ethnic makeup of Las Animas County. Some of the Hispanos on the jury did not speak English and so were dependent on the interpretations of their peers for the content of the testimony and the judge's instructions.[34] Nevertheless, despite pressure from the company and alleged attempts to rig the jury, the defendants were found not guilty and were free to go back to their regular lives.

M. P. Pels, however, had feared that the local jury would acquit McMains, and he had earlier asked that a complaint be sworn out on federal charges of conspiracy to incite a riot and aiding resistance to the service of official papers. A deputy U.S. marshal arrested McMains in the courtroom immediately after the judge read his acquittal. McMains was hurried off to Denver, where he remained for almost a week, until October 17. The company's legal team won the right to have the case against McMains removed to Pueblo, Colorado, but as a result of legal maneuverings on both sides, it did not start for another year. In early October of 1890, a federal jury found McMains guilty as charged of inciting some "of the worst [violence] in the history of the state." Yet, despite the harsh verdict, McMains was sentenced to spend only six months in the Pueblo County Jail.[35]

During the two years between the Stonewall Valley War and the conviction of O. P. McMains on federal charges, the Maxwell Company's agents continued their old policy of issuing ejection suits and legally removing the settlers from the grant with much greater success at bringing the difficult settlers to a compromise. In 1890 they brought sixty-two ejection suits: sixteen were decided in favor of the company, fourteen were dismissed because both sides had agreed on a settlement, and thirty-two were pending; the company averaged an almost 50 percent success rate in getting rid of the settlers.[36] They were also much more successful at getting people to peacefully leave the grant and sell their improvements to the company.[37] The anti-grant movement was slowly dying out.

## POLITICAL AGITATION: RISE OF THE POPULIST PARTY

The anti-grant agitators did make one last attempt to challenge the company through political action. This time, instead of turning to violence, they attempted to bring their plight to the attention of the national Populist movement. Populism in the mountain west historically has been associated principally with the issue of free silver. Recent historiography, however, has shown the movement to be more widespread and complex. As this case indicates, Mexican land grants and settlers' rights played a role in the movement, at least within the New Mexican experience. The early and most influential historians of the Populist movement discounted the impact of Western Populism on the national movement and consigned the region's interest in the movement to a one-issue mantra. John D. Hicks went so far as to claim that if "the Populist program [had] not included free coinage it could hardly have appealed seriously to any of the mountain states."[38] Later historians, including Richard Hofstadter and Lawrence Goodwyn, although they agreed with little else that Hicks had written about the Populists, concurred with his assessment of the Western movement.[39] The resistance on the Maxwell Land Grant provides an example of the diverse concerns that Populists in the mountain west addressed.

Some Western historians, however, such as Robert Larson and Carlos Schwantes, have attacked this interpretation as Eastern-centric and incorrect. Schwantes, in his *Western Historical Quarterly* article "Protest in a Promised Land," argues that what ties the Populist movements of the mountain west together is not free silver, but working people's suspicion of corporations, as well as Westerners' antimonopoly sentiment.[40] Although Western urbanites protested the working conditions under which they labored in factories, and rural people specifically objected to the control of land by the railroads, both agreed, in general, that the monopolistic power of Eastern companies threatened their individualism and livelihoods. What the Maxwell Land Grant settlers hated most about the company was its foreign ownership and monopolistic tendencies in controlling local ranching, farming, mining, and railroad markets and pricing. They were perfect recruits for the Populist movement.

The case of the Maxwell Land Grant and the inhabitants who supported the People's Party provides a good example for the interpretation that

Schwantes puts forth. In 1890, just two years after the confrontation at Stonewall, the settlers formed the Colfax County Farmers' Alliance, which dedicated itself to fighting the cattle and land monopolies that they felt dominated their economic landscape. The Alliance also sponsored a newspaper, the *Nogal Nugget,* which it used to disseminate news of the Alliance and other agrarian movements throughout the country.[41] The creation of the Alliance signaled that residents on the Maxwell Land Grant did not trust either political party to rein in the powerful company. The weakness of the mainstream parties and their refusal to help the settlers on the grant became painfully apparent when the New Mexico Territorial Legislature enacted a change-of-venue law in 1889. Supported by Republicans, the new law allowed an individual party involved in a lawsuit to request a change of venue if the request was supported by the oaths of two disinterested persons. Obviously, acquiring the compliance of two disinterested parties would not be difficult for the company's lawyers. Furthermore, since the judge was not allowed to inquire into the motive behind the request, and the country prosecutors were not allowed to file counteraffidavits, it would be mandatory for the judge to remove the case to another venue.[42] The effect of this was obvious: if ejection suits could be removed to a venue that was less sympathetic to anti-grant sentiment, then the company could pursue removal of the settlers more effectively.

One Alliance newspaper, the *Independent,* also noted that the cost of fighting ejection notices would be higher because of the expense of traveling to a distant court. "Many of these [defendants] are poor, very poor. There are natives among them who have nothing in God's world but a few sheep, the little adobe house, . . . and the little plot of land which gives them and their families their only sustenance."[43] The article referred clearly to the plight of Hispanos, who were at a particular disadvantage because their landholdings tended to be smaller and they rarely understood the language and court system. The Alliance sought to appeal to all ethnicities and races in its quest to battle the company and the new law. Although the sympathetic New Mexico governor, Edmund G. Ross, vetoed the law, the Santa Fe Ring, through the territorial legislature, managed to orchestrate an override and the law went into effect. The new law accounts for the company's sudden success at getting rid of settlers though enforcement of ejection notices in the 1890s.

Despite this setback at the local level, one national paper, the *Anti-Land Grant Monthly,* published in Kansas, took up the cause of New Mexico land grants and settlers' rights to live on them. The paper's editors were particularly interested in the Russell family's struggle against the company and vehemently denounced the death of Richard Russell. An illustration of a bullet was captioned, "The argument used to silence R. D. Russell's objection to ejectment, Stonewall, Colorado, August 25, 1888."[44] The June 1890 issue was devoted entirely to the plight of the settlers on the Maxwell Land Grant. It contained reprinted articles from Denver, Trinidad, and Raton papers, and asked its Populist readership across the country to consider the plight of these citizens and help them gain back their land and economic livelihood. The paper stressed the influence of corrupt government officials who were "forsaking us, her citizens" in favor of "foreigners" who had the money and power. The fact that the Maxwell Company was run by foreigners generated particularly bad feeling among Populists, who saw good, hard-working average citizens removed by corrupt capitalists from Europe with the aid of their own congressmen. An editorial warned, "Hands off, and give settlers a fair show with the foreigners."[45]

The paper's rhetoric focused on the plight of the small, seemingly insignificant citizen who was up against the overwhelming bureaucracy of big government and business. One of the questions posed was how such major incidents of "perjury, fraud, and forgery" could go unpunished when any petty offender who "sold cigars without a license" or "converted his own corn into whiskey" was punished severely and "loaded down with irons and sent to the penitentiary." The paper noted that the U.S. government's policy had been to "take care of the little thieves and the big thieves will take care of themselves."[46] For the settlers on the Maxwell Land Grant and their supporters across the country, who clearly identified themselves as Populists, free silver and monetary policy had very little to do with their day-to-day welfare. The Populist settlers were looking instead for ways to control monopolistic land companies through good government and fair representation, which they saw as the only way to help these "good, hard-working citizens."

Support for the Maxwell settlers was not limited to the national Populist movement. They found another supporter at home in Democrat Antonio Joseph, a Hispano and the New Mexico territorial delegate to Congress. Joseph considered himself a Populist and often stood up for the rights of settlers on Mexican and Spanish land grants. In August 1888, just days before the Stonewall Valley violence, he introduced a resolution in the House of Representatives asking the secretary of the interior to indemnify all settlers who had settled on the grant in good faith, and to reimburse them for their improvements and expenses. The bill failed, but Joseph continued to run in Colfax County as an anti-grant Democrat and, later, a Populist.

During his last two years as delegate, Joseph continued to introduce bills that would reopen the case of the grant's boundaries.[47]

## THE END OF RESISTANCE ON THE GRANT

The final legal blow to the settlers came in 1894, when the Supreme Court heard *Russell v. Maxwell Land Grant Company*. Marian Russell sued to have her ranch returned, citing the fact that she and her husband had settled the land in good faith, believing it to be part of the public domain. Richard Russell had applied for the patent on April 6, 1874, and had received his final receipt for the land in question on September 5, 1876. For the last twenty years the Russells had invested in the American dream of owning land and raising a family. Their 160-acre homestead included a home, several barns, an orchard, and an artificial lake that they used for fishing and watering livestock. When they chose their land, there was no indication that the boundaries were in dispute, and the government confirmed their choice and allowed them to settle.

In this final adjudication of land boundary disputes, the court made two points clear. First, they reaffirmed their holding in *U.S. v. Maxwell Land Grant Company* that only the General Land Office and the Department of the Interior were in a position to determine the boundaries of the land grant. Justice David J. Brewer wrote, "The decisions of that bureau in all such cases, like that of other special tribunals upon matters within their exclusive jurisdiction, are unassailable by the courts."[48] The Court stated clearly that it would not tolerate any more cases that questioned the validity of the survey and the boundaries of the grant. "If in every controversy between neighbors the accuracy of a survey made by the government were open to question, interminable confusion would ensue."[49] Chaos was exactly what the Court was trying to avoid. They had traveled down the path of defending the extended boundaries at all costs, and given their utilitarian concerns, they had to continue to do so.

Second, the Court held that the government had no title when it gave Russell his final patent, and since it had no title, Russell had no claim. Brewer pointed out that citizens possessed the same right to rely upon the regular survey as the company possessed in relying on the validity of the special survey of the grant. He pointed out, however, that "the survey is one thing and the title another." In some of the most strained logic and twisted legalese, Brewer noted that the patent for the Maxwell Land Grant had been confirmed by Congress in 1860, fourteen years before Russell even applied for the land. Therefore, the patent gave title to the company, regardless of the public survey. Brewer conveniently forgot to note that the boundaries of the grant were not determined until 1878, when the surveyor general of New Mexico commissioned the survey, two years after Russell had received his final patent. Brewer concluded that because of the 1860 patent, the United States had no right to the public domain: "If at that time the government had no title, it could convey none."[50] The Russells and other homesteaders were out of luck. With this last question regarding the rights of homesteaders settled, the company had clear title to the land grant.

During the intervening years between the Stonewall Valley "War" and *Russell v. Maxwell Land Grant Company*, a series of violent skirmishes occurred across the grant as individuals continued to resist the company's efforts to remove them from their land. In April 1889 a rash of arsons struck pro-grant homes at three locations on the Poñil River, two locations on the Vermejo River, and one on the Red River. Pels suspected the "Mexicans" and Las Gorras Blancas, but their involvement could not be proved.[51] The Stonewall Valley War was the watershed event for settler resistance on the Maxwell Land Grant. Afterward, never again did an organized resistance of settlers, whether Anglo or Hispano, come together to fight off the company. Perhaps the inhabitants of the grant realized the futility of opposing a large corporation that had seemingly endless resources with which to fight the settlers and which, in the end, had the power of U.S. law behind its claims.

## CHANGING WORLD: THE RISE OF THE
## COLORADO FUEL AND IRON CORPORATION

Perhaps one reason for the settlers' lack of resistance was that they realized the world around them was changing. No longer were they entirely dependent on farming and ranching. Just as the company was stripping their economic livelihood away from them, a new wage-labor economy was emerging in their own backyard. Colorado Fuel and Iron came to replace the Maxwell Land Grant Company as the dominant economic force in southern Colorado and northern New Mexico. By the turn of the century, CF&I was Colorado's largest employer, with almost fifteen thousand employees; approximately one out of ten persons in the state worked for the company. In 1901 the Maxwell Company sold the Colorado portion of the grant to CF&I for $50,000 in cash and $750,000 in Rocky Mountain Coal and Iron Company bonds. CF&I also took a five-year option for ten thousand acres on the New Mexico portion of the grant.[52]

As far as Pels, Whigham, and the Maxwell Company were concerned, the settlers were now CF&I's problem. As these settlers were pushed from their land, there was the simultaneous pull of wage labor within the company towns of southern Colorado and northern New Mexico, where coal was mined from deep underground. Towns like Eagle, Walsenburg, and Gardner began to dot the old Maxwell Land Grant landscape. The displaced settlers, along with migrant labor from as far away as Mexico and eastern Europe, created new communities and provided the perfect labor market for finally making the Maxwell Land Grant a profitable venture.[53]

More research is necessary to understand the changing work and migration patterns of the Anglo and Hispano settlers on the Maxwell Land Grant as they entered the twentieth century. Where did the thousands of men who worked for the coal company come from? Did they ever own any land? Did they work full-time as farmers before the advent of the company towns? Were independent yeoman converted to payroll employees? Or did agricultural roles convert to industrial roles—a somewhat less drastic step? Sarah Deutsch points out in *No Separate Refuge* that the coal camps on the Maxwell Land Grant were part of the regional community she describes in northern New Mexico and Colorado. The camps attracted villagers from northern New Mexico who could no longer make a living on their land and therefore sought wage labor with CF&I. Deutsch argues that these mining towns did not replace the village communities but were unique societies created by their Hispano inhabitants but nevertheless dominated by the ever-present company.[54] I would argue that a significant portion of CF&I's labor force came not only from these northern New Mexico villages but also from displaced settlers of the grant. CF&I did not need to look far to find employees for their mines, coke ovens, and steel works.[55]

When the settlers on the Maxwell Land Grant, some of whom had lived on that land for generations, finally realized they could no longer battle the company, a world was forever closed to them. No longer would they be able to engage in the agricultural economy that had sustained them and their families for years. Like the Jicarilla Apaches of a generation earlier, the company had displaced them from their homeland and left them to find a new livelihood. In contrast to the case of the Jicarillas, however, the company and its subsidiaries still had a place for the settlers on the grant. Although they would no longer work the land for its direct benefits in the form of crops and livestock, they could mine the same land for coal and work for the indirect benefit of a wage.

What does this shift from an agriculturally based livelihood to a wage-labor economy reveal about the changing lives of the people on the grant? In part, the answer depends on the nature of the agriculture that took place there. We must not engage in Jeffersonian rhapsodies about the independence of the small farmer and rancher. As we have seen, the settlers, both Anglo and Hispano, were affected by a national commodities market that dictated the sale of their produce. Especially in the late nineteenth century, once railroads and a Chicago commodities exchange enabled farmers and ranchers to sell their produce on national markets, ostensibly independent farmers were just as dependent on these national market prices and railroad rates as they were on a large coal-mining operation.

At least some local farmers and ranchers did not wholly depend on the national market, even after the advent of the railroad. Many farmers lived a dual life, working for wages while maintaining the small farms they had purchased directly from the Maxwell Company. Eventually, though, the settlers' ability to weather economic downturns and to manage autonomous enterprises was lost forever as they turned more and more to wage-labor work for CF&I. Once the Maxwell Company had deprived Anglo and Hispano settlers of their land, the settlers had to depend on pure labor, the value of which was determined by a vast economic network of corporate decision makers who were as uncontrollable as the weather— and less predictable.

The economic transformation that occurred on the landscape of the Maxwell Land Grant over the last half of the nineteenth century established many of the economic, migratory, and political patterns that still influence the world of present-day Hispanos and Anglos in Colorado and New Mexico. The shift from agricultural work, where a family felt tied to the land they worked, to wage labor for coal-mining companies such as CF&I has left a conflicting legacy. Many Hispanos, particularly those who live on old Mexican land grants, still feel a particular tie to the landscape even though it has become impractical for them to make a living from it. Many of those who work and live in the larger cities of Denver, Pueblo, Santa Fe, and Albuquerque continue to maintain familial and personal ties to the region. It is this historic legacy of land loss and economic transformation as a result of the mistranslation of Mexican property rights in land grants into the U.S. property system that has led to the current litigation, *Espinoza v. Taylor*, that I described at the beginning of this book.

## LAND GRANTS IN THE LATE TWENTIETH CENTURY: THE CASE OF THE TAYLOR RANCH

For the past thirty years, the people of the San Luis Valley in south-central Colorado have been a party to some of the most intense litigation involving the meaning of Mexican land grants, the preservation of private property rights, and the use of a historic commons. The case, *Espinoza v. Taylor*, has pitted the local inhabitants of San Luis, Colorado, against a North Carolina lumberman for control of a 77,000-acre tract of the Sangre de Cristo Land Grant (see map 7). This vast area, known as the Taylor Ranch, became the source of this conflict and litigation when the owner, Jack Taylor, refused to allow the local Hispanos the same access to resources that their ancestors had used as a commons under previous owners. The local Hispanos responded to what amounted to Taylor closing a commons by continuing their traditional uses and, from Taylor's perspective, poaching and trespassing. At the height of the conflict, each side accused the other of violence, and someone even took a few shots at Taylor. Given the intensity of the conflict, the Colorado state government, through the initiative of then-governor Roy Romer, intervened with a rare exhibition of generosity and historical insight by proposing to purchase the parcel from Taylor and return some of the acreage to the original claimants—local Hispanos in Costilla County.

At the heart of the conflict is the meaning of Mexican land grants, what rights they intended to convey, and the status of this particular tract as a historic commons. Since the grant's inception, the Hispanos argue, this mountain tract—*la sierra*—has been used as a common area for grazing, timber cutting, and wood gathering, just to name a few uses. Moreover, the 77,000-acre tract sits at elevations above 8,000 feet and is the watershed for the Culebra River and its tributaries, all of which provide the water that feeds the historic *acequias* used by the Hispanos to irrigate their lands in the valley below. The local people of San Luis fear that Taylor's assertion of his private property rights, as well as the Taylor family's logging activities, threatens both their use of the land as a commons and the stability of the watershed. Perhaps more importantly, Taylor's disruption of the commons threatens the distinct nature of the San Luis community.

Since this litigation began, Jack Taylor has died, and his heirs, particularly his son, Zachary Taylor, would like to either make a profit or sell the parcel: Zach Taylor has no interest in maintaining its historic use. At one point, the State of Colorado proposed purchasing the land for a reasonable

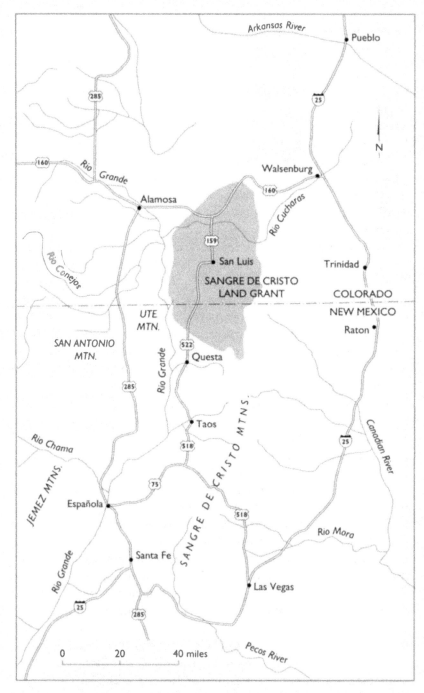

Map 7.  Sangre de Cristo Land Grant in Colorado and New Mexico.

market price through the use of lottery funds in order to save the land from loggers and others whose activities might negatively impact the land. Perhaps a more important goal of the Colorado government was settling the thirty-year-long legal battle between the Taylor family and the residents of San Luis. The seesaw of activity has included both sides winning court cases, but no final adjudication and no signs of a negotiated settlement in the foreseeable future.

For the Hispanos of Costilla County this is not merely a philosophical or legal battle. For them, the outcome of the case, which will determine who owns and controls the tract, directly impacts their quality of life. Hispanos of the rural San Luis Valley depend on subsistence farming, and many live near the poverty level because few industries, agricultural or otherwise, exist to provide local wage labor. The valley has endured a large out-migration of its citizens since World War II, many of whom left to find jobs in Denver, Albuquerque, Los Alamos, and Pueblo.[56] While many emigrants have retained their cultural and familial ties to the area, few economic opportunities remain to sustain them or their families on their traditional homeland. Those who remain in Costilla County and the town of San Luis depend on wood gathering for home fuel consumption (there is no natural gas available, and butane is expensive), grazing for their small herds, and hunting to sustain themselves. When Jack Taylor asserted his individual property rights and excluded them completely from their historic uses, he also cut off a significant portion of their economy. The local Hispano residents have reacted by abandoning local informal solutions and attempts to deal directly with Zachary Taylor; instead they have rejected traditional methods of negotiating conflict in favor of fighting back through the U.S. legal system.[57] Although this story conjures up many of the images Hollywood uses to portray the American West—shootouts, range wars, and quaint local color—it is really about complex ideas regarding property and the problems between conflicting land tenure systems that we have been discussing throughout this book in a historical context.

The history of the Sangre de Cristo Land Grant has its origins, as does the Maxwell Land Grant case, in the administration of the Mexican provincial governor Manuel Armijo. The Sangre de Cristo Land Grant lay to the north of Taos in present-day southern Colorado and northern New Mexico. It abutted the Maxwell Land Grant on the Maxwell's western border. In 1843, Stephen Luis Lee, an American-born Taos distiller, and Narcisco Beaubien, Carlos Beaubien's thirteen-year-old son, teamed up and asked Armijo for the 1,038,195-acre grant in order "to encourage the agriculture of the country and place it in a flourishing condition."[58] Because of the haste with which Armijo made them, land grants during Armijo's regime have had a historical reputation for being suspect, and the Sangre de Cristo grant was one of the most peculiar. First, Stephen Lee was an American— not a Mexican citizen. Although foreigners could obtain land grants if they applied with Mexican citizens, it was not viewed by government officials and other critics as particularly wise given the contemporary fear of American incursions into New Mexico. Second, Narcisco Beaubien was only a young boy and had no stature or ability to lure citizens to the frontier to create new settlements. The grant probably was made as a gift to Carlos Beaubien, the father of Narcisco and the brother-in-law of Lee. Beaubien, however, technically could not receive another grant under Mexican law because Armijo had already granted him half of the Beaubien/Miranda grant.

In 1848, just months after Brigadier General Stephen Watts Kearny had secured the occupation of New Mexico, an uprising in Taos against the American intruders left Governor Charles Bent and others, including the young Narcisco Beaubien, dead. After his son's death, the elder Beaubien gained full control of the Sangre de Cristo grant through inheritance and through purchase of Lee's share. Beaubien then began developing its resources and encouraging settlement. The U.S. Congress in 1860 confirmed that Beaubien owned just over 900,000 acres known as the Sangre de Cristo grant. That same law, of course, also confirmed that Beaubien and Miranda owned their large estate on the other side of the mountains as well.[59]

In 1862, Beaubien was elderly and in failing health. He also owed a significant amount of back taxes on the Sangre de Cristo grant and therefore began looking for a buyer for the entire estate. In William Gilpin, territorial governor of Colorado, he found the perfect entrepreneur to relieve him of his burden.[60] After Beaubien's death in 1864, Gilpin purchased the grant from Beaubien's heirs in 1864 with the intention of turning around and selling the land to European investors at a profit. The contract made clear that the Hispano settlers living on the grant would retain rights to the commons. The following provision for those living on the land grant read, "Certain settlement rights before then conceded by said Charles Beaubien to residents of the settlement of Costilla, Culebra, & Trinchera, within said tract included, shall be confirmed by said William Gilpin as made by him."[61] In 1863, prior to his bargaining with Gilpin, Beaubien had conveyed common areas to the towns on the Sangre de Cristo Land Grant.[62] Beaubien intended to grant the settlers use of the commons and usufructuary rights to firewood, timber, water, and pasture. In short, Gilpin knew he was purchasing the land with certain encumbrances attached, and he explicitly agreed to assume the same obligations that Beaubien had felt toward the settlers living on the grant. Because Gilpin was an outsider, Beaubien felt compelled to write down the conveyances to the Hispanos on the land grant to detail Gilpin's obligations to them. This was not the case with Maxwell, his son-in-law, because Beaubien probably trusted Maxwell to carry out the intentions and obligations associated with owning such a vast piece of land. Beaubien would not have expected Gilpin to know how to act like a *patrón* to the grant's inhabitants.

For the next hundred years, Gilpin and his successors in interest sold most of the grant to various parties.[63] In each of the conveyances from owner to owner, the rights of the local residents to use the commons were duly noted and agreed to by the new purchasers. Even Jack Taylor did not deny that he knew about the interests of the Hispano settlers. In fact, it was precisely because of those rights that he petitioned the court to erase them.[64] Immediately after his purchase, Jack Taylor filed a petition in U.S. district court to register title to his land under the Colorado Torrens Act.[65]

The Torrens Act originated in south Australia in 1858 under the guidance of Sir Robert Richard Torrens. Under this recording system, a landowner could petition the court to wipe away all other claims to a parcel of land. After giving proper notice to all who might have a claim to the land, conducting a hearing, and dismissing other claims, the landowner could then clear his title of rival claims, reducing it to the form of a fee simple absolute.[66] This had the effect of rewriting the legal history of a particular parcel of land. Literally, on the certificate of title, all other landowners, some with complex usufructuary interests in the land, were erased, and the title vested solely in the landowner who petitioned the court. This registration method or analogous ones were particularly effective in Hawai'i, Australia, New Zealand, Canada, and the American West in purging parcels of complex communal rights held by a significant preexisting native population based on their own customary property systems. Jack Taylor, by applying under the Torrens Act, attempted to clear all claims that the grant's inhabitants made for usufructuary rights. In 1967 he found success, and the Colorado court issued Taylor a title that was legally free of any encumbrances.[67] If only the Maxwell Land Grant Company could have had access to such a neat and tidy law that erased prior land title. By 1953, the Colorado state legislature felt that there was enough threat from unclear land titles as a result of Mexican land grants that an arcane and rarely used law was passed to help clear those parcels of prior property rights.

In 1981, however, some of the residents of San Luis filed a new civil action in the Costilla County District Court to regain access to and use of *la sierra*, the mountain tract of the Taylor Ranch. They made three claims for relief: (1) The Torrens Act violated due process of law and therefore did not apply to local landowners. Moreover, when Taylor applied under the Torrens Act, he failed to properly notify the property owners who made use of the commons. (2) The grant inhabitants' usufructuary rights were preserved under the Treaty of Guadalupe Hidalgo. And (3), when Carlos Beaubien conveyed rights to the settlers of the Sangre de Cristo Land Grant in 1863, those were rights and responsibilities that ran with the land and encumbered all subsequent property owners. In the eyes of the plaintiffs, Taylor had an obligation to them to leave the commons open.[68]

The American Southwest has had a long history of Hispano settlers using violence to resist Anglo holders of Mexican land grants. From the nineteenth-century struggles on the Las Vegas Land Grant, when Las Gorras Blancas rode across the landscape cutting fences, to the late 1960s, when Reis López Tijerina occupied the courthouse and shot at police officers in Tierra Amarilla, northern New Mexicans and southern Coloradans have been fighting to preserve their property rights.[69] What differentiates the Taylor Ranch struggle is that Hispanos no longer turn to violence to make their case but instead work within the U.S. legal system to attain their rights. By claiming that their rights to due process of law have been violated, the Hispano plaintiffs have accepted the validity of U.S. law—a concession that earlier land struggle movements would not make. Their legal claims reflect a shift in position from the nineteenth-century inhabitants of Mexican land grants. No longer are the Hispanos of the region foreigners suffering under the domination of a conquering government; they are now fully incorporated U.S. citizens who possess rights that have been violated.

Ironically, the claim that has worked in the Hispanos' favor has not been the more esoteric and principled arguments about the nature of communal rights under Mexican grant law or how Mexican land rights were incorporated into the U.S. system under the Treaty of Guadalupe Hidalgo. Rather, a purely procedural and legalistic objection has kept their claim alive. The plaintiffs claim that when Jack Taylor applied for a clear title under the Torrens Act, he did not give proper notice to all the owners of the commons. Taylor did not even notify all those he knew to have claims, and merely posted notices in the local papers. Furthermore, he did not make any significant effort to track down owners who had long since moved away but still retained property and familial connections to the commons. The plaintiffs believe that since their rights were violated, the clear title issued under this Torrens action should be revoked and the whole issue of who owns the commons should be reopened.

That the courts have almost virtually ignored the plaintiffs' claims made under the Treaty of Guadalupe Hidalgo about the nature of treaty rights and community land grants should not come as a surprise. As described in chapter 5, those protections were slowly eroded as the Supreme Court moved toward other models of protecting property rights. The relative success of the Torrens Act claim illustrates the historic reluctance of the U.S. courts to introduce the Spanish/Mexican conception of complex usufructuary property rights into the U.S. property regime. Unlike their claim under treaty-based rights, in which the plaintiffs assert that they have rights as a *community*, their Torrens Act claim states that they, as *individuals*, were not given adequate notice to vindicate their "individual" interest in the land.

But note the artificiality of the Torrens Act claim: it hardly seems to explain the real nature of the plaintiffs' grievance. The plaintiffs were not merely injured by lack of notice. They were injured by the loss of their communal property rights, an interest that the notice requirements of the Torrens Act would be inadequate to vindicate even if such requirements had been honored by Taylor. Properly notified individual Hispano owners, sometimes located hundreds of miles from the San Luis Valley, may have been less likely to show up in court to vindicate their "trivial" claim to gather wood. Such usufructuary rights are simply too small in value to the individual to justify such expense, especially to an owner who might live hundreds of miles away.

This is not to say that all of these usufructuary rights, taken collectively, would not have considerable value. In fact, they do. But no one usufructuary claimant would have sufficient incentive to defend the rights of all based only on his or her individual share of the commons. The Torrens Act claim is inadequate to protect the real interest of the plaintiffs—the preservation of the commons—because it is a claim designed to protect significant individual interests in the land. The Torrens Act claim simply cannot protect any conception of communal ownership where the vested right in question belongs to a group of persons and where no single individual is institutionally suited to protect the communal interest. Thus, notice to individuals would be insufficient to protect the community interest absent some way to organize all affected community members to challenge the Torrens action simultaneously. The courts, however, have denied the Hispanos the right to act as a class and work together.[70] Rather, they must individually sue Taylor to retain specific rights that had once belonged to the whole community.

216 / Chapter 6

In short, the plaintiffs' claim against the Torrens Act is an inadequate way to recognize Spanish / Mexican communal property rights—a sort of imperfect translation of such communal rights into terms recognized by the Anglo-American system of individual property rights. But its imperfection also indicates why it is the most successful claim of the plaintiffs in the actual litigation: such a theory of individual property rights is more familiar to the state courts than the concept of communal property created by Spanish / Mexican property law. Rather than attempt to reconstruct and enforce the law of these land grants under the terms of the Treaty of Guadalupe Hidalgo, the court preferred to narrowly inquire into whether every owner received a postcard informing him or her of the pending Torrens action. Such a claim might not really reflect what the plaintiffs want: return of their communal interest. But it does reflect what the court feels capable of delivering: enforcement of an Anglo-American system of individual property entitlement.

The Costilla County District Court reheard the case of *Rael v. Taylor*, now *Espinoza v. Taylor*, in the spring of 1998 to determine the extent of these rights. The plaintiffs lost their case before Judge Gaspar Perricone and the Colorado Court of Appeals, but the case has been heard again by the Colorado Supreme Court and is still on appeal. Property rights are still contested.[71] As one can imagine, business interests—and indeed much of the legal establishment, including three justices on the state supreme court —do not wish to see private property rights thrown into such turmoil. In the 1994 remand back to the district court, the dissent of State Supreme Court Justices Vollack, Roviera, and Erickson reads, in part: "The effect of the majority opinion is to reopen a thirty-year-old decision and put into question the ownership of a considerable portion of the land in Costilla County. . . . It is the public policy of this state to make title to property more *secure* and *marketable*, not less. . . . Such a result will introduce chaos and uncertainty in the marketability of land in this state."[72] As the case of the Maxwell Land Grant Company revealed a hundred years earlier, it is bad for business and progress to open up a legal argument that could throw into question the title to thousands of acres.

CONCLUSION

"Thus in the beginning all the world was America," wrote John Locke in 1690.[73] The Maxwell Land Grant Company took this widely accepted European notion and operated on the assumption that the American West was virgin land ready for appropriation. The assumption, however, was false.

This misconception of the West led Dutch and English investors to discount or disregard the established inhabitants, whether Jicarilla, Hispano, or Anglo, and their preexisting property regimes. The Maxwell Land Grant, far from being empty, was rich with history and inhabitants who carried with them their own notions of property.

This history of the Maxwell Land Grant is the story of colliding property regimes, government collusion, expanding markets, and people's loss. Historians have pointed to the Colfax County "War" to illustrate the violent nature of the American West. Others have used the Maxwell Land Grant Company as an example of the institutional order that swept the American West with the advent of industrialization. Finally, others have seen the conflict on the grant as an instance of ethnic conflict between Anglos and Hispanos as they struggled for control of the land. While all of these interpretations illuminate the past, none has pointed out the complexity of the relationships within the grant's boundaries, much less the grant's ties with the larger world markets of the eastern United States and Europe.

When the company's managers first set foot within the grant's boundaries, whether they realized it or not, they faced generations of people who had made their homes and livelihoods off this parcel of land. Rather than immediately executing their idyllic plan to organize the grant into departments that sold land, raised cattle, grew crops, cut timber, and mined gold and coal, the company had to first reclaim the occupied grant so that they could impose their order upon the land. Or so they thought.

In fact, the company never really gained control over the land or the settlers. They either had them removed, as in the case of the Jicarillas; or they left the problem for others to solve, as in the case of the sale to CF&I; or, as in most instances, an uneasy mixture of property rights emerged. By purchasing improvements and selling smaller irregular plots, the company implicitly accepted elements of the prior property regime. Conversely, by selling their improvements and moving off the grant or by purchasing plots from the company, the settlers also accepted and adapted to the changing nature of property. The Jicarillas, however, never had the opportunity to adapt and were made to fend for themselves in a different landscape.

None of this change would have come about if it had not been for the influence of the federal government, particularly the Department of the Interior and the U.S. Supreme Court. The Department of the Interior, with its contradictory policies that first allowed Hispano and Anglo homesteaders to settle 160-acre plots and then reneged on that promise, further complicated the problem of defining property rights. Those conflicting policies had to be clarified by the U.S. Supreme Court, which was intent on creating an outcome that would encourage progress and marketability, quickly clear the company's title, and avoid further litigation over the grant's boundaries.

In all instances of government intervention—from Congress confirming the grant for 1.7 million acres, to the General Land Office approving the Elkins/Marmon survey, to the Supreme Court upholding the company's title—the federal government aided foreign investors and the company while opposing its own citizens, whether Native American, Hispano, or Anglo. Without the powerful aid of the federal government, the battle between the settlers and the company might have been a fairer one. Government collusion, corrupt or legal, was the deciding factor in determining valid property rights on the Maxwell Land Grant.

A second factor influenced the outcome of the battle between the company and settlers: the power of market capitalism. From its nascent beginning, when Beaubien and Miranda first realized the potential of the grant's resources, to Maxwell's first forays into the market by trading with nearby forts and the Santa Fe Trail, to the company's full participation in national markets, the world-system influenced the grant's development. These markets also influenced the people, whether *peones*, landowners, or wage laborers, who worked the land. Whether the farmer thought about these connections every time he sold a bag of grain is doubtful. The same can be said for the rancher who sold a cow, or the miner who dug coal, or even the company manager who sold bonds. Yet all depended to some extent on prices set in Chicago, New York, London, and Amsterdam. It is these larger connections that have illuminated the complexity of the battles on the Maxwell Land Grant.

In the end, however, this is a history of people, their relationships to the land, and, for many of them, their alienation from their homes. Every person who came into contact with the grant had a financial and emotional tie to the land. How these two relationships balanced with each other determined how each group ultimately dealt with its position on the grant. The Jicarillas, who placed spiritual and emotional attachments to their homeland above their economic needs, were the first to lose their place on the grant as Anglos and Hispanos driven by a desire to create farms, and a company driven by its desire to succeed in the world market, chased them from their home. The next casualties were the Hispanos who could not raise sufficient capital to purchase infrastructure and livestock to compete successfully within the emerging market. Their traditional farming practices and adobe homes were incompatible with the company's notions of success in the market and progress on the grant.

One needs only to travel along Interstate 25 today to realize that the company also failed in its desire to control the land. There is no remnant of a Dutch colony except for a few Dutch names that stand out oddly in the Raton and Cimarron phone books; the train runs less and less frequently; and only a few cattle and oil derricks remain to remind the traveler of a market-imposed past. Collinson's, Whigham's, and even Pels's false conception of the land as uninhabited was their downfall. They realized too late that people lived on the grant and would fight back when their property and way of life were threatened. Finally, they sold what they could and exploited what was left. A century later, however, the landscape only hints at the past. What strikes one most is the seeming emptiness of the landscape. In the end, the hostility of the environment prevailed. Today it allows only the most persistent of historical artifacts—the straight fencelines of the grid, adobe structures, and Jicarilla place names—to survive, reminding the traveler of the many people and property regimes that came into conflict and eventually merged on this landscape.

# Notes

INTRODUCTION

1. *Espinoza v. Taylor*, District Court for the County of Costilla, State of Colorado, Civil Action no. 81, May 1998.

2. Regarding the history of property, particularly the place of fee simple absolute property, see A. W. B. Simpson, *An Introduction to the History of the Land Law* (London: Oxford University Press, 1979).

3. Throughout the book I use three terms to describe the Mexican American population of northern New Mexico and southern Colorado. In most cases I use the term "Hispano" in deference to the population that lives there and prefers this term when talking about themselves. I also use "Mexican American" when discussing the early years after the U.S.–Mexican War, when people were attempting to establish their rights. Finally, I use "Mexican" when referring to this population prior to the war, when they were still Mexican citizens. The term "Mexican" also appears in the book when a company agent or government official uses the term in a derogatory manner.

4. For a fascinating discussion of how "the state" is interested in ordering property regimes, and consequently dispossessing prior users, see James C. Scott, *Seeing Like a State* (New Haven: Yale University Press, 1999).

5. See, in particular, the work of David Montejano, *Anglos and Mexicans in the Making of Texas* (Austin: University of Texas Press, 1987); Neil Foley, *The White Scourge: Anglos, Blacks, and Mexicans in Central Texas, 1880–1930* (Berkeley: University of California Press, 1997); David Gutiérrez, *Walls and Mirrors: Mexican Americans, Mexican Immigrants, and the Politics of Ethnicity* (Berkeley: University of California Press, 1995); George J. Sánchez, *Becoming Mexican American* (New York: Oxford University Press, 1993); and Sarah Deutsch, *No Separate Refuge* (New York: Oxford University Press, 1987).

6. In thinking about how people interpreted and made sense of their place on the Maxwell Land Grant, I have been influenced by Katherine Morrissey and her book *Mental Territories: Mapping the Inland Empire* (Ithaca: Cornell University Press, 1998).

7. I would, however, make an exception to this statement by looking at the work of William Robbins, *Colony and Empire* (Lawrence: University of Kansas Press, 1994); Montejano, *Anglos and Mexicans in the Making of Texas;* and Tomás Almaguer, "Interpreting Chicano History: The World System Approach to Nineteenth-Century California," *Review* 4 (winter 1981): 459–507. These works have influenced my thinking about this theme and the place of the American Southwest within the larger context of world expansion and world capitalist markets.

8. One of the most interesting collections that addresses precisely this point is Amy Kaplan and Donald E. Pease, eds., *Cultures of United States Imperialism* (Durham, N.C.: Duke University Press, 1993).

9. The works of Ann L. Stoler, Fred Cooper, and Steve Stern have been particularly useful in thinking about how the history of the American Southwest fits into these larger colonial and imperial circuits. See, in particular, Fred Cooper and Ann L. Stoler's introduction to *Tensions of Empire: Colonial Cultures in a Bourgeois World* (Berkeley: University of California Press, 1997); and the Fred Cooper and Steve Stern essays in Frederick Cooper et al., *Confronting Historical Paradigms: Peasants, Labor, and the Capitalist World System in Africa and Latin America* (Madison: University of Wisconsin Press, 1993).

10. Christine Bold ("The Rough Riders at Home and Abroad: Cody, Roosevelt, Remington, and the Imperialist Hero," *Canadian Review of American Studies* 18, no. 3 [March 1987]: 321) makes some interesting connections between the U.S. military's actions in the American West and their behavior during the Spanish-American War. See also J. Anthony Lukas, *Big Trouble* (New York: Simon and Schuster, 1997), 127, and his discussion of the 24th Cavalry Division's participation in the Spanish-American War, the Indian Wars, and putting down labor insurrections in the American West.

11. Alan Trachtenberg, *The Incorporation of America: Culture and Society in the Gilded Age* (New York: Hill and Wang, 1982).

12. William Cronon, *Nature's Metropolis: Chicago and the Great West* (New York: W. W. Norton, 1993), and John Agnew, *The United States and the World Economy: A Regional Geography* (New York: Cambridge University Press, 1987).

13. The work of Immanuel Wallerstein has been immensely useful in my development of these ideas. See, in particular, "The Rise and Future Demise of the World Capitalist System: Concepts for Comparative Analysis," in *Capitalist World-Economy* (Cambridge: Cambridge University Press, 1979), 1–36. See also Steve Stern and Wallerstein, "American Historical Review Forum," *American Historical Review* 93 (October 1988): 896.

14. For a discussion on the interconnectedness and dynamics of these colonial relationships, see Cooper and Stoler's introduction to *Tensions of Empire.*

15. Regarding how different groups have viewed and used land throughout the world, see the work of Robert Ellickson, in particular "Property in Land," *Yale Law Journal* 102 (April 1993): 1319.

16. Wallerstein suggests that the world-system influenced virtually every aspect of economic and social life in the periphery states. According to Wallerstein, the world-system also required that the colony be run under the control of a strong state machinery. As we will see, the case of the Maxwell Land Grant Company also meets this criterion of the world-system, as the U.S. federal government was always willing to aid the Dutch investors. Wallerstein, *The Modern World System* (New York: Academic Press, 1974).

17. The standard books that have dealt with the history of the Maxwell Land Grant, Lucien B. Maxwell, and the Maxwell Land Grant Company are William Keleher, *Maxwell Land Grant: A New Mexico Item* (Albuquerque: University of New Mexico Press, 1984); Lawrence R. Murphy, *Lucien B. Maxwell: Napoleon of the Southwest* (Norman: University of Oklahoma Press, 1983); Jim Berry Pearson, *The Maxwell Land Grant* (Norman: University of Oklahoma Press, 1961); and Morris F. Taylor, *O. P. McMains and the Maxwell Land Grant Conflict* (Tucson: University of Arizona Press, 1979).

18. In thinking about how whiteness and privilege in the American West are construed together, see Foley, *White Scourge*.

19. Richard White, *Middle Ground: Indians, Empires, and Republics in the Great Lakes Region, 1600–1815* (New York: Cambridge University Press, 1997), 15.

## CHAPTER 1. CONTESTED BOUNDARIES

1. See, for example, William Keleher, *Maxwell Land Grant: A New Mexico Item* (Albuquerque: University of New Mexico Press, 1984); Morris F. Taylor, *O. P. McMains and the Maxwell Land Grant Conflict* (Tucson: University of Arizona Press, 1979); Robert Rosenbaum, *Mexicano Resistance in the Southwest: The Sacred Right of Self-Preservation* (Austin: University of Texas Press, 1981).

2. Patricia Nelson Limerick, *Legacy of Conquest: The Unbroken Past of the American West* (New York: W. W. Norton, 1987), 55. See also Richard White, *It's Your Misfortune and None of My Own* (Norman: University of Oklahoma Press, 1992), 137–54. For a general overview of the New Western History, see Limerick, Clyde A. Milner, and Charles E. Rankin, eds., *Trails Toward a New Western History* (Lawrence: University of Kansas Press, 1991).

3. Regarding the very provocative idea of a "middle ground," see Richard White, *The Middle Ground: Indians, Empires, and Republics in the Great Lakes Region, 1600–1815* (New York: Cambridge University Press, 1991), 52.

4. Veronica E. Velarde Tiller, *The Jicarilla Apache Tribe: A History, 1846–1970* (Lincoln: University of Nebraska Press, 1983), 5.

5. Tiller, *Jicarilla Apache Tribe*, 3; Erdoes and Ortiz, "The Jicarilla Genesis,"

85; James Mooney, "The Jicarilla Genesis," *American Anthropologist* 11, no. 7 (1998): 197.

6. As quoted in Lawrence R. Murphy, *Philmont: A History of New Mexico's Cimarron Country* (Albuquerque: University of New Mexico Press, 1972), 22; Tiller, *Jicarilla Apache Tribe*, 4, 13.

7. Veronica Tiller, "Jicarilla Apache," in Alfonso Ortiz, ed., *Handbook of North American Indians*, vol. 10 (Washington, D.C.: Smithsonian Institution, 1983), 443–44. See also Morris E. Opler, "A Summary of Jicarilla Apache Culture," *American Anthropologist* 38 (April–June 1936): 202.

8. See chapter 3, page 97.

9. "Diario y derrotero de Juan de Ulibarrí," *Provincias Internas* 36, expediente 4 (1706): 362, Archivo General de la Nación.

10. Tiller, "Jicarilla Apache," 441. For an interesting, if somewhat dated, anthropological explanation of gender differences among the Jicarilla, see Morris E. Opler, *Childhood and Youth in Jicarilla Apache Society* (Los Angeles: Southwest Museum Fund, 1946), 85–104. Regarding gendered divisions of labor among the Pueblos in general, see Ramón Gutiérrez, *When Jesus Came, the Corn Mothers Went Away: Marriage, Sexuality, and Power in New Mexico, 1500–1846* (Stanford: Stanford University Press, 1991), 15.

11. Tiller, "Jicarilla Apache," 441–42.

12. Ibid., 441.

13. Regarding Europeans' perceptions of Native American land use patterns, see William Cronon's study on New England Indian/White relations: William Cronon, *Changes in the Land* (New York: Hill and Wang, 1983), 666.

14. Hubert Howe Bancroft, *History of Arizona and New Mexico, 1530–1888* (Albuquerque: Horn and Wallace, 1962), 222–29 passim.

15. For a general discussion of Native American land use, see Richard White, *Roots of Dependency* (Lincoln: University of Nebraska Press, 1983).

16. "Diario," 353.

17. For a discussion of Spanish naming and its consequences, see Anne McClintock, *Imperial Leather* (New York: Routledge, 1995), 1–9; Patricia Seed, *Ceremonies of Possession in Europe's Conquest of the New World, 1492–1640* (New York: Cambridge University Press, 1995); and Mary Louise Pratt, *Imperial Eyes* (New York: Routledge, 1992).

18. "Diario," 361.

19. "Diario," 362v.

20. Ibid.

21. My interpretation of this diary has obviously benefited from my reading of McClintock, *Imperial Leather*, in particular her provocative introduction.

22. "Diario," 363–63v.

23. "Diario," 364v.

24. Ibid.

25. "Diario," 364.

26. Ibid., 366–67v; see also Bancroft, *History*, 222.

27. "Diario," 366–66v.

28. Tiller, *Jicarilla Apache Tribe,* 7–9.

29. Ibid., 9. There is very little information about Jicarilla relationships with either Spain or Mexico during the first part of the nineteenth century. This was a time of increased tension between the two countries, and New Mexico often stood on the outskirts of all the turmoil. For a thorough discussion of New Mexico during this time period, see Andrés Reséndez, "Caught Between Profits and Rituals: National Contestation in Texas and New Mexico, 1821–1848" (Ph.D. diss., University of Chicago, 1997), chapter 4.

30. Guadalupe Miranda and Charles Beaubien to Governor Manuel Armijo, January 8, 1841, in *Translation of the Beaubien and Miranda Petition, & c.* (Santa Fe: Manderfield and Tucker, Printers, 1872), 1–3. Beaubien also faced serious opposition in Taos from Father Antonio José Martínez, and quite possibly he saw this colony on the eastern side of the Sangre de Cristo Mountains as the perfect opportunity to expand his trading post and get away from the hostile eyes of Martínez. See Lawrence R. Murphy, "The Beaubien and Miranda Land Grant, 1841–1846," *New Mexico Historical Review* 42, no. 1 (July 1967): 29.

31. Regarding the differences between these types of landowners and workers, see my discussion in chapter 2, page 69. Regarding the legal meaning of these distinctions, see my discussion in chapter 5, page 188.

32. See entries for Charles Beaubien in Howard R. Lamar, ed., *Reader's Encyclopedia of the American West* (New Haven: Yale University Press, 1998) and LeRoy R. Hafen, ed., *The Mountain Men and the Fur Trade of the Far West: Biographical Sketches of the Participants by Scholars of the Subject and with Introductions by the Editor,* vol. 3 (Glendale, Calif.: Arthur H. Clark, 1965).

33. Reséndez, *Caught,* 359–65.

34. Governor Armijo to Beaubien and Miranda, January 11, 1841, in *Translation,* 3. For a more detailed discussion of the implications surrounding the conveyance, see chapter 5, "The Law of the Land: *United States v. Maxwell Land Grant Company.*"

35. Regarding the Texas expedition into New Mexico, see Howard R. Lamar, *The Far Southwest, 1846–1912: A Territorial History* (New Haven: Yale University Press, 1966), 75–80 passim.

36. E. A. Mares, "The Many Faces of Padre Antonio José Martínez," *Padre Martínez: New Perspectives from Taos* (Taos: Millicent Rogers Museum, 1988), 23. For a complete discussion of the Martínez family, see David J. Weber, *On the Edge of Empire: The Taos Hacienda of Los Martínez* (Santa Fe: Museum of New Mexico Press, 1996).

37. Vigil wrote the boundaries as follows:

> Commencing on the east of Red River, a mound was erected, from whence, following in a direct line in an easterly direction to the first hills, another mound was erected, at the point thereof: and continuing from south to north, on a line nearly parallel with Red River, a third mound was erected, on the north side of the Chico Rica or Chacauco mesa, (Table-land;) thence turning towards the west, and following along the side of said tableland of the Chacauco, to the summit of the mountain where the

fourth mound was erected; from thence following along the summit of said main ridge from north to south, to the Cuesta del Osha, one hundred varas north of the road from Fernandez, to the Laguna Negra, where the fifth mound was erected, from thence, turning again to the east towards Red River, and following along the southern side of the table lands of the Rayado and those of Gonzalitos, on the eastern point of which the sixth mound was erected; from thence, following in a northerly direction, I again reached Red River, on its western side, where the seventh and last mound was erected, opposite to the first, which was erected on the eastern side.

Translation of Beaubien and Miranda Petition, 5.

38. Victor Westphall, *Mercedes Reales: Hispanic Land Grants of the Upper Rio Grande Region* (Albuquerque: University of New Mexico Press, 1983), 45–7.

39. Bent's heirs would eventually sue to gain a portion of the land grant in the 1860s. See chapter 2, page 53, regarding Lucien B. Maxwell's settling of their claims. See also Morris F. Taylor, "A New Look at an Old Case: The Bent Heirs' Claim in the Maxwell Grant," *New Mexico Historical Review* 43, no. 3 (July 1968): 213.

40. David J. Weber, *The Mexican Frontier, 1821–1846: The American Southwest under Mexico* (Albuquerque: University of New Mexico Press), 242–72 passim.

41. Josiah Gregg, *Commerce of the Prairies: or Eight Expeditions across the Great Western Prairies, and a Residence of Nearly Nine Years in Northern Mexico* (New York: H. G. Langley, 1844. Reprint, Norman: University of Oklahoma Press, 1990).

42. Lamar, *Far Southwest*, 8–10, 52; Murphy, "Beaubien," 32–33.

43. Carlos Beaubien remained an influential political figure in both Taos and Rayado. When New Mexico's first Indian agent, James S. Calhoun, arrived in New Mexico, he relied on the political stature and connections of Beaubien. See J. S. Calhoun to Orlando Brown, Esq., Commissioner of Indian Affairs, February 2, 1850, 132–34, and Carlos Beaubien to James S. Calhoun, June 11, 1851, 357–58, in Calhoun, *The Official Correspondence of James S. Calhoun* (Washington, D.C.: Government Printing Office, 1915).

44. Although there is little specific evidence about the early settlements on the Maxwell Land Grant, there is a significant body of research on other early settlements that were intimately linked to it. For instance, the Sangre de Cristo Land Grant was also a Beaubien settlement and probably had a very similar pattern. See *Espinoza v. Taylor*, exhibit no. 148. Furthermore, most of the settlers on the Maxwell grant were moving from the Rio Grande settlements, which conform to the pattern described in the text, and would have created living patterns similar to those they were accustomed to at home. For how New Mexicans established their communities, see Alvar W. Carlson, "Long Lots on the Río Arriba," *Annals of the Association of American Geographers* 65, no. 1 (March 1975): 48; "Rural Settlement Patterns in the San Luis Valley: A Comparative Study," *Colorado Magazine* 44 (1967): 111. See also Margaret Mead,

*Cultural Patterns and Technical Change* (New York: New American Library, 1955), 151–77.

45. Carlson, "Rural Settlement," 117–18; see also Stanley Crawford, *Mayordomo* (Albuquerque: University of New Mexico Press), 1988.

46. Carlson, "Rural Settlement," 119; Lawrence R. Murphy, "Rayado: Pioneer Settlement in Northeastern New Mexico, 1848–1857," *New Mexico Historical Review* 46, no. 1 (January 1971), 37.

47. Murphy, "Beaubien," 34–35.

48. Carlos Beaubien to James S. Calhoun, June 11, 1851, in Calhoun, *Official Correspondence*, 257–58.

49. John Grier, "Overawing the Indians: Captain Judd and Lt. Burnside at Las Vegas," 541A, William G. Ritch Collection, Henry E. Huntington Library, San Marino, Calif. For Maxwell's account, see Henry Inman, *The Old Santa Fe Trail* (Topeka: Crane and Company, 1916), 385–88.

50. Commander to 1st Lt. George F. Campbell, U.S. Third Cavalry, August 25, 1866, Box 24, #1481, Ritch Collection. Prior to being made an Indian agent, Maxwell passed out supplies from his own stock. See Pliny Earl Goddard, *Jicarilla Apache Texts* (New York: American Museum of Natural History, 1911), 251, for a Jicarilla account of Maxwell's generosity. Regarding the skirmishes between the Jicarillas and the Hispano and Anglo interlopers during the 1850s and 1860s, see Tiller, *Jicarilla Apache Tribe*, 36–70 passim.

51. Calhoun to Hon. L. Lea, Commissioner of Indian Affairs, April 6, 1852, *Official Correspondence*, 515.

52. Quoted from Marc Simmons, "The Wagon Mound Massacre," in *Journal of the West* 28, no. 2 (April 1989): 46. See also Morris E. Opler, "Jicarilla Apache Territory, Economy, and Society in 1850," *Southwestern Journal of Anthropology* 27, no. 4 (winter 1971): 311; and Robert W. Frazer, ed., *New Mexico in 1850: A Military View* (Norman: University of Oklahoma Press, 1968), 104. For an account told by Jicarilla informants, see Goddard, *Jicarilla Apache Texts*, 242–43.

53. Grier, "Overawing the Indians," 541A.

54. Burnside was an officer out of West Point. He was also the same Burnside who would assume the command of the Army of the Potomac in 1862 during the Civil War. After a successful military career, he went on to be the state governor and U.S. senator from Rhode Island. Simmons, "Wagon Mound Massacre," 47.

55. Grier, "Overawing the Indians," 541B; *Santa Fe Weekly Gazette*, November 27, 1852.

56. Not surprisingly, we know the names of the White family, but not of the African American slaves or the Mexican teamsters who accompanied them. See Grier, "Overawing the Indians," 541B; Calhoun, *Official Correspondence*, 269–74. See also Donald Chaput, *Francois X. Aubry* (Glendale, Calif.: Arthur H. Clark, 1975), 83–86.

57. Calhoun to Col. W. Medill, Commissioner of Indian Affairs, October 29,

1949, *Official Correspondence,* 64; Calhoun to Orlando Brown, Esq., Commissioner of Indian Affairs, March 29, 1850, 172.

58. Grier, "Overawing the Indians," 541B. We know nothing else of the Indian woman they killed. Grier makes no further mention of the incident.

59. Ibid. There is also an account of the White massacre in Milo Milton Quaife, ed., *Kit Carson's Autobiography* (Lincoln: University of Nebraska Press, 1966), 131–33.

60. Ibid.; however, a different account appears in Simmons's article on the White massacre ("Wagon Mound Massacre," 52 n. 12), suggesting that only Mrs. White was found dead and that the servant and Virginia, the Whites' daughter, had disappeared. The Indian agent, James Calhoun, apparently thought Virginia White might still be alive; he kept sending Mexican and American traders into the field to offer the ransom. See Calhoun, *Official Correspondence,* 269, 293, and 297. Furthermore, a Jicarilla man supposedly told Indian Superintendent Chester E. Faris at the end of the century that a Jicarilla woman named Margarita Inez was actually Virginia White. It is almost impossible to verify such a story, but it does suggest interesting possibilities about captivity and Virginia's desire to remain with the Jicarillas. For an important discussion about captivity, see John Demos, *Unredeemed Captive* (New York: Alfred Knopf, 1994).

61. Quoted from Chris Emmett, *Fort Union and the Winning of the Southwest* (Norman: University of Oklahoma Press, 1965), 172.

62. For details about the violence that followed in the early 1850s, see Hamilton Gardner, "Philip St. George Cooke and the Apache, 1854," *New Mexico Historical Review* 28 (April 1953): 115.

CHAPTER 2. REGULATING LAND, LABOR, AND BODIES

1. Congressmen John C. Calhoun worried that the Mexican elite were not schooled enough in republican and democratic principles to lead their people into an equitable union with the United States. Calhoun said, "Where is the intelligence in Mexico adequate to the construction of such a [republican] government? . . . [T]he owners of the haciendas—the large planters of the country—who comprise almost the remaining mass of intelligence [other than priests], are without opportunities of concert, and destitute of the means of forming such a government." *Congressional Globe,* 30th Congress, 1st session, p. 97.

2. *Boston Times,* October 22, 1847; quoted from Frederick Merk, *Manifest Destiny and Mission in American History* (New York: Vintage Books, 1966), 122. Regarding how Americans viewed the U.S.–Mexican War, see also Robert W. Johannsen, *To the Halls of the Montezumas: The Mexican War in the American Imagination* (New York: Oxford University Press, 1986), 73, 159, 169, 171, 297, and 301; and Reginald Horsman, *Race and Manifest Destiny: The Origins of American Racial Anglo-Saxonism* (Cambridge: Harvard University Press, 1981).

3. Merk (*Manifest Destiny,* 195–201) points out that part of "America's mission" was to stand as a beacon for Europeans who wanted to overthrow their monarchy and take up the torch of freedom and liberty. Many politicians and newspapers saw the war with Mexico as a liberating one that provided a good example for Europe.

4. Regarding the Great Mahele, see Jon J. Chinen, *The Great Mahele: Hawaii's Land Division of 1848* (Honolulu: University of Hawaii Press, 1974).

5. Regarding the specifics of the treaty that ended the U.S.–Mexican War, see Richard Griswold del Castillo, *The Treaty of Guadalupe Hidalgo: A Legacy of Conflict* (Norman: University of Oklahoma Press, 1990).

6. Hunter Miller, ed., *Treaties and Other International Acts of the United States of America,* vol. 5 (Washington, D.C.: Government Printing Office, 1937).

7. To understand the experiences of other Mexicanos as they became Mexican Americans living and working in the greater American Southwest, see the works of David Montejano, *Anglos and Mexicans in the Making of Texas, 1836–1986* (Austin: University of Texas Press, 1987), and Neil Foley, *The White Scourge: Anglos, Blacks, and Mexicans in Central Texas, 1880–1930* (Berkeley: University of California Press, 1997), for Texas. For California, see Albert Camarillo, *Chicanos in a Changing Society: From Mexican Pueblos to American Barrios in Santa Barbara and Southern California, 1848–1930* (Cambridge: Harvard University Press, 1979); David Gutiérrez, *Walls and Mirrors: Mexican Americans, Mexican Immigrants, and the Politics of Ethnicity* (Berkeley: University of California Press, 1995); George J. Sánchez, *Becoming Mexican American: Ethnicity, Culture, and Identity in Chicano Los Angeles, 1900–1945* (New York: Oxford University Press, 1993); and Tomás Almaguer, *Racial Fault Lines: The Historical Origins of White Supremacy in California* (Berkeley: University of California Press, 1994). For Arizona, see Thomas Sheridan, *Los Tucsonenses: The Mexican Community in Tucson, 1854–1941* (Tucson: University of Arizona Press, 1986). For New Mexico the standard work of the period is still Howard R. Lamar, *The Far Southwest, 1846–1912: A Territorial History* (New Haven: Yale University Press, 1966).

8. Even in the midst of the U.S.–Mexican War, the editor of the *Santa Fe Republican* voiced his concern over the problems that would arise as a result of the change in government and people's panic over protecting their property and individual rights. The editor urged the U.S. Congress to move swiftly in deciding what type of government, civil or military, the territory would have immediately after the war. He urged that New Mexico be made a territory so that the process of clearing land titles could move along more smoothly and rapidly. He also wanted specific plans laid out for who would be responsible for implementing the change in legal regimes. *Santa Fe Republican,* September 24, 1847, p. 4, and October 30, 1847, p. 4.

9. Regarding the limitations on married women, see the *Revised Statutes of the Territory of New Mexico,* chapter 44, sections 1, 9, 10, 11, and 12, as quoted in *Edgar and Edgar v. Baca and Gallegos, Report of Cases Argued and Deter-*

mined in the Supreme Court of the Territory of New Mexico, vol. 1, January 1857, reported by Charles H. Gildersleeve (Chicago: Callaghan and Company, 1897). Regarding the New Mexico territorial court's reaction to these laws, see Martinez v. Lucero and Chaves v. McKnight and Gutieres, Report of Cases.

10. Maxwell engaged in a paternalism that is very reminiscent of the world Eugene D. Genovese described in Roll, Jordan, Roll: The World the Slaves Made (New York: Pantheon Books, 1974). See also Charles Joyner, Down by the Riverside: A South Carolina Slave Community (Urbana: University of Illinois Press, 1984), 56 and 231.

11. William Keleher, The Maxwell Land Grant: A New Mexico Item (Albuquerque: University of New Mexico Press, 1984), 40–42.

12. Lucien B. Maxwell was born on September 14, 1818, to Hugh H. Maxwell and Odile Menard Maxwell in Kaskaskia, Illinois. For more information on Maxwell's background and childhood, see Lawrence R. Murphy, Lucien B. Maxwell: Napoleon of the Southwest (Norman: University of Oklahoma Press, 1983), 3–19 passim.

13. Enrique Florescano, "Haciendas." Cambridge History of Latin America, vol. 2, ed. Leslie Bethall (New York: Cambridge University Press, 1984), 171–82; Eric Van Young, Hacienda and Market in Eighteenth-Century Mexico: The Rural Economy of the Guadalajara Region, 1675–1820 (Berkeley: University of California Press, 1981); Francois Chevalier, Land and Society in Colonial Mexico: The Great Hacienda (Berkeley: University of California Press, 1963).

14. For one of the most outrageous caricatures of Maxwell and his life, see Noah Gordon, "The Cowman They Called God," True Men Adventure (November 1956). Copy in Maxwell Land Grant and Family File, Arthur Johnson Memorial Library, Raton, New Mexico.

15. LeRoy R. Hafen, ed., The Mountain Men and the Fur Trade of the Far West: Biographical Sketches of the Participants by Scholars of the Subject and with Introductions by the Editor, vol. 3 (Glendale: Arthur H. Clark, 1965); David J. Weber, The Taos Trappers (Norman: University of Oklahoma Press, 1968).

16. Murphy, Lucien B. Maxwell, 173; see entries for John C. Frémont and Lucien B. Maxwell in Howard R. Lamar, ed., The Reader's Encyclopedia of the West (New Haven: Yale University Press, 1998), 401–2, 685. Although Lucien and Luz married in 1844, it is unclear if they lived together. There is some speculation that he left Taos with Carson and Frémont for California and did not return until after the war in 1848. This seems very plausible because when he returned, Luz would have been seventeen and more prepared to begin a family.

17. See, in particular, Sandra Jaramillo, "The Myth of High Skirts and Loose Blouses: Intercultural Marriage in the Mexican Period," presented at the 1995 meeting of the Western Historical Association in Denver.

18. The similarities between New Mexico and other French trading frontiers should not be overlooked. Comparisons can be made between French alliances made with Native Americans in trapping beaver, and the French alliances made

with Mexicans in trading. For more on French intermarriage with Native Americans, see Sylvia Van Kirk, *"Many Tender Ties": Women in Fur-Trade Society, 1600–1870* (Norman: University of Oklahoma Press, 1980). Regarding the practice of intermarriage in general, and the Maxwells specifically, see Darlis A. Miller, "Intercultural Marriages in the American Southwest," in Joan M. Jensen and Darlis A. Miller, eds., *New Mexico Women: Intercultural Perspectives* (Albuquerque: University of New Mexico Press, 1986). See also Rebecca McDowell Craver, *Impact of Intimacy: Mexican-Anglo Intermarriage in New Mexico, 1821–1846* (El Paso: Texas Western Press, 1982).

19. Milo Milton Quaife, *Kit Carson's Autobiography* (Lincoln: University of Nebraska Press, 1966), 130.

20. Albert W. Archibald testified in *Bent v. Miranda* (p. 190) that Maxwell had thirty to forty families working for him as "lessees" in the early years at Rayado. Victor Grant Collection, Arthur Johnson Memorial Library, Raton, New Mexico.

21. See Lawrence R. Murphy, *Philmont: A History of New Mexico's Cimarron Country* (Albuquerque: University of New Mexico Press, 1972), 58–70 passim. See also Murphy, "Rayado: Pioneer Settlement in Northeastern New Mexico, 1848–1857," *New Mexico Historical Review* 46, no. 1 (January 1971): 37.

22. Regarding the sale and history of the Rayado tract of land, see Murphy, *Lucien B. Maxwell*, 106.

23. Quitclaim deed from Miranda to Maxwells, May 19, 1868, Guadalupe Miranda Family Papers, New Mexico State Records Center and Archives, Santa Fe (hereinafter NMSRCA).

24. Quoted from the *Santa Fe New Mexican*, April 23, 1864, in the *Raton Range*, September 5, 1871, p. 1.

25. Copy of the Will of Carlos Beaubien, Book E, page 417, Colfax County Probate Court Records, NMSRCA. See also the final inventory of the estate of Carlos Beaubien, February 28, 1864, Taos County Records, B-4, pp. 76–79, NMSRCA.

26. For a comparison with Anglo customs regarding inheritance by daughters, see Peggy A. Rabkin, *From Father to Daughters: The Legal Foundation of Female Emancipation* (Westport, Conn.: Greenwood Press, 1980), which has a particularly thorough discussion of the Married Women's Property Acts. See also Carole Shammas et al., *Inheritance in America from Colonial Times to the Present* (New Brunswick, N.J.: Rutgers University Press, 1987).

27. Why did Teodora Mueller sell for only five hundred dollars, the lowest price the Maxwells paid for the Beaubien shares? One explanation might be that Mueller and Maxwell had other business dealings, of which this transaction was just a part. Mueller, along with another brother-in-law, Jesús Abreu, was the executor of the Carlos Beaubien estate, and the three men had several business dealings throughout their careers.

28. *Leonora Beaubien v. Vidal Trujillo*, Bill for Divorce, April 3, 1865, p. 113, NMSRCA.

29. The litigation surrounding the claims of Albert Bent's heirs is tangential and too convoluted to discuss in detail. But the children of New Mexico's first territorial governor, Charles Bent (a close friend of Carlos Beaubien who, along with Beaubien's son Narcisco, died during the Taos Rebellion), believed that their father owned a portion of the Beaubien/Miranda grant. They claimed that when Governor Armijo granted the land to Beaubien and Miranda, a share had also secretly gone to Bent. The transaction had to be kept secret because Bent was an American and known to sympathize with the United States. The Bent suit named all of the Beaubien heirs as defendants, but Maxwell was the one who eventually paid off the claims, thus assuring title for himself as sole owner of those claims. Maxwell personally quieted the two claims by purchasing from Teresina (Bent) and Aloys Scheurichs and Estefana (Bent) and Alexander Hicklin their undivided one-twelfth interests in the grant for six thousand dollars each, which was substantially more than he had paid his sisters-in-law. The final one-twelfth interest of Albert Bent (son of Charles) and his three heirs remained in litigation for the next thirty years, including numerous Territorial Supreme Court cases, district court hearings, and two trips to the United States Supreme Court before their claims were denied. Although Governor Manuel Armijo supposedly had been granted a one-fourth interest in the grant at the same time as Bent, no claim was ever made against Maxwell on his behalf. Few knew of Armijo's interest, and apparently none of his heirs knew enough about his affairs to make a claim.

The only bearing this case has on the discussion in the text is that the litigation threatened to drag on and call into question the validity of the Beaubien heirs' claim to the land grant. Perhaps many of the Beaubien heirs were happy to sell their interests to the Maxwells and let them sort out the legalities and the claims of the Bent heirs. For the particulars of the various suits and the litigiousness of one family, see Morris F. Taylor, "A New Look at an Old Case: The Bent Heirs' Claim in the Maxwell Grant," *New Mexico Historical Review* 43, no. 3 (July 1968): 213. For a brief account of the Taos Rebellion and the career of Charles Bent, see Lamar, *Reader's Encyclopedia*, 91.

30. In 1860 Jesús Abreu entered into a contract with José Pley, a prominent landowner in Rayado, to work Pley's ranch and expand the business. The terms were quite fair, if not generous, and it is likely this arrangement helped make the Abreus one of the wealthier and most respected families in the area. Agreement between José Pley and Jesús Abreu, February 22, 1860, Pley-Abreu, Henry-McGaven Collection, NMSRCA.

31. Testimony from Albert W. Archibald, *Bent v. Miranda*, p. 197.

32. See Frederick and Teodora Mueller to Maxwells and Joseph and Juana Clouthier to Maxwells, April 4, 1864, Book of Deeds A, pp. 74, 75, Taos County, New Mexico; Paul Beaubien to Maxwells, January 1, 1870, Book of Deeds A, p. 67, Colfax County, New Mexico; Vidal and Eleanor Trujillo to Maxwells, July 20, 1864, Book of Deeds A, p. 77, Mora County, New Mexico; Jesús and Petra Abreu to Maxwells, February 1, 1868, Book of Deeds A, p. 35, Mora County, New Mexico.

33. See Murphy, *Lucien B. Maxwell*, 35; Jim Berry Pearson, *The Maxwell Land Grant* (Norman: University of Oklahoma Press, 1961), 11–12; William A. Keleher, *The Maxwell Land Grant: A New Mexico Item* (Albuquerque: University of New Mexico Press, 1984), 30; and Morris F. Taylor, *O. P. McMains and the Maxwell Land Grant Conflict* (Tucson: University of Arizona Press, 1979), 60.

34. In 1860 there were four children and three servants in the Maxwell household. By 1870, the Maxwell household had six children (including an infant) and fifteen servants (including seven Indian servants under the age of fifteen). 1860 Manuscript Census for Mora County, p. 479, Mora County Records; 1870 Manuscript Census for Colfax County, Schedule 1, Precinct 3, p. 22, Colfax County Records.

35. Henry Inman, *Old Santa Fe Trail: The Story of a Great Highway* (Topeka: Crane and Company, 1916), 366–76; William H. Ryus, *The Second William Penn* (Kansas City: Frank T. Riley Publishing Co., 1913), 113.

36. Deed from Lucien and Luz Maxwell to Richard Miller and Taylor F. Maulding, 1870; Deed from Lucien and Luz Maxwell to Agnes Houx, 1871; Deed from Lucien and Luz Maxwell to Taylor F. Maulding, 1871; Mining Deed from Lucien and Luz Maxwell to John Dold and E. H. Bergman, 1871. A number of other deeds in this records collection have only Lucien Maxwell's name. All appear in the Colfax County Records, County Clerk, Misc. Papers and Deeds, NMSRCA.

37. *The Scottish Mortgage and Land Investment Company of New Mexico et al. v. Manuel S. Brazil et al.*, District Court of the Fourth Judicial District, San Miguel County, nos. 4091 and 4092. Reply by Luz Beaubien Maxwell.

38. Letter from Jones and Rogers to Messrs. Bentley and Burlin, Attorneys at Law, Chicago, Ill., June 5, 1902, Land Grants—Maxwell #6, NMSRCA; originally in Acc. 211, Fort Union National Monument, Watrous, New Mexico.

39. "The Last Will and Testament of Ma Gertrudes Barcelo," Misc. Records, Wills, and Testaments, NMSRCA. See also Deena González, "Doña Gertrudis Barcelo," in Adela de la Torre and Beatríz M. Pesquera, *Building with Our Hands: New Directions in Chicana Studies* (Berkeley: University of California Press, 1993), 75.

40. See Angelina F. Veyna, "'It is My Last Wish That . . .': A Look at Colonial Nuevo Mexicanas Through Their Testaments," in de la Torre and Pesquera, *Building*, 91; Deena J. González, "The Spanish-Mexican Women of Santa Fé: Patterns of Their Resistance and Accommodation, 1820–1880," 154–235 passim (Ph.D. diss., University of California, Berkeley, 1985), copy in author's possession; see also González, *Refusing the Favor: The Spanish-Mexican Women of Santa Fe, 1820–1880* (New York: Oxford University Press, 1999), and Janet Lecompte, "The Independent Women of Hispanic New Mexico, 1821–1846," *Western Historical Quarterly* 12, no. 1 (January 1981): 17. For a more general discussion of Mexican women's legal status and property rights during this period, see Silvia M. Arrom, *The Women of Mexico City, 1790–1857* (Stanford: Stanford University Press, 1985), 53–57 passim.

41. More work needs to be done on what rights were preserved for Mexican women under the Treaty of Guadalupe Hidalgo. To date, little research has been done in the area of Mexican and Mexican American women's property rights in the middle of the nineteenth century. One exception is Kathleen E. Lazarou, *Concealed Under Petticoats: Married Women's Property and the Law of Texas, 1840–1913* (New York: Garland Publishing, 1986). Some researchers have addressed how conflicting property regimes have affected women, but only within the East Coast context. See Linda Briggs Biemer, *Women and Property in Colonial New York: The Transition from Dutch to English Law* (Ann Arbor: UMI Research Press, 1983).

42. In 1821, after the United States acquired Florida, President Andrew Jackson declared that only common law was valid in the territory. See Lazarou, *Concealed Under Petticoats*, 44. In Louisiana, the matter was much more complicated, with negotiations between the proponents of civil and common law often reaching heated impasses. See George Dargo, *Jefferson's Louisiana: Politics and the Clash of Legal Traditions* (Cambridge: Harvard University Press, 1975).

43. There is an important historiographical debate about the status of married women and what these reform laws helped them and their husbands achieve in the economically turbulent times of the mid-nineteenth century. For a general discussion about inheritance in the United States, see Shammas et al., *Inheritance in America*, 36. For various interpretations of the Married Women's Property Acts, see Linda E. Speth, "The Married Women's Property Acts, 1839–1865: Reform, Reaction, or Revolution?" in *Women and the Law* (Cambridge: Schenkman Publishing, 1982), 69–99; Norma Basch, *In the Eyes of the Law: Women, Marriage, and Property in Nineteenth-Century New York* (Ithaca: Cornell University Press, 1982); Richard H. Chused, "Married Women's Property Law: 1800–1850," *Georgetown Law Journal* 71 (1983): 1359. Chused argues that the acts were passed to protect family assets and not to give women equal property rights. See also Reva B. Siegel, "The Modernization of Marital Status Law: Adjudicating Wives' Rights to Earnings, 1860–1930," *Georgetown Law Journal* 82 (September 1994): 2127. The historiography of family law, and women and the law, points to the East Coast bias of the field. Traditionally the story has been told as one of great progress, with American women emerging from the patriarchical home of the nineteenth century into the capitalist and individualistic world of the twentieth century where they can finally hold property, make contracts, and dispose of their land at will. See, for example, Mary Ann Glendon, *The New Family and the New Property* (Toronto: Butterworths, 1981), and Stephen J. Morse, "Family Law in Transition: From Traditional Families to Individual Liberty," in Virginia Tufte and Barbara Myerhoof, eds., *Changing Images of the Family* (New Haven: Yale University Press, 1979), 319. While this view has been criticized (see Martha Minow, "'Forming Underneath Everything That Grows': Toward a History of Family Law," *Wisconsin Law Review* 20 [1985]: 819), no one has pointed to the position of Spanish, French, and Mexican women who were incorporated into the

U.S. common law system. For them, the story is a declensionist one because they lost rights they had enjoyed for centuries. More work needs to be done to incorporate the story of these women into the historiography of women's legal history.

44. "Titles," *Laws Passed by the General Assembly of the Territory of New Mexico in the Session of December 1847* (Santa Fe: Hovey and Davies, 1848), 9–11.

45. *Revised Statutes*, chapter 44, sections 1, 9–11.

46. *Martinez v. Lucero*, p. 208.

47. Regarding the ability of women to be heard in a variety of court proceedings in colonial New Mexico, see Ramón A. Gutiérrez, *When Jesus Came, the Corn Mothers Went Away* (Stanford: Stanford University Press, 1989), in which much of his evidence comes from women's testimony before ecclesiastical and secular courts.

48. *Chaves v. McKnight and Gutieres*, p. 147. The court in this case is echoing many reformers' arguments regarding the need to overturn coverture. Given the unstable economy of the 1840s and 1850s, the courts and legislatures sought to preserve family wealth by allowing husbands to place real property in the name of the wife and then overturning coverture laws to protect that familial wealth from a husband's imprudent investments.

49. *Edgar and Edgar v. Baca and Gallegos*, p. 613. It is also interesting that Stephen B. Elkins represented Quirina Baca in this case. She was apparently quite a savvy woman if she could afford to hire one of the best-known, if unscrupulous, lawyers in the territory.

50. Ibid.

51. *Acts of the Territorial Legislature*, HB 118, section 145–2, February 21, 1887, Territorial Archives of New Mexico, roll 6, frame 877.

52. Anne McClintock, *Imperial Leather: Race, Gender, and Sexuality in the Colonial Contest* (New York: Routledge, 1995), 3, 6, and 213.

53. Senator Sidney Breese from Illinois, *Congressional Globe*, 30th Congress, 1st session, p. 321 (February 8, 1848).

54. *New York Herald*, September 30, 1845, and October 28, 1847.

55. *Philadelphia Public Ledger*, December 11, 1847; quoted from Merk, *Manifest Destiny*, 125.

56. McClintock (*Imperial Leather*, 6) also points out that it is the conquering men who implement laws that benefit themselves and the goals of their country.

57. William Pelham, Surveyor General of New Mexico, to Carlos Beaubien and Guadalupe Miranda, Approval of Grant, September 15, 1857, filed April 1, 1873, Book of Deeds A, pp. 321–41, Colfax County Records; Act of Congress, approved June 25, 1860, confirming the grant of land to Beaubien and Miranda, *Congressional Globe*, 36th Congress, 1st session, pp. 2750, 3290.

58. Every historian of the Maxwell Land Grant has agreed that in the early stages of acquiring and running the grant, the Maxwells never realized the exact acreage of the estate, nor did they believe it extended to two million acres.

See Keleher, *Maxwell Land Grant*, 44; Pearson, *Maxwell Land Grant*, 14; Robert Rosenbaum, *Mexicano Resistance in the Southwest* (Austin: University of Texas Press, 1981), 173; and Taylor, *O. P. McMains*, 60.

59. Regarding the refusal to ratify Article 10, see Griswold del Castillo, *Treaty*, 44–45.

60. See Ryus, *Second William Penn*, 109; Inman, *Old Santa Fe Trail*, 374; Josiah Gregg, *Commerce of the Prairies: or Eight Expeditions across the Great Western Prairies, and a residence of Nearly Nine Years in Northern Mexico* (New York: H. G. Langley, 1844; reprint, Norman: University of Oklahoma Press, 1990).

61. For a discussion of how this paternalism worked in the American South, see Elizabeth Fox-Genovese, *Inside the Plantation Household: Black and White Women of the Old South* (Chapel Hill: University of North Carolina Press, 1988), 64.

62. See David J. Weber, *On the Edge of Empire: The Taos Hacienda of Los Martínez* (Santa Fe: Museum of New Mexico, 1996), p. 25, in which he discusses the unique institution of New Mexico's haciendas, which had similarities, but which were not identical to, the Mexican hacienda system.

63. Congress twice attempted to mold property systems in New Mexico. First, in the debates over the establishment of the Office of the Surveyor General of New Mexico, southern congressmen successfully blocked the attempt by northern congressmen to open the territory of New Mexico for settlement to free Blacks (*Congressional Globe*, 33rd Congress, 1st session, May 2, 1854, pp. 1054, 1070–75, 1875). Second, on the eve of the Civil War, in 1860, Congress attempted to declare peonage in New Mexico illegal, but the bill died in session (*Congressional Globe*, 36th Congress, 1st session, 1860, pp. 2059, 2744).

64. Regarding the problems of creating a free labor force, see David M. Potter, *The Impending Crisis, 1848–1861* (New York: Harper and Row, 1976); Eric Foner, *Reconstruction: American's Unfinished Revolution, 1863–1877* (New York: Harper and Row, 1988), 124–75 passim; and Foner, *Free Soil, Free Labor, Free Men: The Ideology of the Republican Party Before the Civil War* (New York: Oxford University Press, 1995), 11–39 passim.

65. Gildersleeve, *Mariana Jaramillo v. José de la Cruz Romero, Report of the Cases.*

66. Ibid., 195.

67. The court talked about three laws: one from Spain, one 1828 Coahuila and Texas law, and an 1852 New Mexico territorial law. Ibid., 196–98.

68. Ibid., 197.

69. Regarding the structure of New Mexican society and households during the early part of the nineteenth century, see Gutiérrez, *When Jesus Came*, 144–75.

70. Ibid., 192.

71. See Howard Lamar, "From Bondage to Contract: Ethnic Labor in the American West, 1600–1890," in Steven Hahn and Jonathan Prude, eds., *The Countryside in the Age of Capitalist Transformation: Essays in the Social*

*History of Rural America* (Chapel Hill: University of North Carolina Press, 1985), 293.

72. See Estévan Rael y Gálvez, "Mal-Criado and Entre-Metido Subalternity: How(!) Is the "old Indian" Luis a Slave?," unpublished manuscript in author's possession.

73. Gildersleeve, *Jaramillo v. Romero, Report of the Cases,* 204. The court refers to an 1852 act passed by the New Mexico territorial legislature.

74. See James Brooks, "'This Evil Extends Especially to the Feminine Sex': Captivity and Identity in New Mexico, 1700–1846," in Susan Armitage and Elizabeth Jameson, eds., *Writing the Range: Race, Class, and Culture in the Women's West* (Norman: University of Oklahoma Press, 1997), 97–121, and Rael y Gálvez, "Mal-Criado."

75. 1860 Manuscript Census for Mora County, p. 479, Mora County Records; 1870 Manuscript Census for Colfax County, Schedule 1, Precinct 3, p. 22, Colfax County Records.

76. Item no. 12, Victor Grant Collection, Arthur Johnson Memorial Library, Raton, New Mexico; interview of Deluvina Maxwell by J. Evetts Haley, June 24, 1927, Fort Sumner, New Mexico, in the Panhandle Plains Historical Museum, Canyon, Texas.

77. There are numerous books on Billy the Kid's life, but the following specifically mention Deluvina's role after his death: Jon Tuska, *Billy the Kid: His Life and Legend* (Albuquerque: University of New Mexico Press, 1994), 103–4; and Robert M. Utley, *Billy the Kid: A Short and Violent Life* (Norman: University of Oklahoma Press, 1989), 160–61, 192, 194. For a fictional account, see Larry McMurtry, *Anything for Billy* (New York: Simon and Schuster, 1988).

78. Murphy, *Lucien B. Maxwell,* 106–8, 114, 117.

79. Inman, *Old Santa Fe Trail,* 374–78, quote on p. 374.

80. Of particular interest in comparing the world of Maxwell and that of the plantation, see the section on paternalism in Genovese, *Roll, Jordan, Roll,* 3–6.

81. Ryus, *Second William Penn,* 109–12; Murphy, *Lucien B. Maxwell,* 118. See also Murphy, *Philmont,* 100–2, for yet more stories of Maxwell's brutality toward his servants and workers.

82. Murphy, *Lucien B. Maxwell,* 111–12, 120; Inman, *Old Santa Fe Trail,* 374; Ryus, *Second William Penn,* 108. See also Irving Howbert, *Memories of a Lifetime in the Pike's Peak Region* (New York: G. P. Putnam Sons, 1925), 163–76 passim.

83. Steve Stern and Immanuel Wallerstein, "AHR Forum," *American Historical Review* 93 (October 1988): 896.

84. For a more complete version of the development of the mining districts near Elizabethtown, see Murphy, *Philmont,* 85–99; and Pearson, *Maxwell Land Grant,* 23–39.

85. Pearson, *Maxwell Land Grant,* 85.

86. Inman, *Old Santa Fe Trail,* 382; Pearson, *Maxwell Land Grant,* 42–44.

87. Murphy, *Lucien B. Maxwell,* 167.

88. Fox-Genovese (*Inside the Plantation Household,* 42) makes an important call for women's historians to look across regions, class, race, and ethnicity to understand the complexities of women's experiences.

## CHAPTER 3. FROM HACIENDA TO COLONY

1. Regarding colonial/native conflicts over perceptions about land use and value, see William Cronon, *Changes in the Land* (New York: Hill and Wang, 1983).

2. Regarding the powerful presence of the "grid" on the American imagination and the settling of the Western territories, see John R. Stilgoe, *Common Landscape of America: 1580–1945* (New Haven: Yale University Press, 1982), 99–107.

3. Peter Onuf, *Statehood and Union: A History of the Northwest Ordinance* (Bloomington: University of Indiana Press, 1987), 40–41. See also John Opie, *The Law of the Land: Two Hundred Years of Farmland Policy* (Lincoln: University of Nebraska Press, 1994), 58–59; and William Pattison, *Beginnings of the American Rectangular Survey System, 1784–1800* (Chicago: University of Chicago Press, 1957), 15–36, 53–55.

4. *Congressional Globe,* 30th Congress, 1st session, p. 96.

5. As quoted from Frederick Merk, *Manifest Destiny and Mission in American History* (New York: Vintage Books, 1966), 159.

6. *New York Evening Post,* December 24, 1847; quoted in Merk, *Manifest Destiny,* p. 158.

7. *Congressional Globe,* 30th Congress, 1st session, p. 98.

8. Waddy Thompson, *National Intelligence,* October 21, 1847; quoted in Merk, *Manifest Destiny,* p. 165.

9. See Richard Griswold del Castillo, *The Treaty of Guadalupe-Hidalgo: A Legacy of Conflict* (Norman: University of Oklahoma Press, 1990).

10. Regarding New Mexico's relationship with Spain and Mexico, see David Weber, *The Spanish Frontier in North America* (New Haven: Yale University Press, 1992), and *The Mexican Frontier, 1821–1846: The American Southwest under Mexico* (Albuquerque: University of New Mexico Press, 1982).

11. Earl Pomeroy, *The Territories and the United States, 1861–1890: Studies in Colonial Administration* (Seattle: University of Washington Press, 1969).

12. George Dargo, *Jefferson's Louisiana: Politics and the Clash of Legal Traditions* (Cambridge: Harvard University Press, 1975); and Weber, *The Spanish Frontier,* 289–91. See also the discussion in chapter 5.

13. William Watts Hart Davis, *El Gringo: New Mexico and Her People* (Santa Fe: Radial Press, 1938).

14. See Howard R. Lamar, *The Far Southwest, 1846–1912: A Territorial History* (New Haven: Yale University Press, 1966); Lamar, "Edmund G. Ross as Governor of New Mexico Territory: A Reappraisal," *New Mexico Historical Review* 36 (1961): 177–209; Robert Larson, *New Mexico's Quest for Statehood, 1846–1912* (Albuquerque: University of New Mexico Press, 1968); and

María E. Montoya, "The Education of a Gilded-Age Politician: L. Bradford Prince," *New Mexico Historical Review* (April 1991): 179–201.

15. See, in particular, John Agnew's map depicting the economic dominance of the North over the rest of the growing nation in *The United States and the World Economy: A Regional Geography* (New York: Cambridge University Press, 1987), 113.

16. Regarding cattle sales to Kansas City merchants and grain sales to Saint Louis Merchants, see Maxwell Land Grant and Railway Company Papers, archive 147 (hereinafter MLGC Papers), item 33, pp. 12–14, Special Collections, Zimmerman Library, University of New Mexico, Albuquerque.

17. Articles and advertisements appearing in an Amsterdam newspaper (name unspecified), March 1, 1890, MLGC Papers, box 45, folder 3; and *De Maxwell Land Grant and Railway-Company* (Amsterdam: Blikman and Sartorius, 1870), 17, Henry E. Huntington Library, San Marino, California.

18. *De Maxwell Land Grant.* The quote was from W. W. Griffin, who was supposed to be conducting the official survey of the land grant's boundaries but found time to comment on the abundant natural resources as well.

19. Ibid.

20. Regarding the appeal of the American West to Eastern and foreign investors, see, for example, Robert G. Athearn, *Westward the Briton* (New York: Charles Scribner and Sons, 1953); and Leland Hamilton Jenk, *The Migration of British Capital* (London: Thomas Nelson and Sons,1927).

21. Deed from the Maxwells to Jerome B. Chaffee, April 30, 1870, box 20, archive 147, MLGC Papers. The sale from the Maxwells to Chaffee was for $1.35 million. However, the most interesting aspect of the deed is that the words "and partly in county of Las Animas in the Territory of Colorado" were added after "situated principally in the county of Colfax in the Territory of New Mexico." It is difficult to say whether Chaffee or Maxwell added the words, but the afterthought clearly shows that there was doubt as to the northern boundary at this early date.

22. Lawrence R. Murphy, *Lucien B. Maxwell* (Norman: University of Oklahoma Press, 1983), 168–69. George M. Chilcott and Charles F. Holly, both of Colorado, also helped secure the sale of the Maxwell estate. See Jim Berry Pearson, *The Maxwell Land Grant* (Norman: University of Oklahoma Press, 1961), 49.

23. Lance E. Davis, "Capital Immobilities and Southwestern Land Prices, 1865–1875: A Case Study of a Historical Market Paradox," unpublished manuscript in author's possession. Regarding the differences in interest rates between different regions in the United States, see Davis, "The Investment Market, 1870–1914: The Evolution of a National Market," *Journal of Economic History* 25, no. 3 (September 1965): 355; and Sydney Homer and Richard Sylla, *The History of Interest Rates* (New Brunswick, N.J.: Rutgers University Press, 1996), 274–326 passim. Regarding the roll of Great Britain's investors in this process, see Allan R. Hall, *The Export of Capital from Britain, 1870–1914* (London: Methuen and Co., 1968). Regarding the importance of eastern cities

as financial centers in the late nineteenth century, see William Cronon, *Nature's Metropolis: Chicago and the Great West* (New York: W. W. Norton, 1991), 281.

24. Herbert O. Brayer, *William Blackmore* (Denver: Bradford-Robinson, 1949).

25. Pearson, *Maxwell Land Grant*, 49.

26. Opie, *Law of the Land*, 36, 47–48.

27. After a considerable amount of debate over whether free Blacks could migrate to New Mexico and own property (they could not), New Mexico eventually got its surveyor general. *Congressional Globe*, 33rd Congress, 1st session (beginning on May 2, 1854), 1054, 1070–75, 1875.

28. Regarding charges of corruption in the surveyor general's office, see the contemporary criticism by George W. Julian, "Land Stealing in New Mexico," *North American Review* 145 (July 1887): 17.

29. *De Maxwell Land Grant*.

30. Murphy, *Lucien B. Maxwell*, 182; MLGC Papers, stock ledger, 1870, box 20, archive 147. Also listed as stockholders were John Collinson, 35,563 shares; W. Waddingham, 9,070 shares; W. A. Bell, 3,380 shares; W. J. Palmer, 1,000 shares; R. H. Longwill (District Judge), 150 shares; M. A. Otero, 100 shares; and Stephen B. Elkins, 50 shares.

31. Regarding corruption in New Mexico's territorial legal system, see Lamar, *Far Southwest*, 444; and Larson, *New Mexico's Quest*, 444.

32. *Congressional Globe*, 41st Congress, 2nd session, H.R. 740, pp. 337, 822; *Congressional Globe*, 41st Congress, 3rd session, H.R. 740, p. 154.

33. Jerome B. Chaffee to J. S. Wilson, Commissioner of the General Land Office, July 17, 1869, Records of the Commissioner of the General Land Office, folder 1, docket 15, division E, National Archives, Washington, D.C.

34. The agreement did not include the Maxwells' personal property or lands that had been sold by Maxwell and registered with the county recorder. Maxwell also agreed to sell to Collinson his remaining Cimarron property that had not been included in the previous transaction. On August 24, 1870, they agreed that Maxwell would sell the thousand-acre ranch at Cimarron, the buildings, his store in Elizabethtown, and $50,000 worth of merchandise, his stock, all farming implements, twenty wagons, his mining properties and leases, for $50,000 and $75,000 to be paid within the year. Pearson, *Maxwell Land Grant*, 52–53.

35. Pearson, *Maxwell Land Grant*, 50; Murphy, *Lucien B. Maxwell*, 185. Murphy asserts that the middlemen in the transaction convinced or cajoled the Maxwells into agreeing that because of the tenuous situation regarding the extended boundaries, they were only entitled to $600,000 for the sale of the land. Since this reduced price was not passed on to the English investors, the speculators made a healthy profit of $750,000. Regarding the intricate financial dealings of the sale, see Pearson, *Maxwell Land Grant*, 50–52.

36. *Santa Fe Daily New Mexican*, August 2, 1870.

37. *Santa Fe Daily New Mexican*, July 22, 1870.

38. Regarding the differences between community, individual, and empre-

sario grants, see chapter 5 for the legal implications of the labels. See also Victor Westphall, *Mercedes Reales: Hispanic Land Grants in the Upper Rio Grande Region* (Albuquerque: University of New Mexico Press, 1983).

39. Secretary of the Interior J. D. Cox to the Commissioner of the General Land Office, December 31, 1869, *Papers Relating to Land Grants in the Office of the Surveyor General of New Mexico*, reel 14 (Bureau of Land Management, Santa Fe, New Mexico; microfilm publication of the University of New Mexico, Zimmerman Library, Albuquerque, 1955–57).

40. Secretary of the Interior Columbus Delano to Messrs. Barton, Laroque, and McFarland, July 27, 1871, *Papers Relating to Land Grants*, reel 14.

41. Amsterdam Committee to Secretary of the Interior, January 25, 1876, Records of the Commissioner, folder 3, docket 15.

42. Julian, "Land Stealing," 28.

43. Willis Drummond to A. G. Thurman, February 12, 1874, folder 3, docket 15; S. S. Burdett to M. W. Mills, July 15, 1875, p. 243; L. K. Lippincott to H. M. Atkinson, March 15, 1876, p. 274; and J. A. Williamson to L. M. Morrill, July 7, 1876, p. 291; Records of the Commissioner, Letters Sent to the Surveyor General of New Mexico, vol. 2, division E; H. M. Atkinson to J. A. Williamson, September 5, 1878, Records of the Commissioner, Letters Received from the Surveyor General of New Mexico, box 90, division E.

44. List of Homesteaders on the Maxwell Land Grant, folder 4, box 1, docket 15, *United States v. Maxwell Land Grant and Railway Company*, case 72100, RG 267, Department of Justice National Archives, Washington, D.C.

45. J. A. Williamson to H. M. Atkinson, September 1, 1877, Letters Sent to the Surveyor General of New Mexico, Records of the Commissioner, p. 357, vol. 2, division E.

46. S. S. Burdett, Commissioner of the General Land Office, to M. W. Mills, July 15, 1875, vol. 2, Letters Sent to the Surveyor General of New Mexico, division E; James K. Proudfitt to S. S. Burdett, May 5, 1875, Letters Received from the Surveyor General, box 89, division E; Records of the Commissioner.

47. W. F. Arny to J. S. Wilson, September 12, 1870, folder 2, box 1, docket 15, Records of the Commissioner.

48. Arny to Commissioner of Indian Affairs E. S. Parker, April 30, 1870, "Report no. 1," Letters Received, Office of Indian Affairs, New Mexico Superintendency, Department of the Interior, RG 75, National Archives, Denver.

49. Veronica E. Velarde Tiller, *The Jicarilla Apache Tribe* (Lincoln: University of Nebraska Press, 1983), 73.

50. Dudley to Smith, June 3, 1873, Letters Received, Office of Indian Affairs, New Mexico Superintendency, RG 75.

51. *Las Vegas (New Mexico) Gazette*, December 25, 1875.

52. Thomas Dolan, "Report of Council Proceedings with Jicarilla Apache Indians, 1873," WA MSS @-1223, file D685, Beinecke Rare Book Library, Yale University, New Haven, Conn., p. 3.

53. Ibid., pp. 9–10.

54. Ibid., p. 10.

55. Tiller, *Jicarilla Apache Tribe*, 96.

56. Maxwell Land Grant Papers, Box 24, item 46, p. 229, Arthur Johnson Memorial Library, Raton, N. Mex.

57. "Notice to the Settlers and Miners," *Railway Press and Telegraph*, September 3 and 17, 1870, box 20, MLGC Papers.

58. William A. Pile, "Proclamation of the Governor," April 19, 1871, Records of the Commissioner, folder 2, box 1, docket 15.

59. William A. Pile to Hamilton Fish, April 28, 1871, Records of the Commissioner, folder 2, box 1, docket 15.

60. *Railway Press and Telegraph*, September 3, 1870, box 20, MLGC Papers.

61. Robert C. Ellickson ("Property in Land," *Yale Law Journal* 102 [April 1993]: 1319) argues that it is virtually impossible to draw a clear distinction between law and custom. Rather, the way most people view their property rights and use their land is a hybrid of law and custom.

62. *Railway Press and Telegraph*, September 17, 1870, box 20, MLGC Papers.

63. Ibid.

64. Robert Rosenbaum, *Mexicano Resistance in the Southwest: The Sacred Right of Self-Preservation* (Austin: University of Texas Press, 1981), 75.

65. Lamar, *Far Southwest*, 153.

66. Of course, this analysis omits any discussion of Native Americans, who were from the outset dismissed by Anglos and Hispanos as unassimilable and unreliable allies against the company. The Jicarillas were left on their own to deal with the federal government's policy of removal.

67. Lamar, *Far Southwest*, 146.

68. Larson, *New Mexico's Quest*, 23.

69. See the entries for Thomas B. Catron and Stephen B. Elkins in Howard Lamar, ed., *The Reader's Encyclopedia of the American West* (New Haven: Yale University Press, 1998), 172, 344; Victor Westphall, *Thomas Benton Catron and His Era* (Tucson: University of Arizona Press, 1973).

70. John M. Dobson, *Politics in the Gilded Age* (New York: Praeger Publishers, 1972), 146.

71. In all of these conflicts over control of the Maxwell Land Grant there is a pattern of clergy defending settlers' rights: Father Martínez, Reverend Tolby, and later Reverend McMains. Because they were some of the only people of authority who had direct contact with the settlers, they became the most likely advocates for those losing control of their land. For accounts of the Colfax County conflict, see William A. Keleher, *The Maxwell Land Grant: A New Mexico Item* (Albuquerque: University of New Mexico Press, 1984), 75–82; Lamar, *Far Southwest*, 152–55; Robert W. Larson, *New Mexico Populism* (Boulder: Colorado Associated University Press, 1974), 21–34; Pearson, *Maxwell Land Grant*, 67–71; Rosenbaum, *Mexicano Resistance*, 75–77; Morris F. Taylor, *O. P. McMains and the Maxwell Land Grant Conflict* (Tucson: University of Arizona Press, 1979), 31–47.

72. Lamar, *Far Southwest*, 153; Taylor, *O. P. McMains*, 40.

73. Here I am indebted to Pervis L. Brown and his dissertation ("Even

Stranger Fruit: An Analysis of Black, Hispanic, and White Lynchings in Texas"; University of Michigan, in progress), which discusses what makes someone "lynchable" in the eyes of the community. Brown suggests that race is not the only category that marks one as "other" and that the crime itself can mark someone as beyond the pale of what society will tolerate. See also Gail Bederman's discussion on the discourse of civilization in *Manliness and Civilization: A Cultural History of Gender and Race in the United States, 1880– 1917* (Chicago: University of Chicago Press, 1995), 23–31.

74. Taylor, *O. P. McMains*, 42; Norman Cleaveland, *The Morleys: Young Upstarts on the Southwestern Frontier* (Albuquerque, N. Mex.: Calvin Horn Publishers, 1971), 101.

75. Deposition of Frank Springer to Frank Angel, Federal Investigator, August 9, 1878, p. 15, no. 1758, William G. Ritch Collection, Henry E. Huntington Library, San Marino, California. Copy also available in the Victor Westphall Collection, New Mexico State Records Center and Archives, Santa Fe.

76. For a complete discussion of the trial and all of its intricacies, see Taylor, *O. P. McMains*, 48–56.

77. Larson, *New Mexico Populism*, 26; Taylor, *O. P. McMains*, 50–52.

78. Regarding the impact of the Panic of 1873 on worldwide investment, see Allan G. Bogue, *Money at Interest* (Ithaca: Cornell University Press, 1955), 82.

79. Pearson, *Maxwell Land Grant*, 75–78.

80. For details about the implications of the *Tameling* decision for the legality of the Maxwell Land Grant, see chapter 5.

81. J. A. Williamson to S. B. Elkins, June 28, 1877, Letters Sent to the Surveyor General of New Mexico, vol. 2, p. 338, Records of the Commissioner; W. J. Baxter, Acting Land Commissioner, to H. M. Atkinson, June 15, 1877, folder 3, docket 15, Maxwell Land Grant, U.S. Department of Justice Papers, National Archives, Washington, D.C., RG 267.

82. Williamson to Atkinson, vol. 2, p. 235, Records of the Commissioner.

83. Chaffee to the Secretary of the Interior, p. 238, roll 5, microfilm M-750, U.S. Department of the Interior Appointment Papers for New Mexico, National Archives, Washington, D.C.

84. R. D. Russell to T. J. Anderson, Assistant Land Commissioner, May 8, 1888, Records of the Commissioner, folder 7, box 2.

85. Benjamin Houx to Carl Schurz, Secretary of the Interior, folder 4, box 1, docket 15, U.S. Department of Justice Papers, RG 267.

86. J. A. Williamson to H. M. Atkinson, May 9, 1879, Records of the Commissioner, folder 4, box 1, docket 15, RG 267.

87. Pearson, *Maxwell Land Grant*, 88.

88. The writings of Immanuel Wallerstein *(The Capitalist World Economy)* and Fernand Braudel *(Capitalism and Material Life, 1400–1800* [London: Weidenfeld and Nicolson, 1973]) have been particularly useful for me in thinking about how the history of the Maxwell Land Grant shows great similarities to other places and times in this history of agricultural peoples and their struggles against emerging capitalist markets. Also, J. M. Neeson's book

*Commoners: Common Right, Enclosure, and Social Change in England, 1700–1820* (New York: Cambridge University Press, 1993) has been extremely useful in pointing out the similarities between enclosure and people's resistance to that movement with the incorporation of the Maxwell Land Grant into the larger political sphere and economic markets of the United States.

89. See David Montejano, *Anglos and Mexicans in the Making of Texas, 1836–1986* (Austin: University of Texas, 1987).

90. There is, of course, a lengthy and excellent bibliography for this field; however, for books that illustrate many of the themes I discuss here, see Richard White, *Roots of Dependency: Subsistence, Environment, and Social Change among the Choctaws, Pawnees, and Navajos* (Lincoln: University of Nebraska Press, 1983) and *Middle Ground: Indians, Empires, and Republics in the Great Lakes Region, 1600–1815* (New York: Cambridge University Press, 1991); and Albert Hurtado, *Indian Survival on the California Frontier* (New Haven: Yale University Press, 1988). For the Maxwell Land Grant in particular, see Tiller, *Jicarilla Apache Tribe.*

91. Gavan Daws, *Shoal of Time: A History of the Hawaiian Islands* (Honolulu: University of Hawaii Press, 1968), 122–24. For a detailed legal discussion of the Great Mahele, see Jon J. Chinen, *The Great Mahele: Hawaii's Land Division of 1848* (Honolulu: University of Hawaii Press, 1958).

92. Daws, *Shoal of Time*, 125–28.

93. William Robbins, *Colony and Empire* (Lawrence: University of Kansas Press, 1995); William Cronon, *Nature's Metropolis: Chicago and the Great West* (New York: W. W. Norton, 1997); and Montejano, *Anglos and Mexicans.*

94. Frederick Jackson Turner, "The Significance of the Frontier in American History," in *History, Frontier, and Section: Three Essays* (Albuquerque: University of New Mexico Press, 1993).

95. Pearson, *Maxwell Land Grant*, 73–76.


CHAPTER 4. PREJUDICE, CONFRONTATION, AND RESISTANCE

1. Throughout this chapter the terms "squatters" and "settlers" are used. "Squatter" was really a company term and could refer to either an Anglo or Hispano who lived on the grant without written title or approval from the company's managers. In most cases, however, the squatters were Hispanos who had lived on Maxwell's hacienda. "Settler" refers to a U.S. citizen (either Anglo or Hispano) who settled on the grant, believed it to be a part of the public domain, and had begun the process of attaining homestead rights. In some cases, like that of Richard Russell, people already held patents from the U.S. government giving them the right to their lands that lay within the declared boundaries of the Maxwell Land Grant Company.

2. Jim Berry Pearson, *The Maxwell Land Grant* (Norman: University of Oklahoma Press, 1961), 80.

3. Meeting of the Board of Directors, May 28, 1880, Netherlands, item 2, Maxwell Land Grant and Railway Company Papers, Archive 147, Special Collections, Zimmerman Library, University of New Mexico, Albuquerque (hereafter, the MLGC Papers).

4. Second Meeting of the Board of Directors, June 10, 1880, item 3, MLGC Papers.

5. Ledger A, 1880 – 85, item 34, MLGC Papers.

6. Frank Sherwin to Harry Whigham, March 18 and 30, 1882, folder 2, Box 24, MLGC Papers.

7. Alex W. Anderson, Secretary, to Harry Whigham, April 1882, folder 2, MLGC Papers.

8. W. F. Thoplan, Vice President in Amsterdam, to Frank R. Sherwin in London, April 25, 1882, folder 2, MLGC Papers.

9. Ziegelaars to Whigham, January 8, 1885, and Alex W. Anderson to Harry Whigham, February 13, 1885, Box 45, MLGC Papers.

10. List of Homesteaders on the Maxwell Land Grant, folder 4, box 1, docket 15, *United States v. Maxwell Land Grant Company*, case 72100, record group 267, Department of Justice National Archives, Washington, D.C. (hereafter, *U.S. v. Maxwell*).

11. Folder 5, Box 24, MLGC Papers.

12. Obituary of Martin P. Pels, *Denver Republican*, February 9, 1906, p. 1.

13. The term "cultural synthesis" comes from the explanation of Dutch colonial practices given by Frances Gouda in *Dutch Culture Overseas: Colonial Practice in the Netherlands Indies, 1900 – 1942* (Amsterdam: University of Amsterdam Press, 1995), 50 – 51.

14. Ibid., 46 – 47. In particular, chapter 2, "A Cunning David Amidst the Goliaths of Empire: Dutch Colonial Practice in the Indonesian Archipelago," is helpful. See also Jean Gelman Taylor, *The Social World of Batavia: European and Eurasian in Dutch Asia* (Madison: University of Wisconsin Press, 1983), 114 – 34.

15. "To Our Constituents in the Matter of the Maxwell Land Grant Company," Maxwell Land Grant Committee, Amsterdam, June 27, 1885, box 45, MLGC Papers.

16. M. P. Pels to Amsterdam Committee, March 3, 1887, p. 1, item 48, MLGC Papers.

17. William Cronon's book *Nature's Metropolis* (New York: W. W. Norton, 1991), pp. 207 – 62 passim, speaks particularly well to this point. In his work readers will find the explanation for what economic forces, in general, might have been pulling the Maxwell managers into this market system. His findings and analysis in the chapter "Annihilating Space: Meat" go quite a long way toward explaining the rapid increase in stock raising on the grant during this time.

18. M. P. Pels to Frank Springer, p. 445, item 48, MLGC Papers.

19. M. P. Pels to the Amsterdam Committee, August 30, 1887, p. 352, item 48, MLGC Papers.

20. Letter reprinted in the *Raton (N. Mex.) Weekly Independent*, February 16, 1889.

21. M. P. Pels to C. Lohman, August 9, 1887, p. 328, item 48, MLGC Papers.

22. M. P. Pels to the Amsterdam Committee, April 8, 1887, pp. 51 and 56, item 48, MLGC Papers.

23. Judge L. Bradford Prince's orders, April 18, 1882, box 20, MLGC Papers.

24. Morris F. Taylor, *O. P. McMains and the Maxwell Land Grant Conflict* (Tucson: University of Arizona Press, 1979), 82–91.

25. The agreement was signed by C. B. Ladd, John Holmes, George Geer, Charles Hunt, Joe Lowry, Abe Sever, M. M. Salazar, Juan González, John E. Lane, Marion Littrell, M. C. Reed, J. L. Woods, and Harry Whigham. Taylor, *O. P. McMains*, 143.

26. Prior to 1887 there is very little correspondence in the MLGC Papers regarding settler problems. The two existing books of correspondence are severely water damaged and illegible. Consequently, this narrative is based on the stepped-up efforts of Pels in 1887, just prior to the conclusion of the suit before the Supreme Court and the final bout of violence in Stonewall Valley.

27. M. P. Pels to the Amsterdam Committee, May 19, 1887, p. 127; M. P. Pels to Harry Whigham, April 29, 1887; both in item 48, MLGC Papers.

28. J. A. Todd to Harry Whigham, May 10, 1887, folder 9, box 28, MLGC Papers.

29. Edward Twitty to Whigham, September 15, 1887, folder 8, box 28, MLGC Papers.

30. Mrs. C. B. Ladd to Whigham, June 24, 1887, folder 8, box 28, MLGC Papers. Here is a case where law did not matter, or people just ignored it. Technically, Mrs. Ladd, as a married woman, probably could not have made a contract without her husband's signature.

31. Mrs. L. R. Thomas to Whigham, November 15, 1887, folder 8, box 28, MLGC Papers. For other examples of land sales to women, see item 1, pp. 3 and 38, MLGC Papers.

32. Anne F. Hyde, "Cultural Filters: The Significance of Perception," in *A New Significance: Re-envisioning the History of the American West*, ed. Clyde A. Milner II (New York: Oxford University Press, 1996), 183; Annette Kolodny, *The Land Before Her: Fantasy and Experience of the American Frontiers, 1630–1860* (Chapel Hill: University of North Carolina Press, 1984).

33. M. P. Pels to F. B. Chaplan, July 4, 1887, folder 8, box 28, MLGC Papers.

34. M. P. Pels to the Amsterdam Committee, July 18, 1887, p. 237, item 48, MLGC Papers.

35. M. P. Pels to Henry Bowlden, August 8, 1887, p. 321, item 48; M. P. Pels to J. D. Dawson, September 1, 1887, p. 364, item 48, MLGC Papers.

36. Pels to Dawson, September 1, 1887.

37. T. O. Boggs to Harry Whigham, November 28, 1887, folder 8, box 28, MLGC Papers. For more discussion of Boggs's problems, see Harry Whigham to T. O. Boggs, November 29, 1887, p. 287, item 47; and T. O. Boggs to Harry Whigham, December 19, 1887, folder 8, box 28, MLGC Papers.

38. Although Taylor did not discuss all of the resistance on the land grant, in his book *O. P. McMains* he posits that McMains was the leader of all opposition on the grant, but this is not true; various types of resistance—legal, violent, and rhetorical—occurred on the grant simultaneously. Furthermore, Taylor almost virtually ignores the Mexicanos and conflates them with the Anglo settlers. In fact, McMains never understood the complexity of the Mexicanos' claims against the company and so never truly acted in their best interest.

39. Boggs to Whigham, December 19, 1887, folder 8, box 28, MLGC Papers.

40. Ignacio, Juan, Guadalupe, and Miguel López; Melquiades Fisher and José Ventura Casados to President Grover Cleveland, November 19, 1887, box 2, folder 6, docket 15, *U.S. v. Maxwell.*

41. Settlers Book, March 1887, item 149.5, MLGC Papers; Harry Whigham to T. O. Boggs, December 22, 1887, p. 360, item 47, MLGC Papers.

42. Settlers Book, March 1887.

43. For a more general discussion on the value of fencing and the meeting of property from a legal perspective, see Robert C. Ellickson, *Order without Law: How Neighbors Settle Disputes* (Cambridge: Harvard University Press, 1991), and Carol M. Rose, *Property and Persuasion: Essays on the History, Theory, and Rhetoric of Ownership* (Boulder, Colo.: Westview Press, 1994).

44. Item 33, pp. 12–14, MLGC Papers.

45. Maxwell Land Grant Company records, item 150, pp. 69–72, MLGC Papers.

46. See William deBuys, *Enchantment and Exploitation: The Life and Hard Times of a New Mexico Mountain Range* (Albuquerque: University of New Mexico Press, 1985), 184–91.

47. Harry Whigham to T. O. Boggs, December 22, 1887, p. 359, item 47, MLGC Papers.

48. Harry Whigham to T. O. Boggs, October 1, 1887, p. 150, item 47, MLGC Papers. Whigham authorized both Boggs and Pels to make leases with settlers "on the terms mentioned in the printed form, . . . but in any case not to exceed a term of five years."

49. Whigham to Boggs, December 22, 1887, p. 362, item 47, MLGC Papers. Regarding financing, Whigham continued,

> We will give them seven to ten years time to pay for the lands, with 7% interest per year on the deferred payments—that means if a man buys, for instance, seventy acres of land at $10 which makes $700 and we sell him on seven years time, he has to pay the first year $70, the next year $70 plus 7% on the unpaid $630, which is $44.10, altogether $114.10, the third $70 and 7% on the unpaid $560, which is $39.20, altogether $109.20, etc.

50. P. H. Van Diest, "Report on the Resources of the Northern Part of the Beaubien/Miranda Grant or Maxwell Grant, Located in the State of Colorado," April 1887, box 20, MLGC Papers.

51. T. O. Boggs to Henry Whigham, December 18, 1886, p. 2, folder 8, box 28, MLGC Papers.

52. "Company History," August 20, 1894, box 23.5, MLGC Papers.

53. M. P. Pels to Charles J. Canda, August 8, 1887, p. 326, item 48, MLGC Papers.

54. Colfax County pamphlet, 1901, p. 5, Bureau of Immigration, New Mexico, box 46, MLGC Papers.

55. Pels to the Amsterdam Committee, October 21, 1887, p. 466, item 48, MLGC Papers; Pearson, *Maxwell Land Grant*, 118.

56. M. P. Pels to Board of Trustees, August 2, 1888, item 51, MLGC Papers.

57. M. P. Pels to Board of Trustees, New York, September 17, 1888, p. 668, item 51, MLGC Papers.

58. Ibid.

59. "List of Settlers Sued in Colorado," item 48, MLGC Papers.

60. *Maxwell Land Grant Company v. R. D. Russell*, August 24, 1887, in the District Court in and for Las Animas County, Colorado. This was an earlier suit by the company to recover $10,000 from Russell for operating a sawmill within the claimed boundaries of the Maxwell Land Grant. See also *Maxwell Land Grant Company v. F. B. Chaplan and R. D. Russell*, 3d District Court, ejectment suit, April 6, 1887, Las Animas County District Court, Trinidad, Colorado; and M. P. Pels to the Amsterdam Committee, August 9, 1887, p. 330, item 48, MLGC Papers.

61. Harry Whigham to T. O. Boggs, December 22, 1887, p. 361, item 47, MLGC Papers.

62. *Maxwell Land Grant Company v. Richard D. Russell*, March 1888, 3d District Court, Las Animas County, Trinidad, Colorado.

63. *Maxwell Land Grant Company v. F. B. Chaplan*, March 26, 1888, 3d District Court, petition for change of venue, Records of the Governor, Alva Adams, archive 26690, Colorado State Archives, Denver, Colorado.

64. Harry Whigham to M. P. Pels, December 23, 1886, folder 1, box 1, T. A. Schomburg Papers, Collection 747, Colorado Historical Society Library, Denver, Colorado.

65. D. F. Wilkens to Harry Whigham, January 31, 1887, folder 9, box 28, MLGC Papers.

66. Ibid.

67. D. F. Wilkens to Harry Whigham, April 18, 1887, p. 2, folder 9, box 28, MLGC Papers.

68. D. F. Wilkens to Harry Whigham, February 20, 1887, folder 9, box 28, MLGC Papers.

69. D. F. Wilkens to Harry Whigham, April 18, 1887, folder 9, box 28, MLGC Papers.

70. R. D. Russell to Secretary of the Interior, March 28, 1888, folder 3, box 2, docket 15, *U.S. v. Maxwell*.

71. R. D. Russell to T. J. Anderson, Assistant Land Commissioner, May 9, 1888, folder 7, box 2, docket 15, *U.S. v. Maxwell*.

72. R. D. Russell to T. J. Anderson, Assistant Land Commissioner, June 3, 1888, folder 7, box 2, docket 15, *U.S. v. Maxwell*.

73. Pearson, *Maxwell Land Grant*, 119.
74. M. P. Pels to Francis Clutton, August 8, 1888, p. 585, item 51, MLGC Papers.
75. M. P. Pels to M. W. Mills, August 20, 1888, p. 602, item 51, MLGC Papers.
76. Ibid., p. 603.
77. Taylor, *O. P. McMains*, 213.
78. M. P. Pels to R. B. Holdsworth, August 25, 1888, p. 620, item 51, MLGC Papers.
79. M. P. Pels to Board of Trustees, August 24, 1888, p. 608, item 51, MLGC Papers.
80. R. B. Holdsworth to M. P. Pels, August 24, 1888, Box 24, MLGC Papers.

CHAPTER 5. THE LAW OF THE LAND

1. *United States v. Maxwell Land Grant and Railway Company* (hereafter, *U.S. v. Maxwell*), 121 U.S 325, 366 (1887).
2. *U.S. v. Maxwell*, 121 U.S. 325, 364.
3. *Interstate Land Company v. Maxwell Land Grant Company* (hereafter, *Interstate v. Maxwell*), 139 U.S. 569.
4. Although the briefs and the Court do not mention it, this territory in 1832 was a no-man's land, with both the provinces of New Mexico and Coahuila y Tejas claiming jurisdiction over the region. The governor of Coahuila y Tejas may not even have had the authority to grant lands in that region, where the political boundaries were so contested.
5. *Interstate v. Maxwell*, 139 U.S. 569, 587, 588.
6. *Interstate v. Maxwell*, 139 U.S. 569, 579.
7. Article 12, Colonization Law, *Compilation of Laws*, vol. 1, no. 416, p. 712, August 18, 1824, as published in *Spanish and Mexican Land Laws: New Spain and Mexico* (Saint Louis, Mo.: Buxton and Skinner Stationery Co., 1895), 122.
8. Ibid., articles 24, 25, and 27, p. 104.
9. Regulations for the Colonization of the Territories, *Code of Colonization*, Mexico, 1893, p. 237, no. 71, November 21, 1828, in *Spanish and Mexican Land Laws*, 121.
10. Drew R. McCoy, *The Elusive Republic: Political Economy in Jeffersonian America* (Chapel Hill: University of North Carolina Press, 1980), 68–75; William B. Scott, *In Pursuit of Happiness: American Conceptions of Property from the Seventeenth to the Twentieth Century* (Bloomington: Indiana University Press, 1977), 53–55.
11. For the founders' view of property, see *Elliott's Debates*. Also, in the Ordinance of 1787, article 4 specifically delineated the right to sell and tax property. 69th Congress, 1st session, House doc. no. 398, as published in U.S. Library of Congress, Legislative Reference Service, *Documents Illustrative of the Formation of the Union of the American States* (Washington, D.C.: Government Printing Office, 1927), 53.

12. For a general discussion of U.S. land law, see Paul W. Gates, *History of Public Land Law Development* (Washington, D.C.: Government Printing Office, 1968); John R. Stilgoe, *Common Landscape of America: 1580–1945* (New Haven: Yale University Press, 1982), 102; and Paul W. Gates, *Landlords and Tenants on the Prairie Frontier* (Ithaca: Cornell University Press, 1973). See also Robert P. Swierenga, *Pioneers and Profits: Land Speculation on the Iowa Frontier* (Ames: Iowa State University Press, 1968).

13. Stilgoe, *Common Landscape*, 99, 106–7; Gates, *History*, 444.

14. Peter S. Onuf, *Statehood and Union: A History of the Northwest Ordinance* (Bloomington: Indiana University Press, 1987), 30–38.

15. Gates, *History*, 59–74; John Opie, *The Law of the Land: Two Hundred Years of American Farmland Policy* (Lincoln: University of Nebraska Press, 1994), 57–69; William D. Pattison, *Beginnings of the American Rectangular Land Survey System, 1784–1800* (Chicago: Department of Geography Research Paper no. 50, 1957); Malcolm J. Rohrbough, *The Land Office Business: The Settlement and Administration of American Public Lands, 1789–1837* (New York: Oxford University Press, 1968), 8–10; Roy M. Robbins, *Our Landed Heritage: The Public Domain, 1776–1970* (Lincoln: University of Nebraska Press, 1972), 3–19; Everett Dick, *The Lure of the Land: A Social History of the Public Lands from the Articles of Confederation to the New Deal* (Lincoln: University of Nebraska Press, 1970), 19–34; Hildegard B. Johnson, *Order Upon the Land: The U.S. Rectangular Land Survey and the Upper Mississippi Country* (New York: Oxford University Press, 1976), 44.

16. Onuf, *Statehood and Union*, 40–41.

17. Richard Griswold del Castillo, *The Treaty of Guadalupe Hidalgo: A Legacy of Conflict* (Norman: University of Oklahoma Press, 1990), 180.

18. Quoted in Griswold del Castillo, *Treaty*, 48.

19. The exact meaning of the Protocol is in dispute between the two countries to this day. The first article of the Protocol clarified the amendment of Article 9 of the Treaty of Guadalupe Hidalgo and reiterated the United States' commitment to the "civil, political, and religious" privileges of the Mexican citizens. Article 2 of the Protocol stated that by deleting Article 10 from the treaty, the United States "did not in any way intend to annul the grants of lands made by Mexico in the ceded territories." Rather, the U.S. government intended to "preserve the legal value which they [the land grants] may possess; and the grantees may cause their legitimate title to be acknowledged before the American tribunals." For more information regarding the political debates in both countries surrounding the meaning of the Protocol, see Griswold del Castillo, *Treaty*, 53–55.

20. See Morton J. Horwitz, *The Transformation of American Law* (Cambridge: Harvard University Press, 1977), 253–66.

21. Although I return to this theme at the end of the book, it is important to note that this reliance on general principle of property was exactly what Judge Perricone did in the 1998 *Espinoza* case when he refused to hear about the specific context of the Sangre de Cristo Land Grant.

22. David Hunter Miller, ed., *Treaties and Other International Acts of the United States of America*, vol. 5 (Washington, D.C.: Government Printing Office, 1937); quoted in Griswold del Castillo, *Treaty*, 179–80.

23. Charles I. Bevans, ed., *Treaties and Other International Agreements of the United States of America, 1776–1949*, vol. 9 (Washington, D.C.: Department of State, 1937), 791–806; quoted in Griswold del Castillo, *Treaty*, 190.

24. Griswold del Castillo, *Treaty*, 180.

25. Ibid., 190.

26. *Tameling v. U.S. Freehold and Immigration Company*, 93 U.S. 644.

27. Ibid., 644.

28. Ibid., 661, 663.

29. Ibid., 663.

30. Ibid., 662.

31. For a general account of the Marshall court's jurisprudence concerning vested rights of contract and property, see G. Edward White, *The Marshall Court and Cultural Change, 1815–1835* (New York: Oxford University Press, abridged ed. 1991), 595–673.

32. *Tameling*, 662.

33. In *Fletcher*, the court had to decide whether the U.S. Constitution's contract clause prohibited the Georgia legislature from rescinding sales of vast tracts of western land in what would later become Alabama and Mississippi to four land companies. *Fletcher v. Peck*, 6 Cranch. 87, 133 (1810).

34. Ibid., 143.

35. See Scott, *In Pursuit of Happiness*, 54–55 (summarizing the 1793 work of Nathaniel Chipman on the conflict between two aspects of property).

36. For a description of numerous instances in which this argument was made either by the United States or legal commentators, see Gates, *History*, 87–119.

37. *United States v. Percheman*, 32 U.S. (7 Pet.) 51, 70 (1833).

38. The conditions requiring, say, production of rope for the Spanish monarch's navy would seem to be either obsolete or illegal after annexation of the grant to the United States. For such a condition, see *Glenn v. United States*, 54 U.S. (13 How.) 250 (1851).

39. *Soulard v. United States*, 29 U.S. (4 Pet.) 511 (1830).

40. Ibid., 512. For a discussion of the difficulties caused by Marshall's delay in the *Soulard* case, see Gates, *History*, 103–4.

41. See, for example, *Delassus v. United States*, 34 U.S. (9 Pet.) 134 (1835) (upholding a claim made under a French grant against the U.S. government's argument that the French lieutenant governor lacked the power to make such a grant under French law).

42. Ibid., 133.

43. As attorney general under Andrew Jackson, Taney had been the leader of the attack on the Second Bank of the United States; as chief justice, he had written the *Charles River Bridge* opinion, which significantly restricted

the broad reading of vested rights that Marshall had given to contract clause jurisprudence.

44. In either case, the grantees had the right to take immediate possession of the land without meeting further conditions, a fact that would indicate that both conditions were, in the classic common law of contingent remainders, a condition subsequent. See Jesse Dukeminier and James E. Krier, *Property*, 3d ed. (New York: Little, Brown, and Co., 1993), 385. I am grateful to my husband, Rick Hills, for pointing out this fact.

45. The claim covered 536,904 arpens. An arpen equals roughly .85 of one acre.

46. Clamorgan's heirs had been aggressively seeking recognition of their claims before the Board of Land Commissioners established by an 1832 statute of Congress and, after the board rejected their claim before Congress itself. Gates, *History*, 106–7.

47. *Glenn v. United States*, 54 U.S.(13 How.) 250, 259 (1851).

48. *Fremont v. United States*, 58 U.S. 542, 557–58 (1854).

49. Ibid., 564.

50. Ibid., 565.

51. *Fremont v. United States*, 556.

52. Ibid., 569–70 (J. Catron dissenting). As Catron noted, Alvarado had never even *seen* the land, because he had never selected the ten leagues from the eligible region.

53. *Fremont v. United States*, 564.

54. *Arguello v. United States*, 59 U.S. (18 How.) 539 (1855). The United States contended that the Mexican governor had violated Mexican law by granting the land without approval of the central government, because the land lay within the "littoral leagues" (i.e., land near the coast) that could not be granted without central government approval. The Court, however, took a generous view of the governor's authority, interpreting the relevant Mexican statutes to apply only to foreign colonization and not to grants to Mexicans.

55. *Arguello v. United States*, 551–52.

56. Ibid., 553–54.

57. *U.S. v. Maxwell*, 362.

58. Ibid., 361.

59. Historians have had clear agendas when discussing this issue of empresario versus individual grant. Most historians who have discussed the legal implications have been very sympathetic to the plight of the settlers. Consequently, they have maintained that the grant could never possibly have been an empresario grant, and therefore there was no legal reason to extend the boundaries. These historians have ignored the reasoning of the court, and furthermore, they should realize that if the grant was an empresario one, as the court stated, then the settlers on the grant would have had some legal claim to the land against the company's claim. Nevertheless, no one has yet given serious consideration to the direct ruling of the court. Regarding the boundaries of the grant, see Victor Westphall, *Mercedes Reales* (Albuquerque: University of New

Mexico Press, 1983), 50, and Malcolm Ebright, "Mexican Land Grants: The Legal Background," in *Land, Water, and Culture: New Perspectives on Hispanic Land Grants*, ed. Charles L. Briggs and John R. Van Ness (Albuquerque: University of New Mexico Press, 1987), 26.

60. "Distribution of Lands to Foreigners Who Come to Colonize," in *Spanish and Mexican Land Laws*, 100.

61. Thomas W. Streeter, *Bibliography of Texas, 1795–1845* (Cambridge: Harvard University Press, 1956), 1: 9. Streeter says that although none of these petitions have survived, there are indications that they did exist at one time.

62. Ibid. There is an original of this form in "1829 Form of Certificate for Colonization," Streeter Collection, Beinecke Manuscripts and Rare Book Library, Yale University, New Haven, Connecticut.

63. Streeter, *Bibliography of Texas*, 1: 10, 13.

64. For accounts of the conveyance of the grant from Governor Armijo to Beaubien and Miranda, see Warren A. Beck, *New Mexico: A History of Four Centuries* (Norman: University of Oklahoma Press, 1962), 175; Charles L. Briggs and John R. Van Ness, eds., *Land, Water, and Culture: New Perspectives on Hispanic Land Grants* (Albuquerque: University of New Mexico Press, 1987), 26; William H. Keleher, *The Maxwell Land Grant: A New Mexico Item* (Albuquerque: University of New Mexico Press, 1984), 13–15; Howard R. Lamar, *The Far Southwest, 1846–1912: A Territorial History* (New Haven: Yale University Press, 1966), 141; Lawrence R. Murphy, *Lucien B. Maxwell: Napoleon of the Southwest* (Norman: University of Oklahoma Press, 1983), 34–35; Jim Berry Pearson, *The Maxwell Land Grant*, 187; Morris F. Taylor, *O. P. McMains and the Maxwell Land Grant Conflict* (Tucson: University of Arizona Press, 1979), 58; Robert Rosenbaum, *Mexicano Resistance in the Southwest: The Sacred Right of Self-Preservation* (Austin: University of Texas Press, 1981), 70–72.

65. Petition from Beaubien and Miranda, signed January 8, 1841, in *Translation of the Beaubien and Miranda Petition, & c* (Santa Fe: Manderfield & Tucker, Printers, 1872), 2, Henry E. Huntington Library, San Marino, California.

66. Beaubien, however, was good friends with Charles Bent, the first military governor after U.S. occupation, and was appointed by Bent to be one of the territory's first judges. Beaubien also had come under attack from Father Martínez, the Mexican nationalist priest who did not trust Beaubien's loyalties. During the Taos Rebellion, in which Padre Martínez may have silently participated, Beaubien's son, Narcisco, was murdered because the rebels believed him to be an American loyalist.

67. *Translation of the Beaubien and Miranda Petition*, 3.

68. Quoted in *U.S. v. Maxwell*, 362.

69. For example, see Ignacio López et al. to President Cleveland, November 19, 1887, box 2, folder 6, docket 15, MLGC Papers.

70. *U.S. v. Maxwell*, 372 (emphasis added).

71. Ibid., 369.

72. Ibid., 360.

73. Ibid., 374, 375.

74. Ibid., 377.

75. Ibid., 379.

76. Ibid., 377.

77. This, however, is precisely the question that arose in *Rael v. Taylor,* which is still in litigation. Descendants of the original tenants who lived under Beaubien's tutelage on the Sangre de Cristo grant claim that they still have rights to a commons that their ancestors were granted by Beaubien. See María E. Montoya, "Dividing the Land: The Taylor Ranch and the Limited Access Commons," in *Land in the American West: Private Claims and the Common Good,* William Robbins, ed. (Tucson: University of Arizona Press, 2000).

CHAPTER 6. THE LEGACY OF LAND GRANTS
IN THE AMERICAN WEST

1. M. P. Pels to R. V. Martinson, item 54, p. 454, Maxwell Land Grant and Railway Company Papers (hereafter, MLGC Papers), Special Collections, Zimmerman Library, University of New Mexico, Albuquerque; Jim Berry Pearson, *The Maxwell Land Grant* (Norman: University of Oklahoma Press, 1961), 130; Morris F. Taylor, *O. P. McMains and the Maxwell Land Grant Conflict* (Tucson: University of Arizona Press, 1979), 200.

2. Pels to Martinson, item 54, p. 455, MLGC Papers; Pearson, *Maxwell Land Grant,* 131; Taylor, *O. P. McMains,* 203.

3. Pels to Martinson, August 21, 1888, item 54, p. 605, MLGC Papers.

4. Pels to Martinson, item 54, p. 458, MLGC Papers. Governor Adams was an investor in the syndicate, which calls into question his ability to act properly when the violence began. Perhaps Adams did not call in the militia because of the bad publicity it would bring his new venture.

5. Quoted from a letter from Pels to Martinson, item 54, p. 457, MLGC Papers.

6. Deposition of C. S. Snyder, October 10, 1889, case numbers 1618–27, District Court of Colorado, Trinidad, Las Animas County Records.

7. Report of Thomas J. O'Neil to James McParland, August 27, 1888, case A, file 17, MLGC Papers; Taylor, *O. P. McMains,* 211–12.

8. O'Neil report, MLGC Papers; Taylor, *O. P. McMains,* 215–16.

9. Quoted in Taylor, *O. P. McMains,* 231.

10. Marian Sloan Russell, *Land of Enchantment: Memoirs of Marian Russell along the Santa Fe Trail* (Albuquerque: University of New Mexico Press, 1981), 131.

11. S. S. Burdett to M. W. Mills, July 15, 1875, Letters Sent to the Surveyor General of New Mexico, vol. 2, record group 49, division E, Government Land Office, U.S. Department of the Interior, National Archives, Washington, D.C.

12. According to the Maxwell Company's records, the Russells had a rather large ranch. Maxwell Land Grant Company Settler's Book, 1887, item 149.5, MLGC Papers.

13. M. P. Pels, in a letter to R. V. Martinson, President of the Maxwell Company, told of the meeting between Pels and Russell in July 1887:

> Mr Russell, an account of whose unfortunate death I will narrate to you hereafter, was one of the first settlers called upon, and after one conversation on the subject, of a quiet character, Mr. Russell made a proposition for settlement which was at once accepted just as he made it, and the same evening a written contract was entered into which he signed in presence of his family and upon his request, fifty dollars was paid to him to bind the contract. Nothing but the insidious influence of McMains, who by repeated representations that Russell was, in making a settlement, becoming a traitor to his cause, ever induced Russell to break his contract, lead a mob against the officers of the law and so accomplish his own death.

M. P. Pels to R. V. Martinson, September 11, 1888, p. 453–54, item 54, MLGC Papers. Regarding the inability of Pels to keep his end of the contract, see also Pearson, *Maxwell Land Grant*, 113.

14. Deposition of Mrs. M. D. Randolf, October 3, 1888, case no. 1627, District Court of Colorado, Trinidad, Las Animas County Records; Pels to E. J. Randolf, August 23, 1888, p. 455–56, item 54, MLGC Papers; M. P. Pels, Report to the Board of Trustees, August 1888, box 46, MLGC Papers; Marian Russell (*Land of Enchantment*, 139) says that Richard went to Stonewall "carrying the flag of truce."

15. Taylor, *O. P. McMains*, 226.

16. Deposition of John Sells, October 3, 1888, case no. 1627, District Court of Colorado, Trinidad, Las Animas County Records.

17. Deposition of Ed Brown, October 3, 1888, case no. 1627, Las Animas County Records; Pels to Martinson, September 11, 1888, p. 457, item 54, MLGC Papers.

18. Deposition of Frank Lewis, October 3, 1888, case no. 1627, Las Animas County Records; Pels to Martinson, September 11, 1888, p. 458, item 54, MLGC Papers.

19. Deposition of William Hunn, October 3, 1888, case no. 1627, Las Animas County Records.

20. R. B. Holdsworth to Pels, August 27, 1888, p. 632, item 52, MLGC Papers; Taylor, *O. P. McMains*, 228.

21. Colonel Benjamin F. Klee to Gov. Alva Adams, August 28, 1888, Infantry Correspondence Outgoing, vol. 2, Records of the Governor, archive 26690, Colorado State Archives, Denver.

22. Pearson, *Maxwell Land Grant*, 125.

23. Pels to Martinson, September 11, 1888, p. 459, item 54; Pels to Harry Whigham, August 29, 1888, p. 647, item 51, MLGC Papers. Who actually started the fire was never discovered. Some suspected that the grant agents were looking for a distraction and caused the blaze; others believed it was merely an accident caused by a careless smoker.

24. Pearson, *Maxwell Land Grant*, 126.

25. Russell, *Land of Enchantment*, 139. In 1895 Marian Russell continued her husband's fight, and her claim was heard by the U.S. Supreme Court. The

court ruled, however, that company rights superseded all rights, even valid homestead rights. *Russell v. Maxwell Land Grant Company*, 158 U.S. 253 (1895).

26. Pels to Martinson, September 11, 1888, p. 459, item 54, MLGC Papers.

27. O. P. McMains, Martin Kephart, F. B. Chaplan, John Heagh, Alphonso Chaplin, Joseph Sagler, George Sagler, George Russell, Sam Bell, William Hadding, Al Kelley, O. B. Abbott, James Cox, A. Gierardt, A. Duling, Joe Duling, Olie McGarty, and A. Harmes were indicted for the manslaughter of Richard D. Russell by the district attorney for the 3d Judicial District of Colorado, Joe C. Elverell. Note that George Russell was indicted for the murder of his own father. Case no. 1627, Indictment for the Manslaughter of Richard D. Russell, October 3, 1888, Las Animas County District Court, Trinidad.

28. The second time that Dunbar brought the indictments before the grand jury, he had them concentrate less on Russell's and Valerio's deaths and more on the attack of the deputies by the anti-grant agitators. Ten indictments were returned against O. P. McMains, Martin Kephart (Sam Bell's brother-in-law, who took over the leadership role after Russell fell), and others unknown. Nine indictments were for the "assault with intent to kill and murder the deputies." The tenth indictment was for the arson of the barn by the Pooler Hotel the night of the riot. Pels to J. M. John, September 3, 1888, p. 661, item 54, MLGC Papers; Taylor, *O. P. McMains*, 228, 243.

29. Taylor, *O. P. McMains*, 241.

30. Those subpoenaed were: "Urbano Vigil, Jose Chavez, Victorio Duran, Albino Vasquez, Juan Sanchez, Pedro Martinez, Prudencio Chacon, Juan Duran, David Espinosa, Vicente Espinosa, Juan Delgado Vigil, Ignacio Duran, Juan Torres, Jose M. Romero, J. Antonio Griego, Vicente Torres, Francisco Gomez, Luis Vallejos, Lazzaro Vallejos, Antonio Valerio, Marcos Vigil, Agapito Vigil, Melquidas Vigil, Vicente Torres, Leandro Torres, Patricio Duran, Francisco Lopez, Juan Martinez, Ramon Gomez, Thomas Bernal, Francisco Chacon, Luciano Gallegos, Melquidas Ortiz, Ignacio Chacon, Justo Sandoval, Francisco Petriquez, and Jose Luis Torres." Subpoenas for Stonewall Cases, September 20, 1889, case nos. 1618–27, Las Animas County Records. Also, José Luís Torres helped put up the bond for McMain's codefendant, Martin Kephart. This indicates that Hispanos and Anglos continued to cooperate with each other after the Stonewall Valley conflict. Bond for Kephart, February 23, 1889, case no. 1627; Las Animas County Records.

31. List of Witnesses, case no. 1627, Las Animas County Records.

32. Depositions of E. J. Randolf, Mrs. E. J. Randolf, and J. W. Llewelling, case nos. 1618–27, Las Animas County Records.

33. One suspects that the defense attorneys realized how overly zealous and temperamental McMains could be in a public setting and decided not to risk putting him on the stand. Russell, *Land of Enchantment*, 139; Taylor, *O. P. McMains*, 249.

34. "William Milliken, Foreman, Verdict," case nos. 1618–27, Las Animas County Records. The jury foreman also wrote to the judge, "We fail to agree

upon a verdict thus far on account of a different construction part upon the instruction of the court by not being able to translate intelligently said instruction into the Spanish language." Milliken, Note to Judge, cases nos. 1618–27. Members of the jury were J. T. Lawson, C. H. Schwatzel, Reginio Archuleta, Manuel J. M. Vigil, William Milliken, Jesús García, J. A. Bell, B. F. Gumm, and Gabino Velpando, List of Jurors in People vs. O. P. McMains et al., case nos. 1618–27, Las Animas County Records.

35. Taylor, *O. P. McMains*, 250–58 passim.

36. Report of the Legal Department, 1890, pp. 183–201, letters A, MLGC Papers.

37. Maxwell Land Grant Company Income and Expenses, October 1888–89, MLGC Papers.

38. John D. Hicks, *The Populist Revolt: A History of the Farmers' Alliance and the People's Party* (Minneapolis: University of Minnesota Press, 1931), 268.

39. See Richard Hofstadter, *The Age of Reform: From Bryan to F. D. R.* (New York: Alfred A. Knopf, 1955), 50; and Lawrence Goodwyn, *Democratic Promise: The Populist Movement in America* (New York: Oxford University Press, 1976), 319.

40. Carlos Schwantes, "Protest in a Promised Land: Unemployment, Disinheritance, and the Origin of Labor Militancy in the Pacific Northwest, 1886–1886," *Western Historical Quarterly* 13, no. 4 (October 1982): 374. Robert W. Larson (*Populism in the Mountain West* [Albuquerque: University of New Mexico Press, 1986], 150–55) agrees with Schwantes that Populism in the West goes beyond free coinage, and he makes a strong case for seeing the movement in even broader terms. According to Larson, Populists in the West were concerned with such broader issues as railroad regulation, direct democracy, and anti-monopoly laws. Consequently, according to Larson, Western Populism should be seen as much a part of the broad-based national movement as were the Midwestern and Southern movements.

41. Robert W. Larson, *New Mexico Populism: A Study of Radical Protest in a Western Territory* (Boulder: Colorado Associated University Press, 1974), 21.

42. Ibid., 28–29.

43. *Raton (N. Mex.) Weekly Independent*, February 16, 1889; quoted in Larson, *New Mexico Populism*, 29.

44. *National Anti-Land Grant Monthly* (July 1890). Collection 374, State Historical Society of Colorado, Denver.

45. *National Anti-Land Grant Monthly* (June 1, 1890): 9, 16.

46. Ibid., 4.

47. Taylor, *O. P. McMains*, 210, 235; Robert W. Larson, *New Mexico's Quest for Statehood, 1846–1912* (Albuquerque: University of New Mexico Press, 1968), 169–91 passim.

48. *Russell v. Maxwell Land Grant Company*, 158 U.S. 253, 256 (1895). Justice Brewer was the circuit court judge who heard the original case of *United States v. Maxwell Land Grant and Railway Company*, 121 U.S. 325 (1887). In

that opinion he had also sided with the company, and his opinion was affirmed by the Supreme Court. Therefore, it seems unlikely that in this case he would have been willing to overrule his earlier lower court opinion.

49. *Russell v. Maxwell*, 258.

50. Ibid., 255, 258, 259.

51. Taylor, *O. P. McMains*, 255.

52. Pearson, *Maxwell Land Grant*, 232.

53. For a good discussion of these emerging communities, see Denise Pan, "Peace and Conflict in an Industrial Family," M.A. thesis, Department of History, University of Colorado, 1994.

54. Sarah Deutsch, *No Separate Refuge: Culture, Class, and Gender on an Anglo-Hispanic Frontier in the American Southwest, 1880–1940* (New York: Oxford University Press, 1987), 87–106 passim.

55. I realize that this section is rather speculative, but preliminary research in Colorado Fuel and Iron records in Pueblo, Colorado, indicates that quite a few employees listed their place of origin as various grant locations. I hope to show how their migratory patterns, work relationships, and union activities developed as they moved from their position as property holders, albeit tenuous ones, to wage laborers.

56. Regarding the historic patterns on migration in the area, see Deutsch, *No Separate Refuge*. On more recent patterns of migration, see Richard Nostrand, *The Hispano Homeland* (Norman: University of Oklahoma Press, 1992).

57. Both Robert C. Ellickson and Hernando De Soto have written on the formal and informal ways that neighbors have worked out property conflicts. See Ellickson, *Order without Law: How Neighbors Settle Disputes* (Cambridge: Harvard University Press, 1991); De Soto, *The Other Path: The Invisible Revolution in the Third World* (New York: Harper and Row, 1990).

58. Victor Westphall, *Mercedes Reales: Hispanic Land Grants of the Upper Rio Grande Region* (Albuquerque: University of New Mexico Press, 1983), 53.

59. The Sangre de Cristo, Maxwell, Las Animas, and Nolan grants were all conveyed by Armijo at roughly the same time. They were later confirmed by the surveyor general of the United States, the secretary of the interior, and Congress with relatively little trouble. Because of the vast acreage and valuable locations, these areas were all ripe for speculation by Anglo land-grabbers. Businessmen and politicians interested in making their fortunes off of these grants were quite influential in seeing that their boundaries were confirmed with outrageous amounts of acreage. See Howard R. Lamar, *The Far Southwest, 1846–1912* (New Haven: Yale University Press, 1966), 136–70; Westphall, *Mercedes Reales*, 147–92, and *Thomas Benton Catron and His Era* (Tucson: University of Arizona Press, 1973), 33–38.

60. For a history of Gilpin's life, see Howard R. Lamar, *Reader's Encyclopedia of the American West* (New Haven: Yale University Press, 1998), 429.

61. *Rael v. Taylor*, 876 P. 2d 1210 (Colo. 1994), p. 3.

62. As recorded in the Costilla County Book of Deeds, book 1, p. 256, as cited by the court in *Rael v. Taylor*.

63. The Sangre de Cristo Land Grant has one of the most interesting legal histories. The sale of the large Trinchera and Costilla tracts led to some of the most influential litigation in land grant history. See *Tameling v. U.S. Freehold and Immigration Company*, 93 U.S. 644 (1876). The Trinchera portion of the Sangre de Cristo Land Grant today is owned by the heirs of Malcolm Forbes.

64. The provision read: "subject to claims of the local people by prescription or otherwise to right to pasture, wood, and lumber and so-called settlements [*sic*] right in, to and upon said land." *Rael v. Taylor*, p. 3.

65. Colorado 1953 Torrens Registration Act, sections 118–01–1 to 102, 5 C.R.S. (1953), currently codified as sections 38–36–101 to –198, 16A C.R.S. (1982 and 1993 supp.).

66. John L. McCormack, "Torrens and Recordings: Land Title and Assurance in the Computer Age," *William Mitchell Law Review* 18: 61, 70–73; U.S. Department of Housing and Urban Development, *Land Title Recordation Practices: A State of the Art Study* (1980); Richard W. Laugesen, "The Torrens Title System in Colorado," *Dicta* 39 (1962): 40.

67. On appeal, the 10th Circuit Court of Appeals held that the 1860 congressional confirmation of the Sangre de Cristo grant extinguished "any conflicting rights prior to the Confirmatory Act of 1860 which might have arisen or existed by reason of the original grant from Mexico." *Sanchez v. Taylor*, 377 F. 2d 733 (1967).

68. *Rael v. Taylor*, p. 6, and the Plaintiffs' and Interveners' Opposition to Taylor Family's Motion for Summary Judgement, April 6, 1998 (copy in author's possession).

69. For examples of resistance, see Robert Rosenbaum, *Mexicano Resistance in the Southwest: The Sacred Right of Self-Preservation* (Austin: University of Texas Press, 1981); Rodolfo Acuña, *Occupied America: A History of Chicanos* (New York: Harper and Row, 1988); Peter Nabakov, *Tijerina and the Court House Raid* (Albuquerque: University of New Mexico Press, 1969).

70. In 1997 the trial court denied the plaintiffs their motion to file as a class action; this ruling is still under appeal. See Opening Brief of Plaintiffs in *Lobato v. Taylor*, Colorado Court of Appeals, 13 P. 3d 821 (2000).

71. Because *Espinoza v. Taylor* (also known as *Lobato v. Taylor*) is still in litigation, I realize that this discussion will become more outdated with each new court decision. Still, I would like the reader to consider the larger implications about commons and their place in the American West.

72. *Rael v. Taylor*, p. 24 (emphasis added).

73. John Locke, *The Second Treatise of Government* (Indianapolis: Bobbs-Merrill Company, Inc., 1952), 29.

# Bibliography

PRIMARY SOURCES

Calhoun, James S. *The Official Correspondence of James S. Calhoun.* Washington, D.C.: Government Printing Office, 1915.

Colfax County Records. *County Clerk Deeds.* New Mexico State Records Center and Archives, Santa Fe.

————. *County Clerk Mining Deeds.* New Mexico State Records Center and Archives, Santa Fe.

————. *County Clerk Miscellaneous Papers.* New Mexico State Records Center and Archives, Santa Fe.

Colorado, State of. *Eighth Biennial Report of the Bureau of Labor Statistics, 1901–1902.* Denver: Smith Books Printing Company, 1902.

*Compiled Laws of New Mexico.* Topeka: George W. Crane and Co., 1887.

*Congressional Globe.* 46 vols. Washington, D.C., 1834–73.

*De Maxwell Land Grant and Railway-Company.* Amsterdam: Blikman and Sartorius, 1870. Henry E. Huntington Library, San Marino, Calif.

"Diario y derrotero de Juan de Ulibarrí." *Provincias Internas* 36, expediente 4 (1706): 353–79. Archivo General de la Nación.

Dolan, Thomas J. "Report of Council Proceedings with Jicarilla Apache Indians, 1873." WA MSS @-1223, file D685, Beinecke Rare Book Library, Yale University, New Haven, Conn.

Grant, Victor. Collection. Arthur Johnson Memorial Library, Raton, N. Mex.

Grier, John. "Overawing the Indians: Captain Judd and Lt. Burnside at Las Vegas." William G. Ritch Collection, Henry E. Huntington Library, San Marino, Calif.

Henry-McGaven Collection. New Mexico State Records Center and Archives, Santa Fe.

Land Grants—Maxwell #6. New Mexico State Records Center and Archives, Santa Fe.

Las Animas County Records. District Court Office, Trinidad, Colorado.

*Laws Passed by the General Assembly of the Territory of New Mexico in the Session of December, 1847.* Santa Fe, N. Mex.: Hovey and Davies, 1848.

Manuscript Census for Colfax County, 1860. Microfilm. New Mexico State Records Center and Archives, Santa Fe.

Manuscript Census for Mora County, 1860. Microfilm. New Mexico State Records Center and Archives, Santa Fe.

Maxwell Land Grant and Family File. Arthur Johnson Memorial Library, Raton, N. Mex.

Maxwell Land Grant and Railway Company Papers (MLGC Papers). Archive 147, Zimmerman Library, Special Collections, University of New Mexico, Albuquerque.

Miranda, Guadalupe. Family Papers. New Mexico State Records Center and Archives, Santa Fe.

New Mexico Counties A–Z File. "Colfax County." Arthur Johnson Memorial Library, Raton, N. Mex.

Office of Indian Affairs, New Mexico Superintendency. *Pueblo-Related Jurisdictions.* Record Group 75. National Archives and Records Center, Denver.

*Papers Relating to Land Grants in the Office of the Surveyor General of New Mexico.* Bureau of Land Management, Santa Fe, N. Mex. Microfilm publication of the University of New Mexico, Zimmerman Library, Albuquerque.

Records of the Commissioner of the General Land Office. Division E, record group 49. National Archives, Washington, D.C.

Records of the Governor. Infantry Correspondence. Archive 26690. State of Colorado Archives, Denver.

Ritch, William G. Collection. Henry E. Huntington Library, San Marino, Calif.

San Miguel County Records. District Court, Civil Records. New Mexico State Records Center and Archives, Santa Fe.

Schomburg, T. A. Papers. Collection 747. Colorado Historical Society Library, Denver.

*Spanish and Mexican Land Laws: New Spain and Mexico.* St. Louis, Mo.: Buxton and Skinner Stationery Co., 1895.

Streeter, Thomas W. Collection of Texas Manuscripts. Beinecke Manuscripts and Rare Book Library, Yale University, New Haven, Conn.

Taos County Records. New Mexico State Records Center and Archives, Santa Fe.

Territorial Archives of New Mexico, Santa Fe. Microfilm rolls 6, 22.

*Translation of the Beaubien and Miranda Petition, & c.* Santa Fe, N. Mex.: Manderfield and Tucker, Printers, 1872. Henry E. Huntington Library, San Marino, Calif.

U.S. Department of Housing and Urban Development. *Land Title Recordation*

*Practices: A State of the Art Study*. Washington, D.C.: Government Printing Office, 1980.
U.S. Department of the Interior Appointment Papers for New Mexico. Microfilm M-750. National Archives, Washington, D.C.
U.S. Department of Justice Papers. *United States v. Maxwell Land Grant Company*. Complaint Case 72100, record group 267. National Archives, Washington, D.C.
Vigil, José Urbano. Papers. Norlin Library, Western History Collection. University of Colorado, Boulder.
Westphall, Victor. Collection. New Mexico State Records Center and Archives, Santa Fe.


NEWSPAPERS

*Cimarron News and Press*, 1875–77.
*Denver Republican*, 1879–1913.
*Las Vegas (N. Mex.) Daily Gazette*, 1881–86.
*Las Vegas (N. Mex.) Nogal Nugget*, 1884–1902.
*Pueblo (Colo.) Chieftain*, 1872–present.
*Railway Press and Telegraph* (Elizabethtown, N. Mex.), 1870–81.
*Raton (N. Mex.) Weekly Independent*, 1884–89.
*Santa Fe Daily New Mexican*, 1881–97.
*Santa Fe Republican*, 1847–49.
*Santa Fe Weekly Gazette*, 1851–69.
*Trinidad (Colo.) Daily Citizen*, 1887–90.


COURT CASES

*Arguello v. United States*, 59 U.S. (18 How.) 539 (1855).
*Beaubien, Leonora, v. Vidal Trujllo*. Bill for Divorce. April 3, 1865. New Mexico State Records Center and Archives, Santa Fe.
*Bent v. Thompson*, 138 U.S. 114 (1891).
*Chaves, Manuela Antonia, v. William S. McKnight and Jose Maria Gutieres*. *Report of Cases Argued and Determined in the Supreme Court of the Territory of New Mexico*, vol. 1 (January 1857).
*Delassus v. United States*, 34 U.S. (9 Pet.) 134 (1835).
*Edgar, Eliza W., and James M. Edgar v. Quirina Baca and Filomeno Gallegos*. *Report of Cases Argued and Determined in the Supreme Court of the Territory of New Mexico*, vol. 1 (January 1875).
*Espinoza v. Taylor*, District Court for the County of Costilla, State of Colorado, civil action no. 81, May 1998.
*Fletcher v. Peck*, 10 U.S. (6 Cranch.) 87 (1810).
*Fremont v. United States*, 58 U.S. 542, 557–58 (1854).

*Glenn v. United States,* 54 U.S. (13 How.) 259 (1851).

*Interstate Land Company v. Maxwell Land Grant Company,* 139 U.S. 569 (1891).

*Jaramillo, Mariana, v. José de la Cruz Romero. Report of Cases Argued and Determined in the Supreme Court of the Territory of New Mexico,* vol. 1 (January 1857).

*Lamy, John B., and Mercedes Chaves de Lamy v. Thomas B. Catron and William T. Thornton. New Mexico Reports,* vol. 5, no. 375 (January 21, 1890): 373.

*Lobato v. Taylor,* 13 P. 3d 821 (Colo. 2000).

*Martinez, Mariana Manuela, v. Tomas Lucero. Report of Cases Argued and Determined in the Supreme Court of the Territory of New Mexico,* vol. 1 (January 1857).

*Maxwell Land Grant Company v. F. B. Chaplan,* Colo. 3d (1888).

*Maxwell Land Grant Company v. F. B. Chaplan and R. D. Russell,* Las Animas County District Court, Trinidad, Colo. (April 6, 1887).

*Maxwell Land Grant Company v. Richard D. Russell,* Colo. 3d (1888).

*Rael v. Taylor,* 876 P. 2d 1210 (Colo. 1994).

*Russell v. Maxwell Land Grant Company,* 158 U.S. 253 (1895).

*Sanchez v. Taylor,* 377 F. 2d 733 (1967).

*Scottish Mortgage and Land Investment Company of New Mexico et al. v. Manuel S. Brazil et al.* District Court of the Fourth Judicial District, San Miguel County, nos. 4091 and 4092 (1895).

*Soulard v. United States,* 29 U.S. (4 Pet.) 511 (1830).

*Tameling v. U.S. Freehold and Immigration Company,* 93 U.S. 644 (1876).

*Thompson, Guadalupe, et al. v. Maxwell Land Grant and Railway Company,* 95 U.S. 391 (1877).

*United States v. Maxwell Land Grant and Railway Company,* 121 U.S. 325 (1887).

*United States v. Percheman,* 32 U.S. (7 Pet.) 51 (1833).

## SECONDARY SOURCES

Acuña, Rodolfo. *Occupied America: A History of Chicanos.* New York: Harper and Row, 1988.

Agnew, John. *The United States in the World Economy: A Regional Geography.* New York: Cambridge University Press, 1987.

Almaguer, Tomás. "Interpreting Chicano History: The World System Approach to Nineteenth-Century California." *Review* 4 (winter 1981): 459–507.

———. *Racial Fault Lines: The Historical Origins of White Supremacy in California.* Berkeley: University of California Press, 1994.

Anderson, Terry L., and Peter J. Hill, eds. "The Evolution of Property Rights: A Study of the American West." *Journal of Law and Economics* 18, no. 1 (1975): 163–79.

————. *The Political Economy of the American West.* Lanham, Md.: Rowman and Littlefield Publishers, 1994.

Arrom, Silvia M. *The Women of Mexico City, 1790–1857.* Stanford: Stanford University Press, 1985.

Athearn, Robert G. *High Country Empire: The High Plains and Rockies.* New York: McGraw-Hill, 1960.

————. *Westward the Briton.* New York: Charles Scribner and Sons, 1953.

Avery, Dianne, and Alfred S. Konefsky. "The Daughters of Job: Property Rights and Women's Lives in Mid-Nineteenth-Century Massachusetts." *Law and History Review* 10 (fall 1992): 323.

Aymard, Maurice. *Dutch Capitalism and World Capitalism.* Cambridge: Cambridge University Press, 1982.

Baade, Hans W. "The Form of Marriage in Spanish North America." *Cornell Law Review* 61 (November 1975): 1.

Bancroft, Hubert Howe. *History of Arizona and New Mexico, 1530–1888.* Albuquerque: Horn and Wallace, 1962.

Barrera, Marío. *Race and Class in the Southwest.* Notre Dame: University of Notre Dame Press, 1979.

Basch, Norma. *In the Eyes of the Law: Women, Marriage, and Property in Nineteenth-Century New York.* Ithaca: Cornell University Press, 1982.

Beck, Warren A. *New Mexico: A History of Four Centuries.* Norman: University of Oklahoma Press, 1962.

Bederman, Gail. *Manliness and Civilization: A Cultural History of Gender and Race in the United States, 1880–1917.* Chicago: University of Chicago Press, 1995.

Biemer, Linda Briggs. *Women and Property in Colonial New York: The Transition from Dutch to English Law, 1643–1727.* Ann Arbor: UMI Research Press, 1983.

Bogue, Allan G. *Money at Interest.* Ithaca: Cornell University Press, 1955.

Bold, Christine. "The Rough Riders at Home and Abroad: Cody, Roosevelt, Remington and the Imperialist Hero." *Canadian Review of American Studies* 18, no. 3 (March 1987): 321–50.

Braudel, Fernand. *Afterthought on Material Civilization and Capitalism.* Baltimore: Johns Hopkins University Press, 1977.

————. *Capitalism and Material Life, 1400–1800.* London: Weidenfeld and Nicolson, 1973.

Brayer, Herbert O. *William Blackmore: The Spanish-Mexican Land Grants of New Mexico and Colorado, 1863–1878.* 2 vols. Denver: Bradford-Robinson, 1949.

————, ed. *The Westerner's Brand Book: Twelve Original Studies in Western and Rocky Mountain History.* Vol. 3. Denver: The Westerners, 1949.

Briggs, Charles L., and John R. Van Ness, eds. *Land, Water, and Culture: New Perspectives on Hispanic Land Grants.* Albuquerque: University of New Mexico Press, 1987.

Brooks, James F. "'This Evil Extends Especially to the Feminine Sex': Captivity and Identity in New Mexico, 1700–1846." In Susan Armitage and Elizabeth Jameson, eds., *Writing the Range: Race, Class, and Culture in the Women's West.* Norman: University of Oklahoma Press, 1997.

Brown, Pervis L. "Even Stranger Fruit: An Analysis of Black, Hispanic, and White Lynchings in Texas." Ph.D. diss. in progress. University of Michigan.

Bryant, Keith. *History of the Atchison, Topeka, and Santa Fe Railway.* New York: Macmillan, 1974.

Camarillo, Albert. *Chicanos in a Changing Society: From Mexican Pueblos to American Barrios in Santa Barbara and Southern California, 1848–1930.* Cambridge: Harvard University Press, 1979.

Carlson, Alvar W. "Long Lots on the Río Arriba." *Annals of the Association of American Geographers* 65, no. 1 (March 1975): 48–57.

———. "Rural Settlement Patterns in the San Luis Valley: A Comparative Study." *The Colorado Magazine* 44 (1967): 111–23.

Chaput, Donald. *Francois X. Aubry.* Glendale, Calif.: Arthur H. Clark, 1975.

Chávez, John R. *The Lost Land: The Chicano Image of the Southwest.* Albuquerque: University of New Mexico Press, 1984.

Chevalier, Francois. *Land and Society in Colonial Mexico: The Great Hacienda.* Berkeley: University of California Press, 1963.

Chinen, Jon J. *The Great Mahele: Hawaii's Land Division of 1848.* Honolulu: University of Hawaii Press, 1974.

Chused, Richard H. "Late Nineteenth Century Married Women's Property Law: Reception of the Early Married Women's Property Act by Courts and Legislatures." *The American Journal of Legal History* 29 (1985): 3.

———. "Married Women's Property Law: 1800–1850." *The Georgetown Law Journal* 71 (1983): 1359–1425.

———. "The Oregon Donation Act of 1850 and Nineteenth-Century Federal Married Women's Property Law." *Law and History Review* 2 (spring 1984): 44.

Cleaveland, Agnes Morley. *No Life for a Lady.* Boston: Houghton Mifflin, 1941.

———. *Satan's Paradise, from Lucien Maxwell to Fred Lambert.* Boston: Houghton Mifflin, 1952.

Cleaveland, Norman. *Colfax County's Chronic Murder Mystery.* Santa Fe, N. Mex.: Rydal Press, 1977.

———. *The Morleys: Young Upstarts on the Southwest Frontier.* Albuquerque, N. Mex.: Calvin Horn, 1971.

Conover, Milton. *The General Land Office: Its History, Activities, and Organizations.* Baltimore: Johns Hopkins University Press, 1923.

Cooper, Frederick, et al. *Confronting Historical Paradigms: Peasants, Labor, and the Capitalist World System in Africa and Latin America.* Madison: University of Wisconsin Press, 1993.

Cooper, Frederick, and Anne Stoler, eds. *Tensions of Empire: Colonial Cultures in a Bourgeois World.* Berkeley: University of California Press, 1997.

Coyle, William. "Common Law Metaphors of Coverture: Conceptions of Women and Children as Property in Legal and Literary Contexts." *Texas Journal of Women and the Law* 1 (1992): 315.

Craver, Rebecca McDowell. *Impact of Intimacy: Mexican-Anglo Intermarriage in New Mexico, 1821–1846*. El Paso: Texas Western Press, 1982.

Crawford, Stanley. *Mayordomo: Chronicle of an Acequia in Northern New Mexico*. Albuquerque: University of New Mexico Press, 1988.

Cronon, William. *Changes in the Land: Indians, Colonists, and the Ecology of New England*. New York: Hill and Wang, 1983.

———. *Nature's Metropolis: Chicago and the Great West*. New York: W. W. Norton, 1991.

———. *Uncommon Ground*. New York: W. W. Norton, 1995.

Dargo, George. *Jefferson's Louisiana: Politics and the Clash of Legal Traditions*. Cambridge: Harvard University Press, 1975.

Davis, Lance E. "Capital Immobilities and Southwestern Land Prices, 1865–1875: A Case Study of a Historical Market Paradox." Unpublished manuscript in author's possession.

———. "The Investment Market, 1870–1914: The Evolution of a National Market." *Journal of Economic History* 25, no. 3 (September 1965): 355–99.

Davis, William W. H. *El Gringo: New Mexico and Her People*. Santa Fe: Radial Press, 1938.

Daws, Gavan. *Shoal of Time: A History of the Hawaiian Islands*. Honolulu: University of Hawaii Press, 1968.

deBuys, William. *Enchantment and Exploitation: The Life and Hard Times of a New Mexico Mountain Range*. Albuquerque: University of New Mexico Press, 1985.

Degler, Carl. *At Odds: Women and the Family in America from the Revolution to the Present*. New York: Oxford University Press, 1980.

de la Torre, Adela, and Beatríz M. Pesquera, eds. *Building with Our Hands: New Directions in Chicana Studies*. Berkeley: University of California Press, 1993.

Demos, John. *Unredeemed Captive: A Family Story from Early America*. New York: Alfred A. Knopf, 1994.

De Soto, Hernando. *The Other Path: The Invisible Revolution in the Third World*. New York: Harper and Row, 1990.

Deutsch, Sarah. *No Separate Refuge: Culture, Class, and Gender on an Anglo-Hispanic Frontier in the American Southwest, 1880–1940*. New York: Oxford University Press, 1987.

Dick, Everett. *The Lure of the Land: A Social History of the Public Lands from the Articles of Confederation to the New Deal*. Lincoln: University of Nebraska Press, 1970.

Dobson, John M. *Politics in the Gilded Age*. New York: Praeger Publishers, 1972.

Dukeminier, Jesse, and James E. Krier. *Property*. 3d ed. New York: Little, Brown and Co., 1993.

Ebright, Malcolm. "Mexican Land Grants: The Legal Background." In *Land,*

*Water, and Culture: New Perspectives on Hispanic Land Grants,* ed. Charles L. Briggs and John R. Van Ness. Albuquerque: University of New Mexico Press, 1987.

————, ed. *Spanish and Mexican Land Grants and the Law.* Manhattan, Kans.: Sunflower Press, 1989.

Echevarria, Evelio, and José Otero, eds. *Hispano Colorado: Four Centuries' History and Heritage.* Fort Collins, Colo.: Centennial Publications, 1976.

Ellickson, Robert C. *Order without Law: How Neighbors Settle Disputes.* Cambridge: Harvard University Press, 1991.

————. "Property in Land." *The Yale Law Journal* 102 (April 1993): 1315–1400.

Emmett, Chris. *Fort Union and the Winning of the Southwest.* Norman: University of Oklahoma Press, 1965.

Erdoes, Richard, and Alfonso Ortiz. *American Indian Myths and Legends.* New York: Pantheon Books, 1984.

Fairman, Charles. *Reconstruction and Reunion, 1864–1888.* New York: Macmillan, 1987.

Florescano, Enrique. "Haciendas." *Cambridge History of Latin America,* vol. 2, ed. Leslie Bethall. New York: Cambridge University Press, 1984.

Foley, Neil. *The White Scourge: Anglos, Blacks, and Mexicans in Central Texas, 1880–1930.* Berkeley: University of California Press, 1997.

Foner, Eric. *Free Soil, Free Labor, Free Men: The Ideology of the Republican Party Before the Civil War.* New York: Oxford University Press, 1995.

————. *Reconstruction: America's Unfinished Revolution, 1863–1877.* New York: Harper and Row, 1988.

Fox-Genovese, Elizabeth. *Inside the Plantation Household: Black and White Women of the Old South.* Chapel Hill: University of North Carolina Press, 1988.

Frazer, Robert W., ed. *New Mexico in 1850: A Military View.* Norman: University of Oklahoma Press, 1968.

Fridlington, Robert. *The Reconstruction Court, 1864–1888.* Millwood, N.Y.: Associated Faculty Press, 1987.

Furer, Howard. *Fuller Court, 1888–1910.* Millwood, N.Y.: Associated Faculty Press, 1986.

Gardner, Hamilton. "Philip St. George Cooke and the Apache, 1854." *New Mexico Historical Review* 28 (April 1953): 115.

Gates, Paul W. *History of Public Land Law Development.* Washington, D.C.: Government Printing Office, 1968.

————. *The Jeffersonian Dream: Studies in the History of American Land Policy and Development.* Albuquerque: University of New Mexico Press, 1996.

————. *Landlords and Tenants on the Prairie Frontier.* Ithaca: Cornell University Press, 1973.

Genovese, Eugene D. *Roll, Jordan, Roll: The World the Slaves Made.* New York: Pantheon Books, 1974.

Genovese, Eugene D., and Elizabeth Fox-Genovese. *Fruits of Merchant Capi-*

tal: *Slavery and the Bourgeois Party in the Rise and Expansion of Capitalism.* New York: Oxford University Press, 1983.

Gildersleeve, Charles H. *Report of the Cases of the Supreme Court of the Territory of New Mexico, January Term 1857.* Chicago: Callaghan and Company, 1897.

Glendon, Mary Ann. *The New Family and the New Property.* Toronto: Butterworths, 1981.

Goddard, Pliny Earl. *Jicarilla Apache Texts.* New York: American Museum of Natural History, 1911.

Godlewska, Anne, and Neil Smith, eds. *Geography and Empire.* Oxford: Blackwell Publishers, 1994.

González, Deena J. "Doña Gertrudis Barcelo." In Adela de la Torre and Beatríz M. Pesquera, eds., *Building with Our Hands: New Directions in Chicana Studies.* Berkeley: University of California Press, 1993.

————. *Refusing the Favor: The Spanish-Mexican Women of Santa Fe, 1820–1880.* New York: Oxford University Press, 1999.

————. "The Spanish-Mexican Women of Santa Fé: Patterns of Their Resistance and Accommodation, 1820–1880." Ph.D. diss., University of California, Berkeley, 1985.

————. "The Widowed Women of Santa Fe: Assessments on the Lives of an Unmarried Population, 1850–80." In *On Their Own: Widows and Widowhood in the American Southwest, 1848–1939,* ed. Arlene Scadron. Urbana: University of Illinois Press, 1986.

Goodwyn, Lawrence. *Democratic Promise: The Populist Movement in America.* New York: Oxford University Press, 1976.

Gouda, Frances. *Dutch Culture Overseas: Colonial Practice in the Netherlands Indies, 1900–1942.* Amsterdam: University of Amsterdam Press, 1995.

Gregg, Josiah. *Commerce of the Prairies: or Eight Expeditions across the Great Western Prairies, and a Residence of Nearly Nine Years in Northern Mexico.* New York: H. G. Langley, 1844. Reprint, Norman: University of Oklahoma Press, 1990.

Griswold del Castillo, Richard. *The Treaty of Guadalupe Hidalgo: A Legacy of Conflict.* Norman: University of Oklahoma Press, 1990.

Gunnerson, Dorris A. *The Jicarilla Apaches: A Study of Survival.* DeKalb: Northern Illinois University Press, 1974.

Gutiérrez, David. *Walls and Mirrors: Mexican Americans, Mexican Immigrants, and the Politics of Ethnicity.* Berkeley: University of California Press, 1995.

Gutiérrez, Ramón A. *When Jesus Came, the Corn Mothers Went Away: Marriage, Sexuality, and Power in New Mexico, 1500–1846.* Stanford: Stanford University Press, 1991.

Hafen, LeRoy R., ed. *The Mountain Men and the Fur Trade of the Far West: Biographical Sketches of the Participants by Scholars of the Subject and with Introductions by the Editor.* Vol. 3. Glendale, Calif.: Arthur H. Clark, 1965.

Hahn, Steven, and Jonathan Prude, eds. *The Countryside in the Age of Capitalist Transformation: Essays in the Social History of Rural America.* Chapel Hill: University of North Carolina Press, 1985.

Hall, Allan R. *The Export of Capital from Britain, 1870–1914.* London: Methuen and Co., 1968.

Hall, Frederic. *The Laws of Mexico: A Compilation and Treatise Relating to Real Property, Mines, Water Rights, Personal Rights, Contracts, and Inheritances.* San Francisco: A. L. Bancroft and Co., 1885.

Hall, Kermit. *The Magic Mirror: Law in American History.* New York: Oxford University Press, 1989.

Hall, Thomas D. *Social Change in the Southwest, 1350–1880.* Lawrence: University of Kansas Press, 1989.

Hibbard, Benjamin H. *A History of Public Land Policies.* Madison: University of Wisconsin Press, 1965.

Hicks, John D. *The Populist Revolt: A History of the Farmer's Alliance and the People's Party.* Minneapolis: University of Minnesota Press, 1931.

Himerich y Valencia, Robert. *Encomenderos of New Spain, 1521–1555.* Austin: University of Texas Press, 1991.

Hobsbawm, Eric J. *The Age of Capital, 1848–1875.* New York: Scribner's, 1975.

Hofstadter, Richard. *The Age of Reform: From Bryan to F.D.R.* New York: Alfred A. Knopf, 1955.

Homer, Sydney, and Richard Sylla. *The History of Interest Rates.* New Brunswick, N.J.: Rutgers University Press, 1996.

Horsman, Reginald. *Race and Manifest Destiny: The Origins of American Racial Anglo-Saxonism.* Cambridge: Harvard University Press, 1981.

Horwitz, Morton J. *The Transformation of American Law.* Cambridge: Harvard University Press, 1977.

Hosen, Frederick E. *Unfolding Westward in Treaty and Law: Land Documents in United States History from the Appalachians to the Pacific, 1783–1934.* Jefferson, N.C.: McFarland and Co., 1988.

Howbert, Irving. *Memories of a Lifetime in the Pike's Peak Region.* New York: G. P. Putnam Sons, 1925.

Hurtado, Albert. *Indian Survival on the California Frontier.* New Haven: Yale University Press, 1988.

Hyde, Anne F. "Cultural Filters: The Significance of Perception." In *A New Significance: Re-envisioning the History of the American West,* ed. Clyde A. Milner II. New York: Oxford University Press, 1996.

Hyma, Albert. *A History of the Dutch in the Far East.* Ann Arbor, Mich.: George Wahr Publishing, 1953.

Inman, Henry. *The Old Santa Fe Trail: The Story of a Great Highway.* Topeka: Crane and Company, 1916.

Jaramillo, Sandra. "The Myth of High Skirts and Loose Blouses: Intercultural Marriage in the Mexican Period." Paper presented at the annual meeting of the Western Historical Association Conference, Denver, 1995.

Jenk, Leland Hamilton. *The Migration of British Capital*. London: Thomas Nelson and Sons, 1927.

Jensen, Joan, and Darlis Miller, eds. *New Mexico Women: Intercultural Perspectives*. Albuquerque: University of New Mexico Press, 1986.

Johannsen, Robert W. *To the Halls of the Montezumas: The Mexican War in the American Imagination*. New York: Oxford University Press, 1986.

Johnson, Hildegard B. *Order Upon the Land: The U.S. Rectangular Land Survey and the Upper Mississippi Country*. New York: Oxford University Press, 1976.

Joyner, Charles. *Down by the Riverside: A South Carolina Slave Community*. Urbana: University of Illinois Press, 1984.

Julian, George W. "Land Stealing in New Mexico." *North American Review* 145 (July 1887): 17–31.

Kaplan, Amy, and Donald E. Pease, eds. *Cultures of United States Imperialism*. Durham, N.C.: Duke University Press, 1993.

Keleher, William H. *Maxwell Land Grant: A New Mexico Item*. Albuquerque: University of New Mexico Press, 1984.

Kolodny, Annette. *The Land Before Her: Fantasy and Experience of the American Frontiers, 1630–1860*. Chapel Hill: University of North Carolina Press, 1984.

———. *The Lay of the Land: Metaphor and Experience and History in American Life and Letters*. Chapel Hill: University of North Carolina Press, 1975.

Lamar, Howard R. "Edmund G. Ross as Governor of New Mexico Territory: A Reappraisal." *New Mexico Historical Review* 36 (1961): 177–209.

———. *The Far Southwest, 1846–1912: A Territorial History*. New Haven: Yale University Press, 1966.

———. "From Bondage to Contract: Ethnic Labor in the American West, 1600–1890." In *The Countryside in the Age of Capitalist Transformation: Essays in the Social History of Rural America*, ed. Steven Hahn and Jonathan Prude. Chapel Hill: University of North Carolina Press, 1985.

———, ed. *Reader's Encyclopedia of the American West*. New Haven: Yale University Press, 1998.

Larson, Robert. *New Mexico Populism: A Study of Radical Protest in a Western Territory*. Boulder, Colo.: Colorado Associated University Press, 1974.

———. *New Mexico's Quest for Statehood, 1846–1912*. Albuquerque: University of New Mexico Press, 1968.

———. *Populism in the Mountain West*. Albuquerque: University of New Mexico Press, 1968.

Laugesen, Richard W. "The Torrens Title System in Colorado." *Dicta* 39 (1962): 40.

Lazarou, Kathleen E. *Concealed Under Petticoats: Married Women's Property and the Law of Texas, 1840–1913*. New York: Garland Publishing, 1986.

Lebsock, Suzanne. *The Free Women of Petersburg: Status and Culture in a Southern Town, 1784–1860*. New York: W. W. Norton, 1984.

Lecompte, Janet. "The Independent Women of Hispanic New Mexico, 1821–1846." *Western Historical Quarterly* 12, no. 1 (January 1981): 17–35.

Limerick, Patricia Nelson. *Legacy of Conquest: The Unbroken Past of the American West.* New York: W. W. Norton, 1987.

Limerick, Patricia Nelson, Clyde A. Milner, and Charles E. Rankin, eds. *Trails Toward a New Western History.* Lawrence: University of Kansas Press, 1991.

Locke, John. *The Second Treatise of Government.* Indianapolis: Bobbs-Merrill Co., 1952.

Logan, J. S. "Early Banking in New Mexico." *New Mexico Banking Review* 9 (1940): 148.

Lukas, J. Anthony. *Big Trouble.* New York: Simon and Schuster, 1997.

Mares, E. A., et al. *Padre Martínez: New Perspectives from Taos.* Taos, N. Mex.: Millicent Rogers Museum, 1988.

McClintock, Anne. *Imperial Leather: Race, Gender, and Sexuality in the Colonial Contest.* New York: Routledge, 1995.

McCormack, John L. "Torrens and Recordings: Land Title and Assurance in the Computer Age." *William Mitchell Law Review* 18: 61–86.

McCoy, Drew R. *The Elusive Republic: Political Economy in Jeffersonian America.* Chapel Hill: University of North Carolina Press, 1980.

McMurtry, Larry. *Anything for Billy.* New York: Simon and Schuster, 1988.

Mead, Margaret. *Cultural Patterns and Technical Change.* New York: New American Library, 1955.

Meinig, D. W. *Southwest: Three Peoples in Geographical Change, 1600–1970.* New York: Oxford University Press, 1971.

Merk, Frederick. *Manifest Destiny and Mission in American History.* New York: Vintage Books, 1966.

Miller, Darlis A. "Intercultural Marriages in the American Southwest." In Joan M. Jensen and Darlis A. Miller, eds., *New Mexico Women: Intercultural Perspectives.* Albuquerque: University of New Mexico Press, 1986.

Miller, David Hunter, ed. *Treaties and Other International Acts of the United States of America.* Vol. 5. Washington, D.C.: Government Printing Office, 1937.

Minow, Martha. "'Forming Underneath Everything that Grows': Toward a History of Family Law." *Wisconsin Law Review* 20 (1985): 819–96.

Montejano, David. *Anglos and Mexicans in the Making of Texas, 1836–1986.* Austin: University of Texas Press, 1987.

———. "Is Texas Bigger Than the World-System? A Critique from a Provincial Point of View." *Review* 4, no. 3 (winter 1981): 597–628.

Montoya, María E. "Dividing the Land: The Taylor Ranch and the Limited Access Commons." In *Land in the American West: Private Claims and the Common Good,* ed. William Robbins. Tucson: University of Arizona Press, 2000.

———. "The Education of a Gilded-Age Politician: L. Bradford Prince." *New Mexico Historical Review* (April 1991): 172–201.

Mooney, James. "The Jicarilla Genesis." *American Anthropologist* 11, no. 7 (July 1898): 197–209.

Morrissey, Katherine. *Mental Territories: Mapping the Inland Empire*. Ithaca: Cornell University Press, 1997.

Morrow, William W. *Spanish and Mexican Private Land Grants*. San Francisco: Bancroft-Whitney, 1923.

Morse, Stephen J. "Family Law in Transition: From Traditional Families to Individual Liberty." In *Changing Images of the Family*, eds. Virginia Tufte and Barbara Myerhoof, 319–60. New Haven: Yale University Press, 1979.

Murphy, Lawrence R. "The Beaubien and Miranda Land Grant, 1841–1846." *New Mexico Historical Review* 42, no. 1 (January 1967): 27–47.

———. *Frontier Crusader: William F. N. Arny*. Tucson: University of Arizona Press, 1972.

———. *Lucien B. Maxwell: Napoleon of the Southwest*. Norman: University of Oklahoma Press, 1983.

———. *Philmont: A History of New Mexico's Cimarron Country*. Albuquerque: University of New Mexico Press, 1972.

———. "Rayado: Pioneer Settlement in Northeastern New Mexico, 1848–1857." *New Mexico Historical Review* 46, no. 1 (January 1971): 37–56.

Nabakov, Peter. *Tijerina and the Court House Raid*. Albuquerque: University of New Mexico Press, 1969.

Neeson, J. M. *Commoners: Common Right, Enclosure, and Social Change in England, 1700–1820*. New York: Cambridge University Press, 1993.

Noble, David. *America by Design: Science, Technology, and the Rise of Corporate Capitalism*. New York: Alfred A. Knopf, 1977.

Nostrand, Richard L. *The Hispano Homeland*. Norman: University of Oklahoma Press, 1992.

Onuf, Peter S. *Statehood and Union: A History of the Northwest Ordinance*. Bloomington: Indiana University Press, 1987.

Opie, John. *The Law of the Land: Two Hundred Years of Farmland Policy*. Lincoln: University of Nebraska Press, 1994.

Opler, Morris E. "The Character and Derivation of the Jicarilla Holiness Rite." *University of New Mexico Bulletin*. Albuquerque: University of New Mexico Press, 1943.

———. *Childhood and Youth in Jicarilla Apache Society*. Los Angeles: Southwest Museum Fund, 1946.

———. "Jicarilla Apache Territory, Economy, and Society in 1850." *Southwestern Journal of Anthropology* 27, no. 4 (winter 1971): 309–29.

———. "A Summary of Jicarilla Apache Culture." *American Anthropologist* 38 (April–June 1936): 202.

Ortiz, Alfonso, ed. *The Handbook of North American Indians*. Vol. 10. Washington, D.C.: Smithsonian Institution Press, 1983.

Ortiz, Roxanne Dunbar. *Roots of Resistance: Land Tenure in New Mexico, 1680–1980*. Los Angeles: Chicano Studies Research Center Publications, University of California, 1980.

Ostrom, Elinor. *Governing the Commons: The Evolution of Institutions for Collective Action.* New York: Cambridge University Press, 1990.

Pan, Denise. "Peace and Conflict in an Industrial Family." M.A. thesis. Department of History, University of Colorado, Boulder, 1994.

Pattison, William D. *Beginnings of the American Rectangular Survey System, 1784–1800.* Chicago: University of Chicago Press, 1957.

Pearson, Jim Berry. *The Maxwell Land Grant.* Norman: University of Oklahoma Press, 1961.

Perry, Richard. J. *Western Apache Heritage: People of the Mountain Corridor.* Austin: University of Texas Press, 1991.

Pomeroy, Earl. *In Search of the Golden West.* Lincoln: University of Nebraska Press, 1990.

———. *The Territories and the United States, 1861–1890: Studies in Colonial Administration.* Seattle: University of Washington Press, 1969.

Porter, A. N., and R. F. Holland. *Money, Finance, and Empire, 1790–1960.* London: Frank Cass and Company, 1985.

Porter, Glenn, ed. *Encyclopedia of American Economic History: Studies of the Principal Movements and Ideas.* 3 vols. New York: Charles Scribner and Sons, 1980.

Potter, David M. *The Impending Crisis, 1846–1861.* New York: Harper and Row, 1976.

Pratt, Mary Louise. *Imperial Eyes: Travel Writing and Transculturation.* New York: Routledge, 1992.

Quaife, Milo Milton, ed. *Kit Carson's Autobiography.* Lincoln: University of Nebraska Press, 1966.

Rabkin, Peggy A. *From Fathers to Daughters: The Legal Foundation of Female Emancipation.* Westport, Conn.: Greenwood Press, 1980.

Rael y Gálvez, Estévan. "Mal-Criado and Entre-Metido Subalternity: How(!) Is the "old Indian" Luis a Slave?" Unpublished manuscript in author's possession.

Reséndez, Andrés. "Caught Between Profits and Rituals: National Contestation in Texas and New Mexico 1821–1848." Ph.D. diss., University of Chicago, 1997.

Reynolds, Matthew. *Spanish and Mexican Land Laws.* St. Louis: Buxton and Skinner Stationery Co., 1895.

Robbins, Roy M. *Our Landed Heritage: The Public Domain, 1776–1970.* Lincoln: University of Nebraska Press, 1972.

Robbins, William. *Colony and Empire.* Lawrence: University of Kansas Press, 1995.

Rohrbough, Malcolm J. *The Land Office Business: The Settlement and Administration of American Public Lands, 1789–1837.* New York: Oxford University Press, 1968.

Rose, Carol M. *Property and Persuasion: Essays on the History, Theory, and Rhetoric of Ownership.* Boulder, Colo.: Westview Press, 1994.

Rosenbaum, Robert. *Mexicano Resistance in the Southwest: The Sacred Right of Self-Preservation*. Austin: University of Texas Press, 1981.

Russell, Marian Sloan. *Land of Enchantment: Memoirs of Marian Russell along the Santa Fe Trail*. Albuquerque: University of New Mexico Press, 1981.

Ryus, William H. *The Second William Penn: A True Account of Incidents That Happened Along the Old Santa Fe Trail in the Sixties*. Kansas City: Frank T. Riley Publishing Co., 1913.

Salmon, Marylynn. *Women and the Law of Property in Early America*. Chapel Hill: University of North Carolina Press, 1986.

Sánchez, George I. *Forgotten People: A Study of New Mexico*. Albuquerque: University of New Mexico Press, 1940.

Sánchez, George J. *Becoming Mexican American: Ethnicity, Culture, and Identity in Chicano Los Angeles, 1900–1945*. New York: Oxford University Press, 1993.

Scharff, Virginia. "Post-Western History." Paper presented at the Western History Association meeting, Albuquerque, N. Mex., 1994.

Schwantes, Carlos A. "Protest in a Promised Land: Unemployment, Disinheritance, and the Origin of Labor Militancy in the Pacific Northwest, 1885–1886." *Western Historical Quarterly* 13, no. 4 (October 1982): 373–90.

Scott, James C. *Seeing Like a State*. New Haven, Conn.: Yale University Press, 1999.

Scott, William B. *In Pursuit of Happiness: American Conceptions of Property from the Seventeenth to the Twentieth Century*. Bloomington: Indiana University Press, 1977.

Seed, Patricia. *Ceremonies of Possession in Europe's Conquest of the New World, 1492–1640*. New York: Cambridge University Press, 1995.

Shammas, Carole, Marylynn Salmon, and Michel Dahlin. *Inheritance in America from Colonial Times to the Present*. New Brunswick, N.J.: Rutgers University Press, 1987.

Sheridan, Thomas. *Los Tucsonenses: The Mexican Community in Tucson, 1854–1941*. Tucson: University of Arizona Press, 1986.

Siegel, Reva B. "The Modernization of Marital Status Law: Adjudicating Wives' Rights to Earning, 1860–1930." *Georgetown Law Journal* 82 (September 1994): 2127–2210.

Simmons, Marc. "The Wagon Mound Massacre." *Journal of the West* 28, no. 2 (April 1989): 45–52.

Simpson, A. W. B. *An Introduction to the History of Land Law*. London: Oxford University Press, 1979.

Sklar, Martin J. *The Corporate Reconstruction of American Capitalism, 1890–1916: The Market, the Law, and Politics*. New York: Cambridge University Press, 1988.

Smith, Henry Nash. *Virgin Land*. New York: Vintage Books, 1957.

Speth, Linda E. "The Married Women's Property Acts, 1839–1865: Reform, Reaction, or Revolution?" In *Women and the Law: The Social Historical*

*Perspective,* ed. D. Kelly Weisberg. Cambridge: Schenkman Publishing, 1982.

Stern, Steve, and Immanuel Wallerstein. "American Historical Review Forum." *American Historical Review* 93 (October 1988): 896.

Stilgoe, John R. *Common Landscape of America: 1580–1945.* New Haven: Yale University Press, 1982.

Stoller, Marianne L. "Grants of Desperation, Lands of Speculation: Mexican Period Land Grants in Colorado." *Journal of the West* 19: 22.

Stratton, Porter A. *Territorial Press of New Mexico, 1834–1912.* Albuquerque: University of New Mexico Press, 1969.

Streeter, Thomas W. *Bibliography of Texas: 1795–1845.* Woodbridge, Conn.: Research Publications, 1983.

Swierenga, Robert P. *Pioneers and Profits: Land Speculation on the Iowa Frontier.* Ames: Iowa State University Press, 1968.

Taylor, Jean Gelman. *The Social World of Batavia: European and Eurasian in Dutch Asia.* Madison: University of Wisconsin Press, 1983.

Taylor, Morris F. "A New Look at an Old Case: The Bent Heirs' Claim in the Maxwell Grant." *New Mexico Historical Review* 43, no. 3 (July 1968): 213–28.

———. *O. P. McMains and the Maxwell Land Grant Conflict.* Tucson: University of Arizona Press, 1979.

Taylor, William B., and Elliot West. "Patron Leadership at the Crossroads: Southern Colorado in the Late Nineteenth Century." *Pacific Historical Review* 42, no. 3 (August 1973): 335–57.

Tiller, Veronica E. Velarde. "Jicarilla Apache." In *Handbook of North American Indians,* vol. 10, ed. Alfonso Ortiz (Washington, D.C.: Smithsonian Institution, 1983).

———. *The Jicarilla Apache Tribe: A History, 1846–1970.* Lincoln: University of Nebraska Press, 1983.

Trachtenburg, Alan. *The Incorporation of America: Culture and Society in the Gilded Age.* New York: Hill and Wang, 1982.

Trefousse, Hans Louis. *Carl Schurz: A Biography.* Knoxville: University of Tennessee Press, 1982.

Turner, Frederick Jackson. "The Significance of the Frontier in American History." In *History, Frontier, and Section: Three Essays.* Albuquerque: University of New Mexico Press, 1993.

Tuska, Jon. *Billy the Kid: His Life and Legend.* Albuquerque: University of New Mexico Press, 1994.

Utley, Robert M. *Billy the Kid: A Short and Violent Life.* Norman: University of Oklahoma Press, 1989.

———. *The Indian Frontier of the American West 1846–1890.* Albuquerque: University of New Mexico Press, 1984.

Van Kirk, Sylvia. *"Many Tender Ties": Women in Fur-Trade Society, 1600–1870.* Norman: University of Oklahoma Press, 1980.

Van Young, Eric. *Hacienda and Market in Eighteenth-Century Mexico: The Rural Economy of the Guadalajara Region, 1675–1820*. Berkeley: University of California Press, 1981.

Veyna, Angelina F. "'It Is My Last Wish That . . .': A Look at Colonial Nuevo Mexicanas through Their Testaments." In Adela de la Torre and Beatríz M. Pesquera, *Building with Our Hands: New Directions in Chicana Studies*. Berkeley: University of California Press, 1993.

Wallerstein, Immanuel. *The Capitalist World-Economy*. Cambridge: Cambridge University Press, 1979.

———. *The Modern World-System*. New York: Academic Press, 1974.

Weber, David J. *The Mexican Frontier, 1821–1846: The American Southwest under Mexico*. Albuquerque: University of New Mexico Press, 1982.

———. *On the Edge of Empire: The Taos Hacienda of Los Martínez*. Santa Fe: Museum of New Mexico Press, 1996.

———. *The Spanish Frontier in North America*. New Haven: Yale University Press, 1992.

———. *The Taos Trappers*. Norman: University of Oklahoma Press, 1968.

Weeks, William Earl. *Building the Continental Empire: American Expansion from the Revolution to the Civil War*. Chicago: Ivan R. Dee, 1996.

Westphall, Victor. *Mercedes Reales: Hispanic Land Grants of the Upper Rio Grande Region*. Albuquerque: University of New Mexico Press, 1983.

———. *Thomas Benton Catron and His Era*. Tucson: University of Arizona Press, 1973.

White, G. Edward. *The American Judicial Tradition: Profiles of Leading American Judges*. New York: Oxford University Press, 1988.

———. *The Marshall Court and Cultural Change, 1815–1835*. Abridged ed. New York: Oxford University Press, 1991.

White, Richard. *It's Your Misfortune and None of My Own*. Norman: University of Oklahoma Press, 1992.

———. *The Middle Ground: Indians, Empires, and Republics in the Great Lakes Region, 1600–1815*. New York: Cambridge University Press, 1991.

———. *Roots of Dependency: Subsistence, Environment, and Social Change among the Choctaws, Pawnees, and Navajos*. Lincoln: University of Nebraska Press, 1983.

# Index

*Page numbers in italics indicate maps and tables.*

Abreu, Jesús, 231n27, 232n30
Abreu family, 53–54, 232n30
*acequias* (ditches), 1, 38, 209
Adams, Alva, 150, 154, 192, 197, 198, 254n4
Adams-Onis Treaty, 173
adobe construction, 6, 138
adultery, 58–59
Agnew, John, 10
agriculture: in Beaubien/Miranda grant, 31, 37–38; corporate, 87; European, 21, 25; Jicarilla, 24–25; markets, 70, 142; Maxwell Land Grant Company and, 85–86, 101–2; Pueblo, 22; sharecroppers, 31, 38, 50, 51, 74; subsistence, 167, 211; in *vara* strips, 37–38, 140; in wage-labor economy, 31, 207–8. *See also* cattle; irrigation; peonage
*ahupuaas*, Hawaiian, 118–19
Allison, R. C. (Clay), 112–13
Alvarado, Juan, 178–80
American South, 64, 65, 69, 71, 74
American West: colonization of, 5, 8, 9–10, 80–87, 117–20; land dispossessions throughout, 117–20; land grant legacy in, 191–219; Maxwell

Land Grant Company property relations and, 79; Maxwell legend and, 50, 54; race in, 13–14; U.S. incorporation of, 2, 9–13, 80–87, 109–10, 117–20, 167–82. *See also* California; Colorado; myths of American West; New Mexico; territorial system, U.S.
Amsterdam Committee, Maxwell Land Grant Company's, 13, 78, 87, 88, 93, 121, 128–36, 146–47, 154
Analla, Juana, 67–68
Ancient Forest Rescue, 13, 14
Anderson, T. J., 121, 153
Anglos, 13–14, 218; American investors, 44, 122–23, 148; on Beaubien/Miranda grant, 35, 39; Colfax County resistance and, 110–13; economic disparity of, with Hispanos, 138–43; environmentalists, 13; *Espinoza v. Taylor* and, 13, 14; fears of encroachment by, 36, 72; Hispano relations with, 13, 14, 51, 107–13, 131–32, 137, 200–1, 214, 217; homesteading and, 11, 12–13, 21, 72, 87, 94–95, 101–7, 146, 217; intermarriage of, 51, 61; and Jica-

Anglos (continued)
rillas, 21, 24, 30, 40–45; land use systems of, 21, 25; vs. Maxwell Land Grant Company, 9, 80, 95–113, 121–56, 200–1, 242n66; Maxwell relationship with, 103–4; on Maxwell's rule, 64; miners, 21, 78, 80, 96–107; myths of male-dominated violence by, 19–20, 120; in negotiations, 133–34, 145–46; prejudice against, 145–46; property conflict position of, 87, 96–107, 106; Sangre de Cristo Land Grant to, 212; and Stonewall Valley trial, 200–1, 256n30; in twentieth century, 207–8. See also Europeans; McMains, O. P.; Russell, Richard D.; United States
anti-grant leagues, 107, 203–4
Anti-Land Grant Monthly, 203–4
anti-Mexican sentiment, 66, 76–83
Apaches: Mescalero, 40; Pícuris founding and, 163. See also Jicarilla Apaches
Aragón, Juan, 131
Archibald, Albert W., 231n20
Archibeque, 28
Arguello v. United States, 180–81, 252n54
Arkansas River, 21, 39
armies. See military
Armijo, Manuel, 167, 258n59; Beaubien/Miranda grant conveyed by, 30–36, 49, 90, 92, 93, 163, 164, 183–86, 189, 232n29, 258n59; and Sangre de Cristo Land Grant, 211–12, 258n59
Arny, William F., 39, 96, 97
Atchison, Topeka, and Santa Fe Railroad, 12, 84–85, 126, 129
Athapaskans, 22, 24
Atkinson, Henry M., 11–12, 115–16, 117
Aubry, F. S., 41
auction, public, 114, 166
Austin, Moses, 182

Austin, Stephen B., 182–82
Australia, Torrens Act and, 213
Axtell, Samuel B., 113

Baca, Quirina, 59–60, 61–62, 235n49
Baldy Mountain, 72, 73, 87
banking, 88, 90
bankruptcies of Maxwell Land Grant Company, 73, 114, 124–25, 148
Barcelo, Gertrudes, 55–56
Barclay's Fort, 41
Beale, Joseph Charles, 161
Bear Flag Rebellion, California, 50, 178
Beaubien, Carlos Hipolite Trotier, 19, 30–37, 49, 226n43, 253n66; Armijo relationship with, 30–36, 49, 184–85, 189; death of, 49, 52–53; as empresario, 184–86; executors for, 231n27; on liquor, 39; marriage of, 31, 51; Maxwell marries daughter of, 48, 50–51; Maxwell meets, 50; Maxwell purchases from, 52; originally named Charles, 51; as patrón, 31, 38; rents paid to, 51; and Sangre de Cristo Land Grant, 1–3, 50, 171, 212–13, 214. See also Beaubien/Miranda grant
Beaubien, Narcisco, 35, 211–12, 232n29, 253n66
Beaubien, Paul, 54
Beaubien, Paula, 31, 51, 52
Beaubien Abreu, Petra, 51, 53–54
Beaubien Clouthier, Juana, 53
Beaubien family, 36–37, 49–54, 62–63, 76, 212, 231n27
Beaubien Maxwell, María de la Luz, 48–49, 50–51, 62–63, 230n16; children of, 69, 233n34; Cimarron home of, 52, 70–71; as property owner, 52, 53–57, 76; sells Maxwell Land Grant, 74, 78–79, 87–95, 239n21, 240n34; slaves and servants of, 49, 68–69, 233n34; widowhood of, 63, 76
Beaubien/Miranda grant, 1, 5, 6, 30–

39, *34*, 48, 50; Narcisco Beaubien
given half of, 212; boundaries of,
30–39, 62–63, 93, 159, 182, 225–
26n37; as empresario grant, 163,
164, 182–86; legalities of, 32–35;
Martínez protests, 20, 32, 35–36,
38, 184–85, 225n30, 253n66;
Maxwell carries out original intention of, 72; Maxwells acquire all of,
48, 49, 52–54, 62; Mexican govern-
ment/Armijo convey, 19, 20, 30–
36, 49, 93, 163, 164, 183–86, 189,
232n29, 258n59; Rayado settle-
ment, 36–38, 40, 51–52, 54; after
U.S. occupation, 49; U.S. troops vs.
Jicarillas on, 20, 40–45; *U.S. v.
Maxwell Land Grant and Railway
Company* and, 159–62. *See also*
Maxwell Land Grant
Beaubien Mueller, Teodora, 53,
231n27
Beaubien Trujillo, Eleanor, 51, 53, 63
Bell, Sam, 196–97, 256n28
Bell, W. A., 92, 240n30
Benedict, Kirby, 53
*Ben Hur* (Wallace), 84
Bent, Albert, 232n29
Bent, Charles, 33, 53, 226n39, 253n66;
murder of, 35, 212, 232n29
Bent's Fort, 39, 41
Billy the Kid, 50, 69
Blackmore, William, 88
Blacks, free, 236n63, 240n27
Blosser, George, 191
Board of Land Commissioners, 119,
252n46
Boggs, Thomas O., 137, 138, 143–45,
147, 149, 154
Bond, Frank, 142–43
borders, defense of, 165. *See also*
boundaries
*Boston Times*, 46
boundaries: authority over Mexican
land grants', 90–95, 171–72, 186,
258n59; Beaubien/Miranda grant,
30–39, 62–63, 93, 159, 182, 225–

26n37; border defense, 165;
Colorado-New Mexico, 5, 149;
grid system, 81, 166–67; Jicarilla,
21–22. *See also* Maxwell Land
Grant boundaries; surveys, Max-
well Land Grant
Bowlden, Henry, 136
Breese, Sidney, 61
Brewer, David J., 205–6, 257–58n48
British: English common law, 4, 179;
investors, 52, 54, 55, 85, 88, 91–92,
118, 122–23, 124, 217. *See also*
Anglos
Brown, Pervis L., 242–43n73
Buchanan, James, 168
buffalo hunting, 22, 25
buffalo ranch, Turner's, 141
Burdett, S. S., 95
Burns, W. T., 156, 197
Burnside, Ambrose E., 40, 227n54
Bustamento family, 67–68

Calhoun, James S., 39, 40, 41–43,
226n43, 228n60
Calhoun, John C., 46, 81, 82, 228n1
California: Bear Flag Rebellion, 50,
178; *Fremont v. United States*,
177–80; Maxwell in, 50, 230n16;
U.S. imperial-colonial ways in, 9, 83
Canadian River, 6, 21
capitalism. *See* market capitalism
captives, war, 29, 40–44, 68–69
Cardenas, Manuel, 110–11, 112–13
Carson, Kit, 43, 50, 51, 68, 230n16
Cass, Lewis, 81
Catholics: French, 28, 29; Mexican,
111, 169–70, 182–83; Spanish, 19,
22, 27. *See also* Martínez, Father
Antonio José
Catron, Thomas B., 109, 114–15, 117,
180, 181
cattle: Maxwell Land Grant Cattle
Company, 130, 136, 140–41; Luz
Maxwell's business in, 55, 63; set-
tlers', 130, 140–42, 146, 195. *See
also* grazing land

CF&I. *See* Colorado Fuel and Iron Corporation (CF&I)

Chaffee, Jerome B., 52, 88–91, 92, 109, 115–16, 239n21

Chaplan, F. B., 135, 148–50, 155, 156

*Chaves v. McKnight and Gutieres*, 46, 58–59

Chávez, Francisco, 58

Chávez, Manuela Antonia, 58–59

Chávez, Mariano, 36

Chávez, Pedro, 137

Chicago, 9, 10, 84, 85

Chihuahua Trail, 30–31

Chili railroad, 142

Cimarron, New Mexico, 6; Jicarillas in, 97, 98–99; Maxwells in, 39, 52, 68, 70–71, 240n34; Pels's business in, 127, 136; White massacre on Cimarron Cutoff, 41

Cimarron River, 24, 36, 52, 105

citizenship, Treaty of Guadalupe Hidalgo on, 169–70

Civil Law, 4, 12, 14, 17, 55, 56, 58

Civil War, U.S., 65, 67, 74, 84, 195, 227

Clamorgan, James, 177, 178, 252n46

Cleveland, Grover, 100, 121, 138

climate, 24, 85–86

coal mining, 8, 207–8

coinage, populism and, 202, 204, 257n40

Colfax County: Farmers' Alliance, 203; Joseph in politics of, 204–5; and Maxwell Land Grant boundaries, 239n21; resistance in, 20, 107–13, 120, 133–34, 137, 191, 196, 217; "War" of, 107–8

Collins, J. L., 60, 61

Collinson, John, 79, 89, 91–92, 102, 105, 240nn30,34

colonization: of American West, 5, 8, 9–10, 80–87, 117–20; Dutch colonial practices, 127; hacienda system replaced by, 78–120; Mexican law and, 163–65, 178, 182–83; worldwide, 9, 117. *See also* imperialism; Spanish; territorial system, U.S.

Colorado, 126; Denver, 10, 84, 88, 127, 150–51; ejections in, 148–51, 156, 191, 197; Las Animas County, 151, 156, 161, 197, 201, 239n21; and Maxwell Land Grant Company fraud, 12, 187; militia of, 197, 198, 254n4; Native Americans in, 22, 96; Purgatory River, 24, 95, 105, 192; Taylor Ranch purchase offers, 209–11; Torrens Act, 213–16. *See also* Maxwell Land Grant; Sangre de Cristo Land Grant; San Luis, Colorado; Stonewall Valley

Colorado Fuel and Iron Corporation (CF&I), 8, 14, 18, 156, 206–8, 217, 258n55

Comanches, 72

*Commerce of the Prairies* (Gregg), 36

common law, 4, 15, 17, 61, 176–81, 234n42, 252n44

commons, in land grants, 1, 37, 38, 184–85, 209–16, 254n77. *See also* communal land rights

communal land rights: Hispano, 1–4, 35, 38, 140, 163, 214–16; Jicarilla, 97. *See also* commons; community land grants

community establishment on Beaubien/Miranda grant, 37–38. *See also* commons, in land grants; plazas, Hispano; settlers

community land grants, 4–5, 12, 163, 165, 215. *See also* communal land rights

confrontation, 19; settlers vs. Jicarillas, 38–39; settlers vs. Maxwell Land Grant Company, 121–56, 191–94. *See also* Martínez, Father Antonio José; McMains, O. P.; negotiations; property system conflicts; resistance; violence

Congress, U.S.: John C. Calhoun, 46, 81, 82, 228n1; and free Blacks in New Mexico, 236n63, 240n27; Hispanos petition, 137–38; Homestead Act (1862), 13, 47, 95, 160, 162,

166, 188; House Bill 740 on land grant size, 90–93; and Jicarilla treaty, 100; Joseph delegated to, 204–5; land grant patents, 122, 153, 159, 171–73, 185, 205–6, 212, 258n59, 259n67; and Maxwell Land Grant acreage, 62, 63, 159–60; and Maxwell Land Grant Company property relations, 78, 109, 115, 117–18, 122, 137–38, 205–6; Maxwell Land Grant plat approved by, 144; and Maxwell Land Grant surveys, 89, 116; Northwest Ordinance (1787), 81, 83, 165, 166, 249n11; and peonage, 47–48, 64–66, 71, 76, 236n63; Supreme Court and property rights authority of, 159–74, 186–87; and territorial system/American South, 65; Treaty of Guadalupe Hidalgo exceptions by, 47–48, 64, 168–70, 188–89; and "unsettled" territory, 81–82. *See also* legal system, U.S.
Constitution, U.S., 65; Thirteenth Amendment, 67
Continental Divide, 70
contingent remainders law, 176–77, 252n44
corporations: CF&I, 8, 156, 206–8, 217, 258n55; land, 20; populism vs., 202. *See also* market capitalism; Maxwell Land Grant and Railway Company; monopoly, populism vs.
corruption, official, 11–12, 13, 108–17, 150–54; and Elkins/Marmon survey, 115–17, 187; populism vs., 204; and racial reporting, 84; Santa Fe Ring and, 11, 13, 108–17, 203; surveyor general and, 11–12, 89–90, 115–16; territorial governor and, 102–3, 109; *U.S. v. Maxwell Land Grant and Railway Company* and, 159, 187; U.S. vs. foreign, 175, 181. *See also* fraud, Maxwell Land Grant Company and
Costilla County, 171, 209–16, 259n63
court cases. *See* legal system, U.S.

coverture, 15, 49, 53, 57, 58, 60, 62, 76, 77
Cox, Jacob D., 92–95, 115, 171
Cox, James, 194
Cronon, William, 10, 120, 245n17
Cuba, 9
"cultural synthesis" tactic, 127, 133
culture: Jicarilla adaptations of European, 30; Maxwell Land Grant Company touts multicultural nature of grant, 146. *See also* ethnicity; land use systems; politics; religion
customs collection in New Mexico, 31–32, 164

*Daily Citizen*, 150
Davis, Jefferson, 81
Davis, W. W. H., 83–84
Dawson, J. D., 136
debt peonage, 65–68
defense, border, 165. *See also* military
Delano, Columbus, 93, 94–95, 103
Delassus, Colonel, 177
democracy: American West as exceptional space for, 9; European colonization and, 127; Jacksonian, 104–5; Manifest Destiny and, 13; populism and, 257n40; republican ideology of, 166; Turner on, 120
Democratic Party, 81, 204
Denver, Colorado, 10, 84, 88, 127, 150–51
De Soto, Hernando, 258n57
Deutsch, Sarah, 207
development. *See* land use systems; market capitalism
ditches, 1, 38, 74, 209
divorce, legal system and, 53, 57–58, 59–60
Dolan, Thomas, 78, 99–100
Donaghue, Florencio, 110, 112–13
Donner party, 135
dowry, 57–59
Dresden, barricade of, 47
Dudley, L. Edwin, 97–98
Dulce, New Mexico, 100

Dummler & Company, 127
Dunbar, W. W., 200, 256n28
Durango, Mexico, 32, 36
Dutch: as desired immigrants, 9, 10, 121, 129–30, 146; imperial-colonial interests, 9, 127; investors, 9, 10–11, 13, 85, 88, 120–36, 140–41, 146–47, 189, 217, 223n16; and Jicarillas, 29; Maxwell Land Grant Company's Amsterdam Committee, 121, 128–36, 146–47, 154. *See also* Pels, Marinus Petrus

East India Company, 127
economy: Anglo/Hispano disparity, 138–43; Beaubien/Miranda development plans, 30–32; ejection-resistance costs, 203; and *Espinoza v. Taylor* outcome, 216; of Gilded Age America, 109; on grant, under Maxwell, 38, 45, 50, 54, 56, 69–75, 87, 89; Hispano decline, 111–12, 211, 218; and incorporation into U.S., 2, 9–13, 80–87, 109–10, 117–20, 167–82, 244n88; Jicarilla, 24–25, 30, 98; Old World, 54, 89; Panic (1873), 114; wage-labor, 31, 206–8, 211, 258n55. *See also* agriculture; finances; gathering; hunting; labor; market capitalism; markets; monetary policy, populism and; natural resources; patronage; property system; trade
ejections: change-of-venue law and, 203; Maxwell Land Grant Company and, 107, 113, 128, 131, 148–51, 156, 191–203. *See also* land loss phenomenon
El Bajado Rancho, Santa Ana County, 59–60
*El Gringo* (W. W. H. Davis), 83–84
Elizabethtown, 73, 74, 102–4, 240n34
Elkins, John T., 115–17, 187; survey with Marmon, 11, 115–17, 120, 122, 153, 182, 187
Elkins, Stephen B., 109, 112; as Baca lawyer, 61–62, 235n49; and

Elkins/Marmon survey, 11, 115–16, 120, 187; shares of, in Maxwell Land Grant Company, 92, 240n30
Ellickson, Robert, 104, 258n57
El Salvador, 80
Emancipation, 65
empresario land grants, 161, 163–65, 168, 174–75, 179–89, 252–53n59
"empty"/"unsettled" space, myth of, 5–8, 80–87, 216–17. *See also terra incognita*
*encomiendas*, 47, 163
English common law, 4, 179
Enlightenment, 81, 166
environmentalists, 13, 14
equality: Mexican laws and, 53, 56, 68, 162–63, 179; republican, 162–63, 166; U.S. legal system and, 48–49, 56–57, 63–64, 162–63, 166, 179. *See also* gender; slaves
Erdoes, Richard, 19
Española Valley, 142
*Espinoza v. Taylor*, 1–4, 188, 208–16, 259n71; ethnicity and, 13, 14, 214, 217; Perricone actions in, 2–3, 4, 216, 250n21
ethnicity, 13–14; Anglo-Hispano relations, 13, 14, 51, 107–13, 131–32, 137, 200–1, 214, 217, 256n30; economy disparity based on, 138–43; Maxwell Land Grant Company touts multicultural nature of grant, 146; populism and, 203. *See also* Anglos; Europeans; Hispanos; Native Americans; racial categories
European investors, 10, 44, 109; British, 52, 54, 55, 85, 88, 91–92, 118, 122–23, 124, 217; Dutch, 9, 10–11, 13, 85, 88, 120–36, 140–41, 146–47, 189, 217, 223n16; Maxwells sell to (1869), 55, 73–79, 87–95, 239n21; populists vs., 204; and Sangre de Cristo Land Grant, 212
Europeans, 26–30; as desired immigrants, 9, 10, 121, 129–30, 146; Jicarillas negotiate among, 21, 26–30, 41; land use systems of, 21, 25;

as migrant laborers, 207; possession-taking modes of, 19, 26–27.
*See also* British; Dutch; European
investors; French; Spanish
"exceptionalism" of American West,
8–10, 120

fees: customs, 31–32, 164; Hawaiian
commutation, 119. *See also* taxes
fee simple absolute, 2, 12–13; empresario system and, 175, 188–89; and
Hawaiian Great Mahele, 80, 119;
and Maxwell Land Grant, 72–73,
78, 97; vs. usufructuary systems,
80, 97
feminization, conquest and, 27, 61.
*See also* women
*femme sole*, 59, 63, 76
fencing, in valuations of settler land,
139–40, 141–42
"fencing in" of Hispanos, 143
feudalism: hacienda system associated
with, 47, 50, 63–66, 71, 72, 75–77,
189; U.S. ideology vs., 46–49, 63–
68, 71, 75–77, 85, 162–67, 189. *See
also* patronage; peonage
finances: banking, 88, 90; cattle business, 142; Maxwell Land Grant
Company's, 10, 73, 75, 85–95, 103,
109, 114–17, 120–32, 146–48,
152–53, 157. *See also* fees; investors; market capitalism; monetary policy, populism and; taxes
Finch, Duane D., 198
First National Bank of Denver, 88
First National Bank of Santa Fe, 90
Fish, Hamilton, 103
*Fletcher v. Peck*, 173–74, 176
Florida, U.S. acquisition of, 56, 83,
170, 234n42
food, Jicarilla shortage of, 97. *See also*
subsistence farming
Forbes, Malcolm, 259n63
Fort Union, New Mexico, 55, 73, 97,
113, 195
Frankfurt Assembly, 47
fraud, Maxwell Land Grant Company

and, 12, 151–52, 182, 187. *See also*
corruption, official
Fredonia rebellion, 183
free Blacks, 236n63, 240n27
free labor, 66, 67, 80
free silver, populism and, 202, 204
Frémont, John Charles, 50, 51, 177–
80, 230n16
*Fremont v. United States*, 177–80,
181
French: fur-trapping by, 21, 26; imperialism of, 12, 21; in Jicarilla territory, 27–29; land grants of, 175–
76; and Louisiana, 56, 83, 173, 175–
76; trading frontiers of, 230–31n18
frontier, Turner on, 120
fur trade, 21, 26, 31, 50

Gallatin, Albert, 167
Gallegos, Filomeno, 59–60
Garrett, Pat, 50, 69
gathering: commons for, 37; Jicarilla,
25
gender: conquest and, 27, 61; in Jicarilla economy, 24–25; and property
system, 11, 12, 47–49, 53–65, 76–
77, 234–35. *See also* women
General Land Office, U.S.: commissioners of, 91, 95, 115–17, 121, 153;
homesteading patents issued by, 95,
125; and Maxwell Land Grant surveys, 91, 95, 115–17, 153; Russell
plea to, 121, 153–54; Santa Fe Ring
and, 109, 115–16; *U.S. v. Maxwell
Land Grant and Railway Company*
and, 205
Gilded Age America, 109
Gilpin, William, 212–13
Girardet, "Frenchy," 197
*Glenn v. United States*, 177–80, 181
gold mining, 71–74, 87, 102
Goldstein, Jeff, 1, 2
Goodwyn, Lawrence, 202
Las Gorras Blancas, 145, 206, 214
government: Mexican Republic, 12,
30, 81–82; miners', 73; New Mexico Mexican, 30–36, 49, 83, 93,

government *(continued)*
163–65, 175; New Mexico Spanish, 26, 29, 30, 83, 175. *See also* government officials, U.S.; law; New Mexico Territory; state; United States
government officials, U.S., 10, 11–12, 108–17, 217–18; Jicarilla negotiations with, 97–101; Justice Department, 187; Maxwell Land Grant Company assistance from, 5, 12, 92, 102–3, 108–17; racial reporting by, 83–84; Sangre de Cristo Land Grant purchased by, 212; Santa Fe Ring and, 11, 13, 108–17, 203; and Treaty of Guadalupe Hidalgo's Article 10, 47–48, 64, 168–70, 188–89. *See also* Congress, U.S.; corruption, official; Interior Department, U.S.; legal system, U.S.; Surveyor General, New Mexico Office of the
grazing land: Beaubien/Miranda grant and, 35, 37, 38; Jicarilla allowance of, to Maxwell, 97; Maxwell Land Grant Company and settlers vie for control of, 135; in Vermejo area, 141. *See also* cattle
Great Mahele (Hawai'i), 16, 47, 80, 118–19, 229n4
Greenhorn River, 39
Gregg, Josiah, 36
grid system, 81, 166–67
Griego, Francisco "Pancho," 110, 112, 113
Grier, William N., 43–44
Griffin, W. W.: field notes of, 85, 126; Maxwell Land Grant survey by, 89–91, 103, 115, 160, 187, 239n18
Guadalupe Hidalgo, Treaty of (1848), 2, 36, 82–83, 168–70; Article 9/citizenship and freedom of religion, 169–70, 250n19; Article 10/property rights, 47–48, 50, 56, 64, 159, 162, 168–69, 179, 188–89, 214, 215
Gutiérrez, José María, 58–59

hacienda system, 236n62; Beaubien/Miranda plans for, 30–

31; colonization replaces, 78–120, 144–45; Maxwell's, 5, 49, 50, 54, 70–72, 75, 89; U.S. lawmakers' view of, 47, 63–66, 71, 75–76, 189, 228n1. *See also* patronage; peonage
Hawai'i: Great Mahele, 47, 80, 118–19; Torrens Act and, 213
Hicks, John D., 202
Hispanos, 11, 13–14, 82, 216, 221n3; Anglo relations with, 13, 14, 51, 107–13, 131–32, 137, 200–1, 214, 217; on Beaubien/Miranda grant land, 35, 37–39; Colfax County resistance and, 110–13, 133–34; communal land rights and, 1–4, 35, 38, 140, 163, 214–16; economic situation of, 111–12, 138–43, 211, 218; empresario rights and, 163, 188; and homesteading, 125, 188, 217; Jicarillas and, 24, 30; land use systems of, 20, 21, 35, 37–38, 105–7, 106, 125, 138–45, 209; in Las Vegas, 40; and Maxwell Land Grant Company, 9, 72–73, 75, 78, 80, 95, 96–113, 121–56, 200–1, 214, 217, 242n66; Maxwell relationship with, 11, 71–73, 75, 96; prejudice against, 13–14, 81–82, 108, 110–12, 134–45, 228n1; property conflict position, 20, 87, 96–107, 106, 188; squatter status of, 9, 72–73, 74, 108, 129–45, 244n1; and Stonewall Valley trial, 200–1, 256n30; in twentieth century, 207–8. *See also Espinoza v. Taylor*; Mexican Americans
Hofstadter, Richard, 202
Holdsworth, R. B., 156, 194, 197
Hollywood myths of American West, 19–20, 211
homesteading, 93, 94, 119, 125; Anglo, 11, 12–13, 21, 72, 87, 94–95, 101–7, 146, 217; Hispanos and, 125, 188, 217; Homestead Act (1862), 13, 47, 95, 160, 162, 166, 188; *Russell v. Maxwell Land Grant Company* and, 206, 256n25; U.S. ideol-

ogy and, 162, 165, 166. *See also*
Russell, Richard D.; settlers;
squatters
Houston, Sam, 81
Houx, Benjamin, 116
Hungarian uprising, 47
Hunn, William D., 194, 197, 198, 199
Hunter, Julius, 200
hunting: commons for, 37; Jicarilla,
24, 25, 35, 39; Plains Indians, 22.
*See also* fur trade
Hyde, Anne, 134–35

imperialism, 8–9; European, 9, 12, 18,
21, 61, 127; U.S., 9–10, 61, 81–84.
*See also* colonization; Manifest
Destiny; territorial system, U.S.
*Imperial Leather* (McClintock), 61
income, Maxwells', 71–72. *See also*
rents
incorporation, 8–11, 18, 47, 65, 80–
86, 90, 119, 217
independence: American movement
(1830s), 183; of Mexico from Spain,
32; of Texas from Mexico (1836),
35, 164
*Independent*, 203
Indian agents: Arny, 39, 96, 97;
Calhoun, 39, 40, 41–43, 226n43,
228n60; Maxwell, 39, 227n50
Indians. *See* Native Americans
individualism, 48, 64
individual land grants, 4–5, 163–65,
180–81, 184–85, 215–16, 252–
53n59
informal property relations, 20, 65,
71–80; conflicts stemming from, 2–
5, 75–77, 89, 96–97, 104, 189. *See
also* hacienda system; patronage;
peonage; squatters
Inman, Henry, 71
Interior Department, U.S., 96, 217–
18, 258n59; and Jicarilla agreement,
100; and limits to grant size, 90–95,
171–72; and Maxwell Land Grant
surveys/boundaries, 90–91, 95,
103, 115–17, 153, 205; and public

domain, 90, 95, 103, 125, 153; Russell plea to, 153–54; secretaries of,
92–95, 103, 115, 171. *See also*
General Land Office, U.S.
intermarriage, 51, 61, 231n18
*Interstate Land Company v. Maxwell
Land Grant Company*, 161, 162,
174–75, 177, 181
investors, 117–20; American, 44,
122–23, 148; Maxwell as investor,
73–74. *See also* European investors; market capitalism; Maxwell
Land Grant and Railway Company
irrigation: Hispano, 37–38, 144, 209;
Jicarilla, 24, 25; Maxwell Land
Grant Company, 107, 130

Jackson, Andrew, 104–5, 176, 181,
234n42, 251n43
Jaramillo, Mariana, 65–67, 68
*Java, or How to Manage a Colony*
(Money), 127
Jay Treaty (1794), 173
Jefferson, Thomas, 167, 208
Jicarilla Apaches, 5, 8, 11, 19, 21–26,
78, 218; and boundaries, 19, 21–22,
33; conflict with Beaubien/Miranda
grant settlers, 38–39; Dolan report
(1873), 78, 100; and Europeans, 21,
26–30, 41, 44; homeland of, 23;
hunting grounds encroached on, 35,
39; land loss of, 20, 21, 39, 80, 97–
101; land use systems of, 20, 24–
25, 30, 38; liquor sold to, 39; as
Maxwell Land Grant's earliest inhabitants, 19, 20, 21–45, 72; Maxwell's relationship with, 25, 39, 70,
71, 72, 96–97; property conflict position, 20, 87, 96–107; removal of,
20, 21, 80, 97–101, 217, 242n66;
U.S. military vs., 20, 40–45, 80, 97;
usufructuary system of, 12, 21, 25–
26, 35, 97; White massacre and, 41–
43, 42, 228n60
Jones, Calvin, 71
Joseph, Antonio, 204–5
Judd, Henry, 40, 43

Julian, George W., 90–91, 94
jumping land claims, 129
Justice Department, U.S., 187

Kaukikeaouli (king of Hawai'i), 118–
    19
Kearny, Stephen Watts, 46, 47, 48,
    212
Kephart, Martin, 256nn28,30
Kiowas, 72
Kolodny, Annette, 134–35

labor: on Beaubien/Miranda grant,
    31, 38; CF&I, 206–8, 258n55; Jica-
    rillas' gendered divisions of, 25;
    market economy and, 85–86; under
    Maxwell, 49, 50, 51, 68–73, 75, 79;
    Maxwell Land Grant Company,
    101–2; migrant, 207, 258n55; popu-
    lism and, 202; wage, 31, 206–8,
    211, 258n55. *See also* peonage; ser-
    vants, Maxwells'; sharecroppers;
    slaves
Ladd, Mrs. C. B., 134
Ladd & Company, 118
Lamar, Howard, 107–8
land grants: communal rights, 1–4,
    35, 38, 140, 214–16; community,
    4–5, 12, 163, 165, 215; conditional,
    161; *de novo*, 172, 185; empresario,
    161, 163–65, 168, 174–75, 179–89,
    252–53n59; *Espinoza v. Taylor* and
    meaning of, 209; incorporation of,
    by U.S., 167–73; individual, 4–5,
    163–65, 180–81, 184–85, 215–16,
    252–53n59; legacy of, in American
    West, 191–219; limits to size of,
    90–95, 163–64, 165, 171–73, 182–
    83; populism and, 202; Supreme
    Court rulings on, 158–90; in twen-
    tieth century, 209–16; U.S. racial
    prejudice toward Mexican system
    of, 82, 170, 181. *See also* Beaubien/
    Miranda grant; boundaries; Max-
    well Land Grant; property system
    conflicts; Sangre de Cristo Land
    Grant

land loss phenomenon, 8–10, 13–14,
    80, 101, 117–20, 208; Hawaiian, 80,
    118–19; Jicarilla, 20, 21, 39, 80, 97–
    101; Maxwell Land Grant settlers,
    20, 72–73, 80, 87, 96–120, 121–56.
    *See also* ejections
Land Ordinances (1784, 1785), 167.
    *See also* Northwest Ordinance
    (1787)
land rights, 3–5; contingent remain-
    ders, 176–77, 252n44; Maxwell's,
    72–73, 75; Maxwell's settlers', 75;
    populism and, 202; Protocol of
    Querétaro and, 168–69, 250n19;
    Supreme Court rulings on, 158–90;
    Treaty of Guadalupe Hidalgo and,
    47–48, 50, 56, 64, 162, 168–69,
    179, 188–89, 214, 215; U.S. home-
    steaders', 72; "vested," 4–5, 173–
    81, 251–52n43; women's, 11, 12,
    47–49, 54–65, 76–77, 234–35.
    *See also* communal land rights;
    *Espinoza v. Taylor*; land loss phe-
    nomenon; law; property system;
    usufructuary systems; *U.S. v.
    Maxwell Land Grant and Railway
    Company*
land use systems: Beaubien/Miranda,
    30–32, 37–38; European, 21, 25;
    Hawaiian, 118–19; Hispano, 20, 21,
    35, 37–38, 105–7, 106, 125, 138–
    45, 209; Jicarilla, 20, 24–25, 30, 38;
    Stonewall Valley resort plans, 153,
    154, 192; U.S. ideology and, 166–
    67. *See also* agriculture; commons,
    in land grants; community estab-
    lishment on Beaubien/Miranda
    grant; market capitalism; natural
    resources; property system;
    usufructuary systems
Lara, C., 112, 113
Largo, José, 78, 99–100
Larson, Robert, 202, 257n40
Las Animas County, Colorado, 151,
    156, 161, 197, 201, 239n21
Las Vegas, New Mexico, 40, 43, 62,
    126

*Las Vegas Gazette,* 98
Las Vegas Land Grant, 214
law: common, 4, 176–81, 234n42,
    252n44; Dutch, 122–23; Spanish, 4,
    37. *See also* land rights; legal sys-
    tem, U.S.; Mexican law; property
    system
law enforcement: ejection service, 131,
    156, 191, 197; and settler violence,
    192–94
lawyers: Baca, 61–62, 235n49; Max-
    well Land Grant and Railway Com-
    pany's, 61, 109, 112, 129, 140, 156,
    161, 197
leases, Pels's institution of, 143–44.
    *See also* rents
Lee, Stephen Luis, 211–12
legal system, U.S., 47–49; change-of-
    venue law (1889), 203; ejection
    suits, 107, 113, 128, 131, 148–51,
    156, 201–2; and equality, 48–49,
    56–57, 63–64, 162–63, 166, 179;
    Hispano defense using, 211, 214;
    incorporating Mexican law through,
    168–73; and informal property re-
    gime, 75–77, 96–97; local corrup-
    tion and, 111–13, 150–53; and
    market capitalism, 36, 158, 189–90;
    and Maxwell Land Grant Company
    finances, 114–17; and Maxwell
    Land Grant Company property
    relations, 78–79, 94–107, 114–18,
    128–31, 157–90; Northwest Ordi-
    nance (1787), 81, 83, 165, 166,
    249n11; and peonage, 47–48, 64–
    68, 69, 71, 75–76, 77; racial preju-
    dice in, 82, 111, 170, 181; Torrens
    Act, 213–16; and "unsettled"
    American West, 80–82; and
    women's property rights, 48, 49,
    54–65, 76–77, 234–35. *See also*
    Congress, U.S.; Constitution, U.S.;
    *Espinoza v. Taylor;* law enforce-
    ment; property system conflicts;
    Supreme Court, U.S.; treaties, U.S.
liberalization of property regimes, 11,
    13–14, 32, 47–48, 56–63, 80

Limerick, Patricia, 19, 120
liquor, 39
literacy of settlers, 101
*llaneros,* Jicarilla, 22
Llewelling, J. W., 192–93, 200
Lobato, María Paula Beaubien, 31, 51,
    52
Lobo (chief), 40, 43
Locke, John, 191, 216
logging, 1, 4, 13
Lohman, C., 130
London, England, 10, 12, 87
Longwill, Robert H., 92, 112–13,
    240n30
López, Ignacio, 138
López brothers, 121
López family, 154–55
López Tijerina, Reis, 214
Los Angeles, 84
Louisiana Purchase, 56, 83, 170, 173,
    175–76, 234n42
Lucero, Tomás, 57–58
lynching, 111–12, 242–43n73

Manifest Destiny, 8, 13, 46–47, 81–
    82, 84. *See also* imperialism
*Mariana Jaramillo v. José de la Cruz
    Romero,* 65–67
market capitalism, 10, 117–20, 218;
    Beaubien/Miranda grant and,
    35, 36, 44–45; and cattle busi-
    ness, 142–43; and Jicarilla econ-
    omy, 98; Maxwell and, 52, 72–
    75, 79, 89; Maxwell Land Grant
    Company and, 8, 78–80, 85–95,
    101–2, 117–20, 127–28, 189,
    245n17; populism vs., 204; Su-
    preme Court and, 158, 189–90;
    and "unsettled" American West,
    84; Wallerstein and, 72, 223n16,
    243n88; and women's property
    rights, 76. *See also* investors; pri-
    vate property
markets: agriculture, 70, 142;
    Maxwell Land Grant Company and,
    78; railroad and, 84–85, 129. *See
    also* market capitalism; trade

Marmon, Walter G., 116–17; survey
with Elkins, 11, 115–17, 120, 122,
153, 182, 187
marriage: Beaubien's, 31, 51; Maxwell's, 48, 50–51, 54, 56, 230n16;
between *ricas* and outsiders, 51, 56,
61, 231n18; and U.S. laws, 48–49,
53, 56–58; and women's property
rights, 11, 12, 47, 48–49, 54–65,
76, 234–35
Married Women's Property Acts, U.S.
states', 47, 56–57
Marshall, John, 173–76, 252n43
Martin, James, 201
Martínez, Father Antonio José:
Beaubien/Miranda protests of, 20,
32, 35–36, 38, 184–85, 225n30,
242n71, 253n66; and Taos Rebellion, 35, 253n66
Martínez, Mariana, 57–58, 63
massacres by Indians, 41–43, 42, 69,
228n60
matrilocal organization, Jicarilla, 24
Maxwell, Deluvina, 69
Maxwell, Lucien Bonaparte, 5, 36–37,
62–63, 189, 230n12; children of,
69, 233n34; Cimarron home of, 52,
70–71; death of, 63; economic position of, 38, 45, 50, 54, 56, 69–75,
87, 89; epitaph on grave of, 46, 48;
Hispano settler relations of, 11,
71–73, 75, 96; as Indian agent, 39,
227n50; Jicarilla relations of, 25, 39,
70, 71, 72, 96–97; marriage of, 48,
50–51, 54, 56, 230n16; Miranda
sells to, 48, 49, 52; as *patrón*, 11, 39,
49, 50, 54, 64, 65, 68–75, 79, 85, 89,
103–4, 213; property system conflicts benefiting, 48–50, 54; and
Rayado, 36–37, 38, 51–52, 68, 70,
74, 231n20; rents paid to, 51, 71–
72, 79, 89; rise to prominence of,
49–54; sells estate (1869), 55, 73–
79, 87–95, 239n21, 240n34; survey
directed by, 89–91, 187
Maxwell, Luz. *See* Beaubien Maxwell,
María de la Luz

Maxwell, Paulita, 69
Maxwell and Brazil partnership, 55
Maxwell Land Grant, 5, 36, 48–50,
*193*, 217, 226n44; acreage of, 62, 63,
159–60, 235–36n58; earlier studies
of, 11–12; economic and social
structure imposed by Maxwell, 38,
39, 45, 49, 50, 54, 64, 65, 68–75; incorporation of, by U.S., 2, 84–87,
109–10, 117–20, 159, 244n88; Jicarillas as earliest inhabitants of, 19,
20, 21–45, 72; labor on, 49, 50, 51,
68–73, 75, 79; Maxwells sell (1869),
55, 73–79, 87–95, 239n21, 240n34;
price of sale, 91–92, 240n35; railroad increases value of, 12. *See also*
Beaubien/Miranda grant; Maxwell
Land Grant and Railway Company;
Maxwell Land Grant boundaries;
Sangre de Cristo Land Grant
Maxwell Land Grant and Railway
Company, 4, 8, 11, 72–73, 78–80,
216–19; bankruptcies of, 73, 114,
124–25, 148; CF&I purchases from,
206–7, 217; compromises and negotiations by, 131–38, 143–50,
153–58, 198; ejections by, 107, 113,
128, 131, 148–51, 156, 191–203;
failures of, 80, 118, 120, 122–26,
131–38, 143; finances of, 10, 73, 75,
85–95, 103, 109, 114–17, 120–32,
146–48, 152–53, 157; and fraud,
12, 151–52, 182, 187; government
officials assisting, 5, 12, 92, 102–3,
108–17; homes of agents burned,
20; *Interstate Land Company v.
Maxwell Land Grant Company*,
161, 162, 174–75, 177, 181; lawyers
of, 61, 109, 112, 129, 140, 156, 161,
197; legal system and, 78–79, 94–
107, 114–18, 128–31, 157–90;
management of, 5, 9, 14, 121–56,
167, 191–95, 217; and market capitalism, 8, 78–80, 85–87, 101–2,
117–20, 127–28; Maxwells sell to
(1869), 55, 73–79, 87–95, 239n21,
240n34; original shareholders of,

91–92; property conflict positions, 80, 87, 96–107, 106; *Russell v. Maxwell Land Grant Company,* 205–6, 256n25; settlers' resistance to, 9, 20, 72–73, 80, 87, 95–157, 190–206, 214, 217, 242n66, 254–57; squatters designated by, 9, 72–73, 74, 96, 103–4, 107, 108, 113, 128–46, 244n1; terms of land sales to settlers, 134, 247n49; valuations of settlers' property, 138–42, *139, 141.* See also *U.S. v. Maxwell Land Grant and Railway Company*
Maxwell Land Grant boundaries, 6–8, *7,* 19, 21, 62, 95–107, 115–17, 128, *193;* Beaubien/Miranda grant, 30–39, 62–63, *93,* 159, 182, 225–26n37; Maxwell sale and, 74–75, 89–91, 239n21, 240n35; *Russell v. Maxwell Land Grant Company* and, 205–6; *U.S. v. Maxwell Land Grant and Railway Company* and, 125, 148, 158, 159–61, 182–87, *189,* 205. See also surveys, Maxwell Land Grant
Maxwell Land Grant Cattle Company, 130, 136, 140–41
*mayordomo,* 38
McCall, George A., 40
McClintock, Anne, 61, 235n56
McCormick, Cyrus, 123
McKnight, William S., 58–59
McMains, O. P., 131, 137, 148, 242n71, 247n38; and Colfax County resistance, 110–11, 113, 191; and Stonewall Valley resistance, 195, 196–97, 198, 199, 200–1, 255n13, 256nn28,33
Merk, Frederick, 229n3
Mescalero Apaches, 40
Mexican Americans, 13–14, 47, 221n3. See also Hispanos
Mexican law: on Armijo conveyance to Beaubien/Miranda, 31–32, *93,* 163, 164, 167, 183–86, 189; and colonization, 163–65, 178, 182–83; and equality, 53, 56, 68, 162–63,

179; incorporated through treaty and statute, 168–73; and informal property regime, 75–77, 189; and peonage system, 47–48, 66–67, 68, 75–77; racial prejudice against, 82, 170, 181; U.S. ideology conflicting with, 4–5, 47–48, 66–68, 75–77, 163–67, 173–77, 181; U.S. Supreme Court property decisions and, 159–63, 172–90; and women's property, 53, 55, 56, 76–77, 234n41. See also property system conflicts
Mexico: Beaubien/Miranda grant made by, 19, 20, 31–36; Chihuahua Trail trade with, 30–31; independence from Spain, 32; Martínez in Durango, 32, 36; migrant labor from, 207; New Mexican government by, 30–36, 49, 83, *93,* 163–65, 175; Republic of, 12, 30, 81–82. See also Guadalupe Hidalgo, Treaty of (1848); property system conflicts; U.S.-Mexican War
"middle ground," concept of, 15, 21, 22, 30, 38, 41, 223n3
migrant labor, 207, 258n55
military: Colorado militia, 197, 198, 254n4; Mexican, 165; Spanish, 29. See also defense, border; U.S.-Mexican War; U.S. military; wars
Miller, Samuel, 159–60, 182, 184–86, 187
Mills, Melvin W., 52, 112–13, 114, 154
miners/mining, 103; Anglos, 21, 78, 80, 96–107, 106; coal, 8, 207–8; gold, 71–74, 87, 102; government of, 73; property conflict position, 96–107, 106
Miranda, Guadalupe, 19, 30–37, 63, *93;* Armijo relationship with, 30–36, 49, 164, 184–85, 189; as empresario, 184–86; sells to Maxwell, 48, 52; U.S. conquest affecting, 48, 49. See also Beaubien/Miranda grant

missionaries, 29–30, 119
Missouri: *Glenn v. United States*, 177;
St. Louis, 84, 85, 177
Moache Utes, 22, 99
monetary policy, populism and, 202,
204. *See also* finances
Money, J. W. B., 127
monopoly, populism vs., 202, 203,
204, 257n40
Montejano, David, 120
morality: land reform and, 94; peonage and, 65; U.S. conquest and, 46–
47. *See also* corruption, official;
fraud, Maxwell Land Grant
Company and
Moreno Ditch, 79
Moreno Valley, 154
Mueller, Frederick, 53, 231n27
murders: of Narciso Beaubien, 35,
212, 232n29, 253n66; of Bent, 35,
212, 232n29; of Cardenas, 113; of
Griego, 112; by Indians, 27–28, 41–
43, 69; by lynching, 111–12, 242–
43n73; Stonewall Valley violence,
197–200, 255n13, 256nn27,28; of
Tolby, 110–13; of Vega, 111–12,
113
Murphy, Lawrence R., 240n35
myths of American West: as
"empty"/"unsettled," 5–8, 80–87,
216–17; as "exceptional," 8–10,
120; Hollywood, 19–20, 211; Manifest Destiny, 8, 13, 46–47, 81–82;
violence dominated by Anglo
males, 19–20, 120

naming as possession-taking mode,
26–27
nationalism, Mexican, 32
Native Americans, 13–14, 22, 68–69,
80–81, 242n66. *See also* Apaches;
Comanches; Plains Indians; Pueblo
Indians; Utes
natural resources, 6–8, 10;
Beaubien/Miranda development
plans for, 30–31; Jicarillas and, 19,
25; Maxwell Land Grant Company

and, 78, 126. *See also* fur trade;
gathering; hunting; land use systems; miners/mining; water
Navajo Indians, 22, 69
Neeson, J. M., 243–44n88
negotiations: *Espinoza v. Taylor* suit
instead of, 211; Jicarilla, 21, 26–30,
41, 97–101; Maxwell Land Grant
Company, 131–38, 143–50, 153–
56, 198. *See also* confrontation
Netherlands. *See* Dutch
New Mexico: Anglo encroachment
feared in, 36; business dealings in
(1800s), 3; Chihuahua Trail trade
with Mexico, 30–31; Mexican government of, 30–36, 49, 83, 93, 163–
65, 175; peonage in, 63–68; property system complexities in, 3–4,
10–13, 19–45, 73, 211; remoteness
of, in U.S. eyes, 83–84; Spanish
government of, 26, 29, 30, 83, 175;
Texas invasion of, 32. *See also*
Cimarron; Las Vegas; Maxwell
Land Grant; New Mexico Territory;
Rayado; Sangre de Cristo Land
Grant; Santa Fe; Taos; U.S.-
Mexican War
New Mexico Territory, 2, 9, 37, 65,
78–120, 229n8; change-of-venue
law (1889), 203; Joseph as congres-
sional delegate of, 204–5; longest
territorial period of any state in the
Union, 170; and peonage, 47–48,
64–68, 71, 75–76. *See also* govern-
ment officials, U.S.; Supreme Court,
New Mexico Territorial; U.S.-
Mexican War
New Orleans, 84
New Western history, 8, 223n2
New York: Maxwell Land Grant Com-
pany connections to, 9, 10, 120,
122–23, 130, 147; Tammany Hall,
108
*New York Evening Post*, 82
*New York Herald*, 61
*New York Sun*, 110
*Nogal Nugget*, 203

*North American Review*, 94
Northwest Ordinance (1787), 81, 83, 165, 166, 249n11
*No Separate Refuge* (Deutsch), 207

*olleros*, Jicarilla, 22
O'Neil, Thomas, 155, 194–95, 201
Opler, Morris, 22–24
Ortiz, Alfonso, 19
Otero, Miguel, Sr., 14, 92, 240n30
ownership. *See* land rights; property system

Palmer, W. J., 92, 240n30
Panic (1873), economic, 114
Paris, barricade of, 47
*partido* system in cattle business, 142–43
patronage: Beaubien and, 31, 38; Maxwell and, 11, 39, 49, 50, 54, 64, 65, 68–75, 78, 79, 85, 89, 103–4, 213; Pels and, 133, 143–44; Republican Party and, 108–9; U.S. ends, 46–48, 49, 64–68, 75–77, 85, 103–4; women's positions and, 64–65, 76–77. *See also* peonage
Pears' Soap, 61
Pelham, William, 62
Pels, Marinus Petrus, 9, 124; and CF&I, 207; Dutch immigrants desired by, 121, 129–30, 146; Jeffersonian ideology of, 167; and settler resistance, 124–58, 191–206, 246n26, 255n13
peonage, 5, 63–68; under Beaubien, 31, 38; under Maxwell, 50, 51, 64, 65, 68–73, 85, 89; U.S. ideology on, 46–49, 64–68, 71, 75–77, 85, 236n63; women's positions compared with, 64–65, 76–77. *See also* patronage; servants, Maxwells'; slaves
People's Party, 202–5
Perricone, Gaspar, 2–3, 4, 17, 18, 216, 250n21
Philippines, 9
Pícuris, New Mexico, 26, 163

Pícuris Indians, 29
Pile, William A., 92, 102–3, 109
Pinkerton agents, 155, 195, 197, 198, 201
Plains Indians: and Beaubien/Miranda grant, 35, 37; Jicarillas and, 21, 22, 24, 96–97; Maxwell trade with, 39
plantation system of American South, 71, 74
plazas, Hispano, 37, 107, 140
Pley, José, 232n30
politics: of American West, 9–13; changing as Americans moved to New Mexico, 38; of Gilded Age America, 109; of incorporation into U.S., 2, 9–13, 80–87, 109–10, 117–20, 167–82, 244n88; in Mexico, 32; populist, 202–5, 257n40. *See also* corruption, official; democracy; feudalism; government; republicanism
Polk, James K., 64, 81, 168
Poñil Park, 141
Poñil River, 24, 36, 105, 106, 137, 206
Pooler Hotel, Stonewall, 154, 155, 157, 190–200
population in land grant region, 6
Populism, 18, 202–5, 257n40
possession-taking modes, 19, 26–27, 33–34, 117–20. *See also* colonization; imperialism; property system
prejudice, racial, 81–82, 121–56; against Anglos, 145–46; against Hispanos, 13–14, 81–82, 108, 110–12, 134–45, 228n1; against Mexican law, 82, 170, 181; against Native Americans, 13–14; in U.S. legal system, 82, 111, 170, 181
Prince, L. Bradford, 84, 131
prisoners of war, 29, 40–44, 68–69
private property: American West as blank slate for, 81, 84; Beaubien/Miranda grant and, 31, 35, 38; *Espinoza v. Taylor* and, 4, 209, 215–16; Hispano vs. Anglo conceptions of, 11, 139–40; Maxwell estate and, 73; Maxwell

private property (continued)
   Land Grant Company conception
      of, 75, 78–79, 93–94, 139–40; re-
      publican ideology of, 94, 173; West
      as culture rooted in, 13. See also fee
      simple absolute; individual land
      grants; land use systems; market
      capitalism
property system: capital-intensive, 8,
      78–80; gender and, 11, 12, 47–49,
      53–65, 76–77, 234–35; liberaliza-
      tion of, 11, 13–14, 32, 47–48, 56–
      63, 80; race and, 13–14, 138–43;
      "vested rights" and, 4–5, 173–81,
      251–52n43. See also boundaries;
      informal property relations; land
      grants; land rights; land use sys-
      tems; possession-taking modes;
      private property; property system
      conflicts; public domain; rents;
      usufructuary systems
property system conflicts, 2–5, 6, 8,
      11, 19–45, 47–48; Beaubien/
      Miranda grant and, 20, 32–36, 38,
      184–85, 225n30, 242n71, 253n66;
      complexities of, 3–4, 10–13, 19–
      45, 73, 136, 173, 211, 215, 217–18;
      and informal property regime, 2–5,
      75–77, 89, 96–97, 104, 189; and la-
      bor system, 65–68, 73; Maxwell
      benefiting from, 48–50, 54; Max-
      well Land Grant Company and, 80,
      87–107, 158–67, 190; and myth of
      "empty"/"unsettled" space, 5–8,
      80–87, 216–17; public domain and
      genesis of, 94–95; republican ideol-
      ogy and, 162–67, 173–77, 181;
      Spanish terra incognita and, 26–27;
      Supreme Court dilemmas, 159–63,
      172–82; surveys at root of, 120;
      women's rights and, 11, 12, 47–49,
      53–65, 76–77, 234–35. See also
      boundaries; ejections; Espinoza v.
      Taylor; land loss phenomenon; legal
      system, U.S.
Protestants, 81, 111. See also
      McMains, O. P.

"Protest in a Promised Land"
      (Schwantes), 202–3
Protocol of Querétaro, 168–69,
      250n19
public auction, 114, 166
public domain, 2, 12, 17, 47, 82, 90,
      93, 103; genesis of legal conflict,
      94–95; government corruption and,
      89–90, 153; Supreme Court and,
      125, 158, 162–67, 171, 174, 176,
      205
Pueblo Indians: community land
      grants to, 12, 163; encroachments
      on, 35, 184–85; Jicarillas and, 21,
      22, 24; revolt of, against Spanish
      (1680), 22; Spanish alliances with,
      26, 29
Puerto Rico, 9, 170
Pullman, George, 122–23
Purgatory River, 24, 95, 105, 192

racial categories, 13–14, 24, 81–84,
      108–9, 221n3; in American South,
      64, 69; free Blacks, 236n63, 240n27;
      intermarriage between, 51, 56, 61;
      and lynching, 112, 243n73; pop-
      ulism and, 203. See also Anglos;
      ethnicity; Hispanos; Native Ameri-
      cans; prejudice, racial
Rael v. Taylor, 216, 254n77
railroads, 44–45, 129; Atchison,
      Topeka, and Santa Fe, 12, 84–85,
      126, 129; Chili, 142; Maxwell Land
      Grant Cattle Company and, 141;
      populism and, 202, 257n40
Railway Press and Telegraph, 104–5
rainfall, 24, 85–86
ranchería grande, Jicarilla, 27–29
Randolf, E. J., 133, 150, 196, 200
rations from U.S. government, 39
Raton, New Mexico, 62, 131, 191
Rayado, 51, 62, 231n20; Beaubien in-
      fluence in, 226n43; Beaubien/
      Miranda grant settlement, 36–38,
      40, 51–52, 54; Maxwells and, 36–
      37, 38, 51–52, 54, 68, 70, 74, 76,
      231n20; Pley ranch, 232n30

Reconstruction, U.S., 65, 84
reformers, U.S. government, 94
religion: clergy defending settlers' rights, 242n71; freedom of, 169–70; Jicarilla, 21–22, 29–30; missionaries, 29–30, 119; Spanish incursions encountering crosses, 26, 28–29. *See also* Catholics; Protestants
rents: to Beaubien, 51; to Maxwell, 51, 71–72, 79, 89; to Maxwell Land Grant Company, 123, 125–26, 129, 131, 143–44, 199
Republic, Mexican, 12, 30, 81–82
republicanism, 94, 162–67, 173–77, 181
Republican Party, 83, 94, 108–9, 167, 203
reservations, removal of Indians to, 20, 21, 80, 97–101
resistance, 121–56, 244n88, 247n38; in Colfax County, 20, 107–13, 120, 133–34, 137, 191, 217; end of, 205–6; Jicarilla, 20, 80, 97–101; to Maxwell Land Grant Company, 9, 20, 72–73, 80, 87, 95–157, 190–206, 214, 217, 242n66, 254–57; Populist Party, 202–5; in Stonewall Valley, 20, 123, 132, 135, 147, 149, 150, 154–57, 192–206, 254–57. *See also* confrontation; violence
resort, Stonewall Valley plans for, 153, 154, 192
rights, constitutional, 65, 67. *See also* equality; land rights
Rio Grande, 21, 22, 26, 32, 35, 70
Rio Grande Valley, 62, 70
Robbins, William, 120
Rocky Mountain Coal and Iron Company bonds, 206–7
Romer, Roy, 209
Romero, José de la Cruz, 65–67
Ross, Edmund G., 203
Royal Community of the Sandwich Islands, 118
Royuela, José Manuel, 161
Russell, Marian, 195, 254n12; and Stonewall Valley violence, 199, 201;

Supreme Court battle of, 134, 205–6, 255–56n25
Russell, Richard D., 95, 195–96, 204–6, 244n1, 254n12; ejection suit against, 148–50; government petitioned by, 116, 121, 153–54; indictments for murder of, 200, 256nn27, 28; and Stonewall Valley violence, 150, 156, 194–201, 204, 255n13; survey questioned by, 116, 153, 187
*Russell v. Maxwell Land Grant Company*, 205–6, 256n25
Ryus, William, 70

Sandoval, Justo, 200
San Francisco, 84
San Francisco Valley, 148, 153
Sangre de Cristo Land Grant, 6, 210, 226n44, 258n59; Beaubien and, 1–3, 50, 171, 212–13, 214; boundaries of, 171–72; commons on, 1, 38, 209–16, 254n77; Congress's confirmation of, 172, 212, 258n59, 259n67; history of, 211–14, 259n63; *Rael v. Taylor*, 216, 254n77. See also *Espinoza v. Taylor*
San Luis, Colorado, 1, 2, 3, 6. See also *Espinoza v. Taylor*
San Luis Valley, 22, 142, 209–16
San Pablo (Jicarilla leader), 99, 100
Santa Fe: Barcelo property, 55–56; First National Bank of, 90; Maxwell Land Grant far from, 62; Texas invasion of, 32; U.S. conquest of (1848), 49
Santa Fe Ring, 11, 13, 16, 108–17, 203
Santa Fe Trail, 30–31, 62, 83, 85; Gregg book and, 36; Maxwell home on, 70; Maxwell markets and, 72; Rayado accommodations, 37; violence on, 39–45, 42
Schurz, Carl, 116–17
Schwantes, Carlos, 202–3, 257n40
secret organizations, Hispano, 145
seison, 19. *See also* possession-taking modes
Seña, Felipe N., 36

servants, Maxwells', 68–69, 233n34.
See also peonage
settlers, 244n1; Beaubien/Miranda,
20, 32–38, 51–52, 72, 184–85,
225n30, 242n71, 253n66; vs. Maxwell Land Grant Company, 9, 20,
72–73, 80, 87, 95–156, 190–206,
214, 217, 242n66, 254–57; property
conflict positions, 20, 87, 96–107,
106, 136, 188; and twentieth-
century changes, 207–8. See also
Anglos; ejections; Hispanos; homesteading; resistance; squatters
Settlers Book, Maxwell Land Grant
Company, 139, 139, 141
sharecroppers, 31, 38, 50, 51, 74
Sherwin, Frank, 122–25, 126,
146–47
Silva, Jesús, 137
silver, populism and, 202, 204
Silvestre, José de, 61
slaves: captives sold as, 29, 68–69;
Maxwells', 49, 68, 69; U.S., 48, 63–
64, 65, 67, 71; Whites', 227n56. See
also peonage
Smith, E. P., 99, 100
Snyder, C. S., 194
South, American, 64, 65, 69, 71, 74
Spanish: Florida of, 56, 83; imperialism of, 12, 21; incursions by, 26–
30; and Jicarillas, 21, 24, 25, 26–30,
44; land grant system, 47, 175–76;
law, 4, 37; Mexico's independence
from, 32; New Mexico government
by, 26, 29, 30, 83, 175; possession-
taking modes of, 19, 26–27; Pueblo
Revolt (1680) against, 22; Reconquest, 47. See also Hispanos;
Spanish-American War (1898)
Spanish-American War (1898), 8, 9
Spencer, Thomas Rush, 89, 90, 92
Springer, Frank, 129, 140–41, 161
squatters: clubs established by, 107;
Maxwell and rights of, 72, 103;
Maxwell Land Grant Company-
designated, 9, 72–74, 96, 103–4,

107, 108, 113, 128–46, 244n1; in
Spanish and French land grant systems, 176; U.S. ideology and, 166,
167, 176. See also homesteading
state: Mexican law privileging, 165;
role in taking possession, 19, 21,
117–20. See also Europeans; government; Mexico; nationalism;
United States
Stilgoe, John, 166
St. Louis, Missouri, 84, 85, 177
Stonewall Valley, 130, 135, 136, 141,
153; resistance in (1888), 18, 20,
123, 132, 135, 147, 149, 150, 155–
57, 192–206, 254–57; resort plans
in, 153, 154, 192
Story, Joseph, 173
St. Vrain, Ceran, 50
St. Vrain family, 31
subsistence farming, 167, 211. See
also gathering; hunting
Sullivan, John L., 82
Summers, Edwin V., 40
Supreme Court, Colorado, 216
Supreme Court, New Mexico Territorial: Chaves v. McKnight and
Gutieres, 46, 58–59; ejection suits,
131; Mariana Jaramillo v. José de la
Cruz Romero, 65–67; and married
women's property rights, 57–58, 60
Supreme Court, U.S., 78, 117–21,
158–90, 217–18; Arguello v.
United States, 180–81, 252n54;
Fletcher v. Peck, 173–74, 176; Fremont v. United States, 177–80,
181; Glenn v. United States, 177–
80, 181; Interstate Land Company
v. Maxwell Land Grant Company,
161, 162, 174–75, 177, 181; Russell
v. Maxwell Land Grant Company,
205–6, 256n25; and state boundaries, 149; Tameling v. U.S. Freehold and Immigration Company,
115, 171–73, 182, 185, 186. See also
U.S. v. Maxwell Land Grant and
Railway Company

surveying, Spanish/Mexican and
American differences in, 166
Surveyor General, New Mexico Office
of the, 89–90, 240n27, 258n59; and
Maxwell Land Grant, 11–12, 89–91,
95, 115–16, 186–87, 206; and Sangre de Cristo Land Grant, 171–72
surveys, Maxwell Land Grant, 95,
115–17; Elkins/Marmon, 11, 115–
17, 120, 122, 153, 182, 187; Griffin,
89–91, 103, 115, 160, 187, 239n18;
*Russell v. Maxwell Land Grant
Company* and, 205–6; *U.S. v.
Maxwell Land Grant and Railway
Company* and, 159, 205; Vigil, 32–
33, 34, 187, 225–26n37
Swartwout, Henry, 43

Tameling, John C., 171
*Tameling v. U.S. Freehold and Immi-
gration Company*, 115, 171–73,
181, 182, 185, 186
Tammany Hall, New York, 108
Taney, Roger, 176, 178–80, 181, 251–
52n43
Taos: Beaubien influence in, 226n43;
Beaubien migration to, 31; Colfax
County trial moved to, 113; Mar-
tínez protests in, 32, 184–85,
225n30; Maxwell Land Grant far
from, 62; Maxwell settles in, 50–
51; Rayado winter retreats in, 37;
Rebellion, 35, 212, 232n29, 253n66;
Texas invasion of, 32
Taos Canyon, 70
taxes: customs collection, 31–32, 164;
Maxwell Land Grant Company,
114, 152–53; on Sangre de Cristo
Land Grant, 212
Taylor, Jack T., 1–2, 3, 4, 209, 211,
213, 214
Taylor, Morris F., 247n38
Taylor, Zachary, 13, 17, 18, 209, 211
Taylor family, 1–2, 209–11
Taylor Ranch, 13. See also *Espinoza v.
Taylor*

*terra incognita*, Spanish naming
of, 26–27. *See also* "empty"/
"unsettled" space, myth of
territorial system, U.S., 4, 65, 170; of
incorporation, 2, 9–13, 80–87,
109–10, 117–20, 159, 167–82,
244n88; Supreme Court and, 173–
74. *See also* American West; California; colonization; Colorado; imperialism; land rights; Manifest
Destiny; New Mexico Territory
Texas, 9; Austin colony, 182; independence of, from Mexico (1836), 35,
164; Republic of, 32
Thirteenth Amendment, 67
Thomas, Mrs. L. R., 134
Thompson, Waddy, 82
Tierra Amarilla, New Mexico, 98, 99,
214
Todd, J. A., 133
Tolby, Franklin J., 110–13, 137,
242n71
Torrens, Robert Richard, 213
Torrens Act, Colorado, 213–16
Torres, José Luis, 148–49, 156, 200,
256n30
torture of Cruz Vega, 110–11
Trachtenberg, Alan, 10
trade: Chihuahua Trail, 30–31; Euro-
pean, 29–30; French frontiers, 230–
31n18; fur, 21, 26, 31, 50; Jicarilla,
22, 28, 29–30; liquor, 39; Maxwell's
plans for, 70; slave, 68–69; U.S.
policy makers' distance from, 83.
*See also* markets; Santa Fe Trail
treaties, U.S., 168–73; Adams-Onis,
173; Jay (1794), 173; with Jicarillas,
40, 99–100. *See also* Guadalupe
Hidalgo, Treaty of (1848)
Trinchera tract, Sangre de Cristo Land
Grant, 259n63
Trinidad, New Mexico, 126, 150, 156,
192–94, 197–99
Trujillo, Vidal, 53
Turner, Frederick Jackson, 5–6, 9, 13,
120

Turner, Ted, 141
Twitty, Edward, 133

Ulibarrí, Juan de, 26–29, 44
United States: American South, 64,
65, 69, 71, 74; Gilded Age, 109;
imperial-colonial ways of, 9–10, 61,
81–84; investors aided by, 10, 44,
223n16; and Jicarillas, 20, 21, 24,
39–45, 80, 97–101, 217, 242n66;
Maxwell as Indians' ally against,
39; Maxwell Land Grant boundaries
set by, 19, 125, 148, 158, 159–61,
182–87, 189, 205–6; Pels as consul
for, 127. See also American West;
Anglos; government officials, U.S.;
legal system, U.S.; property system
conflicts; territorial system, U.S.;
treaties, U.S.; U.S.-Mexican War;
U.S. military
U.S. Freehold and Immigration Company, 171; Tameling v. U.S. Freehold and Immigration Company,
115, 171–73, 181, 182, 185, 186
U.S.-Mexican War, 3, 8, 36, 40–50,
56, 212; as liberation, 46–48,
229n3; territorial system after, 2,
37, 65, 81–87, 229n8. See also
Guadalupe Hidalgo, Treaty of
(1848)
U.S. military: Burnside, 40, 227n54;
and Colfax County violence, 113;
vs. Jicarillas, 20, 40–45, 80, 97;
markets supplying, 70, 72; vs. miners, 102–3; Rayado, 51; rule continuing after war, 83; Russell in, 195;
vs. Stonewall Valley settlers, 155–
56. See also U.S.-Mexican War
usufructuary systems, 1–4, 20; fee
simple absolute vs., 80, 97; Jicarilla,
12, 21, 25–26, 35, 97; on Sangre de
Cristo Land Grant, 212–15
U.S. v. Maxwell Land Grant and Railway Company, 4, 11, 135, 157–90;
analysis of, 182–87; and boundaries, 125, 148, 158, 159–61, 182–
87, 189, 205; Brewer as judge in,

257–58n48; consequences of, 187–
90; overview of, 159–63; Pels and,
132, 135, 157–58; and public domain, 125, 158, 162–67; Russell v.
Maxwell Land Grant Company
and, 205
Utes: massacres by, 41, 69; Maxwell's
relationship with, 96, 97; Moache,
22, 99; Russell homestead and, 195

Van Houghten, Jan, 130
vara strips (of agricultural land), 37–
38, 140
Vega, Cruz, 110–12, 113
Vermejo Park, 141, 191
Vermejo River, 105, 136, 206
Vermejo Valley, 130, 134, 137
Victoria, Guadalupe, 163
Vigil, Cornelio, 32–33, 34, 36, 187,
225–26n37
Vigil, Tenduro, 137
violence, 19, 217; Bear Flag Rebellion,
50, 178; on Beaubien / Miranda
grant, 39; in Colfax County, 20,
107–13, 120, 133–34, 137, 191,
196, 217; Jicarilla, 27–28, 39, 40,
41–44, 97, 98; myths of Anglo
male-dominated, 19–20, 120; on
Santa Fe Trail, 39–45, 42; settlers
vs. Maxwell Land Grant Company,
20, 80, 98, 102–3, 107–14, 120,
121, 132–37, 143, 145, 190–202,
206, 214, 217, 254–57; in Stonewall
Valley (1888), 20, 195–202, 254–
57; Taos Rebellion, 35, 212, 232n29,
253n66; on Taylor Ranch, 209, 214;
after U.S. v. Maxwell Land Grant
and Railway Company decision,
157–58; women and, 135. See also
confrontation; military; murders;
wars

Waddingham, Wilson, 88, 92, 240n30
wage-labor economy, 31, 206–8, 211,
258n55
Wagon Mound, New Mexico, 41
Wallace, A. C., 131

Wallace, Lew, 84
Wallerstein, Immanuel, 72, 223n16, 243n88
wars: allocations to veterans, 166; captives, 29, 40–44, 68–69; Colfax County violence as war, 107–8; Indian, 29, 68–69; Spanish-American War (1898), 8, 9; Stonewall Valley violence as war, 195–202, 206; U.S. Civil War, 65, 67, 74, 84, 195, 227; U.S.-Jicarilla, 20, 40–45, 42, 80. *See also* U.S.-Mexican War
water: ditches, 1, 38, 74, 79, 209; Hispano land use and, 37–38, 140, 209. *See also* irrigation
Watts, John S., 92
West. *See* American West
*Western Historical Quarterly*, 202
Whigham, Harry, 120–26, 131–38, 143–54, 157–58, 207
White, Richard, 15

White family, in Jicarilla-U.S. war, 41–44, 42, 227n56, 228n60
Wilkens, D. F., 128, 151–53
Williamson, J. A., 95, 115–17
Wilson, J. S., 91
Wolf, Al, 13
women: Jicarilla, 24–25; Jicarilla-U.S. war captives, 41–43; on Maxwell ranch, 54; negotiating for land, 134–35; in peonage court cases, 65–68; property rights of, 11, 12, 47–49, 53–65, 76–77, 234–35. *See also* feminization, conquest and; *femme sole*
wool market, 142
Wootten, Richens L. "Uncle Dick," 198
world system, 223n16. *See also* market capitalism

Yeaman, Caldwell, 201

Ziegelaars, W. F., 123, 124

Text:         10/13 Aldus
Display:      Aldus
Cartographer: Bill Nelson
Compositor:   G & S Typesetting Services, Inc.

CPSIA information can be obtained
at www.ICGtesting.com
Printed in the USA
LVHW080044130321
681398LV00023B/290